Speaking Out
Louder

Jack Layton (signature)

Speaking Out Louder

Louder

Ideas That Work for Canadians

Jack Layton

KEY PORTER BOOKS

National Library of Canada Cataloguing in Publication Data

Layton, Jack, 1950–
    Speaking out Louder: ideas that work for Canadians / Jack Layton.

Includes index.
ISBN 1-55263-688-7

1. Canada—Social conditions—1991– 2. Canada—Economic conditions—1991– 3. Canada—Politics and government—1993– I. Title.

FC635.L39 2006   971.064'8   C2005-907185-0

THE CANADA COUNCIL | LE CONSEIL DES ARTS
FOR THE ARTS | DU CANADA
SINCE 1957 | DEPUIS 1957

ONTARIO ARTS COUNCIL
CONSEIL DES ARTS DE L'ONTARIO

The publisher gratefully acknowledges the support of the Canada Council for the Arts and the Ontario Arts Council for its publishing program. We acknowledge the support of the Government of Ontario through the Ontario Media Development Corporation's Ontario Book Initiative.

We acknowledge the financial support of the Government of Canada through the Book Publishing Industry Development Program (BPIDP) for our publishing activities.

This work is a substantially revised edition of *Speaking Out Loud*.

Key Porter Books Limited
Six Adelaide Street East, Tenth Floor
Toronto, Ontario
Canada M5C 1H6

www.keyporter.com

Text design: Jack Steiner
Electronic formatting: Jean Lightfoot Peters

Printed and bound in Canada

06 07 08 09 10 6 5 4 3 2 1

To Olivia Chow, and Sarah and Michael Layton.
And in memory of Dun Leckie and Robert Layton

*If we do not change our direction, we are liable
to end up where we are headed.*
—CHINESE PROVERB

Contents

Preface to the Revised Edition

Since writing *Speaking Out Loud* just over two years ago, much has changed in my life, in Canada, and in the world. Our world has been battered by both natural and political shock waves.

The battering continues. The images have seared scars onto our souls. I will never forget the faces of the tsunami aftermath. News reports and images were stunningly stark. Then, as part of the Canadian delegation visiting devastated areas, I gazed into the faces of those who had experienced violent, rapid, and catastrophic loss of their family and communities in Sri Lanka and Thailand.

I saw despair, determination, and hope—all in the worst of worlds. Old survivors stared at a middle distance, empty, hollow, deeply pained eyes. Adults looked at me with a grim, set-jaw focus as they rebuilt with whatever was available.

But the children's faces were the most striking to me—the ones set permanently in my memory. How could they be smiling? There was a hopefulness in those eyes that it seems that only children can muster in the face of such horror. Surrounded by the devastation of Ampara's seaside fishing neighbourhoods, with a mass grave covered with fluttering white flags, one little boy looked up into our eyes and said: "I lost my mother and my father too." Then, a smile as curiosity took over and he asked, almost cheerfully, "What's your name?"

My heart was breaking as I gave the youngster my name, which he and his friends began to repeat, laughing at the funny sound of "Jack" as foreign to their ears as my skin colour was to their eyes—eyes that had seen things a child should not have had to see. There and then, like many Canadians have already done, I made a commitment to do more personally and politically. It's time to extend the extraordinary outpouring of concern, solidarity, and generosity.

Something more was happening. The extraordinary outpouring of popular support for the tsunami-hit communities seemed to me to embody a message to world governments. The collective generosity of citizens for their fellows suggests that there are values that were tapped by the catastrophe. There's no question that these are core Canadian values: let's ensure that people have the basic necessities of life, particularly when we have so much. But the global grassroots response tells us that these values are universal. I believe people were telling their governments, by their actions, that they wanted government policies and decisions to reflect these values. They were calling implicitly for new choices to be made in the pursuit of human security.

The huge waves and devastation on December 26, 2004 illustrated human vulnerability on a massive scale and in a dramatic, visible way. But human security is threatened daily because of poverty and related diseases. British PM Tony Blair captured this fact when he declared that Africa faces a "tsunami a week" from AIDS and other diseases. So why is there no similar response? Why are the human values that drove so many to give and help in response to the giant wave not propelling us and our governments to respond to the greater and just as real threats facing so many daily?

It is because of the choices that have been made by governments. What are these essential choices?

They have been rather starkly revealed in recent months. On the one hand there has been a rising global call to take on poverty around the world. At the same time, the most affluent nation has ramped up its military spending to unprecedented levels. These are choices being made on behalf of the world's people by the governments that purport to represent them. In early 2005, weeks after the tsunami, a worldwide movement was launched called "Make Poverty History." Nelson Mandela and those others involved were tapping the values that motivated the global response to the tsunami; the challenge is to keep up the momentum and to motivate lethargic or willfully blind governments to achieve the aspirations of the global family: human security for all by ending poverty globally.

A natural catastrophe reminded us that the earth is indeed a lifeboat. So we are faced with key choices and that we must work together in a climate of collaboration, nurtured by an aspiration to equality, fairness, and generosity. Ideas start with dreams—some little, some not so little. "Dream no little dreams!" Tommy Douglas, first leader of the New Democratic Party of Canada, tells us. Why do Canadians respond so well to such a call? I've always believed that Canadians dreamed in big, full-colour panoramas. I also believed that the Canadian capacity to generate ideas that work for Canada and for the world was extraordinary, a conviction that caused me to put this book together in the first place.

On June 28, 2004, I became a Member of Parliament in a minority government headed by Liberal Paul Martin. I was re-elected January 23, 2006 in a second minority, this time headed by Conservative Stephen Harper. Over two million Canadians cast ballots for the NDP in 2004—up one million from 2000—and more than two and a half million chose our party in 2006, demonstrating their confidence in the party that I have had the privilege to lead since January 2003. NDP MPs have worked hard to earn the trust of so many, and we're going to work even harder in the future. In Parliament, we try to do what Canadians want us to do. We have results to show from those efforts. Sure, we're proud of what we've accomplished, but there's so much more to do.

Too often, however, I'm reminded that converting good ideas into parliamentary action is far more difficult than it should be. This, in large part, can be attributed to the failure of some political leaders and parties to recognize certain realities. For instance, when Canadian voters elect a minority Parliament this can be an opportunity, not a problem. Prime Minister Martin appeared to view the minority government he led as a nagging problem, while I viewed it as a golden opportunity. Time will tell how Mr. Harper sees the minority he currently leads, although the first session was not auspicious. "Government by ultimatum" is how I've described his approach. "My way or the highway" seems to be his message to the opposition parties, never mind that they have the majority of seats and votes!

There are also deeper problems and challenges within our democracy. One is that public discontent with government and politicians has increased significantly in recent years because Canadians believe neither is being responsive to their needs. But I firmly believe that part of that negative attitude is due to the way in which we conduct elections in Canada. Since Confederation, we have chosen a winner-take-all system that, almost always, fails to reflect the true wishes of Canadians. Such a system may have been sufficient for earlier elections in our country because there were only two political parties from which to choose. But today we have four recognized parties in the House of Commons. We also have other parties wanting to elect members, and one party—the Greens—would indeed have elected members to the House of Commons in each of the last two elections if we had proportional representation in our political system. The urgent need to change the system and introduce an element of proportional representation is dealt with in the final chapter of this book.

As politicians, we have an obligation to reward the people's trust in us by finding ways to achieve more ethical governance. I am completely mystified by the inability of certain entrenched interests first to recognize truly critical situations, such as climate change, First Peoples' child poverty, and health crises or—having recognized it—to act with any sense of urgency and resolve. Instead of dynamism and principled leadership to implement the best ideas, too often we see instead petty politics, name calling, finger-pointing, and partisan gamesmanship.

In updating this book, I've taken advantage of some of the recent lessons I've learned and reflected on them. Perhaps some of the events, conversations, decisions, and strategic considerations related in the following pages will help others find ways to shepherd their good ideas to a point where they can work for Canadians.

Oftentimes, life's highs and lows are inextricably linked. That has certainly happened to me and, occasionally, the ups and downs were virtually simultaneous. On June 28, 2004, there was the thrill and honour I felt in winning my Toronto–Danforth seat in the House of Commons for the first time, after two previous attempts. Seconds later, elation turned to pain as I realized that my wife, Toronto City Councillor Olivia Chow, would not be joining me in the House of Commons. I knew this would mean many days of separation and lost opportunities to work together—a definite low.

Then, almost exactly a year later, in June 2005 there was the culmination of our efforts to make minority Parliament work for Canadians. For the first time in Canadian history, the House of Commons adopted a budget bill authored by New Democrats. The amendment was the result of negotiations between our caucus and the Liberal caucus that had occurred in April, 2005. (See Chapter 1 for details.) The drama on that warm June evening in the House of Commons was palpable, since defeat of the bill would also defeat the Liberal minority, triggering an election. By a single vote, the amendment passed and an unwanted election was avoided. Instead of unnecessary tax cuts to the largest corporations, $4.6 billion of Canadians' hard-earned tax dollars were invested in education and training—including money for First Peoples; investment in public transit to reduce greenhouse gas pollution; affordable housing; increased foreign aid; and, in a separate bill, protection of workers when their employers faced bankruptcy.

Still, arriving at these very positive results had seen some of the lowest moments in recent Canadian politics: personal insults hurled across the floor of the House of Commons, unbridled heckling from a group of unruly MPs with their horrid finger-pointing; straight-armed salutes accompanied by accusatory, hate-filled glares; conversations, secretly taped, as to whether votes could be swapped in exchange for privileges and positions. These were indeed dark days on Parliament Hill and Canadians were properly disgusted with the whole sordid performance. Ed Broadbent summed up the situation with his usual capacity for plain talking: "It seems to me that the inherent dignity of the individual that should be recognized in this House is not being respected."

Nevertheless, as Canadians prepared to celebrate Canada Day 2005, they could also celebrate a budget that would put some homeless people into homes, commuters into buses, students into colleges and universities that they couldn't otherwise afford, and more Canadian foreign aid into the hands of those around the world in the most desperate need. A "better balanced budget for people and the environment," as we called it, a budget that would not have happened without the uniqueness of a minority Parliament combined with a determination to stick to principles and seize the moment to implement good ideas—ideas that work for Canadians.

While it was exciting to be in the House that night, the true import of the vote sinks in when I am far away from all that self-important pomp and circumstance, away from the electric buzz of the media scrum in the House of Commons foyer.

A few weeks after the House adjourned, Charlie Angus, our tireless MP from the huge Timmins–James Bay riding, insisted that he and I travel hundreds of kilometres north in a small, single-engine plane and spend some time in the impoverished First Nations reserve known as Kasatchewan. We flew in low over the massive delta where the Albany River reaches James Bay and we could see the reserve located smack dab in the middle of the lowlands. Obviously it would be a community prone to flooding. Cree Chief Leo Friday met us at the dirt airstrip. He explained that bureaucrats from Indian and Northern Affairs had insisted on locating the homes where they were, and ignored the pleas from community leaders to situate the village further upstream, away from the inevitable water flows. The bureaucrats recognized that flooding would be a problem all right, but thought they had a better idea. They chose to build an earth wall around the entire community. "Many of our community had lived in the walled-in world of the residential schools," Chief Friday lamented. "Now we find ourselves behind walls again. We can't see over the massive earth wall to see our traditional lands."

Despite the fresh water flowing all around this vast wilderness, the community had to boil its drinking water for the previous four years because the water treatment plant hadn't worked properly since being installed.

Worse still were the atrocious living conditions and overcrowding. With only 240 houses for 1,600 people, it was evident that there simply wasn't enough housing to shelter everyone properly. But the personal toll this extracts on individuals is enormous and simply beyond comprehension for the vast majority of Canadians. Chief Friday wanted the young people to join Charlie and me on a tour of the homes, and one band member was asked by the Chief where his brother was.

"He's sleeping now because that's the only time a bed was available," was the explanation. We visited that home during our tour and found four families—eighteen people in all—crammed into a dilapidated three-bedroom house. The basement had been flooded recently and was still soaking wet after the water had broken through the earth dykes, flooding the whole community. Less than a year later, a four-year-old girl living in one of these dangerous and crammed structures died as a fire destroyed her home. Such an injustice was just waiting to happen, and still is.

The poverty of our First Peoples stands as Canada's greatest shame. No wonder young aboriginal people are losing hope. Chief Friday, sad-eyed, asked if some of the new housing money contained in the NDP budget amendment would allow a few new houses to be built in his community.

"It's our job to make sure that the government gets the housing built. This is exactly the injustice that our budget housing dollars were meant to tackle," insisted Charlie on our return flight. It was an eloquent reminder that passing the budget was only the beginning of the work we needed to do.

And Chief Friday's plea for help for his community underscored the positive reaction we received to the work on our 2005 budget amendment. Canadians believe that politicians, regardless of their political stripe and beliefs, should work together to implement good ideas, rather than simply pursuing the interests of the political party that happened to win the most seats. In this instance, the people saw parties and individual MPs coming together, however awkwardly, behind the proposals we had put forward. And they liked what they saw, because their frustration over political posturing had reached a boiling point. It was indeed time for a new direction. When an opportunity for change suddenly presented itself, we were well prepared and eager to play a positive role in a minority Parliament.

We were prepared because, as the 2004 election campaign was winding down, it was becoming increasingly clear that the first minority government in more than two decades was a distinct possibility. I began to study the ways in which previous NDP caucuses had worked to effect positive change in these delicate minority situations. My long-time friend, retired Ryerson University President Terry Grier, helped pull together options for consideration, and Terry was certainly in a position to know. He had served as the first federal secretary of the NDP, working alongside Tommy Douglas. Terry was an MP working alongside party leader David Lewis and caucus chair Ed Broadbent in the 1972–74 minority Parliament. In 1974, he assumed the chair of Ryerson's political science department (where I was fortunate enough to be hired by Terry as a rookie teacher). Grier's review of the history and experience of minority legislatures made it clear that there was real potential for positive change. His review, combined with conversations with some of our most experienced MPs like Bill Blaikie, now dean of the House as the longest continuously serving MP, our House leader, Libby Davies, and my chief of staff, Dick Proctor, showed me that we were in for a tightrope walk in the months ahead, but that there could be real possibilities for positive change, particularly if we learned lessons from the past.

For older Canadians, seeing minority government work was neither surprising nor new. The NDP had been instrumental in making minority Parliaments work in the 1960s and early 1970s. New Democrat leaders like Tommy Douglas and David Lewis built bridges between parties in the House of Commons and produced some of the defining aspects of Canadian society—medicare, the Canada Pension Plan, Canada's national affordable housing construction strategy, and Petro-Canada, just to name a few. All these and more were created in the political hothouse of minority Parliaments. When no single party controls more than half the seats, it means that no party can lord its dominance and policies over the other parties. In a minority situation, MPs and party leaders have to find ways to work together because, alone, nothing would be accomplished. It means that best ideas actually have to compete for public support and for a majority of votes in the House of Commons. What a wonderful concept!

The most important lesson that I learned from Terry's analysis and talking with the other NDP veterans was: Stick to your principles and be true, in everything you do, to those who cast their ballot for your party. This was Tommy Douglas's message in his famous 1983 speech to the fiftieth anniversary convention of the CCF-NDP, held in Regina. It was not hard for me to remember that the NDP's history of sticking to its principles is the characteristic that first drew me to the party many years ago.

In this revised edition, I decided to continue talking primarily about ideas that work for Canadians. The final two chapters delve into the nitty-gritty of the 2004 and 2006 election campaigns and expand on some progressive ideas that were actually put into practice in the 2004–05 minority that benefited Canadians.

Sometimes I'm asked what I find most frustrating in my job and how I deal with the stress of it all. Oh, there are the frustrating days to be sure, but I said to myself long ago that I would try to put stress and frustration out of my emotional lexicon. So far, I've managed. The main trick I learned from Olivia—exercise. On most days I hit the gym and burn some calories. Calorie burning is essential for survival in politics with lunches on the run, irregular meals, and little control over what you're actually ingesting. I know I'd balloon out of my clothes in no time if I didn't regularly get on a treadmill, ride a bike, or swim lengths. Olivia steered me back into this workout habit when my cholesterol was becoming a concern. It's paid off. This started back when we were both city councillors. We'd inevitably have separate community meetings that would run well into the evening, so we decided to have a regular rendezvous at the University of Toronto gym. The gym has the double advantage of being just a few blocks from our home and remaining open until 11 pm. We'd meet in the field house for some laps—she runs much faster than me— or the pool—where I've been teaching her to do the butterfly. Whenever we have the chance, we also take out our "bicycle built for two" for long outings along the Toronto waterfront and onto the Leslie Street spit. Such outings help keep frustrations in perspective.

Journalists conducting longer interviews about the NDP often get around to a question that is frustrating. It runs roughly as follows: "Mr. Layton, what are you going to do about the perception people have that, while they agree with you on so many issues, they see your party as wanting to just tax and spend. They say they can't trust you to keep spending under control?" While the question is frequently delivered in a sympathetic way, my answer is often not. If facts formed the basis of reportage, instead of repeated myths drawing on isolated circumstances, Canadians wouldn't have that misperception about our party at all. My frustration has been reduced of late because I've had some backup from an unexpected source. "The NDP is right! It's about investment," said former RBC Dominion Securities' Chief Economist and Managing Director at Toronto Dominion Bank Paul Summerville. Mr. Summerville was not only strongly agreeing with the NDP budget amendment, he was also explaining why he had decided to run for us in the 2006 election.

Taking my seat in the House of Commons for the first time was a moving experience. Sitting with my caucus colleagues, including former leaders Alexa McDonough and Ed Broadbent, and Bill Blaikie, gave this rookie some sense of comfort, although it was intimidating, nonetheless. The House should embody the best of Canadian democratic tradition and practice but that old expression "the good, the bad, and the ugly" seemed to sum up my early experiences in the House of Commons, although perhaps in reverse order! The "good" took quite a while to materialize.

Of course, I was thinking of my dad as I addressed Mr. Speaker for the first time. Dad had preceded me as an MP and encouraged me, from an early age, to take an interest in our parliamentary institutions. I was drawn into a church-based parliamentary youth group when I was twelve. Meeting some of the longer-serving MPs from all parties, I was proud and grateful that so many of them had kind words in sharing their memories of my father and his role in the House. Universally, they commented on how respectful he was of all MPs, of all points of view, and of the institutions of Parliament. Clearly, he had practiced what Ed Broadbent describes as the importance of "respecting the inherent dignity and worth of every Member, indeed of every human being." Canadians can only hope that the future will bring more MPs to the House of Commons who believe in tolerance and listening respectfully to the opposing points of view.

This revised edition takes into account political events that occurred up to the end of June 2006. The first session of the thirty-ninth Parliament has just ended, and a second vote on same-sex marriage, the urgent need to begin serious work on reducing the impact of climate change, and Canadian involvement in the war in Afghanistan, the softwood lumber sellout (as I have called it) all will be important topics of debate when Members of Parliament return to the nation's capital in the fall.

In response to the shocks of recent months and with a mandate bestowed by only a minority of Canadians, Mr. Harper and his Conservatives have launched Canada onto a new and dangerous path. Canadian values have been ignored as his government abandoned so much that Canadians hold dear: our environmental commitments to the world and future generations, our role as purveyors of peace, our engagement on the global battle against poverty and AIDS, the emphasis on investments in childcare, housing and education essential for our future—foresaken for expedient tax cuts benefitting most those with the most—and our obligations to the first people of this land.

While the election of 2006 turned on issues of scandal and years of aimless government, Canadians must now face the deeper choices before us. I believe that there is a path, founded in Canadian values and ideas that work. These choices are represented by the New Democratic Party. I hope that what follows will help convince you, the reader, to join with me to help make them a reality.

In creating *Speaking Out Louder*, I have built on *Speaking Out Loud* by adding this new Preface, by adding and updating ideas and events throughout the original text and by adding two chapters that highlight the events and the enormous significance of the past two Canadian elections and Parliaments.

I would like to thank Dick Proctor, Bob Gallagher, successive chiefs of staff, Franz Hartmann, Brian Topp and Sue Milling, Olivia Chow, and Jonathan Schmidt of Key Porter for their invaluable assistance in helping me put together the changes and additions to this book. Also, a big thank you to my caucus and all our staff for their superb efforts. As for errors and omissions, they continue to be my responsibility.

Introduction

My father always said to the four of us kids, "You wouldn't want to miss an opportunity!" He said it most often at the end of a family dinner. We'd groan...then clear the dishes.

But sometimes, usually one-on-one, or with Mom alongside, he'd share his counsel when we faced tougher choices in our lives. In these more serious discussions, I always drew strength from Dad's focus on taking the opportunity to serve. He saw a problem, or someone would bring one to him, and he'd want to pull people together to develop ideas that would work. He'd call on people to take the opportunity to serve their community, putting the best ideas into action.

Now I find myself with a wonderful opportunity to serve. I wish Dad were still here to advise me. I do get regular emails from my mother, who, of course, was always the one with the best advice on practical matters anyway. Lately she's been telling me that one of our best new constituencies as New Democrats is to be found among "informed seniors." To quote her: "They're not only worried about themselves and the future of things like health care, Jack," she writes. "They're worried about the air their grandchildren breathe." According to a Toronto Board of Health report prepared by Dr. Sheela Basrur, the medical officer of health widely regarded as the most sane voice during Toronto's SARS crisis in 2003, each year in Toronto alone one thousand people, mostly children and seniors, die before their time because of smog.

I've always found it immensely rewarding to join with others in speaking out about issues and collaborating with people to find ideas that work and to put these solutions in place. Over the twenty years I've spent in public life, working in local government and in Canada-wide organizations, I've had hundreds of these opportunities. Now, as leader of the New Democratic Party of Canada, I have a chance to infuse into our national dialogue a full range of positive ideas and strategies for solving the serious problems we face as a nation.

The NDP is a great place to pursue this work because it has always been about building a better world, taking positive action together. Think of Tommy Douglas bringing medicare into being as the first provincial premier to carry our political banner (at the time it was the Co-operative Commonwealth Federation, or CCF). I was one of many who celebrated Tommy's legacy by voting for him in the CBC Greatest Canadian contest in the fall of 2004. Tommy Douglas was selected for the honour. I believe the million votes were cast for a vision of Canada as much as they were for a great leader from Saskatchewan who, as one New Democrat Youth T-shirt put it, "never was Prime Minister." Or think of Manitoba premier Gary Doer putting into place a remarkable sustainable energy strategy for the twenty-first century that will reduce pollution and at the same time strengthen the economy of the province. The NDP's focus is to tap that positive energy that Canadians have in abundance. And to draw on their best ideas and make them work.

This book isn't about the NDP platform. We have election campaigns for that. It's about the experiences I've *had*—as a city councillor, community activist, and Federation of Canadian Municipalities president—that make me believe that by working together, citizens can be the catalysts for the adoption of good ideas in government at all levels.

Over the past two decades, however, political debate has been about how we should accomplish less together, not more. Whether it's tax cuts that effectively download responsibility for paying for good ideas onto individuals through user fees; or whether it's trade deals that restrict governments' capacity to act in their citizens' interests; or whether it's handing over the collective role of government to corporations through privatization, we've been taught to abandon the concept that we can build together.

I reject that analysis because I'm a pragmatist who's seen good ideas in action. This book shares just some of those ideas and solutions, and the role they played in making me believe federal politics matters. All politicians speak with hope about the future. But I believe that experience—where someone has been, the choices he or she has made, his or her solutions to problems—is equally important. Rhetoric is easy. Results are what count.

Friends suggested to me that I should share some of these experiences with a broader range of Canadians. I'd like to tell you a bit about where I've been, the people I've met, and some of the ideas I'm proud to have put in effect.

We have opportunities to make our world a better place. The question is, Are we going to take them? I know what Dad would have said.

Good ideas come from many directions. Since I started working on this book, many people have generously shared their ideas with me. I want to single out the following: Greg Allen, David Bell, Lisa Caton, Martha Friendly, Michael Hough, Phil Jessup, Richard Johnston, Gordon Laird, Hugh Mackenzie, Burkhard Mausberg, Michael Rachlis, Wayne Roberts, Mary Rowles, Michael Shapcott, Rick Smith, Jim Stanford, Ross Sutherland, Dan Tatroff, Ralph Torrie, Mel Watkins, Michael Wiggin, Armine Yalnizyan, and Peter Zimmerman.

I could not have completed this project without George Ehring and Dennis Mills (the editor, not the former MP) and my team in Ottawa, especially Franz Hartmann, Jamey Heath, Donne Flanagan, Bruce Cox, and Chris Watson. Others who have been instrumental in the project are Jim Laxer, Alison Reid, and Marjan Farahbaksh. Pierre Ducasse,

Karl Belanger, and André Cardinal have assisted me in various ways with the French edition, prepared by the superb translator Isabelle Allard. I also want to thank my French publisher, Guy Saint-Jean, for his patience and faith.

Various friends encouraged me to write this book but some went further and offered me their homes as getaways. Svend Robinson and his partner, Max Riveron, provided a haven on Parker Island, and Pat Martin and his wife, Barbara, loaned us their Saltspring Island farmhouse for secluded writing.

Serendipity intervened when I called Key Porter's Meg Taylor at a moment she had been considering calling me. Little did she know that at the behest of her astonishingly demanding and supportive employer, Anna Porter, she would be compelled to virtually move in to my home to supervise the completion of the book, which otherwise might well still be on the go.

Olivia Chow devoted the better part of two erstwhile holidays to organizing ideas and editing drafts—with constant encouragement and creativity.

To all of these and to the many hundreds of friends and acquaintances who have shared their good ideas with me over the years, I offer my deepest thanks. Any shortcomings in capturing the full extent of the possibilities embodied in their ideas are mine alone.

[CHAPTER 1]

Why Does Politics Matter?

Politics matters. Ideas matter. Democracy matters, because all of us need to be able to make a difference. This book is about all three—politics, ideas, and democracy. The chapters that follow are about ideas—ideas that work. As outrageous as it sounds, coming from one, politics is too important to leave just to politicians. That's where you come in. You, the Canadian citizen, or someone who is on the way to becoming one. Canada is your country. Democracy should ensure that you are engaged and involved in setting the course for your country. You should feel right at the centre of the political process but, all too often, you feel pushed aside. You're told that politics doesn't really matter. That message is often delivered by politicians closely linked with the corporate elite. At the heart of their message is, keeping you out of politics creates more space for them. Power has been slipping away from Canadians. Have you noticed? I remember the optimism of Canadian politics years ago—we could build together and were proud of it. We built health-care systems for all, the best affordable housing in the world, great education systems for our kids, railways and public transit systems, communities where quality of life was second to none. But now, we feel all that slipping away. Even as communities across Canada are showing the way with creative local solutions, grabbing every opportunity that comes within their grasp, our federal government has cynically slipped into the role of naysayer.

For at least ten years, we've been told we cannot build and innovate anymore because we have no financial capacity to do so. As we turn away, discouraged, from voting, from participating, from building together, the vacuum that's created allows powerful elites to be free to negotiate cozy deals behind closed doors, deals that often cost Canadians their livelihood. They want to sell off our public resources without your knowledge. There is a growing CEO atmosphere around government these days with the direction of the country being directed from Bay Street boardrooms, well away from pesky questioners. Powerful interests want to spend your money on astoundingly expensive projects such as the Star Wars missile defence program. And the fewer opportunities that Canadians are given to have meaningful input, the easier it is for the corporate elite to proceed, maximizing their bottom line in the process.

There's another reason why so many people come to believe that politics doesn't matter. Sociologists call it "feeling alienated," left outside, as though there is nothing that we can do about the problems we face. It's sad. I've met Canadians across the country who refer to Ottawa, not as a place, but as a bad idea. These folks think that government, with its complex processes and shenanigans, doesn't represent them, or speak for them, or act on their behalf. The federal sponsorship scandal and other debacles have only served to rub more salt in the wounds. Our confidence is further shaken when governments act to dismantle public services or social programs that people have come to rely on. But think about it—shouldn't this alienation be driving us to become more involved in politics, not less? People should be working with their neighbours, their co-workers, and with others who share their concerns, coming together to make sure their voices are heard, their interests protected, and their ideas and concerns treated seriously.

For two decades at least, corporate think tanks and the politicians who promote their messages have been telling Canadians, essentially, that citizens do not matter in the political process because they lack the capacity to build the country of their dreams. This feeds a sense of alienation. With every election, it seems, fewer people turn out to vote. That's just as well from the point of view of the corporate players. According to them, the country we dream of is possible only if we leave the decision-making to the private sector. They promise prosperity but then dismantle the public sector for corporate profit, at heavy cost to all. It's time to build again. I'm a typical Canadian in that I've always loved building. Canadians are builders. But year after year, we've been taking apart what we built: medicare, affordable housing, industrial strategies, and public power systems. The past ten years have been all about tax cuts. These years have focused on privatizing our public services and on empowering the corporations through trade deals that handcuff citizens wanting to build better communities. I intend to show in this book that we can once more build to achieve a new prosperity for Canadians, even a prosperity for those corporations that have been maximizing their success when people are poor.

In the world of 9/11, SARS, mad cow disease, tsunamis, hurricanes, AIDS, famine, and grinding poverty, the need for collective action has been brought into sharp relief. We can almost see the faces of those courageous nurses, volunteers, caregivers, and peacemakers.

With the SARS health crises of 2003, Canadians recognized the need and value of public services and the taxes that pay for them. Let's face it: our taxes pay for nurses on SARS wards, for our soldiers on peacekeeping and peacemaking missions, for forest-fire fighters, for childcare workers, and much more. As the American jurist Oliver Wendell Holmes said a century ago, "Taxes are what we pay for civilized society." Or, as my disarmingly insightful wife, Olivia Chow, put it so clearly on national TV (as she provided commentary on a

CTV panel), "Taxes are what we put on the table, to do the things we want to do in common."

When the government removes itself from public housing and the private sector fails to provide affordable housing, the poor end up homeless, living on the street. This is hardly the time to advocate less government.

I have always found it interesting that no politician who is caught up in this corporate drift when referring to the military proclaims: "We should privatize or do more with less." Why, then, do these same people say we should privatize and cut health care, education, or environmental protection? It's because corporations want it that way, and their powerful influences have permeated government much too extensively.

The end result has been to teach Canadians to expect less. Do not expect solutions now for cities, for long-term or home care, for child care, or for assisting the people afflicted by desperate poverty and disease around the world. Lower your expectations, you Canadians. Abandon your dreamy, idealistic ways, your optimism, your capacity to construct the future you wish for your communities or elsewhere in the world. What a sad and demoralizing message it has been. No wonder people do not want to be associated with politics at all and stay home when voting time comes.

That explains why so many Canadians have turned to alternative ways of challenging the way things are by building what they believe in. Community organizations, non-governmental organizations, movements of citizens have sprung up related to peace, the environment, sovereignty, health care, human rights, education, worker safety and salaries, international development assistance, equality. These groups, said General Romeo Dallaire, as he spoke to journalists working for free speech in the fall of 2003, are the places where hope for the future resides. It's called "civil society," society outside the traditional governmental/electoral processes, and it is rising up. I'm not the only one to have said that "a new superpower is emerging"—people in communities around the world, connecting in novel ways, exercising their aspirations in positive initiatives locally and globally. These are the builders of the future. Let's become part of that process, and turn politics on its head.

When Canadians get up in the morning, we turn on the tap, and without thinking about it, we expect safe, clean water to come out. That water is treated and delivered by public-sector workers toiling away for a public utility. We flush the toilet, and without thinking about it, we expect the sewage to disappear and be properly treated by yet another publicly owned utility. We drive to work on public highways or ride there on public transit. Our children go to public schools. In most of Canada, the electricity that powers our workplaces and our homes has been generated and delivered to us by a public utility. In the rest of the country, our power is publicly regulated. We expect police officers to maintain law and order. We expect firefighters to protect our communities. If we need health care, we expect doctors and nurses to minister to us in public hospitals. All these services (and hundreds of others) are provided to us in one way or another by our government. What's really unthinkable is that we would ever want to do without public services. But our governments are now selling them off to private companies or creating cozy-sounding "public-private partnerships" (P3s). Can that be good?

Fortunately, the message that private multinational corporations bring us closer to the divine has worn a little thin. The past two decades have been the Era of Corporate Corruption, aptly demonstrated in the United States by Enron and WorldCom, and in Italy by Parmalat, and by so many others. For those who still believe that corporations are reliable and trustworthy, every week brings a new tale of CEOs raking in multi-million-dollar salaries, while their corporations lose money and lay off workers—Nortel is the most insidious example because it's ostensibly a Canadian company—plus pension-fund rip-offs, insider trading, "cooked" accounting books, and profits diverted to offshore tax havens.

The reality is that for a number of very good reasons, many aspects of our economy and society are better delivered by government than by the private sector. That's because governments are typically more transparent, accountable, and efficient than the private sector. Many others are better left to the private sector, and, when they are, we should let them be. It's important for us to find the balance—and to know the difference. However, if we think it's best for the private sector to deliver certain goods or services, we, the people, need to make sure that we have good regulation and oversight to protect us and our environment. I don't think that government needs to run a mine, but we must not rely on the mining company to tell us it's safe for workers—the families of the dead Westray miners can testify to that. Thankfully, the families and the Steelworkers Union never gave up and pressed the Canadian government to adopt laws with penalties in situations where worker safety is jeopardized. They did so with the help of our NDP MPs Alexa McDonough and Yvon Godin, a miner himself. While I think a great deal more shipping should be done by the railways and getting trucks off our highways, I don't have a problem with private trucking. But I think rules need to be in place to ensure that drivers are only licensed after passing a demanding test, that they are restricted in the amount of hours they are behind the wheel, and that the trucks are reliable and inspected regularly so other motorists aren't killed by flying tires on highways.

When it comes to food inspecton and safety, I want to be assured that the meat being purchased has been inspected and okayed by a qualified individual employed by the government, not someone employed and in the pay of the meat-packing company.

When people in Walkerton died painful deaths because the Ontario government had decimated its water inspection services, it is not the time to advocate less government.

When hospital waiting lists grow to unacceptable and dangerous lengths because we have underfunded the health-care system and failed to provide adequate numbers of trained nurses, doctors, and other medical staff, it is not the time to advocate less government.

We need to advocate for positive change. To move from opposition to proposition. To build instead of diminish. I came by this belief in many ways. One of the pathways has deep family roots.

An early memory for me—providing an important political lesson—is hearing about the work of my great-grandfather, Philip E. Layton, who had been blinded as a teenager in a woodcutting accident. After otherwise recovering from that, he immigrated to Canada from England and settled in Montreal, starting a music business in Montreal that can still be found at St. Catherine and Stanley streets (now under the name Layton Audio). Then he did something very romantic: he sent a message across the Atlantic asking for the hand of Alice Gilbert, the young nurse who had cared for him back in England. She agreed and sailed for Canada in 1887 and they made their lives together in Montreal.

He was dismayed that blind children had no opportunity for schooling, and that blind adults had nowhere to work. He was appalled at the meagre lives blind people eked out, too many of them reduced to selling pencils on street corners. On one occasion while he napped, his two sons—both notorious pranksters—took his dark glasses, his white cane, and a cup, and pretended to be poor blind kids, collecting coins at the corner of Guy and Sherbrooke, near their little house.

They were caught by their father and given a scolding they never forgot. The world of those with disabilities, they were told, is not to be made fun of or exploited. It is, rather, a world inhabited by people who deserve the same rights and opportunities as any other citizen. My great-grandfather and Alice were determined not only to provide for their family, but to improve the plight of blind people in Canada as well. Although Philip Layton became a successful piano tuner and salesman, his real achievement was in organizing members of the Montreal blind community to fight for themselves.

In the early 1900s, Philip and Alice found a farm property west of the city (on what is now Sherbrooke Street West) that they hoped to buy in order to build a school and workshop. They began a fundraising drive, using networks of volunteers to hold Montreal's first "tag day," selling tags that could be hung off coat buttons in support of the cause. Out onto Montreal streets they flooded to sell their tags, young people, boys and girls alike, yes, including blind girls, which was considered scandalous at the time—all to build a dream.

In 1908, that dream became a reality, and Montreal's blind people had a lending library, sheltered workshop, and social club. Shortly after, a school was built, and thousands of Montreal's blind children have studied there for almost a century. My great-grandfather's vision became the Montreal Association for the Blind (MAB). For blind people themselves, the project provided an early step toward full participation in the community and helped them realize their rights of citizenship.

Even though I never knew my great-grandfather, I will not forget the stories handed down to me of his ability to organize and empower people. Several of Philip's descendants were politicians. My grandfather Gilbert became a cabinet minister in a government formed by newly elected reformers determined to throw out the arrogant and corrupt Liberal government of the day. They called themselves the Union Nationale and were led by Maurice Duplessis. Premier Duplessis was an ardent French-Canadian nationalist who would later oppose forced participation of young francophone Quebeckers in the Second World War because he regarded it as Britain's conflict. My grandfather resigned his cabinet post and his seat in 1938 and later broke completely with the Union Natonale over this "conscription crisis." Gilbert believed that all Canadian young people should fight the fascists. After the war, he returned to Montreal to follow in his father's footsteps as chair of the MAB. Gilbert's brother, George, won a seat on Montreal's city council. My father, Robert, also served as chair of the MAB. My sister, Nancy, now serves on the board, carrying on the family tradition. That people can advocate for change and then actually make it happen has been an essential part of our family's tradition.

My path grew out of the tumultuous days of the October Crisis. It was 1970. Quebec's Quiet Revolution had moved to a much more active and aggressive form of protest against inequality. Self-determination movements were forming and gaining support. I was an early supporter of a community movement in my neighbourhood. Front d'Action Politique (FRAP) was a democratic municipal political organization concerned about good planning, affordable housing, the environment, and local democracy in the era of Montreal's autocratic mayor, Jean Drapeau. It was exciting, canvassing and building support among low-income tenants for the idea that their neighbourhoods should be protected from ruthless plans to evict them and tear down their homes. We knocked on doors, talked to residents, and built a movement to save old affordable housing. It was my first direct local politics experience. I thought of it as a real-life version of the democracy I was studying in my political science courses. A few years later, FRAP was renamed the Montreal Citizens'

Movement and became the duly elected majority government of the Montreal City Council, under the leadership of my friends Mayor Jean Doré and Deputy Mayor Thérèse Daviau.

Sadly however, some Quebec political movements strayed far beyond the limits of protest that any democracy can tolerate or accept. Over several months, terrorist bombings of Westmount mailboxes by the Front de Libération du Québec (FLQ) escalated into the kidnapping of the British trade commissioner, James Cross, and the murder of Quebec's Labour Minister, Pierre Laporte.

I was in my last year of studying politics, economics, and philosophy at McGill University when Laporte was murdered. I found myself at first agreeing with the popular sentiment calling for drastic action in response to the threat the FLQ seemed to represent. When Prime Minister Pierre Trudeau said he would suspend civil liberties through the use of the War Measures Act, I was inclined to go along with the vast majority of Canadians and even Quebeckers behind the get-tough plan.

Then one parliamentarian, Tommy Douglas, leader of the New Democratic Party of Canada, gave a widely reported speech decrying the suspension of civil rights. I said to myself: "That's a very unpopular position this NDP leader is taking." Still, as I listened to his powerful arguments and his brilliant capacity to deliver them, I realized that his stance, while unpopular, was indeed right. Mr. Douglas displayed eloquence, logic, and passion in a way I had never heard before. Here's just some of what Douglas said that made such an impression on me. It's from his October 16, 1970 address to the House of Commons on the introduction of the War Measures Act. "We are prepared to support the government in taking whatever measures are necessary to safeguard life and to maintain law and order in this country. But, Mr. Speaker, we are not prepared to use the preservation of law and order as a smokescreen to destroy the liberties and the freedom of the people of Canada. The government, I submit, is using a sledgehammer to crack a peanut!"

In the subsequent three weeks, as many as 424 people were detained under the War Measures Act. Most of them were never charged. Jean Marchand, Pierre Trudeau's Quebec lieutenant, and Jean-Pierre Goyer, the Solicitor General, accused all kinds of groups of being terrorist suspects. Some of the people arrested were from FRAP, the very group that was contesting the municipal election—I had canvassed on behalf of their local candidate. As developments were reported to the House on November 4, Douglas made an impassioned plea for human rights: "I think it is significant that to date most of those detained seem to be members of either FRAP or the Parti Québécois. Although I disagree with the separatists, it is not a crime to be one as long as they do not seek to use violence or unconstitutional means to advance their objectives. We in the New Democratic Party recognize the need for prompt and energetic steps to stamp out terrorism, but we have insisted from the beginning that in the process of stamping out terrorism we must not abridge the freedoms that our people and our forefathers have won for us over the years."

I joined the NDP at the very next opportunity.

• • •

Just a few months ago, I met the organist at the Anglican church where my uncle was being memorialized. He told me that he supported the work I was doing as leader of the NDP. As we chatted, the conversation turned to how it was that I had joined the NDP. Then he said, "Perhaps it is significant that I was one of those arrested and jailed without charge during the October Crisis in Quebec." He was a South

African who had moved to Canada and was working on justice issues, including an end to apartheid. Travelling in these circles evidently made him suspicious to the Canadian military and the RCMP. Under the War Measures Act, no reasons were needed to scoop him up and detain him for questioning, without any of the normal protections granted to Canadians.

Events of the sixties and seventies were formative for me— protesting against the Vietnam War, riding one of many buses to the U.S. border to denounce the testing of nuclear weapons, joining the march down Sherbrooke Street in Montreal as part of the "McGill français" demonstration to make the big English-language university bilingual, studying political philosophy with Charles Taylor while he was writing his magnum opus on Hegel and dialectics. Taylor's book *The Pattern of Politics* laid out the idea that debate and conflict can produce positive transformations. I had never thought of it that way. Compromise had been the watchword of Canadian politics, especially among the elites. Professor Taylor told us that this was the politics of status quo and privilege. He encouraged us to "challenge the way things are."

With Taylor's urging, I headed to Toronto to broaden my academic horizons. At York University, young professors turned me on to all manner of new thinking. I met and studied under Jim Laxer, a young leader of the Waffle movement. The Waffle was the name chosen by a group on the left within the New Democratic Party that felt the party was waffling on fundamentals like socialism and Canadian independence, hence the tongue-in-cheek moniker. Credit for the name goes to Ed Broadbent who flirted with the ginger group and said at one meeting: "If we're going to waffle, we may as well waffle to the left!" I found very compelling the concept that Canadians on the left had to be much more clear in our denunciation of certain government policies and more ambitious in our work to prevent Canada from being swallowed up by the United States and its multinational corporations. The well-known Canadian economist Mel Watkins had been writing about the need to place controls on foreign investment to protect our ability to make decisions in Canada that represented our values, rather than those of the U.S. administration and its supporters in corporate America. By the time I had become immersed in my doctoral studies, I decided to study how nations had attempted to influence and restrain the movement of foreign capital to achieve national goals—like employment, research and development, environmental benefits, regional economic development, and the like. As I was beginning the work, the NDP won sufficient seats in the 1972 election to create a minority government for the Liberals. Prime Minister Trudeau now needed the support of the new leader of the NDP, David Lewis, in order to govern. Lewis supported Trudeau's Foreign Investment Review Agency (FIRA), which tried to make transnational corporate expansion in Canada more palatable. I ended up completing my doctoral thesis on the operations of this agency. After studying the thousands of foreign takeovers that were approved by FIRA and the very few that were refused, I concluded that this instrument of public policy had largely failed because of a lack of will on the part of the federal government to insist that its objectives be met. In the process, I developed an early appreciation of the growing power of multinational corporate capital flows in determining the shape of national societies, even undermining democratic institutions. Years later, the concern about this globalization process reached a fever pitch as a growing movement of young people, environmentalists, social justice advocates, and international development proponents rose up against the whittling away of people's power through trade deals of all sorts. My early assessment of the threats to sovereignty that globalization could pose has proven, sadly, to be all too true. We'll come back to this key challenge in later chapters of this book.

At the same time as I was researching the global, my professor of urban studies at York immersed me in the local. Professor Michael Goldrick, a friendly mentor in my early days at the windswept campus, brought me into contact with the ideas of thinkers like Jane Jacobs and the activism of a young lawyer and Toronto city councillor named John Sewell. Their work was exciting, hands-on focussing on stopping bad projects like the Spadina Expressway and promoting livable communities through affordable co-operative housing and neighbourhood preservation policies. Goldrick became a candidate in the famous 1972 municipal election in Toronto, the one that elected the "tiny perfect mayor," David Crombie, and his reform council. I threw myself into the campaign with a vengeance and learned about street-to-street electoral politics and community organizing from some of the best in the city. The win was unpredicted, huge, and enormously exciting.

I was hooked on local politics and neighbourhood engagement. After that election, I became involved in many urban reform movements and coalitions that formed around fair transit fares, that pursued community policing to reduce harassment of visible minorities and gays, that worked for rent controls to protect tenants from being gouged by unscrupulous landlords, and much more. We won some of these long struggles. Perhaps the most significant was the effort to build a rent-control system in Ontario, where tenants were being hammered with massive rent increases they simply couldn't afford. They had virtually no rights with which to protect themselves. I learned about how to help tenants organize to protest impossible rent increases and poor maintenance of their rented homes and apartments. The key concept I was taught by people like Norm Brudy, who had been empowering tenants for years. Brudy's main message was help tenants understand that, by acting collectively, they can be much more effective than acting alone. Step by step, we would walk through the process of building a tenant association, taking on the landlord together, withholding rents, and pressing governments to insist that landlords enforce basic building standards. We formed the Federation of Metro Tenants' Associations to convince political parties to establish rent controls and developed a communicatons strategy to ensure the media reported positively on our work.

I will never forget the powerful speeches of Stephen Lewis, then the young leader of the Ontario NDP, who relentlessly took the tenants' sad stories to the public forum of the legislature. The combination of grassroots organization and a political party that would present their case effectively and generate media proved to be a potent mixture. Rent controls came into place as a result of the combined pressure. Nightly meetings and weekend rallies and conventions were piled on top of my duties as a professor in the politics department at Ryerson Polytechnic Institute. I taught classes in local government, Canadian government and politics, and political theory to a succession of budding journalists, social workers, public health inspectors, engineers, and librarians.

My first wife, Sally, and I lived in North York, fiefdom of its outspoken mayor, Mel Lastman, who later became the first mayor of the megacity. Our children, Sarah and Michael, were born there, and we became involved trying to preserve the quiet family neighbourhood from Lastman's big developer friends who wanted to overrun the communities with high-rises. A trip to North York today will demonstrate that we weren't entirely successful.

By 1982, we had moved to downtown Toronto, and I decided to put my years of political theory into direct action.

I ran for Toronto City Council and won in what the Toronto *Star* reported was the big upset of the election. Our huge team of volunteers took on a much-touted incumbent conservative alderman named Gordon Chong, who had big-time financial backing from the business elites on Bay Street. We were given no chance to win, but the hundreds of tenants who had worked with us for fair and affordable housing over the past few years turned out to help. We ended up with six hundred volunteers. On election night, when some pundits declared me defeated, I said: "Six hundred workers can beat $60,000 anytime!" That's just what occurred when all the votes from the big high-rises rolled in. I learned that night that democracy is finally about people, not money. It's a lesson we need to relearn periodically.

The next twenty years as a city councillor would show me every day how much politics matters in very down-to-earth ways. Sometimes the issues had an impact on only a limited number of people: a community garden, a bicycle repair service run by formerly homeless men, an income-generating recycling program in Toronto's oldest public housing neighbourhood. Yet even these "small" issues were important and worthwhile to the people involved. Other times, the scope was larger. With other councillors, I helped initiate Toronto's first blue-box curbside recycling program to pick up glass, plastic, and cans. I also chaired the Toronto Board of Health for many years, with its $50-million budget involving six hundred-plus health-care professionals. This agency helped put in place Canada's first AIDS Defence Plan, and assisted in developing a labour-business-city partnership to retrofit building spaces, which created jobs, saved energy, cut costs, and reduced pollution. Some projects took a long time, like the seventeen years to try to persuade city council to remove the ugly Gardiner Expressway in the part of the port lands that I represented and replace it with a tree-lined boulevard, bike lanes, and public art. Others projects were elegantly simple ones that community groups could achieve, as long as they had some political support, like the installation of an elegant wind turbine on Toronto's waterfront. In that case, I was able to help the turbine come into being as the vice chair of the $2-billion-a-year publicly owned energy company known as Toronto Hydro.

It comes as a surprise to many, but municipal governments all across the country are putting together some of the most progressive, innovative solutions to practical problems facing their residents. You will read about lots of examples in this book. Cities, towns, and villages have the power to build programs that really work to meet people's immediate needs, implement ideas, and create change. And they are doing it now, from coast to coast. Local democracies and community governments are where the real innovations are happening and the best ideas are being originated with public participation and creativity. The problem? No money! It's that simple. But at the federal level it's a much different story. The federal government is so awash in revenue that it can easily afford to give tax cuts to the corporate world with abandon, while community governments put needed projects and creative initiatives on hold and raise taxes just to tread water. Changing this unfortunate reality was a key motivation for me when I decided to move to federal politics and leave behind the exciting world of local government and its emphasis on direct contact with people and their ideas and solutions. I want community democracy to be able to flourish, so I headed to Parliament Hill, apparent fount of our national aspirations, but too often the problem rather than the solution.

I am desperately worried that the Canadian government is losing, or has already given away, its will to act on behalf of citizens.

43

During those same twenty years I served on Toronto City Council, the federal government signed away significant democratic and sovereign powers in international trade deals like the North American Free Trade Agreement (NAFTA) and through the World Trade Organization (WTO). Why would our government do this? The goal was to create a legal environment globally that would make it easier for governments to reduce services, while opening the door to their corporate replacements. To shrink the public provision for people's needs while enshrining a legal latticework that would facilitate multinational corporate expansion. Just look at how services like care for seniors, drinking water supply, and even our energy utilities have come under the growing influence of multinational corporations instead of public institutions or community organizations. This transition from a mixed public-private-sector economy to one where privatization is increasing and public services are sent packing was mandated by trade arrangements never approved by democratic processes. Critics will say that the 1988 federal election was the Free Trade Election, and Prime Minister Mulroney, campaigning in favour, won a majority government. But Mr. Mulroney's Progressive Conservatives did not receive 50 per cent support. Majority support went to the combined Liberal and NDP, which both campaigned vigorously against the idea of free trade. A better set of ideas for trade in the context of well-functioning and just democracies needs to be constructed.

During the same period, the federal government and our chartered banks have facilitated the foreign takeover of thousands and thousands of Canadian companies. Think about this: from 1985 to 2002, foreign corporations applied to Industry Canada's Investment Review Division for the takeover of 10,052 Canadian companies. Not a single takeover was rejected. Not one.

Of the new foreign investment spending in Canada during that time, only 3.4 per cent was actually used for new business investment in real machinery or factories or buildings. A staggering 96.6 per cent went for corporate takeovers. Is this really what we mean when we talk about encouraging investment in Canada?

In his book, *The Vanishing Country*, Mel Hurtig describes this takeover scene and the threats to Canada's independence. He and writers like Linda McQuaig, Maude Barlow, Tony Clarke, and others have chronicled the wholesale sell-out of Canada, and it is very alarming.

Not to put too fine a point on it, but corporate powers are taking over our country and threatening our independence by utilizing their friends in federal and provincial governments as "business partners." Our governments are allowing this takeover through downsizing and privatizing, the slicker packaging of public-private partnerships, and abdicating democratic decision-making. We find an example in the text of NAFTA's Chapter 11, which blithely gives foreign corporations the right to sue Canadian governments for lost profits whenever our legislation limits their freedom in Canada. (Canadian companies, however, do not have this right in the United States.) As Hurtig says, "The potential for future U.S. corporate claims relating to health care, education, social services, municipal water delivery, federal and provincial resources and cultural policies are real and ominous."

Perhaps the most symbolic example has been the decision of the federal Liberal government, in the fall of 2003, to turn over the Canadian census-taking job to Lockheed Martin, the world's largest munitions manufacturer. Asked why an American multinational was contracted to count Canadians, the hapless minister responsible at the time cited the provisions of trade agreements as the reason this couldn't be prevented. As NDP MP Bill Blaikie put it in yet another of his wonderful contributions to parliamentary debate, "In just which corner of the Pentagon will the Canadian vital statistics be stored?"

All this has to change if Canadians are to be able to create solutions in our own interests. In the end, this is why Canadian independence is important. Politics is about people, not just corporations. Sovereignty lets people decide. And we are losing our sovereignty.

I know that sounds dramatic. But we are losing our independence and that ought to concern every Canadian. At the local level, we still have the power to put in place community gardens so people can grow their own food. At the national level, however, our agricultural policies are subject to scrutiny by foreign governments. Community decisions in a whole range of policy areas are based on Canadian values, determined by our democratic processes, as awkward as they can sometimes be. International trade arrangements are jeopardizing our ability to make these decisions and are increasingly turning over the direction of our society to huge corporate entities that do not necessarily share our values.

What values? Let's start with the notion that Canadians believe communities are places where we help one another. We don't just leave people to fend for themselves when it comes to health care, to housing, to education, or to safe communities. That's why Canadians say they are proud of our health-care system. In fact, for many of us, it's what we cite first when asked about what makes us different from Americans. We also highlight our diversity and the welcome we give to people from around the world. The diversity and welcome are founded on public services that help people adjust and make their way in a new land, while also ensuring that they can preserve as well as celebrate their cultural communities in enduring ways. These public services need support, including financial support. Yet another value is our belief in peace. Canadians support their soldiers abroad by citing their key role in pursuing peace. Blessed are the peacemakers. Ask Canadians what the proudest achievement of 2003 was, and the most frequent answer is that we refused to participate in the invasion of Iraq.

So Canadians have their values and are justifiably proud of them. But our recent governments, which have pushed international trade deals sacrificing democratic rights and accountability and given ever-increasing rights to powerful and profitable multinational corporations, have been totally out of touch with the Canadian bedrock. We need to confront this challenge directly. We need federal and provincial governments that put the interests of Canadians first. That's why, when I was president of the Federation of Canadian Municipalities (FCM), I created the team of municipalities that challenged the unbridled implementation of the General Agreement on Trade in Services (GATS). It was going to lock municipalities into a decision-making straitjacket. The most dramatic example happened at the Greater Vancouver Regional Council. To save some money, some councillors were preparing to agree with a plan by a huge multinational water company to build a treatment plant. But then council discovered that, if the voters and their elected representatives became unhappy with the private operator and wanted to bring the water system back into the public realm, it would first have to pay compensation for lost profits to the multinational corporation. It also might well have to bid competitively for its own water system against other giant companies. Vancouver sought out the help of the FCM, which just so happened to have a president (me) who was alarmed about the prospects. FCM's worries about potential implications for local democracies were forcefully expressed to flummoxed federal trade bureaucrats who treated us with patronizing contempt. As a result, municipal opposition to the trade deals continued to grow, together with protests by community groups and young people in the streets.

Though I am convinced that we have already signed over far too much of our sovereignty, it is not too late to get it back. But, the clock is ticking.

In case there are any doubts about urgency, let's remember that Canada has already been forced to pay a penalty to the U.S.-based manufacturer of the toxic gasoline additive MMT. This additive is not permitted in the U.S., but because of the wording of the NAFTA rules, the manufacturer, Ethyl Corporation, was able to sue Canada successfully for prohibiting its sale. Their case was that Canada had to pay the forgone profits of the company. In other words, when the Canadian government wants to prevent a toxic compound from being used here in order to protect our citizens and the environment, it must pay a penalty to the U.S.-based multinational firm! Imagine if something similar happened with hundreds of decisions made by Canadian democracies—from local governments and provinces to the federal government? Well, that's the future we have in store, unless we act and transform our politics.

The final approach to politics that I want to present here is about connections. Connections of people and connections of processes and systems. The incarnation of the best politics would point out the great extent to which our economy, our environment, our health, our social safety net, our democracy, and, yes, our independence itself are all interconnected. How can we even think about building a healthy society without thinking about what we eat, what kind of housing we have, how much income we earn, the quality of the air we breathe? And so on. Each of these affects every other one. Let me take a simple example. We all want to live in safe neighbourhoods. When we say "safe," that brings up the subject of crime. But a neighbourhood downwind from a polluting, coal-fired generating station is not safe. A community that draws its drinking water from a polluted river is not safe. A one-industry town is not safe. A society that neglects its children will not be safe for long.

We all need to think more about how interconnected we are, how much we depend on the environment and on the economic and social systems that weave society's fabric together. That's why in this book, when I talk about public health, for example, I hope you will be thinking not just about prenatal services, preventing the spread of AIDS, or community clinics. We also need to realize that public health is also about the air we breathe and the polluted air a lot of us who live in big cities have to breathe causes asthma in tens of thousands of people; it's about designing communities and encouraging transportation alternatives so people don't always have to rely on using cars to get around; and it's about eliminating the chemicals in our surroundings that cause cancer in so many people.

We can't think about the economy without thinking about its environmental impacts—and vice versa. The disappearance of some of our fisheries on both the Atlantic and Pacific coasts is a perfect example of the connection between environment and economy. So also is the way we generate the energy we need and dispose of the waste we create.

It's all about the choices we make as a community. We can choose to build nuclear power plants and import toxic waste—which we do, by the tonne: between 1987 and 1999, toxic waste imports into Canada grew from 129,476 tonnes to 660,000 tonnes! Or we can choose instead to retrofit buildings and improve public transit. We can make choices that respect the links between our economy and our environment and society. Or we can carry on making choices that create the appearance of prosperity now, passing on the problems to our children and their children.

So, what is this alternative vision of the economy inter-connected to environment and to society? It's a vision that reflects the reality of a complex twenty-first-century economy. It recognizes that the fundamental goals of an economy are to create financial well-being, improve environmental quality, increase social equity, and promote human development. In other words, it's no longer exclusively just about making profits. In the business community, this is being called the "Triple Bottom Line" approach: economic progress, environmental protection, and social equity. I agree with those three but would add one more—human rights for all from childhood to old age—as Dr. Trevor Hancock has suggested. Others who have been using this approach refer to this Quadruple Bottom Line as sustainable development.

Businesses have always been motivated by the financial bottom line, the last line in the accounting statements, showing the profit or loss for the year. This one-dimensional approach has limited our possibilities. If we added bottom lines for our social and environmental well-being and measured our success accordingly, we would be making the connections required to ensure that our world and our societies within it are to be sustainable for the long term. Canada should adopt this approach in its policy-making.

A successful twenty-first-century economy will be one that recognizes that public and private organizations should be structured to use capital efficiently, that improves environmental quality, contributes to solving social inequities (not watch them increase), that creates good-quality and safe jobs, practises true corporate responsibility, extends human rights, enhances democracy, and invests in products and services that people want and need. These organizations can be large or small, organized as non-profits, public-sector entities, or privately owned firms. What matters is that we create a context in which all of us have the opportunity to help meet the Quadruple Bottom Line goals. This vision celebrates the idea that democratically elected and sovereign governments by the people can provide the flexible and purposeful framework for our economy.

What do I mean? Here's a for instance. The public sector has to provide many essential services because only elected government has the potential to be directly accountable to the people. I say "potential" because true accountability requires a democracy that works well. I join most Canadians in putting education, health care, key community services like water and child care, energy, and most transportation into this "public sector" category. Moreover, our government has to invest in social and physical infrastructure, the nuts and bolts, because elected and engaged governments can reflect the balance and interconnectedness needed to reflect the priorities of the public. Someone has to look out for the common good, challenged, as it almost always is, by private greed. Who better to take responsibility for this than all of us together, through our votes and through our engagement in our communities?

This Quadruple Bottom Line vision is certainly not mine alone. Such new thinking is, happily, sprouting up here and there, often in places least expected. I am simply acknowledging what is already happening on the ground every day. Consider what Bill Hunter, president and CEO of Alberta-Pacific Forest Industries, one of the largest pulp mills in North America, was quoted in the *Globe and Mail*, December 1, 2003, as saying: "There is a new wave of CEO thinking about the triple bottom line [profit, environment, and social effects]. It's ethical; it's moral; it's access to raw materials in the long term. Society should demand that and will demand that."

It is a vision that no longer accepts the black-and-white division of the economy into the public and private sectors. It is a vision that has a much more sophisticated view of the economy—it sees it in full colour.

Thinking outside the box, and considering multiple simultaneous benefits, also opens doors to new ways of looking at things. An NDP member, a jeweller in a resource town, told me about his day. He used to berate the other business leaders of the community when they griped about the workers wanting higher wages. The jeweller told the others that when those workers don't have a few dollars left over from their pay packets after purchasing necessities, they don't buy jewellery. That means he couldn't hire sales staff, who, in turn, would have shopped in local stores. So giving raises to workers not only helps their quality of life, it spreads economic activity through a community as well.

Quadruple-bottom-line sustainability:
- **encourages everyone to live by four "bottom lines" simultaneously;**
- **rewards businesses that truly practise the quadruple bottom line;**
- **penalizes businesses that sacrifice environment, social equity, and human development for personal or institutional greed.**

In short, what differentiates this vision from the status quo is not public versus private: it's the new multiple-bottom-line economy versus the unidimensional-greed economy. We can draw some hope from some of the leading businesses and corporations that are beginning to "get it" by adopting a new approach to measuring corporate success. We can also draw hope from those catalysts for change that emerge from local community democracies.

In fact, the story that is unfolding today is about conflicting visions of collective goals, even conflicting visions of whether there is such a thing as collective goals (versus individual objectives). Parroting eighteenth-century theorists, many corporate think tanks, their tribunes, and representatives still contend that the true goal of an economy remains the maximization of profits. They continuously lobby governments and support political parties to develop and maintain laws and tax policies that affirm their concept of the greed economy. Why? Greed breeds Growth and is therefore Good. These interests don't want to share power with the rest of us. They are happier when other people don't bother to vote because they can continue influencing politicians and hoarding their wealth with the help of favourable government policies. Declining democracy is beneficial to this agenda.

The worst nightmare of the greed economy is the quadruple-bottom-line economy—a successful, just, green, and equitable economy in which humanity develops and flourishes in a sustainable equilibrium with nature. A truly balanced economy. Such a positive vision of the economy would redirect the existing huge government subsidies away from the unbridled acquisitive economy toward one in which businesses and government activities are truly focused on all the interconnected bottom lines that make up a harmonious community of communities and ecosystems. If effectively transformed into policy, this vision could unleash our collective capacities, our "commonwealth," through community action, the enhancement of the health of ecosystems and the plants and animals that inhabit them, as well as through innovation and wealth creation.

Much of this book is therefore about relationships, both short and long term. More than thirty million people live in Canada, in different circumstances and facing different obstacles. I've tried to focus on some of the issues that have the greatest impact on the greatest number of people. I raise some issues that, it seems to me, people aren't thinking all that much about. I want to get people thinking. I hope this book stimulates discussion. And I've chosen innovative solutions that are working, to encourage discussion.

No matter how vast a country we occupy, we all live together—a point so obvious that we forget its implications. What we do affects each other in ways that we've lost sight of. People want to be connected—with each other, in their communities, and with a government that they feel is responsive to their concerns and able to help them achieve their goals. Like the issues, people are connected to each other in ways that are both obvious and subtle.

When we talk about the love that connects us to our partners, our parents, and our children, we know what we mean. We want their world to be a better place, somewhere they can live their lives in justice and dignity, a place where their dreams can come true. We hope for a place where they don't suffer hardships, where they grow and prosper, and where the future is a little brighter than the past.

We also talk about loving our country. That's a different kind of passion. But like everything else, the future of our country and the future of the people who live in it depend on each other. Ultimately it's the love of humanity, of all people, that should drive us forward. Canada is a natural breeding ground for such a powerful perspective. That's why all of us have to be involved, making a difference.

Things are beginning to change in Canada, even affecting the holy mantra of the right—tax cuts above everything. Canadians understand that when they stopped being described as citizens and started being defined as taxpayers, they lost something. Canadians understand even better than corporate leaders that there's no free lunch. That you can't keep cutting taxes without paying the price in reduced public services. Canadians understand that high-quality public services—public infrastructure, livable cities, excellent education and training—are the keys to success in the new economy. It is clear to most Canadians now that, thanks to tax cuts, some governments across the country no longer have the resources they need to provide the basic services that we require from our governments. Canadians also understand that Canada needs to secure its future.

From one end of the country to the other, people are rebelling against the mantra that everything government does is bad, and everything the corporate sector does is good. Over and over again, people tell pollsters that they would be prepared to pay higher taxes to buy improvements in public services. Over and over again, from provincial elections in Saskatchewan, Manitoba, Nova Scotia, New Brunswick, and Ontario to municipal elections in Vancouver, Toronto, and Montreal, to name just a few, voters are rejecting the siren call of tax cuts in favour of a return to responsible, progressive government—government committed to public service.

Politicians who cling to the old tax-cut mantra are stuck in a time warp. And by steadfastly refusing to see the downside of tax cuts and downsizing, they are standing in the way of the new prosperity.

Canadians have been losing faith in their politicians. Election after election, they voted for progressive ideas yet received a doctrinaire dose of precisely the opposite. As Canadians conclude that their voices are not reflected in election results, they drop out, stay home. Voter turnout is falling rapidly. Soon we'll have caught up with the poorest performer among the G8 countries when it comes to democratic participation—the U.S., with turnout at or below 50 per cent. Later, I'll touch on some of the ideas that can turn this around, that can rejuvenate our democracy from the federal level to the local community level. From proportional representation in our national elections to enhanced funding and powers for local governments and the community sector. There are viable solutions that work.

And just in case someone is holding on to the view that politics does not matter, remember that Canada stayed out of the war in Iraq because people decided they wanted to make a difference. Into the streets they poured, by the thousands, saying no to the war. From the 250,000 people gathered in Montreal to the grade 7 class I met in Moose Jaw that started the ball rolling for a community protest and anti-war website, Canadians decided to make a difference. And we did!

I had been the leader of the party only for about a month when Jean Chrétien decided to agree with Canadians, and with my party, by refusing to join George W. Bush's invasion. It was the highlight of my first year. I knew the New Democratic Party had made a difference on an important issue. And we made a difference because we worked with the peace movements across the country. We set up advocacy teams in our caucus. One of them was the Peace and International Development Team, which I asked Alexa McDonough to lead. She has been our peace advocate. She and I pulled together the peace groups and said, "How can we help you achieve your goals?" We went to them—a reversal of the usual relationship between political parties and groups in the broader civil society. Non-government organizations (NGOs) are usually compelled to come on bended knee to the politicians. We changed that dynamic by going to them first. It's a new way of doing politics, and it's going to be much more effective.

Olivia Chow was the source from whom I shamelessly cribbed the concept for our six caucus "advocates"—for peace, health, diversity, democracy, sustainability, and communities. She had developed the concept and process that supported her invention of the child and youth advocate on Toronto City Council, allowing her to move effectively from opposition to proposition, with many well-informed partners in the community. The result for her was astounding. City council began supporting initiatives, including spending, for children and youth. It was so positive. It was about making a real difference instead of just spouting off for the cameras. This, I thought, was politics as it should be.

We duplicated this kind of work on other key issues with our various advocacy teams. In addition to the Women's Caucus, these teams brought the power of positive vision and practical proposals to our daily work: proportional representation, softwood lumber policy, the green car manufacturing strategy, a national pharmacare program, the inquiry into Maher Arar, the "once in a lifetime" bill to help immigrant extended families reunite in Canada, the modernization of marriage laws to give human rights to same-sex couples, and much more. In working through the advocacy teams, helped by active partners in the NGO and civil society organizations, our tiny group in the House of Commons was making a difference.

And people across Canada noticed. Many have joined with us in this building project. I welcome you too.

Let's make it a habit to make a difference. That's why politics matters.

[CHAPTER 2]

Sharing Our World

In summer, when a fisherman in St. John's, Newfoundland, wakes up at dawn and gets ready to head out to sea, the sun has just set within the hour at the western edge of Canada. From east to west, this country spans more than 5,500 kilometres, in six different time zones. North to south, we cover nearly half of the northern hemisphere.

Most people in the world love their country. Canadians love their country, and countryside. And although many have never seen the Arctic tundra, an old-growth forest, a teeming marsh, Canadians identify with those landscapes—and with good reason. We are fortunate enough to inhabit some of the most magnificent natural environments in the world. And it is our responsibility to protect this natural heritage.

But instead of being a leader in environmental stewardship, we are actually laggards. Canadians use more energy per capita than almost all other countries—including the United States—and we can't just blame our northern climate. We use significantly more energy per person than the people in Finland or Sweden. We produce the third-highest per capita emissions of carbon dioxide, after the even-more-wasteful U.S. and Australia. More than 750,000 square kilometres of our country are covered by freshwater lakes and rivers, but every year Canadians are subject to at least six hundred boil-water orders.

Over half of our land area is covered by forests, but each year we cut trees that cover more than ten thousand square kilometres—nearly twice the size of Prince Edward Island—and about 90 per cent of the logging in our boreal forest is clear-cut, causing soil erosion and loss of biodiversity. Solutions such as certified, sustainable logging and the creation of secondary wood-based manufacturing so that we don't just export raw logs and jobs are lagging badly.

When it comes to garbage, we have little to be proud of. Only 15 per cent of the waste we generate is recycled or composted, 5 per cent is incinerated, and 80 per cent of it winds up in landfills. Our national government does little to help change this situation.

On the most important environmental issue of our time, global climate change, Canada has not led the way, as it should have. I attended the worldwide "Conference" of the "Parties" in Bonn, Germany, in the summer of 2001 and was distressed to see the Canadian delegation adopting positions that potentially threatened the very viability of the Kyoto Protocol. The official policy of the Liberal Party, laid out in its 1993 Red Book, called for Canada to improve energy efficiency and increase the use of renewable energies, with the aim of cutting carbon dioxide emissions by 20 per cent from 1988 levels by the year 2005. Instead of meeting these targets, the Liberal government dithered and watched emissions increase over 20 per cent above 1990 levels! There were real international leaders. During the same period, the United Kingdom reduced its emissions by 11.7 per cent, Germany by 18 per cent, and France held to a zero increase. We were one of the last countries to ratify the Kyoto Protocol on the reduction of greenhouse gases. And during the debate at the time, Paul Martin raised serious doubts about his commitment to the protocol. In December 2003, days before he became prime minister, the media reported that Martin refused to say he would follow through on Canada's Kyoto commitment should the deal die. Instead, according to press reports, he said, "What I have said very clearly is you need a plan to determine whether in fact you can meet those targets.... That plan is going to determine our capacity to do so [meet targets], our ability to do so and really what are the very important steps. And we have not yet developed that plan, certainly not to my satisfaction." He had ten years since making the Red Book commitment to devise a plan to deal with the biggest environmental issue facing our time. But the best he could do was to complain that no plan had been developed, as if the blame for this lies elsewhere. Canadians are way ahead of their federal government. Individual Canadians are committed to protecting the environment. In poll after poll, Canadians have said that they consider the environment among their highest priorities, and that they are prepared to spend money to protect it.

As if to demonstrate their level of personal commitment, in communities and neighbourhoods, in households and on farms, Canadians are working hard to improve their own environmental performance. And they're showing that this can be done while at the same time they are enhancing economic activity and strengthening our social relations.

Yet, despite all this grassroots enthusiasm and public support for programs to reduce greenhouse gas emissions, in December 2004, when the governments of the world got together for the tenth time under the United Nations Framework Convention on Climate Change, it was revealed that Canada was one of the worst offenders as measured on a per-person basis. I was a member of the Canadian delegation at the gathering. I thought my little Canadian flag lapel pin would win me the usual accolades and friendly greetings. Not this time. As one representative said in addressing the entire assembly: "No standard of living justifies emissions of twenty tonnes of greenhouse gases per year per person." It was a stinging indictment. Many countries have standards of living as high as Canada's but emit less than half this level of pollution. And poor countries with GDP per capita less than a fifth of ours have emissions that are also a fraction of ours. I learned at Buenos Aires that many countries around the world are mobilizing their citizens, not with advertising, as Paul Martin's government did—and I say this with respect for Rick Mercer and his TV spots on the "one tonne challenge." But other countries have developed policies and programs that are showing real improvements instead of publicity. In many other countries, real change is underway with a fierce determination to achieve the targets agreed to by the global community in the Kyoto Accord. For Canada, this target would be a reduction of 6 per cent in total emissions from the 1990 baseline year. Yet, Canada still has no plan in place.

One of the key reasons that I decided to run federally was to help Canada shoulder its responsibilities for the environment. That's why, once elected to the House of Commons, I took on the role within our caucus as energy and climate change critic. That's why I conscripted Peter Tabuns, former executive director of Greenpeace Canada, to work with me as special adviser on energy and climate change. Peter and I worked with the knowledge gained from many of Canada's best minds in the field, as well as with my new caucus, to develop a comprehensive plan for Canada to achieve its Kyoto target. Canadians had never been presented with such a plan by their government. I felt that, first of all, Canadians should have the chance to see what it would take for their country to become a responsible world citizen. Second, I knew that such a plan would open up many doors for new approaches to economic and business development. It would save money and make profits for firms in the new economy of the twenty-first century, and it would also create hundreds of thousands of new jobs every year. What was stopping us? We needed to have the federal government break out of the political straitjacket imposed by the clout and influence of those powerful firms and interests who make their profts from the most rapid burning of non-renewable fossil fuels possible. Any imaginable future will require fossil fuel. But we simply can't continue to accept the reckless abandon of a government that grants more incentives and tax loopholes to the rich and powerful oil cartel that wants to accelerate fossil fuel combustion than to those who are trying to at least slow it down. So my plan was designed to ensure that Canadians had an option. The plan can be read in its entirety at www.ndp.ca. While we cannot celebrate much that the Canadian government has done for the environment in the past decade, examples abound of Canadians doing the right thing. As I describe later, my hometown of Hudson, Quebec led the way in battling multinational chemical companies to reduce pesticide use. The little town had to go all the way to the Supreme Court to do it, with no help from the feds! In Halifax and Guelph, incredible strides in waste reduction and composting have been made. In Calgary, the city council endorsed the building of a new rapid-transit line extension, and they contracted with a wind-power manufacturer to provide all the electricity needed to run it. In a marketing masterstroke, they call it Ride the Wind. That initiative will get people out of their cars and into public transit; more important, the wind power will reduce carbon dioxide (CO_2) emissions by 26,000 tonnes a year. When you ride Calgary's C-Train, it's like sailing—the wind is pushing you along, with no pollution at all. Now, if Calgary, the oil capital of Canada, can pull this off, anyone can. And there are countless more projects like these that improve our environment.

It's time—well, it's long past time—that we took control of our environmental future, building on best practices and carving out exciting new approaches to public policy. We have to free local communities to innovate. We should facilitate their exchange of winning ideas. We should be encouraging municipalities to act as catalytic agents for environmental rehabilitation. And we should be applauding those people who walk softly on the planet and rewarding those who create economic opportunities while widening the spaces for nature to thrive.

The country is full of ideas that work. Let's promote them. Let's open our imagination and dare to take new directions. At our 2003 NDP leadership convention, my friend Pierre Ducasse put it well: "To have the results you have never had, you must do what you have never done."

Renewing Our Resources

Like a lot of kids these days, especially those who live in cities, our son, Mike, has asthma. When he reached his teens, we were lucky that he could go to camp as a counsellor for a few weeks every summer and get out of the smog of Toronto.

A few years ago, we were looking forward, as always, to the time when he came home. Within a day of his return from the clean air of Northern Ontario, I was standing beside him in an emergency ward while the doctor put the third oxygen mask on his face. His mother, Sally, had experienced this moment many times, too. The smog had brought his asthma to a critical level. It was the most terrifying moment any parent could have.

The doctor looked at me and said, "You're lucky you brought him in here in time." Not long before, a Scarborough teenager, struggling to breathe, was rushed to hospital, but the first emergency ward had been full, and by the time he arrived at a hospital that could care for him, it was too late. This is not something you forget—ever.

But because Canada has failed to act, the horrors return. When my mom went to the funeral home to pick up the ceremonial urn containing my dad's ashes, she saw, in the corner of the director's office, a child's bike. Attempting a lighthearted aside in the awkwardness of the moment, she said, "That's an odd way to commute to work."

"Oh no, Mrs. Layton," soothed the funeral home manager. "The bicycle was the favourite toy of the five-year-old we buried today. He died from asthma only a day after the city's last smog alert."

That story made something burn deep inside me. This is the injustice of pollution, the uncounted cost. A child's bike in a funeral home. A child choking to death because of smog. All because we pollute recklessly by burning fossil fuels in spite of the public's clear desire to use existing technologies to do better.

Health Canada reports that every year more than 5,000 Canadians die prematurely as a result of air pollution. Other government estimates put the figure as high as 16,000 a year. In 2000, the Ontario Medical Association estimated that air pollution resulted in 9,800 hospital admissions and 13,000 visits to emergency rooms in that province alone. Most of the fatalities are among children and the elderly, the people whose respiratory systems are the most fragile. The OMA report, called *Ontario's Air: Years of Stagnation*, also notes: "These serious health effects that we are now experiencing in Ontario at current levels of air pollution also have significant economic impacts. Annually, air pollution is estimated to cost Ontario over $1 billion a year from hospital admissions, emergency room visits and absenteeism. When the pain and suffering and loss of life from polluted air are added into these costs, then the total annual economic loss from polluted air was estimated at $10 billion a year."

Needless to say, if we spent just a fraction of that amount addressing the causes of air pollution, rather than the health effects caused by it, we would save both lives and money.

Around the world, people have recognized the urgent need to clear the air. This call for action finally resulted in the signing of the Kyoto Protocol in 1997, which set national targets for the reduction of greenhouse gases. Canada's original target was a mere reduction of 6 per cent from 1990 levels. But because the federal government has dithered, our emissions have increased during the past seven years, and are now over 18 per cent higher than 1990 levels and going up.

The Kyoto Protocol

Faced with record world temperatures, increasing air pollution, and unusually severe weather patterns, the United Nations created the International Panel on Climate Change (IPCC) in 1988. That panel brought together leading scientists from around the world to study if, how, and why our climate was changing. In that same year, Toronto hosted one of the world's first major scientific conferences on climate change. The Changing Atmosphere Conference called for a 20 per cent reduction from 1988 greenhouse gas emissions by 2005.

Two years later, the IPCC issued its first report, which said that the planet was warming, and that it was caused primarily by human activity. The IPCC called for further study.

In 1992, another Earth Summit met, this time in Rio de Janeiro. (The first had been held twenty years earlier, in Stockholm.) This summit resulted in the Rio Convention, which called on nations to stabilize greenhouse gas emissions at 1990 levels by 2000. Canada and the United States both agreed to the Rio Convention, which recognized that developing nations would be able to increase their emissions, at least temporarily.

In 1995, the IPCC issued its second report, now concluding that the best scientific evidence pointed to a "discernable human influence on the global climate system."

In 1997, representatives from more than 160 nations met in Kyoto, Japan, to review new targets for greenhouse gas emissions. The Kyoto Protocol was signed by many countries, including Canada and the United States. The accord set global targets for reduction of 1990 emissions by 5 per cent between 2008 and 2012. Canada's target was set at a reduction of 6 per cent. Many poor and developing nations did not have targets set in this first phase because such targets would have prevented even modest efforts to improve living conditions.

Further meetings were held (in Bonn in 1999, and The Hague and Ottawa in 2000) to devise more specific mechanisms for the reduction of emissions. These meetings failed because the world's leading nations could not agree on a number of important issues.

Finally, on July 29, 2001, back in Bonn, the meeting I attended, 180 countries agreed to new rules for implementing the Kyoto Protocol. These rules would become legally binding only after the protocol was ratified by at least fifty-five countries, covering at least 55 per cent of the emissions from developed nations. Significantly, the United States and Australia, the countries with amongst the highest per capita emissions, refused to ratify. Fortunately for the world, Russia, which had equivocated, finally decided in late 2004 to ratify this most significant worldwide collective effort to deal with the earth's biggest environmental challenge. As a result of Russia's historic move, on February 16, 2005, the Kyoto Protocol came into legal force and effect for all fifty-five countries which had signed. We know that such international initiatives can work. The Montreal Protocol on CFCs, for example, helped to reduce signficantly our emissions of ozone-depleting chemicals. Now, we have to show that the same can be achieved with greenhouse gases (GHG), even without commitments from the United States and

Australia. It will be tough, very tough. But inaction will be much tougher indeed.

The government of Canada ratified the Kyoto Protocol on December 10, 2002 with a vote of the House of Commons. Then PM Jean Chrétien and then Minister of Environment David Anderson, under pressure from a broad range of Canadians, community groups, and the New Democrats as well as the Bloc Québécois, seemed genuinely committed to the idea. While Prime Minister Paul Martin appeared to support this commitment, his actions—or lack of them—told a completely different story. Under his watch, as both finance minister and prime minister, Canada's greenhouse gas emissions went significantly up, not down. By 2003, the most recent year for which data are available, Canada's greenhouse gas emissions exceeded 1990 levels by 24 per cent, up from an already high 18.42 per cent in 2001. Therefore, for Canada to meet its goal of a 6 per cent reduction from 1990 levels, it must reduce total greenhouse gas emissions by 32 per cent by the year 2012.

Finally, after years of talking about a plan to reduce emissions, former Environment Minister Stefan Dion revealed the Liberals' much-delayed Kyoto Implementation Plan in April 2005. Within minutes of its release, eleven key environmental groups slammed it, saying it was "inadequate to achieve Canada's Kyoto emission reduction target." One of the key problems of the plan—and there were many—was that it let Canada's large polluters off the hook of having to reduce their emissions. As a David Suzuki Foundation press release stated, "...even though individual Canadians are only responsible for about 28 per cent of Canada's emissions, they may end up being responsible for at least 74 per cent of emission reductions according to the current version of the plan."

As I write this, it is unclear what the new Harper government will do on the Kyoto file. During the election campaign, the new prime minister stated he believes Canada should withdraw from the Kyoto Protocol and develop Canadian-made targets. This would be a grave mistake politically, economically, and ultimately for the planet.

With a greater commitment to the use of hydroelectric power and other renewable energy sources, the production of more fuel-efficient vehicles, and modest, practical efforts by corporations and individuals to use less energy, the Kyoto goals can certainly be achieved. As noted above, throughout the fall of 2004, I worked with the brightest energy experts and climate change specialists in Canada to develop a detailed strategy that would guide Canada in meet its Kyoto commitments. In January 2005, I released the NDP's Kyoto Plan, which sets out exactly how Canada can meet our Kyoto targets, clean the air, and create over eight hundred thousand new jobs.

The Canadian unions whose workers are likely to be most affected by implementation of the Kyoto Protocol—the Communications, Energy & Paperworkers Union, the Canadian Auto Workers, and the Steelworkers Union—all support it. Yet Kyoto represents only the first step toward resolving climate change issues. In order to stabilize the earth's carbon cycle, leading scientists worldwide agree that reductions in greenhouse gases of up to 60 per cent or more will be necessary. According to the IPCC, global greenhouse gas emissions in this century will likely increase somewhere between 47 and 164 per cent from 1990 levels. That means the concentration of GHGs in the atmosphere could approach 1,000 parts per million (ppm) by 2100, compared with about 370 ppm in 2000 and 280 ppm in the pre-industrial era. Climate models predict that, as a result, the global temperature will rise in the range of 1.4 degrees to 5.8 degrees Celsius by the year 2100. Such a dramatic change over such a short period of time would probably result in abrupt, unwanted changes in the earth's physical and biological systems.

Scientists studying biodiversity over the past thirty years report numerous changes in the distribution and abundance of species as a direct result of climate change. A recent study published by *Nature* magazine predicts that 15 to 37 per cent of species in the geographical sample studied will be "committed to extinction" under the various climate scenarios.

Reducing greenhouse gas emissions will slow down and reduce damage caused by climate change. Kyoto is only a start. Far more dramatic reductions are required. In order to stabilize GHG emissions at, say, 450 ppm in the atmosphere, human emissions would have to drop below 2000 levels in a few decades and eventually decline to a very small fraction of current emissions.

Such reductions appear difficiult to obtain but are, in fact, doable. A David Suzuki Foundation and Torrie Smith Associates joint study indicates that Canada can reduce its GHG emissions by almost 50 per cent by 2030, putting the country on a trajectory to reduce emissions even further in the longer term. The study suggests that by a smart use of best available technology and innovative regulatory measures and financing, Canada can dramatically reduce its emissions. And we can begin realizing the huge job potential and cost savings that come from a green economy.

In 1903, petroleum supplied 2 per cent of the world's energy needs. That's just about what the worldwide supply of renewable energy provides today. Thankfully, renewable energy supply is on the rise. Here are just a few examples of how Canadian communities are leading the way in fighting pollution.

Edmonton brought in a Fuel Sense Program and worked with the one thousand municipal employees who had logged the highest fuel consumption in city vehicles. Employees were trained to drive for better fuel efficiency, and the results worked. Then the program was expanded to the city's transit operators' training program. In one year, fuel consumption was down by more than 10 per cent, double the city's original goal. It produced savings of $175,000 and lower vehicle emissions. No doubt heath costs from respiratory disease fell, too.

In St. John's, Newfoundland, the city councillors approved plans to renovate their city hall and other municipal buildings, and they paid for the work entirely from energy savings. They anticipate annual reduced energy costs of $600,000, along with better air quality, improved workplace lighting and comfort, and lower maintenance costs. Far from the economy "suffering," as the opponents of the Kyoto Protocol contend, the economy was enhanced.

Toronto has also made an early start. Inspired by the Changing Atmosphere Conference, the city council approved an emission reduction target of 20 per cent in 1990, the first municipality in the world (along with Hanover, Germany) to do so. In 1991, the council established the Toronto Atmospheric Fund (TAF) to finance community projects to reduce greenhouse gas emissions. Council endowed TAF with $23 million from the proceeds of a profitable sale of property. At about the same time, the city council also established the Office of Energy Efficiency to spearhead local greenhouse gas reductions further.

In 1997, I had the honour of being president of TAF, a position I held until I was elected leader of the federal NDP in January 2003. TAF is the only municipal agency in the world today dedicated to combating global warming, though the model is now being considered by Vancouver and a number of European jurisdictions. TAF-sponsored projects have brought multiple benefits to the city, including cumulative carbon dioxide emission reductions of about 250,000 tonnes and energy savings in city operations of over $2.7 million annually. (For more about the Toronto Atmospheric Fund, go to www.toronto.ca/taf.)

In 1996, I was involved in bringing together an association of private-sector companies, leaders of construction unions, bankers, municipal agencies, publicly owned energy companies, and community representatives to develop a plan to retrofit building stock in Toronto, while saving money and energy in the process. We called it the Better Buildings Partnership (BBP). This program is an example of sustainable economics. It creates jobs, helps businesses be more efficient, saves governments and consumers money, makes heating more affordable (especially for low-income people), and reduces pollution—all at the same time.

Here is how the program works. A building owner is offered the possibility of having renovations done, essentially at no cost because the type of work done reduces the building's energy use significantly, thus saving money. For example, insulation, windows, lights, motors, heating, ventilation and cooling systems, and control systems are all upgraded with much more energy-efficient materials and technologies. The energy reductions produce a financial saving that repays, over an agreed period of time, the cost of the work. Investors are found who are interested in predictable and moderate rates of return to put up the cash. (That's why such a project holds great promise for pension funds.)

Initially, the BBP was a pilot project with a target of retrofitting 2 per cent of all the buildings in Toronto. The pilot exceeded our hopes, and the city decided to expand it and has set a target to retrofit 40 per cent of industrial, commercial, and institutional floor space in Toronto by 2010. To date, the partnership has retrofitted 39 million square feet of space in 433 buildings, creating 3,850 person years of employment, with a local economic impact of $132 million. At the same time, the owners of those buildings (private and public) reduced their annual operating costs by $16 million and cut carbon dioxide emissions by 172,000 tonnes a year. Hundreds of workers had good jobs. Buildings were made more energy efficient, reducing their heating and cooling costs, which in turn produced lower greenhouse gas emissions. (For more information on the Better Buildings Partnership, go to www.toronto.ca/bbp.)

Imagine if cities around the world all pledged themselves to retrofit on such a scale. Work would be created for millions, pollution reduced by huge quantities, and all our buildings—our physical capital—would be in better shape. That's why I've proposed that Canada take the lead and develop a national energy retrofit program, which I describe in more detail in Chapter 6.

Another innovative community initiative in Toronto that will cut pollution, create jobs, and save building owners money is called Deep Lake Water Cooling. Air conditioning is becoming increasingly important as the temperature rises. It's also really rough on the environment. From the huge chilling machines on big buildings to the small noisy air conditioners in home windows, cooling the air uses lots of electricity and heats up the planet. A brilliant engineer by the name of Bob Tamblyn convinced me that we should use the cold water at the bottom of Lake Ontario to cool our buildings instead of burning tonnes of coal to create electricity to power our air conditioners. I was skeptical. How could taking cold water from the lake be good for the environment? The trick is to use the cold water in the lake—instead of burning fossil fuels—to chill the air in office buildings. Here's how Bob's proposal works.

Downtown office towers need a constant supply of "coolth" to cool the air that is circulated through the buildings. This is done with heat exchangers, remarkably simple devices that transfer heat from the air to water. Like a furnace in reverse, an exchanger passes warm air over a radiator full of cold water. Thanks to the immutable laws of thermodynamics, heat flows from the hotter to the cooler medium so that the water gets warmer as the air gets cooler. The cooled air is then circulated back through the building, and the warm water is sent off to get cooled again.

And how does this water that just chilled the air get cool again? This is where Lake Ontario comes into the equation. Lake Ontario is very cold—just ask anyone who has tried to swim in it. Because it's so deep, the water at the bottom of the lake is only four degrees Celcius. Tamblyn proposed to draw this very cold water through a large pipe into a special facility near Toronto's downtown office towers. There, the lake pipe containing cold water would meet the pipe from the office towers. This large heat exchanger would, once again following thermodynamic principles, transfer the coolness from the water in the lake pipe to the water in the pipe leading back to the office towers, water that would once again cool the air that is circulated through the office towers. And the warmer water from the lake would still be cool enough to be used for municipal drinking water.

The beauty of Deep Lake Water Cooling is that the natural cooling of the lake that takes place during the winter—not the burning of fossil fuels—air conditions our buildings.

The challenge to turn Bob Tamblyn's idea into reality was to convince all kinds of people—from big-building owners to public works officials in several levels of government to environmental groups in the city to politicians at all levels—that replacing polluting air conditioners with environmentally advanced central cooling using cold water as the basic cooling source was technically workable, economically viable, and politically achievable. I have to admit some ideas seem to take a long time to be put into place. The first meeting I convened on this topic, with then councillor Richard Gilbert, was in 1989. Thirteen years later, I stood on a stage with

Robert Kennedy Jr. to announce that the project was going ahead on Toronto's waterfront. (To find out more about this, go to www.enwave.com.)

A growing number of large downtown office towers are now being cooled with cold lake water. These include Adelaide Place, TD Centre, Royal Bank Plaza, Metro Toronto Convention Centre, Air Canada Centre, 151 Front Street West, Steam Whistle Brewery, 123 Front Street West, and One University Avenue. Enwave, the company that is providing the service, has enough capacity to air condition one hundred office buildings, or 3.2 million square metres of office space, the equivalent of 6,800 homes.

Overall, Toronto has achieved a million-tonne reduction in greenhouse gas emissions from city government operations, helping bring Canada's biggest city a third of the way toward Kyoto compliance. City government cut its emissions by 42 per cent, helping Toronto achieve a 2 per cent citywide decrease in greenhouse emissions between 1990 and 1998.

Sudbury has initiated a joint venture with a private-sector company to develope at least fifty megawatts of wind power. That will provide power to about 40 per cent of the city's residents, all of it non-polluting. The city has succeeding in convincing manufacturers to build portions of the wind machines in the community as part of the deal.

Sequoia Energy, a company in Victoria, B.C., has negotiated with Manitoba Hydro to build the country's largest wind farm near St. Leon, in central Manitoba. It will produce as much as one hundred megawatts of energy, enough to power forty thousand homes. This project will generate more electricity than the wind farm in southern Alberta that powers Calgary's light-rail transit. That wind farm produces seventy-five megawatts and is currently Canada's largest.

Believe it or not, few of the components required to build wind turbines are manufactured in Canada. That's why they have to be imported from Europe at a cost of over $1 million for each one, plus $100,000 for each windmill in transportation costs.

I've been meeting with Bombardier officials and the leadership of the Canadian Auto Workers union. They are considering how we could meet some of the rapidly growing demand for turbines (thousands a year in Canada and the U.S.) by building them here. After all, the arms of wind turbines are like airplane wings set vertically. We know how to build planes in Canada, so let's get going.

Some countries have the national will to make a real effort to counteract global climate change. Denmark already produces 21 per cent of its electrical power by wind generation. (Canada's percentage is less than one, but increasing.) Today, wind turbines supply electricity to forty million Europeans.

Germany, which has a goal of reducing its carbon emissions by 40 per cent by 2020, is the world's leader in wind generation. In 2003, that nation passed its 2010 goal by producing 12,500 megawatts of wind power. It has done this in part by restructuring its tax system to encourage alternative energy and discourage the use of fossil fuels.

After studying wind resources, Greenpeace and the European Wind Energy Association concluded that our planet's wind-generating potential is twice as great as the entire world demand for electricity projected for 2020. Meanwhile, the cost of generation continues to decline. The Greenpeace–Wind Energy Association study predicts that the average cost per kilowatt hour of wind-generated electricity will drop to 3.4 cents (Canadian) by 2010, and to 2.7 cents by 2020 (from its current 8 to 12 cents per kilowatt hour). In addition to these huge savings, there are no more pollution costs. And once the turbine is paid for, the fuel is free.

Another renewable energy resource that is commercial today is geothermal. Heat pumps tap into the earth's natural temperature, which remains relatively the same throughout the year, to provide both heating and cooling for buildings. In winter, when the ground is warmer than the air, underground pipes pump up the earth's heat to provide warmth. In the summer, when the earth is cooler than the air, the reverse happens. Today there are about thirty thousand homes across Canada with geothermal heat pumps—the systems, while having almost no operating costs, remain fairly expensive to install. However, Manitoba and Manitoba Hydro are on the cutting edge in Canada in developing and offering programs to install heat pumps in that province. They are working to ensure Winnipeg's newest and largest subdivision will have heat pumps in thirteen thousand new homes, making it Canada's first entirely geothermal subdivision. While heat pumps use some electricity to operate, they are incredibly efficient when compared with furnaces and air conditioners because they use renewable energy from the earth. Manitoba Hydro also offers a heat pump loan program that allows people to pay off the installation costs over a number of years. So instead of paying for polluting fossil fuels to heat and cool their homes, Manitoba residents pay off a capital asset that is environmentally friendly.

In four short years, Manitoba has quadrupled the number of heat pumps installed in the province and has become the Canadian centre for training the men and women who install them. Instead of seeing the earth solely as a source for fossil fuel extraction, Manitoba sees it as a source for renewable energy. That's why they describe their heat pump program with the phrase "Where the earth is on your side." Manitoba is a model of what can and should happen across all of Canada.

One of the other renewable energy sources we should be plugging into is the oldest one available—the sun. Imagine if we could use the immense power of the sun right away rather than the solar energy stored in fossilized hydrocarbons created millions of years ago, the coal, oil, and natural gas we burn today. My dad, a heating and air-conditioning engineer, urged my brothers and me to consider these possibilities thirty years ago. My mom, an avid swimmer, had convinced Dad to put a narrow pool in the backyard so she could get her exercise by swimming lengths. The problem was the weather. The Ottawa River valley is cool for a good part of the spring and fall. If we could heat the pool, said my dad, then Mom could swim longer, and so could we. "What if you boys set up a system so that the pool water could be heated by the sun, keeping the pool swimmable longer each season?" My younger brothers, Rob and Dave, were the inventive ones and produced four systems on the roof for heating the water. We installed all four systems and tested their cost and effectiveness. We found that a coil of black plastic pipe did the best job. The pool's water was pumped into a tight coil of two-inch-diameter black pipe. The sun heated the black pipe and the heat was transferred to the cooler water inside. The result? We all swam in the pool— from May until October.

None of this surprised Dad, always an innovator. He was one of those who helped install wind turbines on the Gaspé Peninsula and on P.E.I.'s west coast after the oil crisis in the mid-1970s. His firm also pioneered a strategy for putting water on the huge, flat roofs of industrial buildings so that evaporation, caused by the sun's energy, would cool the buildings in the summer, reducing the need for air conditioners.

The sun's energy can also be used to heat water, or it can be used to create electricity. This all came nicely together in a story that former NDP leader Alexa McDonough told me, the morning after Hurricane Juan hit Nova Scotia in the fall of 2003. All the electricity in her neighbourhood had been knocked out by the force of the hurricane. The next morning she took a shower. Then she thought, Wait a minute! How come I have hot water when I have no electricity? The eureka moment came when she realized that her solar hot-water heater system on the roof was still working. It had fully stocked her water tank with cozy hot water. Falling electrical wires couldn't stop her solar system from providing energy.

We had the same experience at our house during the big summer blackout earlier that year, because we also have a solar hot water heater on our roof.

There are two lessons here. First, small-scale and local production of energy is more resilient than huge central energy plants connected through incalculable lengths of transmission wires. Second, renewable energy sources work better during crises. In some places and in some circumstances the sun's energy is less expensive than electricity or gas for some key needs like heating water. Modest rooftop solar hot water heaters are now in use in many countries and communities. When we were travelling around the Carribean Island of Dominica on a snorkeling and hiking holiday break, Olivia and I were struck by the presence of hot water tanks and solar panels on just about every rooftop. Sure, there's lots of sun, but another reality is that incomes are low and electrical infrastructure modest.

The technology for producing electricity from solar power is still expensive, but with improvements—and expanding acceptance and use—costs are dropping. Sales of solar photovoltaic cells increased by 21 per cent a year from 1995 to 2001, which means that the costs will likely decrease even faster in the future.

In many villages in developing countries, where connecting to the electrical grid isn't feasible or is simply too costly, solar cells are already competitive for residential lighting. Families pay for the installation and then draw power essentially for free; the initial investment pays for itself in a couple of years (by not having to pay for kerosene or candles). Almost one-third of the world's population is not connected to any electrical grid. Solar energy is the best source for hundreds of millions of these people. And in these more remote locations, solar power provides a direct health benefit in two ways. First, it provides electricity to refrigerate vaccines and other medicines. Second, it reduces the amount of indoor smoke from open flames, which create numerous health risks. When Olivia and I travelled through the Yunnan province of China a few years ago, we found ourselves choking on smoke as seniors stirred the coals and generously poured us hot tea in the dark, dense air. We both thought, there has to be a role in Canada here. Canada could and should be a leader in developing a multiplicity of solar technologies, but we have no effective national plan. Solar electricity infrastructure can be established or re-established more quickly to get basic services to people in need after disasters like the horrific tsunami. Large central systems are cumbersome and expensive to repair and restore.

Even in major urban centres, solar-powered electricity is a source not only for the future, but for today.

Japan is the world's leader in solar photovoltaics—driven by a smart national program of incentives, a desire to reduce their dependence on imported fossil fuels, and a commitment to clean up their air. The Japanese government introduced a 70,000 Roofs Program in 1996, subsidizing domestic solar photovoltaic systems by 50 per cent. In 2001, Japan installed 120 megawatts of new solar generation, and the amount is steadily increasing.

Meanwhile, the United Kingdom has committed to source 10 per cent of its energy supply from renewable energy by 2010. In addition, the U.K. government is providing $728 million to support renewable energy projects to 2006. Funds to support solar energy are administered by the Energy Savings Trust, and some forty thousand photovoltaic panels have been installed on the roofs of U.K. homes.

A few years ago, the electrical utility in Sacramento, California, began to sell solar-electric systems to homeowners. These rooftop systems are connected to the grid, and the utility buys back the electricity they produce. On rainy days and at night the homeowners draw power from the grid, eliminating the need for batteries to store the energy. On sunny days, when the demand for electricity is the greatest (primarily because of air conditioning), the solar panels provide electricity to the utility company, and the consumer reaps the benefit.

A community I visited in the Netherlands, Eindhoven, is powered entirely by such a solar-energy swap. The people there, several thousand of them, reap the benefits of the sun's energy every day.

In 2003, a new apartment building was unveiled in downtown Manhattan that used photovoltaic cells to generate electricity as part of its basic design. Canada could have been a real leader in this area. In 1992, a consortium of Canadian companies came together to design and build the most advanced energy-efficient apartment building in the world. The group included Greg Allen and his partner, Mario Kani, innovative Canadian designers; the Green Catalyst Group, a small business I created to bring together some of the best minds, nationally and internationally, to develop advanced building and community design; Quadrangle Architects; and Windleigh Developments, as well as the Peel Non-Profit Housing Company. Our building was actually constructed in Mississauga and was cited by the United Nations Habitat program as a world leader. Allen took this award-winning design and added many new features similar to those found in the Manhattan building. The project would have been built and housed hundreds in need of affordable accommodation had Mike Harris, the Conservative premier of Ontario at the time, not cancelled this and all other social housing projects in 1995. Since then, many buildings around the world have been constructed with very advanced environmental features. Canada could have been a world leader but lost the chance. Will we keep slipping, or will we become leaders?

Through energy efficiency and renewable energy sources, we can meet most of our power needs. Canada already produces about 58 per cent of its electricity from hydro power. We could also be a leader in wind, geothermal, and solar energy.

The job-creation potential for green energy production and energy efficiency is enormous. But the reality is that jobs will also be lost in the fossil fuel sector. As a nation, we have a responsibility to ensure the transition to a green energy future is a just one so that all workers and communities share the benefits.

The Communications, Energy and Paperworkers (CEP) union, which represents tens of thousands of energy sector workers in Canada, has developed a comprehensive and innovative strategy that will smooth the way to what they call the Just Transition to sustainable development. Unlike much of the oil and gas industry, the CEP embraced the ratification of the Kyoto Protocol and rolled up its sleeves to figure out how its members, and all Canadians, could benefit from the opportunities possible from ratifying Kyoto. This proactive, solutions-based attitude is at the heart of the Just Transition strategy: "Solutions to environmental problems address the interests of workers and the communities where they live. The cost of change should be fairly distributed throughout society. No worker should be asked to choose between his/her livelihood or the environment. Sustainable employment must be part of the solution along with a sustainable economy and healthy ecosystems. Just Transition is about planning for these changes in a fair and equitable way."

Key elements of the strategy include:
- taking advantage of the knowledge and skills that energy-sector workers have by involving them in defining the problems and developing solutions to reducing energy use;
- ensuring that government plans for meeting our Kyoto targets include a detailed analysis of employment impacts as well as funded programs for employment adjustment;
- requiring employers to include local employment adjustment plans, in particular for projects with limited lifespans such as mines;
- making sure communities—and their municipal leaders and local labour leaders—are part of any local Just Transition plan;
- working with all levels of government, local employers, and various community leaders to develop economic strategies that are truly environmentally sustainable;
- providing government support for research and development into sustainable businesses;
- making education and training available and economically accessible to all those who need them, especially workers displaced by job loss in the fossil fuel sector.

The good news is that the funding for the Just Transition strategy could be paid for by using less than half of the federal tax revenue generated by all the new jobs and economic activity created by a national energy retrofit program—about $100 million a year over ten years!

This sort of innovative policy or idea put into practice would ensure that Canada has a secure energy future. But our federal government has not been willing to listen. It doesn't want to annoy the big fossil fuel and nuclear power producers. In fact, the situation has become worse. According to a January 2005 report, the federal government provided a $1.4-billion annual subsidy to the fossil fuel industry in 2002, the last year for which data were available.

And that brings me back to the Kyoto Implementation Plan released by the Liberals in April 2004, the one immediately criticized as inadequate by eleven environmental groups. There was no mention in that plan of eliminating current subsidies to non-renewable energy production. In fact, there were only token, vague words designed to suggest the appearance of action.

Imagine if the federal government treated cancer and second-hand smoke in the same way it treated our Kyoto commitments. After thirteen years of study after study showing the links between cancer and smoking, the federal government finally releases a plan about how to reduce the number of smokers. Unfortunately, the plan has few details and no timelines and follows a federal budget that only allocates a small fraction of the money needed to realize the plan. The government, however, does nothing to stop its annual large subsidies to big tobacco companies, money that is used to develop and market cigarettes. Canadians would rightly be in an uproar if such a flagrant misuse of public dollars were to continue.

Yet this is exactly what the Liberal government proposed with their Kyoto Plan. This is why I spent much of 2005 talking about an alternative vision, one that not only made common sense, but would help clean the air and create jobs.

Unlike the Liberal plan, the NDP Kyoto plan, presented in 2004 and then updated by our Energy Critic, M.P. Dennis

Bevington from the Western Arctic and by M.P. Nathan Cullen, our Environment Critic, in June of 2006, outlines a detailed set of strategies that will help us meet our Kyoto commitments. It's based on simple, but powerful logic. Help Canadians cut their energy consumption; use energy more efficiently; and build and shift to green, renewable energy. And finance these initiatives by reallocating the subsidies now going to the fossil fuel sector, through the savings realized from using less energy and by strategic government investments that will help create jobs and sustainable, economic activity in all regions of the country. The plan contains a wide variety of programs, most of which promote conservation, energy efficiency, and/or green energy production and use in homes, communities, industries and internationally.

Key elements include:
- **support for public transit energy retrofit programs for homes, workplaces, industries, and institutional buildings across Canada;**
- **new requirements for energy-efficient appliances and upgraded building codes for new construction;**
- **financial support for cogeneration;**
- **financial support for green energy production and the development of an east-west power grid.**

The plan also includes a Just Transition Strategy for affected energy workers and the communities they live in, a program to set up an emissions trading system, and a way to work with other nations to promote greenhouse gas reductions across the planet.

My small team, led by Peter Tabuns, came up with this plan over the space of a few months, a plan that received plenty of praise from key climate change groups, including the David Suzuki Foundation. So you can imagine my shock when I saw the Liberal plan, released three months later, that had significantly less detail. I have no doubt that Environment Canada staff were as anxious as I was to see real federal action on climate change. It's frustrating and disappointing that the Liberal government never gave them the resources or the encouragement to come up with the forward-looking, innovative planning that this country needs.

Prime Minister Harper has a chance to correct this history of federal inaction. While he may disagree with elements of the Kyoto Protocol, surely he cannot side with George W. Bush or lobbyists for fossil fuel corporations that continue to insist, against all logic, that climate change is not a problem. Anyone who still needs convincing should have a close look at the Arctic Climate Impact Assessment, released in the fall of 2004 in Iceland. Sheila Watt-Cloutier, Canadian Inuit leader and chair of the Circumpolar Innuit Conference, walked me through the shocking conclusions as we talked about strategy at the Buenos Aires climate change conference in late 2004:

- About four million hectares of boreal forest in Russia were burned annually over the past three decades, and the amount more than doubled in the 1990s.
- An average of one to two million hectares of boreal forest were burned annually in North America (read Canada) from the 1940s to the 1980s, but this jumped to two to three million in the 1990s.
- Arctic warming is happening at twice the rate of the rest of the world.
- Melting of sea ice and the Greenland icefield is accelerating, adding fresh, colder water to the oceans' circulation patterns, threatening to disrupt them and producing potentially very significant increases in sea level.

- Glaciers are melting and will disappear in many parts of the world in a matter of decades, drying up the sources of many key rivers in the northern hemisphere.
- Permafrost is melting, increasing greenhouse gas releases and causing buidlings and transportation infrastructures to be damaged.
- Ways of life based for many centuries on ice and hunting are threatened.
- Polar bears will likely be extinct by the end of the twenty-first century, as predictions say most of the Arctic summer ice cap will have melted by then.
- Animal habitat, including that provided in the Arctic to hundreds of millions of migratory birds from all over the planet, is changing rapidly. For animals like polar bears and seals, the future is grim indeed. Invasive species of insects are appearing in unprecedented outbreaks.
- Arctic vegitation zones are shifting faster than species can migrate.
- Transportation may become possible through the Arctic, opening up development, which will have more consequences for the climate.

Increased growing seasons will open up agricultural possibilities much farther north than Canadians now farm. All this produces a monumental challenge for the global community. Around the world, people are responding to that challenge. They are doing so internationally, with accords like the Kyoto Protocol. They are doing it nationally, with a whole variety of incentives, disincentives, policies, and programs. And people are doing it locally, in dozens of imaginative and practical ways. I know this from the work I've done over the years at the Federation of Canadian Municipalities. I also know this from my work as part of a federal government process to develop a climate change response plan, known as the

National Climate Change Process (NCCP). I was privileged to be one of the four-hundred-plus specialists involved in the NCCP. Many good ideas were thoroughly developed and investigated as part of this three-year process. The problem is that federal governments have not had the political will to move aggressively and take advantage of the opportunities to lead.

- New electrical capacity brought on line in 2001 by wind power in megawatts: 6,700; by nuclear power: 1,505
- Potential cost of restarting four mothballed nuclear reactors in Pickering, Ontario, that would supply 2,060 MW of electricity: $4 billion
- Estimated cost of building 2,667 1 MW wind turbines that would harness roughly 27 per cent of current viable wind energy potential in Canada: $4 billion
- Number of compact fluorescent lamps in use world-wide in 2001: 1.8 billion
- Number of coal-fired generation stations not needed because of the energy the lamps saved: 40
- Percentage change in carbon emissions in the United States between 1990 and 2000: +18.1; In Europe: −1.8

If the earth were the size of an apple, our atmosphere would be much thinner than the peel. It would be more like a layer of skin on an onion. That's pretty fragile. You think we'd be more careful with it. What this country needs is a comprehensive strategy for energy that captures the possibilities for a truly sustainable approach to energy economics, environment, job-creation potential, and human well-being, all at the same time. I will say more about the shape of such a plan when I discuss new prosperity for Canada in Chapter 6.

Waste Not, Want Not

In nature, there is no such thing as waste. Organisms consume; extract what they need for survival, growth, and reproduction; and discharge or leave behind what they cannot use. What remains becomes food for other organisms. This cycle means that some plant or animal's waste bcomes another's resource.

But human beings have managed to think their way out of this cycle. The idea of human "domination" of nature—not to mention domination of other humans—combined with an oversimplified, linear idea of "progress," has taken us to new levels of arrogance about our place at the "top of the food chain." Instead of using our capacity to think about coexistence, to take us to places of humility, inquiry, and wisdom, we have used it to become unparalleled masters of wasteful consumption.

For a magnificent example of this arrogance of waste, we need look no further than my own city, Toronto.

Most Canadians have heard about Toronto's "big idea" to ship a trainload of its garbage every day, six hundred kilometres north, to Kirkland Lake, Ontario. The brilliant scheme involves dumping a million tonnes of green-bagged refuse into the deep lake that was formed in an abandoned hollowed-out iron mine. That lake sits at the top of one of the highest points in the great ridge that runs down the middle of the Canadian Shield. Yes, Toronto looked for the biggest hole it could find, far away from its own territory, so that it could dump garbage into it—with impunity. With impunity, yes, but with a price tag. The city was prepared to pay $50 a tonne, for at least twenty years. That's $1 billion!

Torontonians would pay $1 billion to have someone else live with the stinking pile of garbage generated by Canada's most profligate city. It's no wonder that Canadians think Toronto is arrogant.

The proposed landfill threatened fisheries, border waters between Ontario and Quebec, as well as First Nations lands and communities, all legitimate and clear reasons for a federal environmental assessment.

The good news is that once the people of Toronto learned more about this idea—as a result of a brilliant, community-based coalition of Toronto environmentalists and a farmer/Aboriginal alliance from the North—and once people had an opportunity to think about the absurdity of the scheme, the citizens of Toronto soundly rejected the madness.

How this turnaround happened is a wonderful tale of democracy, toiling as it should—from the grassroots up. The full saga would take a book, or a miniseries, with sequels. But, briefly, heading the Brown team: Texas-based Waste Management, reportedly the largest garbage company in the world—with every high-paid lobbyist conscripted to do its bidding. Close at hand were several local politicians, including former mayor of Toronto Mel Lastman and the chair of the Works Committee. They were joined by business interests from Kirkland Lake, a community devastated by mine closures and struggling with high unemployment.

On the Green team: Northerners who relied on the pristine environment—plus dairy farmers, ecological tourism operators, people who enjoyed Adams Ale made with water drawn from the Kirkland Lake water table, and First Nations communities who relied on traditional fishing and hunting. Also on the Green team were groups of Torontonians who wanted to compost their waste, recycle packaging, and reduce garbage—the Toronto Environmental Alliance and a broad network of citizens and other groups. I represented the Green team on the Works Committee and at city council, with lots of help from then councillor, now mayor, David Miller.

This titanic struggle, as Montreal Canadiens hockey broadcaster Danny Gallivan used to put it, raged over three years—and we thought we'd been beaten, but we were wrong. The Green team triumphed. We won for two reasons.

First, in the late stages of the contest, we were able to force a secret document onto the table which showed that Toronto City Council would bear responsibility for most of the environmental liabilities. Even Mayor Lastman admitted that this condition was a deal breaker and had to be removed. At that point, Waste Management and the Brown team withdrew. They were unwilling to take the "business risk," as their lawyers put it in a letter.

Second, the Green side had gone beyond mere opposition to the folly by proposing viable alternatives. We laid out an alternative strategy for treating waste as a resource. The proposal included building recycling plants and large composting factories to turn kitchen and restaurant waste into nutrient-rich soils for gardens and produce energy at the same time. All this was based on the wonderful work of citizens and city councils in Halifax, Guelph, and Edmonton, which had earlier established advanced models of waste resource management.

A classic model for merging environmental and economic goals had been created by some visionary citizens. First, ask Toronto's citizens to do some work—separate wet kitchen waste and allow the city to collect it in green boxes. Then take this beautiful muck to composting plants right in the city, instead of shipping the putrefying mass to far-off landfill sites or dumps in Canada's North, or west on Highway 401 and across the border to Michigan. (There it would rot for decades to come, releasing methane gas into the atmosphere, each molecule doing twenty-one times more damage to the environment than carbon dioxide.) The Green team plan recommended using the gases from the composting plants to create energy, reducing our dependence on fossil fuels piped in from thousands of kilometres away.

Composted material would be used on gardens in the city, avoiding the need to manufacture and ship artificial fertilizers over great distances to feed the city's plants.

We predicted that Torontonians would embrace these new ideas enthusiastically. Bureaucratic and political naysayers forecast doom and gloom. Yet, faced with no mine in Northern Ontario, no cheap dump site, and nothing else to offer, City Council was forced to implement the citizens' plan. Still, narrow thinking led the bureaucrats to recommend a high price to collect the compost and recycling materials.

That's when some councillors joined with me in suggesting a radical idea. We recommended that market mechanisms be employed to reward good behaviour while bad behaviour would be tolerated at a higher price! Council adopted our plan to have compost and recycling collected at no charge, but to set a high price for collecting unsorted bags of garbage beyond a fixed minimum. The message was crystal clear: do the right thing, and save money!

Lo and behold, Torontonians embraced the plan. Small businesses put out their composting in much greater quantities than the "experts" and naysayers had predicted. Ditto, citizens. The latest numbers show that people are putting out so much of their waste as pre-sorted, compostable material that the city is having to build or purchase more composting plants, creating even more local jobs.

In fact, Torontonians like composting so much that 95 per cent of eligible households participate. When fully implemented, the City of Toronto expects over 110,000 tonnes of composting will be diverted from landfill, helping the City achieve its target of diverting 60 per cent of its waste by 2008.

In Halifax, the city council put in place a new waste-resource management strategy that diverted about 40 per cent of its solid waste through recycling and composting in its first nine months of operation. The program saves energy, reduces waste sent to a landfill, produces useable compost, reuses materials through recycling, and reduces greenhouse gas emissions by half a megatonne. As a result, Halifax is one of the world's leading cities in solid-waste management. And in that city, citizen power also made it happen.

Treating waste once it's produced is one thing; reducing waste in the first place is even more important. It's all about efficiency. Natural ecosystems constantly redefine themselves to become more and more efficient. The best examples I've seen close up are found in the astounding coral reefs. Constant adaptation over millennia produces more efficiency and specialization of the species in the reefs. Nature has been rather wise about such things. In nature, inefficient organisms die.

Human activity, at least our economic activity, is different. When humans are inefficient, the short-term consequences sometimes seem "profitable." Usually, the costs of the inefficiencies are passed on to others and all too often fail to show up in the accounting books at all. Costs of fraud, of pollution, of unsafe workplaces, of below-poverty wages are all borne by others. The price is paid, but not by the firm. Such profits are false profits!

For example, if pollution goes up the smokestack or down the river, the costs of addressing the harmful effects almost never appear on the balance sheet of the offending corporation. People toss old batteries into the "garbage," and they're toted off to landfills, where, years later, the chemicals leak out into the groundwater. While the purchaser of the battery may have paid an environmental tax, neither the company that produced the batteries nor the retailer who sold them ever paid anything to offset the cost for pollution caused later. The price is paid eventually—by future generations, by other organisms with which we share this degraded planet, and by our fellow citizens who get sick with cancer. (Then, as taxpayers, we also pay for the health-care costs.) But nowhere do all these costs ever become attached to the producer or the retailer. Economists call these uncosted effects "externalities." But they're not external at all—they're just outside the profit-and-loss statements of the corporations that produce and sell the goods. When you don't have to absorb the costs, you'll carry on being inefficienct. That's what we all do. But that's what we all have to stop doing. We can use market principles to address some of these issues, to shift markets and product design. We can also steer product management toward waste reduction and recycling, and create more jobs.

Recycling costs more initially. But it creates jobs which, in turn, generates more economic activity and a more robust, healthier, and efficient community and, therefore, one more likely to succeed. Polluters, like the Brown team, always object by saying that if we force them to do these things, they'll have to close down.

Mandating original product manufacturers to take responsibility for the goods they produce is called Extended Producer Responsibility (EPR). A national EPR system in Canada would be a step in the right direction toward reducing and recycling millions of tonnes of material that now becomes "waste."

EPR policy shifts the responsibility upstream, to the producer and away from municipalities and consumers. EPR provides incentives to producers to take environmental considerations into the design of their products. Consequently, the environmental impacts of production are reduced at the initial stage. "Polluter pays" is the underlying principle.

The Netherlands, for example, approved a National Environmental Policy Plan in 1989. Through their plan, companies voluntarily enter into covenants with the government; the provisions of the covenants are then enforceable by law. There are now more than one hundred such covenants in place in the Netherlands.

Dutch industry and government worked together to reduce packaging significantly, eliminate any hazardous materials (for example, heavy metals) in packaging, prohibit the disposal of packaging in landfills, and develop recycling capacity. They have already exceeded their targets.

A 1998 OECD (Organization for Economic Co-operation and Development) study of the Dutch plan concluded that "the competitiveness of the Dutch industry neither increased nor decreased because of the packaging measures, while the competitiveness of the food production sector increased.... The available results regarding market trends may indicate that packaging overall has only a marginal role in terms of competitiveness."

That is just one example. At least twenty-eight countries (and the number is growing) have mandatory rules for packaging. Another sixteen have laws that require the recovery of batteries. An increasing number of countries —including Switzerland, Taiwan, the Netherlands, Italy, Japan, and Norway—have implemented recycling and EPR laws to deal with the wide variety of electronics, and others have such laws in the work. It makes environmental sense. It also makes economic sense.

IBM has opened a number of Routinization and Materials Recovery Centers around the world to reclaim computer parts and reuse the electronics. In 1999, these centres processed more than 59,000 tonnes of equipment. Over 90 per cent was recycled; less than 3.7 per cent wound up in landfills.

Nike shoes (whose Asian sweatshops have rightly brought the company a lot of justifiable criticism) created a reuse-a-shoe program, which provides for the recycling of used athletic shoes. The outer rubber sole and inner foam are ground up and reused in running tracks, courts, gym floors, soccer fields, and playgrounds. The cloth upper part is turned into carpet underpadding. The program diverts at least ten million outworn shoes from landfills every year.

Xerox saves at least $200 million a year by recovering and remanufacturing used copiers.

In the United Kingdom, DuPont, which manufactures the paint used by Ford, is paid by how many cars are painted, not by how much paint they sell. Because DuPont and Ford split the savings, they both have an incentive to develop paint applications that minimize waste from the painting process. DuPont has increased its market competitiveness because other companies don't offer this service.

The materials in used cars have long been recycled; commonly, about 75 per cent of a car, measured by weight, is reused or recycled. Still, in the United States, between ten and eleven million cars are scrapped every year and, when measured by volume, what isn't being recycled represents about 75 per cent of a car. This includes much of the plastics, fibres, foams, glass, and rubber. In the U.S., it amounts to about five hundred million cubic feet of waste headed to the landfill every year. That's enough to fill 55,125 garbage trucks!

In Europe, they don't allow this environmental nightmare. In 1996, German vehicle manufacturers voluntarily accepted responsibility for the return of their cars, no matter how many owners they may have had. It's the "polluter pays" principle: you made it, you take it back. The European Union recently approved what they call the End of Life Vehicle (ELV) Directive. The ELV Directive calls for the recovery of 85 per cent of all automobiles now, and 95 per cent by 2015. And the EU also expects automakers to cut back or eliminate the use of lead, mercury, cadmium, and other toxic metals.

In Canada, no such mandatory legislation is in place, and the automakers are only studying ways to improve the reuse and recycling of materials. But the Canadian Auto Workers (CAW) union is urging Canadian automakers to accept Extended Producer Responsibility. Why? Because the CAW knows it's good for the environment, and because it also creates jobs.

The amount of waste that North Americans generate is staggering. But with careful product design, proper corporate responsibility, and increased consumer awareness, we can dramatically reduce the amount of "garbage" we create. And we can learn to reuse and recycle it much more efficiently. If single-celled organisms can be models of efficiency, so can we.

Sustaining Our Lives

Canada is graced with an abundant, and one might think inexhaustible, supply of fresh water. In fact, Canada's lakes and rivers contain enough water to cover our entire country (about ten million square kilometres) to a depth of two metres! That's a lot of water. Fresh water, however, represents less than 3 per cent of all the world's water, and of that 3 per cent, two-thirds is locked in glaciers and the polar ice caps. This means that the world's entire supply of available fresh water amounts to less than one-half of 1 per cent of all water, or about one teaspoon per litre.

With climate change, glaciers and ice caps are rapidly melting, and forecasters predict that all of Canada's glaciers south of the territories will have melted by 2030. As a consequence, rivers such as the North and South Saskatchewan and the Bow will lose much of their volume because of depleted headwaters. Bob Hawkesworth, a Calgary alderman, told me that the Bow River glacier is predicted to melt completely within a decade, after which the river's volume will be reduced by as much as 40 per cent during late summer. This 644-kilometre-long river supplies irrigation water to more than 200,000 hectares and provides drinking water for many communities in southern Alberta.

You might assume we'd all be more careful with the water we all depend on. Without water, there's no life. Without clean water, everyone's health is at risk. But, as with air, humans continue to pollute water with little regard for future generations or the big environmental picture. Some analysts predict that fresh water will be the most important economic and environmental issue of the twenty-first century—one that will force dramatic decisions about growing and importing food, put great pressure on water-rich countries like Canada to export their water, and even provoke threats of war. As a recent World Bank report notes, "Water is vital for life, human life, life of our ecosystem, economic and social well-being. With water resources threatened in so many parts of the globe, and especially in developing countries, life itself is threatened. Action is, therefore, needed worldwide to reverse this trend and to better manage our water."

Worldwide, about two-thirds of all fresh water is used to irrigate crops. To grow a tonne of wheat requires about one million litres of water; one kilogram of potatoes requires about one thousand litres of water. Food supply and water supply are inextricably linked. One recent study suggests that in about twenty years, water scarcity will cause annual global losses of 350 million tonnes of food—slightly more than the entire current U.S. grain crop. Parched lands will not be able to produce agricultural crops as they once did, forcing people living there to import food.

And climate change is expected to intensify this devastation. The world's breadbaskets (the Canadian prairies, the U.S. southern plains, China's north plain, and India's Punjab region) are all expected to suffer from increasingly hot and dry weather. This will significantly reduce the ability of farmers in those breadbaskets from continuing to grow staples like grain. In recent years, the world's grain harvest has been declining, partly because of a warmer climate and partly because of water shortages. With worldwide water consumption doubling every twenty years, a crisis of Malthusian proportions may be just around the corner. For some people, the lack of clean water is already a deadly fact of everyday life.

Lest you think this is alarmist rhetoric, here are a few dry facts about the state of the world's fresh water:

- In developing countries, about 80 per cent of all illnesses are water related. Every year, three million children under the age of five die from diarrhea.

- More than one billion people lack access to safe water, and 2.4 billion—over one in three of the world's population—don't have adequate sanitation facilities.

- Clean water is so scarce in Mexico's maquiladora zones that parents give babies and children Pepsi and Coca-Cola instead.

- About 90 per cent of the developing world's waste water runs untreated into local rivers and streams.

- Eighty per cent of China's rivers no longer support fish life.

- In 1972, China's Yellow River failed to reach the sea for the first time in thousands of years of recorded history. Since 1985, it has run dry every single year.

- Three-quarters of Poland's rivers are so polluted by chemicals, sewage, and agricultural runoff that the water is unfit even for industrial use.

- In 1999, a federal government study revealed that one-third of Ontario's rural wells were contaminated by E. coli bacteria—and in that same year, the provincial government dropped testing for E. coli from its Drinking Water Surveillance Program. In 2000, the same government dropped the entire program. In June of that year, seven Ontarians died and more than two thousand people became seriously ill in Walkerton because of E. coli bacteria in their drinking water.

Every year, Canadians—particularly those living in rural communities and on reserves—suffer through hundreds of boil-water orders. Canadians should be shocked to learn of polluted waters in hundreds of communities in pristine Prince Edward Island, in Newfoundland and Labrador, and in British Columbia, with its snow-fed streams. Living in our fresh-water-rich country, most Canadians are barely aware of the consequences. But then, Canada has no strategy for the stewardship of its fresh water, over which we have been blessed with custodianship. Shouldn't this change?

Friends of the Don River

One in every three Canadians depends on the five Great Lakes for fresh water. These imortant bodies of water constitute a major underpinning of our economy—in agriculture, transportation, industrial uses, and much more.

Pollution is killing this natural habitat and seriously affecting people's health. Lake sediment contains polychlorinated biphenyls (PCBs) about a hundred times higher than safe levels. Alien invasive species like zebra and quagga mussels, sea lampreys, and more than 150 other non-native species continue to invade and destroy this environment and negatively affect the economy. Mercury (the greatest source of which is atmospheric pollution from coal-fired generating stations) continues to work its way up the food chain, causing cancer, reproductive and neurological diseases, and immunological abnormalities. Despite years of efforts to reduce them, toxic industrial releases are actually increasing. Health authorities estimated that some one thousand premature deaths and at least forty thousand hospitalizations occurred along the Ontario side of the Detroit River between 1986 and 1992 alone. Evidence of thyroid gland disorders among young women in Windsor is twice as high as in Ontario as a whole.

While scientists continue to study contamination of the lakes and issue dire reports about its consequences, we need a national action commitment to restore one of our most essential natural resources. As always, our environment, our economy, and our health are inextricably intertwined.

Cleaning up the Great Lakes will take time, money, and a genuine international commitment. The International Joint Commission (made up of representatives from Canada and the U.S. to oversee the Great Lakes and the St. Lawrence River) calls upon the governments to "complete the cleanup of all known sites [of major sediment pollution] in the basin by 2025." That goal is achievable. And though cleanup costs would likely reach into the hundreds of millions of dollars, those costs will certainly be much less than treating generations of sick people or dealing with the destruction of so many industries and jobs.

In 1990, my right hand at city hall, the brilliant Dan Leckie, came into my office one day with mud on his boots. He was raving about a wonderful citizens' group called Friends of the Don, whose members had been hauling out tires, engine blocks, and other junk from this river that runs through the heart of Toronto. (A photography student once developed film in water taken straight from the Don, just to show the level of chemical contamination.) Before long, working with city councillors Marilyn Churley and Barbara Hall, who represented the neighbourhoods near the Don, we sent out a letter that started: "Have you ever imagined swimming in the Don River?" We included photos of people swimming in the once-great recreational river half a century before. "Have you ever imagined fishing in the Don River?" More photos, then we asked, "Have you ever imagined drinking the water of the Don River?" It flows into Lake Ontario—the source of Toronto's drinking water, so even if people can't imagine it, they're doing it, every day! "If you

don't think we're nuts yet," the letter went on, "we are invit-
ing you to a public meeting to talk about the river and how it
could be restored."

Being optimists, we prepared for a modest group of ten to
twenty people at city hall. When lineups reached down the
corridor, we shifted to a larger space. We had touched a
nerve. Within two meetings, we had a full committee with
vision documents, budgets, proposals, and a step-by-step initiative to bring city council on side. Some councillors wanted
to leave all matters relating to the flow of water to the engineers. Incredible as it may seem, the engineers' plans
included a $1-billion scheme to put most of the watershed's
storm water into large pipes under the river valley. Such folly
would only have exacerbated the problem of stress on the
watershed's ecosystems. Fortunately, many citizens with
diverse expertise had stepped forward to be part of that revitalization movement, and city council accepted our
proposals, over the objections of some senior bureaucrats
and councillors.

In the years since, that community project has involved
more than ten thousand volunteers, schoolchildren, local
businesses, and service clubs like my own Rotary Club, who
have planted about thirty thousand native trees, shrubs, and
wildflowers. Marshes have been created, which have reduced
pollution-laden runoff and brought countless species back to
the valley. Cycling and walking trails have opened up the
area to tens of thousands of city dwellers. Salmon have been
documented in the river for the first time in decades.
Pollution sites have been cleaned up. Now songbirds, foxes,
muskrats, and herons all make their homes there, right in the
heart of the city.

Perhaps best of all, the Bring Back the Don Task Force
concept was infectious. Across Canada, a network of watershed councils sprang up, mobilizing citizens, all of them

linked to similar groups. Imagine what more could have been achieved had the federal government become involved by providing significant resources toward these projects.

Not even an army of dedicated volunteers could restore the ten thousand kilometres of the Great Lakes' shorelines or clean up the thousands of tonnes of contaminated sediment. This is the painful lesson we've learned with the Great Lakes Water Quality Agreement, which is a Canada-U.S. pact to clean up the Great Lakes. The agreement focuses on what are called in the agreement Areas of Concern: some forty-two communities identified as hot spots. Citizens and communities in the hot spots were asked to participate, by identifying areas that required cleaning by preparing a Remedial Action Plan and implementing its recommendations. By all accounts, the citizens were keen and excited, and after millions of volunteer hours identified many practical and workable solutions.

During this time, a whole network of citizens organized under an umbrella group called Great Lakes United (GLU) to share their solutions, learn from each other, and propose cost-effective and successful cleanups. For years the people of Canada and the U.S. had shown they were ready to implement these solutions. But a lack of meaningful federal funding from Ottawa meant solutions were never properly implemented. The International Joint Commission, an independent joint Canada-U.S. agency, repeatedly criticized our federal government for its funding inaction. But purse strings still weren't loosened. What should have been a steady flow of funds to co-ordinate citizens' volunteer involvement ended up being a trickle. And as a consequence volunteers became frustrated and disillusioned. They lost interest.

The lesson is clear: the only hope to restore the shores of the Great Lakes is a well-funded international program that involves local communities and volunteer groups who are empowered to speed up and enhance the work of governments.

Once again, while restoration is essential, the key is preventing pollution in the first place. That means stringent controls on the use of agricultural chemicals, tougher restrictions on toxic industrial output, a reduction in the number of coal-fired generating stations, strict enforcement against dumping of ballast water from ocean-going ships, because ballast water introduces non-native species into the lakes, banning pesticides for lawns and gardens, and phasing out municipal waste incinerators. We don't need more Love Canals. But we do need more people like Lois Marie Gibbs. For those too young to remember, the Love Canal was a chemical dump in Niagara Falls, N.Y., over which a housing subdivision was built. In 1978, the New York State Department of Health declared a state of emergency at Love Canal after a lengthy battle with residents about how to respond to the many health problems facing residents. A huge class-action lawsuit was launched, President Jimmy Carter called the Love Canal a national disaster, and the residents were eventually evacuated. Today, the neighbourhood remains a ghost town.

Had it not been for the courageous efforts of Lois Marie Gibbs, a resident of Love Canal, people might still be dying in the Love Canal subdivision. A wife and mother who had no previous political or activist experience, Gibbs mobilized her neighbours and turned the injustices facing residents of the Love Canal into a national issue. And thanks to her, an entire generation of grassroots environmental activists have been inspired to fight toxins before they are produced.

Preventing toxic pollution is another reason for governments to enact Extended Producer Responsibility (EPR) legislation. EPR requires manufacturers to eliminate toxins before they ever reach the waste stream; places the burden on the manufacturers for all recovery costs associated with their products; and requires them to take back their products once consumers are finished with them.

These strategies should be used across the country, of course, not just in the Great Lakes basin. Groundwater supplies about 90 per cent of rural Canadians with their drinking water—including everyone on Prince Edward Island. Once an aquifer is polluted, it can be decades, or lifetimes, before restoration makes the water safe to drink. Despite those hundreds of boil-water orders that Canadians endure every year, we still have no federal standards for drinking water quality and no overall water policy. Incredible.

As usual, innovative solutions to reduce water use and provide clean water are available—and in effect now—in parts of the world.

In developed countries like Canada, addressing the world's shortage of fresh water is often a matter of public education and public policy. People can vastly reduce their own use of water simply with low- or no-cost, common-sense remedies and by changing their daily habits and routines. Don't let the tap run while you brush your teeth or wash the dishes. Install low-flush toilets and low-flow shower heads. A soaker hose or a drip system can keep your garden healthy but uses 80 per cent less water than a sprinkler or regular hose nozzle. People have it in their power to save millions of litres of water every year.

Because of our normally abundant rainfall, about 70 per cent of water used in Canada is for industrial, rather than agricultural, purposes. Significant reductions in water use will mean that industrial practices have to change.

Treating water and pumping it to households is a major part of every urban infrastructure in Canada. Despite the fact that only about 3 per cent of treated water is actually used for drinking, Canadian cities and towns—at great public expense—bring all treated water up to drinking quality. This requires massive amounts of energy, and for what? To flush most of it down toilets (the biggest personal use of water), to wash cars, to cool machinery, to heat radiators, and for countless industrial processes. In the summer, about half of our treated water is used on lawns and gardens.

The most effective way we can reduce the costs of water treatment systems—and save water along the way—is to reduce the amount of water that's treated and delivered in the first place. Let's talk about something as basic as a shower head. If you use a low-flow shower head in your home, you save water, and that's good. But, more important than saving water, you also save the energy required to heat the extra water and pump it to your shower. People usually don't think about how much energy is needed to move water from its source to a shower. So imagine carrying several buckets of water from wherever your community draws its potable supply all the way to your bathroom. A pretty good workout, right? That gives you some idea of the energy used by our cities and towns to make sure you've got your shower on demand. If you use half the number of buckets by changing that shower head, you save half the energy. You also save the money used to produce that energy. Your own hydro bill goes down. Great. When an entire city of people use low-flow shower heads, the public utility that generates electricity can save tens of millions of dollars by not having to build extra capacity, not to mention the environmental benefits from less fossil fuel pollution or fewer nuclear power stations

It's in a city's interest to give away low-flow shower heads to residents, because overall they save the city money. And bulk-buying means they can be purchased at a very good price. The brilliant environmentalist Amory Lovins has a strategy for distributing low-flow shower heads to people. He suggests we put a box of them on every street corner with a sign saying: "Government Property. Do Not Steal."

So here's a choice. On the one hand, government can spend millions of dollars to construct a generating station that contributes to environmental pollution, and use the energy produced to pump water. Using that alternative, the consumer will also use more energy to heat the water for showers and then watch it go down the drain. Alternatively, government could spend less money by buying shower heads from a local manufacturer, if possible, and either giving them away or making shower-head replacement part of a comprehensive water-saving retrofit program. By using this alternative, the government continues to reap the benefits through lower energy costs and less pollution.

The City of Barrie, Ontario, chose such an alternative. Faced with a rapidly growing population and a proposal for a huge new brewery that would need lots of water (to be converted to a very useful purpose!), the city needed to consider the options for additional water supply and treatment. The "logical" way was to build a $41-million addition to its treatment plant and draw more water from Lake Simcoe by constructing a new $27-million intake facility. (This itself would have required a further $20 million to upgrade later.) But Barrie city councillors decided to think outside the box. The city installed low-flush toilets, plus low-flow shower heads and aerator faucets, in about 11,000 homes. This option saved about 1,800 cubic metres of water a day, and at least $9.3 million over the construction option. Additional energy savings to homeowners, accruing from having to heat less water, amounted to another $18.4 million in savings. On top of that, about 2,400 new jobs were created (eight hundred more than would have been created by building the new facilities), virtually all of them local.

The mayor of Santa Monica, California, told me the history of his city's terrible water shortage. It looked as if the city could not construct any more homes or apartment buildings because there was no more water. Then they came up with a challenging idea: a new building could be constructed, but only if it effectively used no water. Not possible? Well, it turned out that the existing wasteful faucets, shower heads, and toilets in the homes and apartments of the good citizens of Santa Monica held the key. Developers wanting to build new units would approach owners of older buildings and ask, "Can we take out your old toilets and faucets and give you free new ones that use less water? Yes, of course, we'll pay for all this work. You'll see the savings on your water bill." Not surprisingly, just about everyone said yes. So the new building went up at the same time as the installation of the efficient water appliances—with no net increase in water use at all. Bingo!

"Now that's thinking outside the pipe," I told the mayor, and looked for a similar opportunity in my own city. Not long afterwards, Toronto officials brought forward a plan to expand the city's water treatment plant—and a $1-billion expansion to the sewage treatment plant to provide water for suburban sprawl spreading over the agricultural lands north of the city. Some of us said, "Wait a minute." What would it cost to replace a million old-fashioned, water-wasting toilets (twenty-four litres) with models that used 75 per cent less water (six litres)? And could we also avoid all the new pipes and pumps—and the energy to move water through them and treat it all when it's contaminated? Would it make sense to give Torontonians a million new "thrones," all paid for, plus savings on their energy and water bills? In that way, the water not flushed could be diverted to the suburbs, without a single new pipe or pump. Naturally, the city council's conventional thinkers attacked my million-toilets plan. Some said that the low-flow toilets didn't work or that they usually had to be flushed twice. I pointed out that all of Western Europe was using them, with no evidence of social breakdown. But then, water is more scarce in Europe and much more expensive. Here, we are profligate wasters, and water is cheap, so why change? To roars of derision and amusement from the media gallery, I invited the doubting councillors to visit our home and try out three different types of low-flow toilets. (We had no takers. Even Toronto politicians avoid some publicity!)

Nevertheless, the commissioner of the Works Department and a few of his more creative staff saw potential in the idea. They tried a pilot project, replacing forty thousand toilets in apartment buildings. The owners loved the scheme because it saved water and reduced pumping costs. Tenants liked the new fixtures. And the savings far exceeded the conservative projections. Now the Toronto Council is involved in a multi-year program to replace almost a million toilets. In addition to energy savings from not havng to pump extra water, the results will include lower demand on the coal-burning electricity plants, thus reducing smog and climate-changing gas emissions. Not only that, but the toilet manufacturing business got a boost, and plumbers installing all the new fixtures were hiring apprentices to keep up with the demand. This is sustainability—the new prosperity.

The Federation of Canadian Municipalities' Green Municipal Funds are advancing this kind of thinking. Now we need an industrial strategy related to water and municipal infrastructure that ties together the opportunities to enhance our economic and environmental capital simultaneously.

I confess that it's fun to see policies of governments, big and small, change for the better, especially when the ideas have been initially laughed off. There's something special about last laughs.

Yet all these innovative conservation ideas flowing from local communities could be undermined if the federal government fails to protect the public ownership of our precious water resource. Thanks to the excellent work of Maude Barlow and the Council of Canadians, Canadians are becoming aware of how federal inaction may result in transnational private corporations controlling and depleting our fresh water supply, if nothing is done to stop their bulk exports of this precious commodity. As Barlow eloquently outlined in 2003, giant transnational corporations want to export Canada's fresh water to the rest of the world. They want to turn our precious resource into a commodity to be sold to the highest bidder. Barlow writes:

> So far, Canada has not allowed these exports. But if we do allow them it will be impossible to stop them. (Yes, you read correctly: impossible)... Canada is bound by the North American Free Trade Agreement (NAFTA). And the NAFTA deal clearly says that once we start exporting water we cannot stop. Furthermore, Canadian and American corporations will have the actual legal right to come in and buy as much of our lake water as they want—without restriction. Should our government try to pass a law prohibiting these exports, American corporations can sue for lost revenue.

Canadians are not sitting idly by as federal government inaction threatens our water. They are telling the federal government in no uncertain terms that water is not like a soft drink. It should not be controlled by private, unaccountable transnational corporations. It should not be bought and sold to make a profit. As Maude Barlow rightly points out, water belongs to the earth and its species and accordingly should be declared a basic human right.

> •Litres of water used in a five-minute shower with a regular shower head: 100; with a low-flow shower head: 35
> •Litres of water used by the average Canadian household annually: 500,000

Living Machines

The smallest and most natural water treatment plant is literally that—a plant. Wetlands filter water, their vegetation cleans the air, and marshes provide an environment for wildlife. Canada has about a quarter of the world's wetlands, covering about 16 per cent of our country's land mass. As with so many other resources, we are truly fortunate.

The small town of Roblin, Manitoba, created its own engineered wetland. It's only sixteen hectares, but it manages water flow and reduces flooding and chemicals on irrigated land. A waterfowl habitat developed. Nutrients from the wetlands' effluent feed crops. And the town has potential revenue from the sale of timber, which also benefits from the effluent.

Private companies can make their own wetlands. Around the world, businesses are adopting "living machines"—systems of shallow ponds and plants in greenhouses in which bacteria treat waste water that is then recycled for reuse.

During my time as an environmental consultant with my Green Catalyst Group, I had a chance to work with and promote an astonishing Canadian biologist, John Todd, who developed the living machine concept. The Body Shop, Ben & Jerry's, and a growing number of other companies have installed living machines in their own commercial spaces, treating their own water and reusing it.

Living machines vary in size. The City of Burlington, Vermont, built a living machine that treats 80,000 gallons (300,000 litres) of municipal sewage a day—and the effluent quality far exceeds standards and targets. That living machine produces no odours, and it fits into a residential environment. By the way, the system's greenhouses are manufactured by one of the most advanced firms in the field, located in Hamilton, Ontario. It's yet another Canadian exporter to the United States that's underappreciated here at home.

As John Todd and I sat in the lush greenhouse environment of the living machine in Frederick, Maryland, he explained: "We don't know exactly why, but the water purification via the natural organism is so complete that it's removing trace elements that cannot be removed by traditional technologies." He laughed and added, "The snails. We think it has something to do with the snails, but we're not sure what!" For me, Todd was underlining the sense of mystery that humans—especially decision makers—should have about natural systems. A little humility and respect for nature would serve us well, instead of behaving like "the dominant species."

Todd made a return visit to Toronto from his post at Harvard University. In a lecture about our waterfront, he outlined a vision for the role that living machines and natural systems could play in a sustainable urban future. He said Canada could lead the world using natural processes to purify previously polluted waters and keep ecosystems in better balance. We could rise to the challenge and the opportunity to use waste as a resource, to convert sewage and industrial discharge into useful plants and organisms rather than spreading them on farmland or incinerating them into our atmosphere. Our federal government should embrace and encourage such innovation. But water is a provincial concern, say the constitutional gurus. A national will would be required. And I believe that Canadians would jump at the chance to become world leaders in the preservation and purification of fresh water. There would be no problem establishing such a mandate for our national government, if only the people of the country were asked. Given half a chance, they could become engaged and excited at the prospects. Then the federal government could announce support for cross-country engagement strategies and community-based projects. These would include new industrial development, as well as job creation in the enhancement of watercourses, wetlands, moraines, and threatened aquamarine environments. What an exciting prospect. Gary Doer's NDP government in Manitoba recently announced a water initiative that is capturing the imagination of Manitobans. Imagine if the entire country were enlisted in similar challenges. Canadians would excel—doing good things for the whole planet, starting here at home and sharing our knowledge abroad.

From the Ground Up

If the polluter-pays principle applies to the products we manufacture, it should certainly apply to the cleanup of toxic chemicals that corporations have left in our soil.

Contaminated industrial lands litter our cities. These sites, called brownfields, total about thirty thousand in Canada. In many situations they pose enormous health hazards, and cleanup costs are often very expensive. All too often, the companies that contaminated the land assume no responsibility for cleaning up the mess they've left behind. Area residents suffer the health consequences, and taxpayers suffer the economic consequences. In October 2003, in a case brought by Quebec against Imperial Oil, the Supreme Court of Canada upheld the right of provincial governments to sue corporations based on the principle of polluter pays. This landmark case from the nation's top court makes clear that corporations are liable for the contamination they leave behind.

Ironically, as cities and towns grow in Canada, most brownfields are now valuable real estate, often on strategically located sites near downtowns or along rivers or waterfronts. Once located on industrial lands that were on the periphery of a much smaller centre, the community has grown around them. In the wake of the Supreme Court ruling and because the land is much more valuable, corporations seriously consider cleaning up their brownfields, especially when limits on liability and taxpayer subsidies can be negotiated.

Cities are often interested in these projects for several good reasons. They create tens of thousands of jobs, add millions of dollars in property tax, revitalize neighbourhoods, allow for planned communities or facilities, reduce urban sprawl, and rehabilitate toxic land or wasteland, thereby reducing or eliminating the health hazard. Canada has many success stories of rehabilitated brownfields.

False Creek in Vancouver, is an early example. Begun in the 1970s on thirty-two hectares of decaying industrial land, False Creek, created on the designing table with the participation of city planners, became a benchmark for new communities. This planned community now provides housing for mixed ages and incomes, both market and non-market, with co-operatives, condominiums, rental, and ownership.

The Moncton Shops Project in New Brunswick is another interesting development. For nearly a century, the soils on the 115-hectare site had been polluted by industrial contaminants from Canadian National Railways' repair shops. This site, when restored, will comprise forty-four hectares of recreational area (including ten baseball diamonds, two football fields, and four soccer fields), a sportsplex with four regulation-size hockey rinks, twenty-six hectares of residential units, and twenty-four hectares for a business and technology park. By the time it's finished—construction is expected to last about ten years—the project will have created about 2,100 person years of employment. An additional five thousand permanent jobs are anticipated in the business and technology park, and the potential property tax base is almost $9 million a year.

In Montreal, more than 485 hectares of former Canadian Pacific Railway lands are being rehabilitated, and in Voisey's Bay, Argentia, in Newfoundland and Labrador, 3,600 hectares of an old military base are also being cleaned up for industrial and commercial use. Dozens of smaller projects are under way across the country.

However, brownfield redevelopment requires careful planning and thorough cleanup. The residential community of Lynnview Ridge, in Calgary, illustrates why.

For fifty years Imperial Oil operated a refinery on the site. That closed down in the 1970s, and the land was later rezoned for residential use. Now, two-thirds of the property's soil has lead levels several times higher than the allowable provincial guideline of 140 parts per million—and dust in Lynnview Ridge homes has lead levels up to ten times higher than in homes elsewhere in Calgary. In 2001, Imperial Oil offered owners a buyout package of 120 per cent of the homes' market value. To date, about 135 of the 160 homeowners have accepted the deal.

Imperial Oil said the lead came after they closed down, from topsoil brought onto the site by a development company that no longer exists. The Alberta government and the Lynnview homeowners weren't buying that story. The government sued Imperial Oil and won. Imperial Oil appealed while the remaining residents worry about their health and watch the ongoing legal battle with dismay. In April 2005, Imperial Oil reached an agreement with the Alberta government to test, remove, and replace contaminated soil.

Although local and provincial initiatives are a good start, we must do better. As the National Roundtable on

Environment and Economy (NRTEE) has been suggesting, it's time the government of Canada, steward to a magnificent land, took a leadership role in cleaning up brownfields. In May 2002, the NRTEE convened a task force, with the Federation of Canadian Municipalities (FCM) as one of its members, and produced important recommendations on how to deal with brownfields. These included changing the federal tax system to remove disincentives to redevelopment, expanding Canada Mortgage and Housing Corporation's mandate so that they can provide mortgage insurance to qualified sites, providing grants to municipal governments to fund brownfield redevelopment, and creating a revolving loan fund for brownfield redevelopment.

As I found out during my years at the FCM, on this issue leadership is not hard to find in local communities. But a significant investment fund needs to be created nationally to stimulate action and capture a share of the benefits of cleaning up polluted sites over the long term. Canadians want to invest in making their country a better place, if only their government would enlist their support and create the investment vehicles to do so. Revolving funds and investment bonds designed to achieve such exciting goals as cleaning up and restoring polluted sites in cities to useful purposes are exactly the kinds of investments that Canadians, their pension funds, and their governments should be encouraged to make. And, as a 2003 David Suzuki Foundation report notes, brownfield redevelopment would help solve another problem that concerns Canadians: urban sprawl.

It was heartening to encounter a reference to contaminated sites in the 2004 federal budget, which allocated modest funds for cleanup. Our collective diligence was required to ensure that the full vision of a major investment fund became a reality. Just such an infusion of finances materialized when the 2005 federal budget was adopted and the FCM Green Municipal Funds received further federal investment and an expanded mandate to include brownfield remediation.

Even though many brownfield rehabilitation projects are worthy and successful, an important lesson remains. We must be far more vigilant about soil contamination before it happens. We need strict standards to regulate the use and discharge of pollutants, because many contaminants remain in the soil for centuries. The legacy of contaminated industrial sites endures long after the corporations have moved on or amalgamated, and what is left affects the health of people and the environment. We also need strict enforcement of those standards—and, in an era when governments have reduced services, eliminated inspectors, and cut back enforcement, we must demand accountability. As conservative governments clamour for "less government" and "business-friendly" environments, the consequences will have to be paid, sooner or later. Should our lack of foresight and oversight—let alone the reckless behaviour of governments and corporations—be dumped on future generations?

As Henry David Thoreau is often quoted, "What good is a house if you don't have a decent planet to put it on?"

Last time I checked, ours was the only planet we've got to put our houses on. Relocation opportunities are limited. Imaginative people, working with far-sighted governments, both local and national, are creating ways to protect our planet and stimulate our economy. It's time Canada took a leadership role.

Asphalt Is the Land's Last Crop

Protecting what you've got is a lot easier than reclaiming what you had. This is especially true of Canada's agricultural land.

Only about 7 per cent of Canada's land can be reasonably used for farming. Prime agricultural land (what we call Class 1) makes up less than one-half of 1 per cent of the total—and over half of that land is in Southern Ontario. On a clear day—yes there are still a few—from the top of the CN Tower in Toronto, a person can see about one-third of the best food-producing land in Canada—and this terrain is subject to the most rapidly rising population and prone to the worst kinds of urban sprawl.

We are losing our best agricultural land fast. Once it's gone, it's almost impossible to reclaim. As one wag put it, "Asphalt is the land's last crop." Ontario now loses about one square kilometre of prime agricultural land every day. In the past thirty years, urban uses across Canada have eaten up about six thousand square kilometres of quality agricultural land. Picture the whole of Prince Edward Island built on and paved over.

Not only is agricultural land being squandered, but the number of farms in Canada is declining as well. Since 1941, we have lost about two-thirds of our farms. Correspondingly, the average size of a farm has grown about 2.5 times. Traditional family farms are disappearing, and the number of larger corporate farms is increasing.

In British Columbia, agriculture occupies less than 5 per cent of the province's territory, but it provides food for over half the province's people. Employment in B.C.'s farms and food processing industries tops two hundred thousand, and the agricultural sector contributes $2.2 billion to the provincial economy. Realizing the importance of protecting its scarce food-producing land, B.C.'s first-ever NDP government (1972 to 1975) under its exuberant Premier Dave Barrett created what is known as the Agricultural Land Reserve. The government set aside areas almost exclusively for agricultural purposes. (Land can be withdrawn from the ALR, but it's not easy.) The

Commission de protection du territoire agricole du Québec has similar objectives enshrined in law. We need the federal government to support agriculture and protect agricultural lands—particularly close to our cities. Food grown locally is cheaper and better, and Agriculture Canada should have programs to help farmers adapt to markets on their doorsteps.

In the 1990s, another NDP government in B.C. directed a portion of its gasoline tax revenue to Vancouver, with the stipulation that the city put restrictions on land use. This sensible solution provided funding and agricultural land protection at the same time.

Just as the provinces can do smart things to protect agricultural land, so could the federal government. For instance, Ottawa could work with provinces to tie infrastructure funding to the control of urban sprawl, assisting provinces to create ways of keeping farmland in farmers' hands. Smart federal funding for municipal infrastructure can help achieve national goals, for example preventing urban sprawl, especially on Class 1 and 2 farmland. We're losing these lands and farmers, but there are remedies.

Food Security

Like all elected politicians, I receive my share of politely indignant proposals telling me what to do. But a letter I received in 1985 kept nettling me.

It was addressed jointly to me and to my (then new) partner, Olivia Chow, who had just been elected to the Toronto School Board, representing the same downtown ward as I did on city council. The letter came from Dr. Cyril Greenland, a professor of sociology at the University of Toronto and a constituent to boot. The essence of his letter: too many thousands of children were going to school hungry, and we needed to address that issue.

"Mr. Layton," he said, "you are the new chair of Toronto's Board of Health. Ms. Chow, you are the school trustee for downtown, where there are many hungry kids. You two should propose a program to feed kids in schools, not just in Toronto, but across Ontario."

Over lunch, Olivia and I had a long chat about the idea. What would it cost? How could it be delivered? Later, we turned on the computer and sketched a plan to provide every child in Ontario's school system with one hot nutritious meal every day. With funding of roughly $1 a day for each child plus some set-up costs, our plan totalled $180 million. Given the size of the provincial budget, and considering the health and educational benefits that would flow in the long term, this was not an impossible number.

On the day before Christmas that year, we had tea with Professor Greenland at his kitchen table. He helped us with the details of the concept, and he emphasized the importance of feeding every child every day. "Surely this is a responsibility of a well-functioning society," he said. Of course, he was right.

After checking our calculations and our facts, Olivia and I presented the idea simultaneously to the Toronto School Board and the Board of Health. A key to bringing the idea to fruition was the mobilization of community groups in support. They quickly lined up behind the plan. Both boards were energized by the idea, and supported it. Of course, provincial funds would be required because local governments are chronically starved for cash. We sent the proposal and our appeal to the Ontario Liberal government of the day. Sadly, they ignored it.

Despite that rejection, the city initiated pilot projects with its own funding, and gradually the program grew. Today, sixty-five thousand Toronto kids benefit every day from nutritious snacks and meals. Governments, the private sector, and parents all provide funding for the program.

I know Stephen Harper and Gilles Duceppe will remind me that education is a provincial responsibility, but it's time Canada had a national school meal program like every other OECD (Organization for Economic Co-operation and Development) country, including the U.S.

School meal programs do a lot more than just feed kids:
- They provide a head start for kids from low-income families who might otherwise have their learning interrupted by hunger or be involved in misbehaviour.
- They cut health-care costs, especially those associated with childhood obesity, by making sure all our kids, even those from middle-class families whose parents might be squeezed for time, are provided with nutritious food.
- They support our farmers by providing a large local market for local foods.
- They educate our students about our agricultural system, how composting works, and how food preparation differs across cultures.
- They create local jobs for micro-producers and for short-order cooks.

Let's start helping our kids—and ourselves too!

The Most Fundamental of Human Rights

According to the United Nations Food and Agricultural Organization (FAO), more than eight hundred million people in the world go hungry every single day. Most of them are children. That's a daily tragedy, but the real disgrace is that the world already grows more than enough food to feed all of them.

The director general of the Food and Agricultural Organization, Jacques Diouf, writes, "We do not have the excuse that we cannot grow enough or that we do not know enough about how to eliminate hunger. What remains to be proven is that we care enough, that our expressions of concern... are more than rhetoric, that we will no longer accept and ignore the suffering of 840 million hungry people in the world or the daily death toll of twenty-five thousand victims of hunger and poverty." Diouf calls on us to ensure that people have "the most fundamental of human rights— the right to food that is essential to their very survival and existence."

- Percentage of Ontario farms that were family owned in 1976: 91; in 1996: 57
- Number of people in the world who suffer from malnutrition as a result of hunger: at least 852 million
- Number who suffer from malnutrition as a result of overconsumption: at least 1.2 billion

Many factors "explain" the world's failure to provide people with access to food. In the developing world, armed conflict, unequal land distribution, and natural disasters are among the most prevalent reasons. But so-called market forces are often the underlying cause.

A study released in the fall of 2003 showed that over 750,000 Canadians use food banks every month. The 482 food banks that participated in the study (there are 639 food banks in Canada) distributed about 3.2 million kilograms of food and about 2.3 million meals a month. Children make up 39 per cent of the recipients.

In 1989, Ed Broadbent—on his final day in Parliament as leader of the NDP—called on the House of Commons to work toward the elimination of child poverty in Canada by 2000. His resolution passed unanimously. But the numbers have not declined, and today almost 1.1 million Canadian children are living in poverty. More children are homeless. More children go hungry. More children are being denied a decent future. In a country as fortunate as Canada, with the natural resources we have at our disposal, it is an absolute disgrace that Ottawa has not dealt with this tragedy.

Fifteen years later, Ed was back! Ed was in the House! Good news for Canadians. But this time, Ed was damn mad. Why? Because the Conservative and Liberal hypocrites who had unanimously supported his motion had, instead, presided over the next sixteen years with cuts to the modest, now fraying social fabric that Canadians had created to protect those most in need.

People have asked me how I managed to hook Ed Broadbent back into the political fray. When I asked Ed out for dinner to pop the question about his running again for the House of Commons, I'd consulted with his good friend, and my mentor, Terry Grier—a former NDP federal secretary and staffer to Tommy Douglas. I had a plan. Ed suggested one of his favourite outdoor cafés in Ottawa when I asked him for advice on a number of issues. At that time, I'd been party leader for about six months, in no small measure because Ed had decided to support my candidacy. He had done so, despite his deep respect for others in the race, particularly Manitoba MP Bill Blaikie, who had worked alongside Ed in caucus from 1979 until Ed retired a decade later. After a glass or two of wine and his wise answers to and advice about my questions, I moved the conversation to child poverty. Immediately, I could see the flash in his eyes as we talked about his important motion of 1989, passed unanimously. Passage of that motion had helped spawn a coalition called Campaign 2000, the campaign to end child poverty by the turn of the millenium. Despite the creative and passionate efforts by the Campaign 2000 leadership, child poverty had increased not decreased. I paused, took a deep breath—knowing that my next question could set an important course for the NDP in the next election—and said: "Ed, I don't want you to answer the question I'm about to ask you—not now, not tonight. I want you to promise me you'll sleep on it before you answer . . . unless of course your answer is yes! If you are going to say no, don't do it now. Agreed?" Ed accepted the rules of engagement, with a twinkle in his eye. I'll never know if he saw the question coming, or if he secretly hoped I'd ask, or if Terry Grier had prepared him. "The Liberals have appointed Mac Harb, the MP for Ottawa Centre, to the Senate. There will be a by-election. I'd like you to come back to federal politics Ed, and run in that by-election." Ed honoured his commitment and did not say no, but he did say: "Jack, I don't want you leaving this dinner with the wrong idea. The idea that I would ever say yes is very, very, very remote." He pointed to his age—I scoffed. He worried about his sweetheart's health. Lucille had been battling cancer, but was, it turned out, very keen on Ed's running. After rhyming off the reasons why not, Ed began to talk about what he would do if he were to return. Of course, tackling child poverty was the top item on his list. Second was reforming democracy with proportional representation—more on that in the final chapter of this book. But it was the passion in his eyes when he talked about the injustices of poverty in Canada and around the world that told me he would make the right decision. As it happened, the "Who's back? Ed's back" rap video that we used in the campaign was the most popular section of our website. Sadly, after serving one wonderful term in our caucus, Broadbent decided not to run again in order to be with Lucille as she tackled cancer one more time.

The reasons for Canadian childrens' poverty vary—and are almost always surmountable. However, the consequences are clear. Growing up in poverty puts children at risk of physical, social, and psychological damage. Children in poverty are more susceptible to disease, less resilient to stress, and more prone to anxiety and aggression. Poverty inhibits children's ability to learn at school and increases the likelihood that they will drop out.

The interconnections between feeding people properly, improving health outcomes, and reducing poverty while increasing economic growth are direct. Right-wing politicians and economists have been telling us for years that the best way to stimulate the economy is to cut taxes, when what we really should be doing is making sure that everybody has enough to eat.

But food security is not a worry only to those people who have to wonder where their next meal might come from. Food security is everybody's concern. If overfishing, changes to the environment, pollution, and habitat destruction deplete the world's supply of fish, that's everyone's problem. When the world's breadbaskets are affected, it's an issue for all of us. As more and more crops are being genetically modified by multinational corporations (which own and control these new life forms)—and we don't know how they will affect people—everyone's food security is at risk. Big cities usually have only about three days' supply of food. In a disaster such as the flooding Hurricane Katrina delivered to the residents of New Orleans in the summer of 2005, food cannot be delivered daily, and the city's residents will soon run out. When the power went out during August 2003 across much of eastern North America, refrigeration and freezers didn't work—and that became everyone's problem. So although it hits poor people hardest, food security isn't just a poverty issue. It's also a people issue.

War, however, constitutes the biggest threat to food security. War prevents people from growing food—and receiving it—and the dislocation of families and communities only makes a bad situation worse. Land mines—millions of them—make both farming and grazing animals either impossible or enormously dangerous, and minefields often cut people off from their access to water and food.

Now, consider the impact of drought and flood, climate change, loss of habitat, soil erosion, depletion or chemical contamination of aquifers, or salt-water intrusion preventing irrigation, and so on. Environmental changes that affect our ability to grow food, catch fish, or raise livestock all directly affect our food security. So do catastrophic events like the tsunami in south Asia on December 26, 2004 or floods or hurricanes.

In case you thought that was all, there's one more main threat. Oddly enough, it's the price of food itself. The number of farmers in Canada is already incredibly small, relative to our population—only 1 per cent of Canadians are now classified as farm operators. Obviously, many more work in the food sector (it's one of our largest employers), but only one person in a hundred is a full-time farmer. And when farmers can't earn enough money growing the food we all eat, they get out of the business. Between 1996 and 2001, the already minuscule number of Canadian farmers dropped by more than 10 per cent. While food processors, supermarkets, and middlemen are all making solid profits in the food system, most farmers are struggling to eke out a living for themselves and their families. Our former agricultural critic, MP Dick Proctor, told me about many farm families throughout Canada that survive only by having a family member work off the farm to bring in enough income enough to keep the farm going. "Show me any other business, worth at least a million dollars, where the owner-operator has to work somewhere else just in order to keep his business alive," Proctor said.

Subsidies also constitute a major factor in keeping food prices artificially low. Developed countries use subsidies to support their export-oriented agricultural industry. In the European Union, for example, the average cow is subsidized to the tune of about three dollars a day—which, incidentally, is about three times what a typical person in India is likely to earn. Farm subsidies, especially in Europe, the United States, and to a lesser extent Canada, put great pressure on farmers in developing countries and are a serious bone of contention between first- and third-world nations.

Subsidies are a rich country's way to prop up their farmers' incomes (and others in the agricultural industry) while keeping prices low. Tariffs are one way for a less-developed country to protect itself. Tariffs don't cost the local taxpayer any money while they protect local markets for local producers. The battle over subsidies versus tariffs has placed international trade at an impasse. Developed countries, with their large agrcultural subsidies, argue for the elimination of all tariffs, while developing countries argue for the elimination of subsidies in order that their farmers can compete.

When it comes to subsidies and support systems for North Amercan agriciulture, Canadian governments have not been nearly as generous with our farmers as the Americans have been with their farmers. The impact of large U.S. subsidies to help its farmers often makes U.S.-grown food and food products cheaper than food Canadian farmers can grow it here. Once again, this affects our own farmers' ability to earn an income, and it affects our food security.

It also reduces Canadians' capacity to grow our own food. If Canadian farmers can't compete with crops grown in the U.S.—and dumped in the Canadian market (permitted under the trade deals we've already signed)—they will be forced out of the business of growing food for local consumption. Amazingly, most of the Grade A fruit grown in British Columbia's Okanagan Valley is sold in Europe, while B.C. consumers buy a lot of fruit grown in

Washington, Oregon and California. This makes no environmental sense. It frequently means lower quality and reduces our own food security.

Finally, there's the issue of our retail food industry. In this business area, Canada has the highest degree of corporate concentration of any country in the world. Two retailers drive this sector—Loblaws and Sobeys. These retailers squeeze the food processors, who, in turn, squeeze the farmers. It's a nasty chain, and with most farmers holding the bottom link of that chain, they have virtually no bargaining leverage. Most Canadian farmers are price takers, not price makers. Food, which ought to be a highly important national issue, has the least government intervention of any major sector of our economy. Is there a national program to produce food? No. A national program to distribute food? No. A national program to sell food? No. Though we understand the need for a public presence in making and selling electricity, for instance, we have no Food Canada to offset the power of corporations, no public ownership, and very little regulation. And, as we have seen in other sectors, when governments cut back on enforcement and inspection, everyone's food security suffers, and we run a higher risk of buying and consuming tainted meats and other products.

Our marketing boards (eggs, milk, and wheat) help control the supply while guaranteeing a floor price to farmers. Yet these efficient, public, accountable regulatory bodies are also on the trade chopping block, with the federal government sharpening the axe. The U.S. government keeps attacking the Canadian Wheat Board in expensive legal proceedings, claiming the board is a state-trading enterprise and that its presence distorts the wheat market. The U.S. has appealed and lost the case on ten successive occasions but it shows no interest in letting up and simply files another appeal. Preserving our right to organize the sale of wheat through the co-operative mechanism of our Canadian Wheat Board is important, not just for farmers and agricultural sustainability, but also as a matter of Canadian sovereignty. Canada should be helping other countries develop similar mechanisms to help their farmers. But Canadians have recently elected a minority Conservative government that wants to kill off the CWB, without even giving grain farmers who market their products though the board a vote on its demise. So much for the grassroots democracy that the Reform and Canadian Alliance parties used to preach about.

Healthy Cities

Is there anything new we can do about the emerging food problem? Yes. I found out, however, while chairing Toronto's Board of Health, that the good model comes from England—not Canada.

In 1990, the Toronto board was implementing the concept of a "healthy city," talking with people from every kind of interest group in Toronto. It took no time for food to emerge as a common issue for people of all interests, in every community. We asked ourselves, Where in the world are people dealing with food issues in cities? The answer resided in the Greater London Council, where a Citizens' Food Council had been set up as a catalyst. A Ryerson social work professor, Marvyn Novik, had returned to Toronto from London raving about how successful it was. In no time, we pulled together community groups, farmers, local grocers, and environmental and public health groups to learn about the idea. Soon afterwards, I took a proposal to City Council.

Opponents of the idea slammed our plans, saying, "Food is not municipal business!" Or "Why should we have farmers telling us what to do?" Fortunately, the 1988 municipal election had produced a majority of council seats for our allies, and we were able to establish Canada's first urban Food Policy Council.

A key lesson I learned from my friend and right hand at City Hall, Dan Leckie, was this: "Always create a structure with a clear goal, made up of diverse constituencies who believe in that common goal." We put that lesson in place with the Food Policy Council. As a result, farmers from the Toronto environs were dealing directly with consumers. As a result, many ideas emerged that had economic, environmental, and social benefits. Two of the best were the "green box" organic foods delivered to homes directly from the farm, with no giant retail middleman skimming off the biggest share of the revenue, and the community kitchen concept, where a large kitchen is built or commandeered and used by community members to prepare collective meals and cater to community events, or share cooking knowledge across cultures, and to feed the neighbourhood kids.

The Toronto Food Policy Council (TFPC) has been the only organization of its kind in Canada for years, though other communities, like Vancouver and Saskatoon, have adopted similar ideas. It's a municipal food initiative, with a small number of staff paid by the city's Department of Public Health but under citizen control—and with a big mandate. The city recognizes the importance of food to public health and pays its staff to be advocates on behalf of food security, and they bring together people concerned with all aspects of food questions. Participants include farmers, retailers (big and small), nutritionists, urban growers, environmentalists, schoolchildren, transportation industry members, churches, local food agencies and processors, specialists in community and economic development, composters, and others.

The TFPC lobbied to have access to food and other food security issues incorporated in Toronto's official Community

Charter and, as a result, the city is now one of a select few that has made this kind of commitment.

May They Rust in Peace

As leader of the NDP, I get to travel a lot, but not as much as the average American grape. It clocks more than 3,400 kilometres to get from vine to table. A tomato travels almost as far. Food travel tends to be costly, bad in terms of food value for the person eating the grape and the tomato, and no good at all for the environment. The fundamental requirements for food security include a Canada-wide food strategy, regional food programs, and local food initiatives. Those aren't contradictory objectives.

Local food initiatives are springing up all over the world—even in cities. In China's eighteen largest cities, for example, vegetables grown locally supply 90 per cent of the residents' needs. Finally, we're starting to do the same thing in Canada. People are realizing that they can grow their own food in community gardens and on the rooftops of apartment buildings. Growing food on an urban roof has the side benefits of insulating the building from heat and cold, thus lowering energy costs, and of storing rainwater and keeping it out of the stormwater-sewage system. The *Globe and Mail*'s rather straight-talking columnist Margaret Wente wrote that she had opened this book at precisely this page as she flipped through to find out what, if anything, might be on the mind of the NDP leader. Encountering this brief discussion of roof gardens for food, she easily settled on "airhead" to capture her reaction. To her credit, she sat with me on our campaign plane during the 2004 election and found that I was a genuine zealot when it came to the untapped potential of hot city roofs to produce food and other goodies, like cooler buildings and happier residents.

She also accepted my explanation that, among other advocates, I could count renowned Toronto architect Jack Diamond, who had sat me down years ago to extol the virtues of green roofs. Roof gardens are catching on around the world and there's a whole Canadian organization devoted to the cause (www.greenroofs.net). After the sky-high interview, she issued a friendly revision of her initial less-than-complimentary initial assessment.

And while we're at it, backyard vegetable gardens have always been expected in neighbourhoods—and why not in the front yard, too? People are realizing that they can replace grass with something edible while letting their noisy air-polluting lawn mowers rust in peace. Psychiatric patients at a mental health facility in Toronto are growing vegetables in a garden, and their caregivers call it the best therapy available.

Of course, the food grown in yards and community gardens doesn't have to be for personal use; it can supply an urban market hungry for fresh produce. Local markets are popping up like crocuses, providing revenue for growers and good food for consumers.

Brilliant regional programs linking urban dwellers with nearby farmers are also on the increase across Canada. Two of the best are Farm Folk/City Folk, in B.C.'s lower mainland, and FoodShare in Toronto. These ventures bring together farmers and consumers with a range of services that put local food on the table and help keep the family farm profitable.

In Quebec, Équiterre (from the French words for "equity" and "earth") is a not-for-profit organization dedicated to promoting ecological, socially just choices through action, education, and research from a standpoint that embraces social justice, economic solidarity, and the defence of the environment. As part of its program, Équiterre promotes local agriculture, and about fifty farms across Quebec assist new farmers to get started.

Through these programs, city dwellers can buy into community-supported agriculture programs, purchasing in advance a share of a farmer's crop. Farmers get the cash in the spring, when their costs are highest and there's no money coming in. In return, their customers receive a weekly box of fresh local produce throughout the growing season. An alternative is that consumers can opt into buying clubs and other bulk-purchasing programs, pooling resources and paying wholesale prices for their fruit and vegetables. Urban communities are also finding more locations to establish farmers' markets, which draw the farmers directly into the community neighbourhoods.

Innovative strategies like these provide for more than just good nutrition. They reduce the environmental impact of long-distance transportation. They spur local economic growth—not only among farmers but also among local processors and retailers. These projects help ensure that agricultural land remains in active agricultural use, with the farmers assured an income and a market, so they're not obliged to sell out to suburb-hungry land developers. In short, these strategies help preserve the family farm. They also make consumers more aware of where their food comes from and how it's grown. And, of course, they increase our food security and our food safety.

Organizations like Farm Folk/City Folk and FoodShare operate with very little government support or input. Municipal governments across the country ought to be facilitating programs like these, because good food policy makes good sense. The Federation of Canadian Municipalities Sustainable Communities project is moving in this direction, especially with its exchanges of best practices. More federal assistance and encouragement could move these solutions along more quickly.

In Finland not long ago, I picked a gorgeous tomato from a four-metre vine in a vast greenhouse. The farmer and her team proudly pointed to the pipes coming all the way to the greenhouse from a factory-like building on the horizon. That factory produced wood products; wood chips and sawdust were burned in a cogeneration system that supplied electricity for both the factory and the neighbouring town; and the waste heat from that process was used to create hot water that was piped to the greenhouse. (In most similar factories in Canada, the heat simply goes up the stack, contributing to air pollution.)

Finland went a step further. The relatively cool combustion gases from the cogeneration plant contained lots of carbon dioxide. And guess what tomato plants need? Yes, that nasty greenhouse gas. So the factory in Finland pipes the carbon dioxide right into the greenhouse, creating a supercharged atmosphere for photosynthesis and tomato growth. Without this inventive approach, tomatoes in Finland would have to be trucked long distances from southern Europe. So the pollution from those heavy trucks is avoided. There is no wasted heat—it is used to create warmth at no cost. And the greenhouse gases contribute to the production of hothouse tomatoes for the Finns to eat.

For five years I tried to get such a cogeneration plant and greenhouse onto Toronto's parklands—with Toronto Hydro in partnership with the Boralex cardboard recycling plant. But the Conservative governments of first Mike Harris and then Ernie Eves so badly mauled Ontario's electricity system that the project was unable to proceed. Premier Dalton McGuinty could have seen the light but instead proposed a massive gas-fired electricity plant without co-generation. The City of Toronto and Toronto Hydro began work on a more modest proposal in the summer of 2006 with the help of the city councillor for the area, Paula Fletcher. To give such projects an incentive, the federal government should begin redirecting some of the hundreds of millions of dollars it currently gives to subsidize fossil fuel production toward innovative businesses that want to improve energy efficiency through cogeneration. Perhaps it's time for a national green energy greenhouse initiative: locally produced Canadian tomatoes in the winter without genetic modification or toxic chemicals, grown with the help of waste heat and carbon dioxide.

Get Out the Transfat-free Mayonnaise!

Playing Russian Roulette

Have you ever met kids who didn't play with their food? Me neither. That's why all parents have to tell their children not to do it. Now, however, we aren't just saying that to our kids, we're telling it to big corporations: "Don't play with our food."

I don't really know the consequences of eating a tomato that's been modified with fish genes. I do know that the soybeans that go into my tofu are almost certain to have been genetically modified (GM), I just don't know how that's likely to affect me. And that's precisely the problem. We just don't know—and neither does anyone else. Genetic modification is like playing global Russian roulette: fish genes in the tomato may be an empty chamber. Maybe they're not. I'd rather not find out the hard way.

We do know some things about genetic modification. Multinational corporations want it so they can control a farmer's use of seeds. A corporation cannot patent a native seed, but it can patent a genetically modified seed—and corporations can sue (and have sued) farmers for planting seeds of GM crops they've saved from a previous season. Corporations can also deliberately use what they call "terminator technology" so the plant produces sterile seeds, thus making sure that no crop can be grown from them. Corporations can also modify crops by building in compatibility with their own particular brand of chemical fertilizers, herbicides, and pesticides. This compels the farmer who has purchased the seed to to buy these additional products and no other. No wonder "designer genes" is the term du jour. And the long-distance shipping, already mentioned is another motivational factor behind the genetic modification of food. Corporations like Monsanto are looking for ways to get food to ripen after it's been harvested, so it won't spoil during shipment.

At the 1992 Rio Summit on the Environment, most of the world's nations agreed to adopt what's become known as the Precautionary Principle about the environment. It applies on many fronts, but perhaps none more important than the genetic modification of food. Principle 15 of the Rio Declaration says, "In order to protect the environment, the precautionary approach shall be widely applied by States according to their capabilities. Where there are threats of serious or irreversible damage, lack of full scientific certainty shall not be used as a reason for postponing cost-effective measures to prevent environmental degradation."

"Lack of full scientific certainty" undoubtedly applies in the case of GM foods—and we should never go down that road until we learn exactly where its taking us.

Labelling of all foods as GM and non-GM should be mandatory. Consumers must have the right to know what they're buying and eating. The corporate line—"It's too complicated to label products"—is pathetically self-serving. (Labelling food must be far easier than splicing genes.) Once more, Europe has led the way on the labelling and restricting of GM foods. However, the most dramatic illustration of resistance to GM crops can be found in Africa. In Zimbabwe, Mozambique, and Zambia, countries with many desperately hungry people, officials have refused shipments of genetically modified U.S. corn. But the pressure is on. One of the last things that the Americans did when they "handed over" power in Iraq was to include a provisions on intellectual property rights that forbids Iraqi farmers from saving their seeds. This disgusting clause shows more than an underlying cause of the war and the Americans' slavish coporate interests. It is of course a gigantic agricultural affront in another breadbasket of civilization.

Sometimes a "good idea that works for Canadians" is a good old-fashioned protest. A grassroots campaign against genetically modified wheat spread like wildfire through communities in Saskatchewan. Petitions were signed. Municipal councils adopted resolutions against the proposals by global food giant Monsanto to bring DNA-rigged seeds to the Canadian breadbasket. The NDP raised the issue in the House of Commons. The movement against the aberration grew. And Monsanto, very publicly, announced that it had backed off.

Just when we thought sanity was catching on, I met with the executive of the National Farmers' Union, who were concerned about a proposal that was wending its way through the Canadian bureaucracy. This one would prevent Canadian farmers from using the age-old practice of seed-saving to cut costs, to manage product, and to maintain a degree of autonomy and independence from the multinationals that have increasingly taken charge of the seed supply. A piece of legislation is percolating in the backrooms of Agriculture Canada, ready to pounce when unsuspecting Canadians are least expecting it. To date, the legislation hasn't been introduced in the House of Commons, thanks to the excellent Seed Saver Campaign launched by the National Farmers' Union, which has resulted in farmers and other Canadians putting pressure on government MPs and agriculture officials to stop this dangerous legislation.

It's unclear how the new Harper government will deal with this issue. One thing is for certain, though: working with the National Farmers' Union to keep up the pressure on Ottawa to make sure farmers continue having the right to save seeds is a good investment for any Canadian concerned with helping our farmers.

At the same time, and behind the closed doors of the World Bank and World Trade Organization, corporate moguls are working out the rights of investors to do whatever they want. The intent of these two powerful organizations is to fashion trade agreements that suit corporations and maximize profits, even at the expense of human health, the viability of the ecosystem, and every human being's right to decent food.

It's clear that when they have the opportunity, the citizens of the world are saying no to GM crops and trade agreements designed to maximize profits at the expense of human health and ecosystem viability. Monsanto may have backed off for the moment, but the federal government must ban GM wheat. Farmers, environmentalists, and communities all agree on this one. How can Canada continue to be one of the breadbaskets of the world if we alllow the introduction of GM wheat and then 90 per cent of our current wheat customers refuse to buy our product? As well, the federal government should put a moratorium on all new genetically engineered crops, and it should change current regulations so that biotech corporations must prove new technology is environmentally safe—before it is used. Not only would these measures protect Canadian markets oversees, but they would mean Canada could once again be a leader in environmental protection.

If ever we should err on the side of caution, it's with what we eat. Don't play with our food.

The Web of Life

Scientists call the complex, interconnected relationships among living things "the web of life." This very apt phrase symbolizes the way things are woven together to sustain one another. Through millions of years of history, human beings have worked their way to the top of the food chain, and now we seem intent on gobbling up our precious resources with the same insatiable appetite we have brought to our conquest of every other living thing on earth.

There is another way, a way that respects the other forms of life with which we share this planet—and that respects the planet itself. We can live and flourish without destroying our atmosphere, polluting our waters, and fouling our land. We can support each other—environmentally, economically, and ethically—in ways that are sustainable. Let's construct Canada's way forward by building according to these principles.

[CHAPTER 4]

A Caring Society

Every year since 1990, the United Nations has published a Human Development Report, assessing trends and measuring countries in a wide variety of categories. Part of that report is its Human Development Index, which compares societies for their citizens' life expectancy, educational attainment, and standard of living. The index serves as a kind of international report card.

For many years, Canada stood at the top of the list. Our "human development," though not without fault, was the best in the world as measured by these standards—and we were proud of that, particularly former Prime Minister Jean Chrétien, who boasted endlessly about our standing.

But we've begun to slip in recent years, and the Liberals reduced their rhetoric. In 2001, when Canada fell to third place, I gave a speech and warned: "Mimic those below us and we'll end up there. If we keep trying to copy the conservative policies of the U.S., which is in sixth spot, rather than copy the social democratic policies of Norway, which is above us, we will continue to fall." And that has been exactly the case. We hung on to third place in 2002, and have been slipping ever since, down as low as eighth in the 2003 report, fourth in 2004 and fifth in 2005.

Years of cuts in public services and community investment have started to unravel the fabric of our society. We need to reconsider that direction, review its consequences and, once again, assess the value we place on what the UN calls human development. Sweden, which has moved from sixth place in 1999 to third in 2003, would be a good model for Canada to follow.

In Canada, our defining social program, the one most valued by its citizens, is public health care. Indeed, Canadians consider universal access to health care a right of citizenship, not a privilege for those who can afford it. Public health care is one of our principal measures of a caring society—a system that is not supposed to be based on income, age, ethnicity, or place of residence. At least that's the idea.

Olivia emigrated from Hong Kong with her parents. When asked why her family chose Canada rather than the U.S., she says, "We chose Canada because we wanted to be a part of a society that put the health of everyone ahead of everything else and made sure that everyone had equal access to take care of their health needs." Frankly, like a lot of people born here, I sort of took our health system for granted. When Olivia said that I thought to myself: "We should listen more to recent immigrants to our country about what is good here."

As Tommy Douglas used to remind us: "The real measure of a nation is not the height of its skyscrapers. The real measure of a nation is the quality of its national life, what it does for the least fortunate of its citizens and the opportunities it provides for its youth to live useful and meaningful lives."

Our country hasn't always stood for the principle that everyone should have equal access to care for their health needs. Older Saskatchewan farm families still vividly remember the grim desperation of drought, dustbowl, and the Great Depression of the 1920s and 1930s. They know, too, that out of poverty, misery, and deprivation came community will and creativity.

As I was campaigning for the NDP leadership leading up to the 2003 convention, I had a chance to talk with some Saskatchewan farmers in rural legion halls around the province. "We weren't allowed to meet in halls like this back then," one of them told me. "No, we were branded revolutionaries and Communists and shut out. All we knew was that we had to co-operate with each other to make it through the hard times, and that we needed our government to respond to our basic needs." Another man spoke up: "We needed health care for our families, and electricity, like they had in the cities."

Those farmers had to create their own credit unions to lend them money fairly, instead of suffering under the harsh hands of the Eastern Canadian banks. With community halls closed to them, they met in fields, standing in circles out in the cold—small groups that organized the Co-operative Commonwealth Federation (CCF). Their dream was a political party that would give expression to those needs.

"It was Tommy Douglas, the young preacher from Weyburn, who showed us how. He just wouldn't accept the reality of families with their sick children waiting on hospital steps, unable to afford care and being refused,"declared one Saskatchewan old-timer, proudly.

Public Health Care Comes to North America

Determined that there had to be a better way, the voters of Saskatchewan elected the first social-democratic government in North America on June 15, 1944. Called the Co-operative Commonwealth Federation (CCF), it would be the forerunner of the New Democratic Party, and Tommy Douglas was the party's leader and premier.

Douglas's government introduced free hospital care; free medical and dental services for old-age pensioners; and free treatment for cancer, tuberculosis, and mental illness. The government also lowered the voting age to eighteen, introduced the first public auto insurance plan in North America, began a government-operated air ambulance service, and issued a Bill of Rights. Saskatchewan's civil servants became the first in the country to receive collective bargaining rights, and the government created a provincial bus line, timber board, power corporation, and airline. And that was in just their first term of office.

On January 1, 1947, the Saskatchewan government launched its Hospital Insurance Plan, the first public hospital coverage in North America. Family premiums were $10 a year. The very first patient to benefit showed up at Regina General Hospital shortly after midnight on New Year's Day. She delivered a healthy baby.

For ten years, Saskatchewan funded its hospital coverage without a dime from the federal government, even though Ottawa had been promising a national program since 1919. Canadians had to wait until 1957 for a partial national health-care plan, the Hospital Insurance and Diagnostic Services Act.

In 1961, the Saskatchewan government passed legislation that provided universal medical coverage in doctors' offices. The province's doctors and the Canadian Medical Association launched bitter opposition, but the people's support for public medicine was simply too great. In 1962, the doctors backed down. In 1966, the federal government finally passed the Medical Care Act, bringing health-care coverage to all Canadians, thanks to the foresight and determination of the CCF/NDP as well as the people of Saskatchewan. If the NDP shies away from trumpeting its role in creating Canada's medicare system, people who think it should be protected or expanded might not realize how it came about. Modesty is tough when you're trying to convince people to support your party because of what the team has been able to produce in response to real needs.

You'll even find other parties trying to claim the credit. Still, Paul Martin went too far in 2003 when he compared himself to Tommy Douglas. His rationale was that Douglas was a fiscal conservative with a social conscience. (People who knew Douglas know that he would have succinctly dismissed such a self-congratulatory opinion.) Besides, unlike Mr. Martin, Tommy Douglas believed in translating the social conscience into something meaningful, something beyond rhetorical pap. Just as the NDP tries to do today, Mr. Douglas put into practice the concept of investing in those essentials that all should be able to access equally. For Tommy, as premier of Saskatchewan, this meant electricity for all in rural areas in the 1940s and 1950s. Aydon Charlton former chief of staff for Intergovernmental Affairs Minister Roy Romanow, found himself sitting beside Tommy on an airplane travelling from Lloydminster to Regina long after Mr. Douglas had retired from public life. Aydon asked Douglas what he thought his greatest accomplishment had been:

"I expect you will think that I will say medicare and there's no question that I'm enormously proud of that. But a lot of other people besides me had a big hand in that." It was a clear summer evening and the small charter was flying along the Saskatchewan-Alberta border. Tommy looked out the window and said: "The thing I am most proud that I did you can see in all the lights down there." He was referring of course to the rural electrification program that, within a decade, had transformed Saskatchewan.

Of course there was a great deal more than bringing electricity to far-flung Saskathewan farm families. Education, health-care, public insurance, co-operative economic institutions like credit unions, retail and wholesale co-ops where the benefits could be equally and democratically shared and determined. Today, we would add public child development programs for all, post-secondary education that does not discriminate, programs for clean air and water through federal investments in local infrastructure such as transit and water treatment.

During the final days of the 2004 election, Canadians heard the cynically desperate call of the Martin Liberals urging NDP supporters to vote for the Liberals in order to stop the Conservatives. The Liberal logic, incredible as it was, suggested that both the Liberals and the NDP grew out of the same well-spring of social values. It was the latest version in the old Liberal trick—claim to represent progressive values during the election, then govern largely for their rich, comfortable, and powerful friends. Unfortunately for my party and for Canada, this old Liberal chestnut proved to be effective once again. Liberal advertisements highlighted the evils that were sure to follow if the Harper Conservatives were to win the election. Daunting images of George Bush's foreign policy flashed across the screen, suggesting that by voting Liberal Canadians could be assured of going in a different direction. Of course right after the election, the Martin Liberals were eagerly lining up behind the Bush Star Wars missile defence scheme.

During that election, voters saw other Liberal ads with images of dramatic increases in pollution and climate change that a Conservative administration would bring, since the Conservatives had announced they would reject the Kyoto Protocol. But at the swearing-in ceremony of the new cabinet after the election, left on the sidelines was David Anderson, the former environment minister who had been a strong proponent of Kyoto and of meeting Canada's climate change targets. Mr. Anderson was replaced by Stephane Dion, whose first lame pronouncements suggested that Canadians shouldn't be preoccupied with meeting targets for reducing pollution. This strategy left me, and I hope a lot of Canadians, asking this question. Is it less honourable to say that, if elected, you will tear up an important internatonal agreement, or to boast about having signed the agreement but with no action plan, and perhaps even no intention of meeting the commitment made by your predecessor?

The Liberal advertising in 2004 also featured images evoking the fear of credit-card medicine. But, since that election, more and more Canadians have found it necessary to use their credit cards to get health care. That's because Liberal policies did nothing to protect public delivery of health care. The public health system that Tommy Douglas and the Pearson Liberals brought to life in the 1960s for all Canadians lies critically wounded from billions of dollars in cuts made by Paul Martin. Part of the original health-care agreement was that the federal government would pay 50 per cent of the hospital and physician costs of provincial health care. This commitment was honoured from the 1970s, then modified by Trudeau with a transfer of taxation points to the provinces, bringing the federal share to 25 per cent. During Mr. Martin's years as finance minister, these federal transfers were drastically chopped without consultation or negotiation. The much vaunted $41-billion health-care accord negotiated in the fall of 2004 with the provincial premiers only partially restored the previous funding but did not achieve the 25 per cent level as the NDP had argued it should.

Two months after the June 28 election, I finally secured a meeting with Paul Martin at the prime minister's residence, the famous 24 Sussex Drive. During our discussion, I reminded him of his electioneering phraseology concerning the "common wellspring of values" that, ostensibly, the Liberals shared with the NDP. I said that I would be invoking that phrase to remind him of his commitment quite often in the months to come. I added that, as long as he were true to that claim, we would support initiatives such as a pan-Canadian child-care program and a climate-change plan that ran true to those principles. He responded by joking that "the wellspring may run dry from time to time!" It did not take long to find out that he wasn't kidding!

To be sure, Tommy Douglas and his finance minister Clarence Fines administered Saskatchewan finances with great care. They never wanted to become beholden to the chartered banks or the money lenders in New York, Chicago, or Zurich. Instead of doing what Paul Martin did as Liberal finance minister—slash programs in 1995 in order to spend $100 billion on tax cuts in 2000—Douglas used a system of fair taxation to fund provincial programs. Paying taxes is like buying insurance. It ensures that health, education, and electricity (among other services) are available to everyone. Tommy once said to a young Lorne Nystrom, the NDP's long-serving MP, who used to drive with him on the long, straight roads of rural Saskatchewan, "If they don't trust you at the till, they won't trust you at the ballot box." Two years before his death, in a glorious speech to the 1983 NDP federal convention in Regina, Tommy warned the party faithful that each generation had to stand and fight to preserve what had been won previously. As usual, Tommy was right, and today's generation must fight to save many of the the services and programs that the CCF-NDP pioneered.

Protecting Canada's Health-Care System

During his ten-year tenure as prime minister, Jean Chrétien appointed a string of Liberal hacks, hangers-on, backroom boys, wealthy contributors, and corporate buddies to an array of agencies, boards, commissions—and the Senate.

Yet he had the courage, in April 2001, to appoint former Saskatchewan NDP Premier Roy Romanow to head the Royal Commission on the future of Canada's health-care system. The PM was well acquainted with Mr. Romanow as they had worked together in the early 1980s, co-chairing a federal-provincial committee trying to devise a way to repatriate the Canadian constitution with an amending formula and a Charter of Rights that would be acceptable to all the provinces. The two became known as "the tuque and the uke."

The report of the Romanow Commission, appropriately titled *Building on Values*, could serve Canadians well for a long time to come. It is thoughtful, comprehensive, and visionary. It is on a par with the 1964 report of another Saskatchewan hero, Supreme Court Justice Emmett Hall, that helped advance public health care in Canada. While the Pearson minority government implemented Mr. Justice Hall's recommendations swiftly, the Martin minority government did little toward enacting Mr. Romanow's recommendations.

Much has been written about the Romanow Report, and it's available on the Internet at www.cbc.ca/healthcare/final_ report.pdf. I do want to make a few comments and summarize some of Romanow's conclusions and recommendations because they point the way to a more accessible, affordable, and work-able health-care system. In his report Mr. Romanow states:

> Early in my mandate, I challenged those advocating radical solutions for reforming health care—user fees, medical savings accounts, de-listing services, greater privatization, a parallel private system—to come forward with evidence that these approaches would improve and strengthen our health-care system. I have also carefully explored the experiences of other jurisdictions with co-payment models and with public-private partnerships, and have found these lacking. There is no evidence these solutions will deliver better or cheaper care, or improve access (except, perhaps, for those who can afford to pay for care out of their own pockets). More to the point, the principles on which these solutions rest cannot be reconciled with the values at the heart of medicare or with the tenets

of the Canada Health Act that Canadians overwhelmingly support.

Amen.

Privatized services, parallel systems, user fees, co-
payments, and the like all have no place in a universal, public,
accessible health-care system. They betray the fundamental
Canadian values that gave birth to this special national protection. In November 2003, a report called *Funding Hospital
Infrastructure: Why P3s Don't Work, and What Will*, was
issued by five well-respected senior economists, including the
former director of audit operations for the auditor general.
Their report exposed the fact that the latest fad in hospital
privatization—the so-called public-private partnership (P3)
approach—is not only at least 10 per cent more expensive
than the public system Canadians have valued since the
1960s, but it also lacks accountability. They concluded that
Ontario would be ill-advised to proceed with plans made by
its former Conservative government to allow the privatization
of two hospitals. That was good advice proffered by experts
who can read a bottom line and understand value for money.

The Romanow Report also recognizes that our system is
now seriously underfunded. Though some provincial governments can be faulted, the main culprit in creating this
financial crunch has been successive federal governments,
which significantly reduced their funding commitments to
the provinces for more than twenty years between 1977 and
2000. As a result of these federal cutbacks, people began saying that we can no longer afford our health-care system. But
that's simply not the case. Public spending on health care
increased by about one-third between 1985 and 2000. But
that increase represents only 0.8 per cent of our gross domestic product. The major amputation in federal funding came
in 1995 when Finance Minister Paul Martin declared that

reductions in transfers to the provinces for health and other social programs were required to eliminate the deficit. When Ottawa began running up large supluses in the years after 1995, Mr. Martin and Prime Minister Chrétien chose to cut taxes rather than restore the health and social funding to the provinces. Canadians know that lower taxes benefit the elite and the corporate community much more than working-class Canadian families.

It's also important to remember that when people talk about the need to reduce spending on health care, they always mean reducing *public* spending. Of course, that doesn't make health care any less expensive. It only shifts the burden to the credit cards of individual Canadians, many of whom will be unable to pay. With prescription drug costs driving up health-care costs faster than any other component, it's no wonder that a growing number of Canadians cannot afford the medications prescribed by their physicians. As a result they either don't have the prescription filled or take the medication in lower doses so that it lasts longer. Either is a denial of universality, one of the five principles of the Canada Health Act.

Like everything else, projections of costs of maintaining our health-care system into the future show that financial demands will grow over time. These should be funded with a step-by-step strategy based on the actuarial analysis of future needs. Without this information, Canadians are asked just to "trust the government." That's increasingly difficult to do since that trust has not been well placed recently. We don't need more studies and waffling. We need clear and decisive action and the political will to ensure it.

Romanow recommended "the establishment of a minimum threshold for federal funding," and recommended $15.3 billion in new spending over the next three years. This requirement is only about 15 per cent of the massive tax cuts implemented by Paul Martin and Jean Chrétien in 2000. At that time, Canadians could have enjoyed more modest tax cuts plus a fully funded health-care plan.

It's worth quoting one more section of the Romanow Report at length:

> We also need to renovate our concept of medicare and adapt it to today's realities. In the early days, medicare could be summarized in two words: hospitals and doctors. That was fine for the time, but it is not sufficient for the 21st century. Despite the tremendous changes over the past 40 years, medicare still is largely organized around hospitals and doctors. Today, however, home care is an increasingly critical element of our health system, as day surgery has replaced the procedures that once took weeks of convalescence in hospital. Drugs, once a small portion of total health costs, are now escalating and among the highest costs in the system. The expense associated with some drug therapies or of providing extended home care for a seriously ill family member can be financially devastating. It can bankrupt a family. This is incompatible with the philosophy and values upon which medicare was built. It must be changed. I am therefore recommending that home care be recognized as a publicly insured service under medicare and that, as a priority, new funds be invested to establish a national platform for home care services. I am also recommending the creation of a national drug strategy, including a catastrophic drug insurance program to protect Canadian families.

Deep cuts by the federal government in health-care funding over many years have made Ottawa a junior partner in the process and effectively eroded the federal government's credibility to enforce the Canada Health Act and provide real leadership in health-care reform. This became abundantly clear when the federal government failed to prevent Alberta from establishing a private hospital, in violation of the Canada Health Act. Perhaps we shouldn't be surprised, given that many of Paul Martin's staff, when he was finance minister and later prime minister, were former corporate lobbyists employed by health privatizers.

Despite the federal cuts, overall government health-care spending in Canada has averaged a 2.5 to 3 per cent per-capita per-annum increase since the 1970s. These increases had to be borne by the provinces, which also had to backfill the gaping financial hole left by the federal government's reduced contributions. All this has created much of the "fiscal disequilibrium" often referred to, and rightly so, by our premiers. It is important to realize however that key issues in health care have as much to do with new ideas as with money.

A National Drug Strategy and Community Health-Care Delivery

Canadians now spend more on drugs than on doctors. The average family spends over $1,200 a year on prescription drugs, yet 27 per cent of Canadians have no drug coverage. Families that can't afford prescription drugs just go without or cut back on the dosage. In the past ten years, drug companies in Canada had a phenomenal 41 per cent average rate of return each and every year. Our party has been citing this statistic from an in-depth academic study out of Quebec, by Léo-Paul Lauzon and Marc Hasbani, during our campaign around pharmacare in Canada. During those ten years, drug costs to governments in Canada have increased by 87 per cent. Some also suggest that increased drug costs are, at least in part, driven by the propensity of doctors to prescribe expensive newer drugs when the old reliable ones work just as well or even better.

Ever thought about all those drug company ads on TV, you know the ones that brag about how much money they're spending on research? I wish they would, because in the past decade, drug companies spent three times more on advertising and marketing their products than on research. When I see the ad featuring the middle-aged guy having a heart attack and his family in a panic, urging people to get their blood cholesterol tested, I wonder about those people who couldn't afford the medication should their cholesterol turn out to be high. If you're not on a medical plan, how do you afford the thousands of dollars a year for Lipitor or similar medications? I guess you just tough it out and hope your heart doesn't stop. And eat celery. But not the celery that has been laced with pesticides! (You don't want prostate cancer, because the drugs for that are even more expensive.)

It also burns me to know that some families that need puffers for their kids can't afford them. With my son covered through my drug plan at work, the hundreds of dollars we spent every month on puffers so Mike could breathe were reimbursed. But what about the kids in his class whose parents don't have a drug plan and live on a modest income? Don't they have the same right to breathe as my son has? Or does the right to breathe now depend on income in Canada?

- **Number of drugs licensed for human use by Health Canada: 5,200**
- **Number of "essential drugs" classified by the World Health Organization: 326**
- **Amount Canadians spent on prescription drugs in 2002: $12 billion; Increase from 2001: $1.2 billion**

- **Number of new nurses who could have been hired with the increase alone: 24,000**
- **Number of children who live in poverty in Canada: 1.1 million**

The Liberal government did nothing to reverse the Mulroney government's doubling of drug companies' patent protection (from ten to twenty years), while it slashed the budget for the Health Protection Branch by 50 per cent. Now called the Health Products and Food Branch, it allows the health minister to enforce legislation and regulations that ensure our food, drugs, and health products are safe. The time has come to put in place a national pharmacare plan so that all Canadians have coverage for the prescription drugs they need. We need to roll back patent protection to ten years and introduce, as the Romanow Commission recommended, a national drug agency to make bulk purchases. Such a system would keep the price down by forcing the multinational manufacturers to compete for Canadians' business while ensuring that more Canadians could have access to reasonably priced drugs. The NDP government in Saskatchewan purchases generic drugs in bulk for its drug plan. They estimate that it saved the province and consumers about $6 million in 2002–2003. We advanced such a plan in the 2004 election. The Liberals promised something similar, but nothing happened. We'll continue our push in the House of Commons for this relatively simple initiative to be introduced.

And do we need all these high-tech drugs in the first place? After I started living in a Chinese family, I had a chance to discover the magic of ten thousand years of Chinese medical wisdom. Our drug companies may do double-blind tests on drugs for several years, but when herbs and plants have been studied for some four hundred generations, you'd think we might accord these traditional medical approaches some level of credibility. It's true that the teas brewed by my mother-in-law taste terrible, but that's not reason enough to avoid them. We put the traditional Chinese medicine retail industry through every kind of hoop imaginable rather than opting for traditional medicine. Some of the best medication ideas come to us from immigrants who know all about them because they've been handed down in their cultures for centuries. Let's remove the barriers and start learning about what we have available right in our own communities.

Finally, Mr. Romanow demonstrates how much better it would be to shift health services out of hospitals and into smaller clinics, which would become models for a new delivery of a wide range of health-care services. The network of clinics in Quebec (CLSCs—Centres locaux de services communautaires) and the Group Health Centre in Sault Ste. Marie, Ontario, are good examples.

Sault Ste. Marie's clinic houses about 350 health-care professionals, including nurse practitioners, doctors, dieticians, physical therapists, speech pathologists, and others. The nurse practitioners can provide 85 per cent of primary care. That means that eight out of ten patients who come to the clinic have their needs met without being examined by a general practitioner. Patient records are computerized, and doctors can consult electronic records from their offices. The clinic provides day surgery, lab analysis, a women's health centre, cardiology, physiotherapy, vision and auditory care, diabetes prevention, and many other services. Patients and health-care professionals benefit from the comprehensive services and team approach; the community benefits from health promotion and disease prevention. It's also less expensive for the government because fewer tests are repeated, and there is less overlap in care. Quebec's CLSCs provide similar services; many also provide social services.

Again, as the Romanow report suggests, "We must transform our health care 'system' from one in which a multitude of participants, working in silos [isolation], focus primarily on managing illness, to one in which they work collaboratively to deliver a seamless, integrated array of services to Canadians, from prevention and promotion to primary care, to hospital, community, mental health, home and end-of-life care."

Community clinics have other benefits. They provide faster access to care for small ailments and reduce reliance on expensive emergency rooms. They also build positive relationships and strengthen neighbourhoods in powerful ways. Having had a small hand in creating the new Regent Park Community Health Centre, I've seen the benefits up close. Here was a group of mothers, living in the lowest-income community in the whole city of Toronto, deciding that the health of their families needed better attention. They came from every continent, so services had to be available in many languages. Cultural traditions concerning health had to be infused into the daily operations, otherwise depressed and isolated women and their families suffered. The low income of the community produced predators—drug dealers and pimps who looked for weakness to attack—giving the neighbourhood a bad reputation. Fighting back, mothers such as Betty Hubbard and young people like her daughter, Joy Henderson, struck out to create a positive image and reality for the community. Targeting an abandoned and polluted gas station on the tough corner of Parliament and Dundas East, their committee surmounted every conceivable hurdle to realize their vision. As the local councillor, I witnessed their tenacity and honesty as we canvassed the surrounding houses to tackle the inevitable opposition that arose from a few homeowners just next door who imagined the worst. Even more difficult was securing the support of bureaucrats. Thankfully, the NDP government in Ontario had brought the financial commitments sufficiently far along that the Mike Harris Conservatives could not stop the momentum. The building, designed by award-winning architect Jack Diamond and his team, has breathed new life into the community. This initiative became the epicentre of energy for the complete redevelopment and revitalization of the entire Regent Park housing project, now moving forward amid optimism and hope.

Good ideas in health promotion, disease prevention, and health care can all be combined. As the experience of such clinics suggests, many health-care services can be provided by health-care professionals other than doctors—in particular, Canada's well-trained nurses. Yet in the recent passion to reduce health-care expenditures, we have eliminated hundreds of nursing positions, and overworked registered and licensed practical nurses are at the point of exhaustion and burnout.

Statistics show that Canada had 897 nurses for every 100,000 people. Finland had 2,162; Norway 1,840; and Ireland 1,593. Many other countries also had higher ratios than Canada's. But young, potential nurses here are well aware of the stressful, underpaid positions that our nurses are forced to endure, and enrolment in nursing schools has declined. (Between 1990 and 2000, admissions to basic-entry registered nursing programs dropped by 28 per cent.) The high number of anticipated retirements is another major factor. The number of nurses who provide long-term care, for example, has been declining by about 20 per cent. An earlier study estimated a shortage of sixty-nine thousand nurses by 2011, while more recent studies confirm these figures. One of the reasons is the lack of training of new nurses to replace the growing numbers who are retiring and as the average age of nurses reaches the mid-fifties. To illustrate present shortages, the physician who heads one of the larger non-profit Chinese seniors' nursing homes in Canada told me his biggest problem is finding experienced nurses to staff the new beds being opened. This is why the NDP program in the 2006 election included a specific plan to train thousands of nurses as soon as possible. Following the release of his film *Bowling for Columbine* at the Toronto International Film Festival in 2002, maverick filmmaker Michael Moore held a press conference. He said, "You Canadians actually think that everyone, no matter who you are or the size of your wallet, has the right to high-quality health care from the moment you're born until you die. Everyone! We don't have that idea in the U.S.A!"

He's right, of course. Canadians do have that idea. And we're going to keep it. And we're going make sure we keep it—with Roy Romanow's Royal Commission Report.

Public Health Versus the Medical Model

In 1886, after having achieved justifiable and lasting fame in the Crimean War, Florence Nightingale was asked to open a children's hospital in London. The world's most famous nurse refused. She knew that the most important factors in improving children's health were not to be found in hospitals, but in their communities. What hospital could adequately treat the young boys forced to crawl on their bellies into wet, airless coal seams and to work there for fourteen or sixteen hours a day? What doctor could repair their lungs? What nurse could restore their health?

The coal dug by boys and men was used to heat people's homes, and the smoke that polluted their homes and their neighbourhoods caused innumerable respiratory diseases. Their diets were poor, their hours of work incredibly long, and the city's sanitation system was a horror.

Nightingale knew then what we are finally catching on to now—that the most important factors in achieving a healthy population are not, strictly speaking, "medical." They are social, environmental, and economic. (The "medical model" is about the delivery of health care. The "public health model" is about improving overall health and preventing disease or injury.) Nutritionists know that a healthy society is not possible unless people have good food and a wholesome diet. Organized labour knows that a healthy society is not possible unless workers have clean and safe workplaces. Environmentalists know that healthy people need clean air to breathe and clean water to drink. And anti-poverty activists know that having a healthy society depends on reducing income inequality and bringing people out of poverty.

> *I find myself standing by the shore of a swiftly flowing river when I hear the cry of a drowning man. So I jump into the river, put my arms around him, pull him to shore and apply artificial respiration. Then, just as he begins to breathe, there's another cry for help. So back in the river again, reaching, pulling, applying, breathing, and then another yell. Again and again, without end, goes the sequence. You know, I am so busy jumping in, pulling them to shore, applying artificial respiration, that I have no time to see who the hell is pushing them all in.* —IRVING K. ZOLA, 1970

You'd think that Canadians would excel at promoting health and preventing disease. Not so. We spend over 95 per cent of our health dollars treating illness and less than 5 per cent on prevention. We have to get our spending priorities straight—helping prevent illness rather than spending money to treat people after they've become sick.

Numerous studies show a clear connection between economic conditions and a person's health. A recent report by the Canadian Public Health Association says that "life expectancy depends more on the internal distribution of wealth than increases in income. The narrower the spread of income in a given society, the higher will be its overall health status." The *British Medical Journal* agrees: "The more equally wealth is distributed, the better the health of that society." A rich nation with an unequal distribution of wealth is not necessarily a healthy nation. Among the twenty-nine OECD (Organization for Economic Co-operation and Development) nations, the richest is the United States, yet it ranks twenty-second in life expectancy for men and nine-teenth for women. And the U.S. has the greatest gap between rich and poor. So policy that increases the gap between the well-to-do and the rest turns out to be literally lethal. Years of life are lost as a result.

The distribution of income in Canada is very unequal, too, and that disparity is increasing as we copy more and more American economic policies. In 2000, the wealthiest 10 per cent of families earned $18 for every $1 earned by the lowest 10 per cent. In richer provinces like Ontario and B.C. the ratio is twenty to one. And the gap is getting wider. Through the 1990s, Canadian families with the highest incomes had the biggest percentage of income gains (after adjusting for inflation): 14.6 per cent. The lowest-income families gained just 0.8 per cent.

The Canadian Public Health Association estimates that if the bottom half of income earners received just a 1 per cent increase in the share of income, the mortality rate would decline by twenty-one deaths per one hundred thousand people. That's equivalent to eliminating the deaths from all motor vehicle accidents and breast cancer among people of working age. If such a modest change in income distribution would save that many lives, imagine the impact it would have in reducing non-fatal illnesses, improving overall health, and reducing health-care costs!

Infectious and communicable diseases are directly linked to living conditions. Poor nutrition, contaminated water, overcrowded and unsanitary environments, and similar factors result in tuberculosis, pneumonia, diarrhea, measles, and other common diseases. These days, medicine can treat them all, but their causes are not medical. And if we want to create healthy societies, the answer is not more or better health care but improved living conditions, a cleaner environment, and a more equal distribution of income.

In 1999, the U.S. Centers for Disease Control and Prevention listed the greatest public health achievements of the twentieth century. These included vaccines for children, safer and more healthful foods, control of infectious diseases, motor vehicle and workplace safety, healthier mothers and babies, and reduction of tobacco use. In Canada, for example, we've seen a 95 per cent reduction in preventable diseases among children and the total elimination of polio as a result of vaccines. Promoting the use of bicycle helmets and seat belts is another successful public health measure. An estimated twenty-two thousand fewer injuries and permanent disabilities per year result from the use of helmets and seat belts, with net savings of $500 million in health costs.

It's unfortunate that the links between public health and health-care costs weren't made by Roy Romanow. Perhaps he saw public health as beyond his mandate. Nonetheless, it remains a serious shortcoming of the report. Almost nothing was said about strengthening public health. As the examples above suggest, federal investment in public health would create significant financial savings in the health-care system, to say nothing about making us healthier! Romanow missed an opportunity to make this crucial point, and he missed the opportunity to note that the federal government should also make healthy public policy—that is, public policy in non-health sectors that is good for public health. For instance, designing our cities to encourage more walking and cycling not only helps us clean the air and combat climate change, it makes us more fit.

Developing agricultural and food policies that support the production and consumption of non-GM and organic food not only helps our farmers and the natural environment, it means people eat more wholesome fare. And the healthier our natural environment is, the healthier we are and the fewer health-care dollars must be spent on treating preventable illnesses.

In developed countries like Canada, the primary causes of death are no longer communicable or infectious diseases but chronic ones—cancers, heart disease, and stroke. And the main causes of these diseases are social, environmental, and economic—stress, addiction to tobacco and alcohol, toxic chemicals in our food and in our surroundings, unhealthy diets, and inactive lifestyles.

A shocking study released in November 2003 shows deteriorating health in Canada's kids. Toronto's Hospital for Sick Children studied a group of Boy Scouts and Girl Guides age ten to eighteen and found that one-third of them were overweight. As a group, they were 5 per cent above normal weight, which is considered "dramatic" in a population, according to Dr. Brian McCrindle, head of the hospital's cholesterol clinic. Tests on the boys and girls showed their arteries already thickening and having trouble dilating—key markers of metabolic syndrome and the precursor to heart disease. McCrindle said, "We're getting to a point where 'normal' weight is associated with disease."

There's no question that many people have lifestyles that are deteriorating, not just kids who park themselves in front of a television or computer. Obesity in Canadian society doubled between 1985 and 2001, from 6 to 16 per cent in men and from 7 to 14 per cent in women. "We live in a culture that promotes gluttony but glorifies thinness," says Heather Maclean, from the Centre for Research and Women's Health at the Sunnybrook and Women's College Health Sciences Centre in Toronto.

We must all take responsibility for our own health—getting regular exercise and avoiding junk food and fast foods. But as a result of industry hoping to supersize our fast-food portions, we're beginning to "supersize" the population. The "sickening" rendition of the life we're called upon to lead by daily advertising is well captured in the film *Supersize Me*. So the food industry has a responsibility and a role to play here, just as it does with respect to the excessive amounts of dangerous transfats in our foods. What about governments? When governments cut funding for schools, and schools cut physical education programs as a result, or sign contracts with junk-food companies to earn some money for their programs, social and health problems result. So healthy lifestyles are a personal, a corporate, and a public responsibility. We have seen some moves against the corporations selling soft drinks in schools. In some cases, the corporations are moving to sell other products like bottled water (even though the schools have water fountains with free water, tested by public health departments more often that any bottled water is tested). Such considerations, and my personal addiction to late-night scoops of peanut butter, prompted the NDP initiative to ban transfats in Canada, presented successfully to the Martin minority government in the fall of 2004. This resulted in my awkward appearance on several cooking shows to demonstrate how to cook without transfats. We had more calls and emails in support of this initiative than we had on most other issues. In 2006, the report prompted by the NDP motion called for strong action by the federal government and we intend to pursue these measures agressively.

Preventing disease is a central function of public health. It's also essential to promote healthy communities and healthy living. It's smarter, it's cheaper, and it's usually easier than treating disease.

Our national government should consider how some health-care resources could be focused on healthy human physical development. Let's comb the world for best practices and adapt them to the Canadian context, working with provinces and communities, promoting and engaging Canadians with a focus on kids' health and physical fitness.

In 1985, just after being elected to my second term on Toronto City Council, I entered another contest—for the position of chair of the city's Board of Health. A new and mysterious disease had begun attacking gay men. My opponent for the board position was a councillor whose strategy for dealing with this issue was to close down the bathhouses frequented by gay men. Deliberately, in the midst of the 1981 provincial election, Toronto police had raided four of these establishments, arresting nearly three hundred men. I had joined with those who opposed the police action because the raids violated privacy rights. Tragically, several of those arrested committed suicide because police released their names to the press. It was against this background that the vote for chair of the Board of Health was taken. I was fortunate enough to win—and serve six years in that position.

Immediately, we set about the process of developing a strategy to address this new disease that had no name. It became known as acquired immune deficiency syndrome (AIDS). Instead of closing the bathhouses, we needed to turn them into centres for safe-sex education by providing condoms, health advice, and treatment.

In the midst of developing this plan, a bureaucrat from the blood diseases section of the city's Health Department came to see me in my office after hours. It was like talking to a spy who was acting contrary to orders.

"I shouldn't be meeting with you," he said quietly. "But the problem we're facing with HIV and AIDS is potentially so large that my conscience demands that I talk with you.

There's a possibility that HIV is being carried in the blood of people who don't even know they're infected. They could be blood donors." I began to get the picture. "Their blood could contain the virus that is making people sick," he continued. "If this is happening, then blood products used in transfusions could be infected. Without knowing it, we could already be facing a disease that has spread well beyond those who are visibly ill." His voice was hushed. "My son is a hemophiliac," he said.

The gravity of what he had told me and the extent to which this disease might already be spreading were terrifying. "What do you think should be done?" I asked. "I need a big increase in my education budget," he replied. "How much is your budget?" "It's $25,000 right now." "How much of an increase do you need?" "I think I need to double my budget!" "You know that council has just finalized its budget discussions and set a 5 per cent cap on budgetary increases for all departments?" "But we have to get the information out," he almost pleaded.

He was right, of course. And I also knew that another $25,000 wasn't going to do the job. "I tell you what," I said. "Let's pull together the best minds we can find, people who know the most about AIDS. Let's find out how large the problem is, according to the best information available. Let's invite the new groups that are forming to deal with AIDS and some of the doctors working with people with HIV."

We did. Through this, as on so many other issues, I worked with my executive assistant, Dan Leckie. We brought together, for the first time, a number of people who had been involved in the various aspects of this disease, all operating within their own silos, with little communication among them about what the others were doing. The meeting produced a legion of ideas—and some of the most fascinating hours of my life. It was also horrifying.

HIV was moving through the community much faster than the "authorities" were saying—or admitting. Information wasn't being communicated to the public; it wasn't even being tracked.

We talked about how to control the disease, how to educate people, how to inform the public. We helped set up networks in the community and among the specialists. We began to lay out a plan. And over the next few weeks, Dan and I also figured out the costs. In the end, instead of the $25,000 my friend from the Health Department asked for, we persuaded city council to give us $6 million for two and a half years.

Without a doubt, the public money we spent on the AIDS Defence Plan was only a small fraction of what would have been spent treating countless more victims of HIV/AIDS, let alone the appalling toll in human suffering.

This was public health in action. I'm very proud of our AIDS strategy, and of all the people in the community, the medical profession, and the Health Department who collaborated to make it work. I shudder to think what would have happened without it.

Unfortunately, the federal government appears not to have learned the valuable lessons we learned at the local level. The government is currently two years into developing a new strategic plan for fighting HIV/AIDS. But as Ralph Jurgens, executive director of the Canadian HIV/AIDS Legal Network, noted in early 2004, "The federal government must show leadership and immediately develop a highly specific plan that clearly defines what its contribution will be.... The plan should include a timetable, performance targets, and accounting mechanisms." We need action, not just consultation.

Jurgens also rightly points out that marginalized groups suffering from HIV/AIDS have been largely ignored by existing federal programs. There need to be specific plans for dealing with the epidemic in our federal prisons as well as among injection drug users. But as is usually the case, plans are not enough. There must also be a financial commitment to make these plans real. Since the early 1990s, the federal government has spent on average about $42 million a year fighting HIV/AIDS. This funding has not changed, even as inflation has eaten away at what this money can do and as the number of Canadians living with HIV has increased by 40 per cent since 1996. The government must invest more in dealing with HIV/AIDS. We cannot wait.

But federal involvement does not end here. We also have a moral responsibility to deal with HIV/AIDS at an international level. Stephen Lewis's passionate and seemingly endless work on behalf of AIDS victims in Africa is testament to the nightmare that happens when there is no strategy, no public health policy, and no money. For too long, the international community has stood by and done nothing while the HIV/AIDS pandemic has swept through Africa, killing millions and millions. In January 2004, Lewis gave a moving speech to my Rotary Club in Toronto. He laid out in stark detail the challenges and hopes facing the people in Africa ravaged by this disease. One of the most chilling points he made was the role played by the so-called developed nations: "At some point in the future, historians are going to look back at this period and ask, quite simply, how in God's name the world allowed this to happen. More than twenty million people have already perished, the vast majority in the developing world. It's of the same genre as General Romeo Dallaire's question, How did the world stand by and watch the genocide in Rwanda without lifting a finger? There seem to be these historical moments, these historical periods when moral resolve either freezes or evaporates. It's not just unconscionable; it's inexplicable."

Thankfully, as my friend Stephen suggested later in his speech, the world's moral resolve was beginning to awaken. In Canada, the NDP's Peace Advocacy Team (made up of MPs Alexa McDonough, Bill Blaikie, Svend Robinson, and Judy Wasylycia-Leis) spent much of 2003 demanding the federal government become proactive in dealing with the HIV/AIDS pandemic. The team campaigned for the federal government to contribute a fair share to the Global Fund, inspired by UN Secretary General Kofi Annan, and set up to deal with AIDS, TB, and malaria. NDP MPs worked tirelessly with NGOs and Canadians from coast to coast to push the federal government to introduce legislation that would make it easier to export generic drugs (in particular drugs that dramatically improve the life expectancy of people with HIV/AIDS) to countries that need them. The government finally responded in November 2003 and introduced Bill C-56, the Act to Amend the Patent Act and the Food and Drugs Act. The bill contained fatal flaws favouring multinational drug companies, thus effectively and cynically undermining the achievement of its stated goal.

There is no doubt that dealing with the HIV/AIDS pandemic will cost money. But as Stephen Lewis reminded us in his speech, had the industrialized world put resources into dealing with the pandemic when it first began, "millions of people would still be alive today, and millions of others would have a fighting chance of prolonging life, and you wouldn't have between eleven and fourteen million orphans, no different in any way from your children and mine, from your grandchildren and mine, wandering the landscape of Africa, bewildered, forlorn, anguished, abandoned, exploited, hungry, despairing... cared for by grandmothers or older siblings or communities already reeling and further impoverished by the impact of AIDS."

I want to return to another important lesson I learned from my experiences with the Toronto AIDS Defence Plan.

It's fine to have an expensive, ambitious new program to address important issues, but it's also crucial for those people responsible for the dollars—in this case, me, as chair of the Board of Health—to keep a close eye on exactly how the money is spent. It is also essential that program leaders be able to shift direction if the problem alters or if solutions aren't working. Sometimes politicians come up with grand ideas, but they don't follow through to ensure that the ideas are indeed implemented in a timely and efficient way. The politicians who propose the ideas and put them in place need to be accountable.

Watching the federal government mismanage file after file through the late 1990s illustrates the importance of this basic lesson. A perfectly reasonable idea like firearm registration for long guns mutated into a massively expensive program. Horrendous costs aside, it plunged the simple concept of registering firearms into disrepute and made further advances in real gun control, for example prohibitions on more types of guns, more difficult. If accountability is ever to have any real meaning, a basic operating principle must be that each cabinet minister take responsibility for monitoring, adjusting, and correcting each program he or she initiates. Without this, government programs can never be effective or efficient. And without this, we will not do justice to the urgency of the HIV/AIDS pandemic.

Often it's nearly impossible to calculate money not spent. In health care, the pressure is always on to provide more money for treatment, because how can you possibly deny treating the injured, the ill, and the aging? As I mentioned earlier, spending on public health is less than five per cent of our health dollars. That's shameful. Because every dollar spent on public health—on education, nutrition, prenatal care, immunization, screening for disease, encouraging safe practices and healthier lifestyles, and so on—saves many,

many more dollars down the road. More to the point, it keeps people and communities healthier. That's what a caring society does.

Aboriginal Communities and Public Health

I can't leave this topic without raising one more critical problem we must face.

There is no more urgent need for public health than in Aboriginal communities. The appalling levels of poverty, disease, substance abuse, and suicide suffered by indigenous peoples living in Canada are a national disgrace. To witness, as I have on many occasions, the dignity and humanity so common on their reserves and elsewhere, in the midst of so much tragedy and poverty, is both powerful and astonishing.

In 1996, the Royal Commission on Aboriginal Peoples anxiously called for federal government action on many fronts to redress the disadvantages that so mark life in too many First Nations, Métis, and Inuit communities. The Royal Commission's study was called *Gathering Wind* but it should have been called *Gathering Dust*. Years have gone by while successive governments have disgracefully failed to act. No civilized nation should allow its First Peoples to live the way they do in Canada.

In those communities, you can plainly see the direct social, environmental, and economic connections to the health of a population. The commission noted that infant mortality among so-called registered Indians is twice as high as it is for the rest of the Canadian population—and it's three times higher among the Inuit. Tuberculosis is more than twenty times as common among Aboriginals as it is among non-Aboriginal Canadians, and the prevalence of diabetes is at least three times higher. Alcohol-related motor vehicle fatalities, fatal fires, and other accidental deaths are also much more common among Aboriginal peoples, and so are suicides. The high rates of poverty and unemployment, poor housing and sanitation, and lack of clean drinking water all create unhealthy and unsafe living conditions that contribute to appalling rates of infectious diseases and despair.

In March 2003, I visited a remote First Nations reserve called Pauingassis in northern Manitoba. The distinguishing feature of this community is its very high rate of youth suicide, perhaps the highest in Canada. But it's small wonder the people there are struggling. I walked through the sole store in the community and couldn't believe my eyes. I wrote down some of the prices facing mothers shopping for their families. Apples: four for $7.79; oranges: six for $6.37. A dozen eggs were $21. Three litres of milk were on sale for $8.99, down from the normal price of $11 when the winter road isn't in. But 1.5-litre plastic bottles of Pepsi were going for just $1.99! With a monthly stipend of $476 for a mother and one child, plus a housing allowance, residents have little hope of enough money left to provide a wholesome diet. No wonder Aboriginal people suffer from poor nutrition, obesity, and diabetes.

And yet, solutions abound. Empowering Aboriginal communities by dealing with them all as First Nations—rather than in the paternalistic way that has driven public policy for so many years—is a key first step. Imposing stumbling governance models from above, as proposed by the Chrétien government in the closing days of its mandate, will not improve the situaton. That's exactly what NDP MP Pat Martin and Bloc Québécois MP Yvan Loubier drove home during their marathon filibuster of Bill C-7, the dreadful First Nations Governance Act, in the House of Commons during 2003. Laws such as this fundamentally perpetuate dependency, not self-sufficiency. That's never a recipe for long-term community health.

The 1996 Royal Commission recognized this paternalism and named it, then called for all levels of government "to support the assumption of responsibility for planning health and social services by regional Aboriginal agencies and councils." The commission also understood that Aboriginal peoples have a particular cultural approach to health care and healing, which we must respect, and called for the establishment of healing centres and healing lodges under Aboriginal control.

Sharing power and resources with indigenous peoples would be a good starting place—indigenous peoples who often willingly shared what they had with waves of European immigrants, only to see the newcomers fence off, mine, harvest, and pollute their traditional lands, waters, and forests. I've learned from my years in municipal government that healthy public policy should shift resources to communities themselves. That way it's possible to empower people who live in those communities to implement their ideas, rather than live under the dictates of others. In the case of First Peoples, the principle of social justice demands it.

And, of course, we also need to be much more in tune with the needs of Aboriginal people living off reserve, often in cities, who are frequently victims of racism and violence in addition to the dislocation and loss of community they suffer.

I recall watching the birth and growth of the amazing Anishnawbe Health Centre in downtown Toronto. It seemed such a modest request when the centre's wise director asked if we could find a van so that soup and blankets, as well as respectful advice and transportation, could be offered to homeless First Nations men, women, and teenagers. Chairing the Board of Health allowed me to rummage around in the budgets, and we found an eight-year-old van that was being sold off—sent to an auction where it would have fetched little. The medical officer of health at the time,

Dr. Sandy McPherson, pulled the van off the auction block, spent $1,000 on repairs, and gave it to the Anishnawbe group. They used it for years, with the help of hundreds of unpaid volunteers from urban First Nations and from the broader community. In 2006, I know lives are still being saved by the Street Patrol Service, and many a politician has driven in the van's late-night shift to learn about the faces of homelessness. That little van may actually have helped encourage political will to build affordable housing like the new First Nations housing we all worked to create on Coxwell Avenue, near the railroad tracks. From homelessness to housing, in a recycled van!

Shifting the focus to our seniors allows me to make a personal comment about the people who cared for my dad. The need for services for seniors really hits home when you actually have to start looking after your own parents. In my case, this experience started when our family had to go get nursing home care for my father. As my dad's Parkinson's worsened, it became clear that my mom, Doris, wasn't going to be able to take care of him at home. The children all set to work to try to find a place where he would be given dignified care, and where he could receive visitors, friends, and family in a way that would make everybody feel comfortable. We immediately ran up against the crisis in long-term care for seniors. My brother Dave, who was leading the effort, discovered that there were virtually no beds in the non-profit or public long-term-care facilities in the Toronto area. Waiting lists were long, and we didn't have much time. So, without other options available, we turned to the list of private long-term-care providers. We visited one that was not far from my brother's home and was easily accessible to my mom.

Sure enough, the facilities for seniors who could mostly look after themselves seemed friendly enough, the common areas were nicely appointed, pretty plants grew here and there, and the cafeteria had the feel of a friendly restaurant. A quick visit to the secure floor, where seniors requiring care live, seemed to indicate that this might be suitable. The sales staff who led the tour seemed agreeable and competent. But what a difference a week can make.

When my father moved into the facility, we quickly realized that the service wasn't going to measure up to our hopes. There was a telltale odour of urine and other unpleasant smells, not enough to make you sick, just unpleasant. Maybe this was just the way it was in seniors' homes, we thought. How could we have known differently?

Our next experience was with the care levels. The workers were certainly earnest, and they tried their best to be friendly, but from the outset we could tell that they were overworked. Frankly, they looked exhausted much of the time. Their shifts seemed to be terribly designed as far as their personal lives were concerned, and there was no question that their wages would make it tough for them to support their own families. Most of the workers had many different functions, from cleaning up after seniors who had had accidents to cleaning the rooms and hallways, and even to performing some services that really seemed to require a nurse.

But you could see in their eyes a real sense of unhappiness and strain. Naturally this was transferred to the seniors under their care. We didn't blame the workers. It wasn't their fault. The place just wasn't organized or designed for the caregivers to feel very positive about their work. We wondered if this was common in all seniors' homes.

And then there was the price we were paying—over $3,000 a month. How many families could even consider this? Fortunately, my father's pension, from a lifetime in business and political service, did cover it, but few working families today can afford such an expense without major hardship.

We watched my father's spirits deteriorate day by day. He had always been one of the most optimistic, upbeat people in any circle he travelled or worked in—his positive energy was his most distinguishing feature. I assumed at first that it was the Parkinson's disease, combined with the effects of the medication he was taking for prostate cancer, that was affecting his mood and making him unhappy.

Then he began to whisper the suggestion that maybe it wasn't worth carrying on. This is a very, very tough thing to hear from your father, someone who has always been the tower of strength in your life. It made me angry that he was having these feelings. I was angry at myself, I was angry at the situation, and I became increasingly angry at the treatment he was receiving. My dad had spent his whole life making other people happy, and for him not to be able to be happy in his last years seemed to me to be fundamentally unjust.

So we began to investigate other long-term-care options, and we tracked down a few possibilities, provided that we were willing to wait. One was very attractive. It was a non-profit, long-term-care facility that had been built with a lot of help from the Rotary Club of Toronto, and it was located right behind City Hall. This was going to be perfect—if there was any chance that my dad could move in.

I dropped in to visit, and from the very first moment the difference was absolutely clear. First, I smelled home cooking, not urine. A warm, welcoming receptionist, just inside the front door, greeted me and a cat strolled by, getting a pat from some of the seniors in their wheelchairs. They were having conversations and keeping an eye on the comings and goings at the front door. My instant reaction was that this felt like home rather than "a home."

As I toured the kitchen and the residential areas with the director, I felt I was not being given a sales job. The underlying message was that this was a place that provided dignity and care for seniors. When I asked how long the workers had been there, I was told that the average length of tenure was many, many years. Obviously, this meant that the caregivers were treated with real respect. Frankly, you could see it in their eyes and in their smiles. And when I visited the floors where the care was being given, I could see it in the eyes and smiles of the seniors themselves.

At the end of the tour, I said to my tour guide, "It looks as if you give tender loving care here." And she said, "Well, of course we believe in TLC. It's our motto, and it's our name: The Laughlen Centre—TLC," and she laughed.

Naturally, I expected that the costs here would be at least equal to or greater than at the private operation where my dad was living; there were more staff here, and more attention was being given to the seniors. Wrong. The Laughlen Centre offered accommodation at a little over half the price a month that the private, corporate facility was charging.

So on one hand, we experienced a private, multinational corporation's long-term-care facility, with low wages for its workers, poor shift arrangements for its staff, and problematic care bordering on the denial of dignity to the seniors. On the other hand, we experienced a non-profit, long-term-care system that manages to provide everything that seniors need, from dignity to food to physical care, and all at a considerably lower price.

Eventually my father was able to move into The Laughlen Centre. And, if anything, the reality proved to be even better than the tour. My father was happy as he lived out his last months. Ultimately, pneumonia took him when a chest infection overpowered his immune system. Now I understand why pneumonia is sometimes called "the old man's friend"—it took him quietly and without pain. And he was surrounded by his family. By then, his "family" included many of the people at the Rotary's Laughlen Centre.

I'm grateful to everybody there, for what they did for my father. Mostly, I'd like to hope that we, as a nation, develop a plan that ensures that high-quality, non-profit, long-term care is available for our seniors, no matter what their incomes, no matter what their backgrounds, and no matter what circumstances have necessitated their families' need.

Seniors' health issues are wider ranging than just residential long-term care. Home care is another important issue. Home care refers to a wide range of services used to help people with health problems stay in their homes. Historically, most of these services were provided by non-profit charitable organizations like the Victorian Order of Nurses and the Red Cross. Their work included homemaking services and nursing services such as insulin injections, eye drops, dressing changes, and health assessment. In the past fifteen years, with the drive to close hospital and in-patient mental health beds, there has been a dramatic switch in home-care services, to meet the needs of the acutely ill. Home care frees up hospital beds by allowing people who need IV antibiotics, dialysis, complex dressing changes, and palliative care to stay at home and get care. As the demand for acute care has increased, funding for services to allow the frail elderly to stay in their homes has taken second place.

In the 1970s, provincial governments started to take over the funding of some of these programs. Since home care falls outside the Canada Health Act, there is a disparity across the country in which services are funded through government programs and who delivers the services. Some provinces, for example Manitoba, provide their home-care services though public agencies, while Ontario contracts out all its services, a majority delivered by for-profit companies. Services may include homemaking, personal support, social work, the full range of therapy services, nursing, and medical supplies.

It's time we had public or non-profit-based home care available in all parts of Canada. Every Canadian should have access to the same level of service: our elderly deserve it, and the women who disproportionately care for elderly relatives deserve it. And it will save us money, too. Care in hospitals is $9,000 to $16,000 more expensive per year per patient than community-based home care.

Canadians who are sixty-five or older in 2006 total about 3.5 million, and that number is growing as the baby boomers move into their sixties. While most seniors feel that they receive good health care, provincial and national policies are not encouraging. In British Columbia, cuts by the Campbell Liberals to home-care services resulted in a decline of seniors' health, increased hospitalization, higher admissions to residential care, and more deaths. These cuts didn't save money and, more to the point, they were cruel and counterproductive.

Seniors take more prescription drugs than other age groups, and the national pharmacare program I mentioned earlier would lessen the financial burden on them for medicines they need beyond the provincial plans that cover some costs now.

Better public-health programs would encourage more physical activity in seniors and provide more opportunities to get together with other seniors. Such programs improve health and extend longevity and are major contributors to the quality of life.

Environmental programs that reduce smog, for example, would have a marked effect on seniors, who are especially vulnerable to respiratory diseases. Of the five thousand people who die prematurely each year in Canada from the effects of smog, significant numbers are seniors and the young. These are probably the least responsible for smog, yet the most affected. Another of our world's nasty ironies.

Improvements in public pensions would help seniors, especially women, avoid the poverty trap that so many of them fall into.

What gets me is that seniors don't complain much. I remember the time we were petitioning against the cancellation of significant senior discounts on the transit system. As we knocked on doors in a seniors' apartment building looking for signatures, one kindly woman said to me, "Oh, it's not so bad, Jack. I do need to use the streetcar to get to my doctor. I'll just stay in touch by phone instead of taking those trips to have tea with my friends." It just about made me cry. Here's a woman who has made her contributions to our society for eighty years or more. Now we're going to make it impossible for her to have that little joy—tea with her friends. What sort of definition of "quality of life" or "prosperity" do we use that does not include a well-deserved cup of tea? The health of our seniors depends as much on that tea—and on that affordable streetcar ride—as any high-tech medical intervention.

A caring society would meet these needs. Surely ours is capable of doing so.

In fact, it seems to me that seniors have been getting the brush-off in Canada in recent decades. In the 1960s, New Democrats like Tommy Douglas and Stanley Knowles talked about the importance of having basic income support for the people who built the country when they reached retirement age. The Canada Pension Plan and the Quebec Pension Plan were put in place effectively during minority Parliaments in the mid-1960s and were augmented by the guaranteed income supplement of the 1970s. Since then, there's been virtually no talk at election time about seniors' issues. In fact, judging from the discourse in the House of Commons you'd never know that we have a major demographic shift going on in Canada with a rapidly aging population. In the 2006 election, I talked about the need to address senior issues as a priority for working families, but we were unsuccessful in developing traction on it. We were unable to bring it to the forefront of public debate, and it was clear that we were going to have to work harder. Following the election, our caucus spent time figuring out how we could honour this commitment to follow through for seniors. We appointed a critic for senior's issues—newly elected Chris Charlton (Hamilton Mountain), who picked up on work begun by Brian Masse (Windsor West) in the previous Parliament. Brian had called it the Seniors' Charter. What we decided to do was work to have Parliament adopt a charter laying out what seniors had a right to expect from the country they had helped build. It contained six basic points—income security, affordable housing, wellness, universal health care, opportunities for self-development (including affordable access to education, recreation, and training), and timely access to all federal services, including family reunification.

We highlighted the need for a seniors' pharmacare program because we knew there were many people doing without medication either because there wasn't a pharmacare program available in their area or because that pharmacare program didn't cover a particular drug. We know that sometimes seniors are not refilling prescription or taking only half the prescribed amount in order to put food on the table and pay their rent. This is wrong. We also pushed for a national dental care program for seniors because dental care is so important for overall health, well-being, and self-esteem.

We brought our revamped Seniors' Charter to a vote in the House at the end of the June 2006 session, and it turned out to be a real success. All of the parties, with the sole exception of the Bloc, decided to support our Seniors Charter. The vote by Gilles Duceppe's party underlines yet again how utterly shallow the Bloc's understanding of what their role in Parliament really is.

Now that we have taken the Seniors' Charter to this stage,

we have to turn the motion, which is really just an expression of intent, into something more meaningful and tangible. We have to build support for legislation that we intend to introduce to give effect to the basic elements of the charter. We are confident that in doing this work we are honouring our commitment to working people and making important progress in the lives of our seniors.

Reawakening Our Communities

A young friend of mine, Joy Henderson, once told me about her first time at a summer camp outside the city. Joy grew up in the low-income community of Regent Park in Toronto, and when she returned from her trip, she said to her mom, "You never told me about the stars!" She'd never seen the miracle of a night sky. Having grown up witnessing hundreds of star-filled nights in rural Quebec, I was shocked to realize that big-city kids, especially poor ones with little access to the countryside, think the Milky Way is only a candy bar, and that they're denied the spectacle the heavens reveal on a clear night.

Country and small-town life are special. I grew up in the quiet little town of Hudson, so there's a part of me that still nods secretly in agreement when friends in rural Canada tell me that they'd never want to live in a big city. Clean air, the smells of forests and flowers, and those countless stars.

But we are a nation of city dwellers. Statistics Canada says that 80 per cent of us live in cities, defining "urban" as any place larger than ten thousand people Almost two-thirds of us live in fairly large cities—more than one hundred thousand people—and over half the Canadian population lives in one of the four urban regions of Toronto, Montreal, Vancouver, and the Calgary–Edmonton axis. For all our vast geography, we are one of the most urbanized countries in the world. And as is happening around the world, the population continues to gravitate toward cities—out of the countryside—including about 75 per cent of newcomers to Canada.

Towns and cities are now the heart of our country's life. Rural Canada is vital to our economy and our future—especially as resources are depleted and valuable non-urban ways of life are threatened by depopulation. However, it is time to recognize the social transformation that has taken place—and to take advantage of the opportunities that our cities provide.

Two elements of a new agenda are essential to keep the blood pulsing through healthy communities: reforming the basis on which cities are financed, and reforming the decision-making structures of all governments to achieve healthier democracy through community engagement.

A Raw Deal for Cities

In Canada, cities have been considered "creatures" of the provinces. That, in a nutshell, is a big problem with the way we govern municipalities. The role, function, and structure of municipal governments in Canada derive from the Baldwin Act of 1849. At that time, fewer than 15 per cent of Canadians lived in urban areas, and local governments were concerned with problems like running cattle in public places, noisy disturbances, public drunkenness, profanity, and itinerant salesmen. (Some problems just won't go away.) The Constitution gives the provinces control over municipal institutions In fact, constitutional recognition of municipalities as a form of government doesn't exist. Cities are the poor cousins of the Canadian political family, the neglected relatives—except that our towns and cities are also the engines of the economy, the driving force of our society, and the centres of our culture.

Way back in 1901, towns and cities across Canada realized they needed to band together so they could speak to provincial and federal governments with one voice. They formed the Federation of Canadian Municipalities, an umbrella group that now has a membership of more than one thousand towns and cities. The FCM serves as a forum for mayors and other elected officials to share experiences, as a clearing house for ideas and innovation, and as a lobbying organization on behalf of municipalities. I was honoured to serve a term as FCM president recently.

My predecessor as president of the FCM, Kitimat Regional Councillor Joanne Monahan, used to say, "Somewhere between asylums and saloons, that's where you find municipal government in the Canadian Constitution." And it's true. Our cherished local democracies—the creation of which required rebellions, for heaven's sake—languish in a mundane list of the various responsibilities of the provinces!

Yet, as I've noted in many examples, true innovations come from municipal governments. So many of our best ideas first emerged locally, where creativity and experimentation can thrive. The idea that the most important public-health measure is a secure roof over everyone's head produced the first affordable public housing through local medical officers of health and city councils. Infrastructure to create safer sewage treatment and drinking water first came from city governments. Public transit. Transport infrastructure for industry. Parks and playgrounds. Libraries. Concert halls. Health clinics. Bicycle lanes and recreational trails. Tree-planting programs. Food banks. Shelters for the homeless. The list of local policy innovations is long.

Now, more Canadians have come to recognize the importance of cities to Canada's future. In May 2002, the Toronto Dominion Bank issued a special report called *A Choice between Investing in Canada's Cities or Disinvesting in Canada's Future*. The title makes the options pretty clear. In the report, the bank writes, "The bottom line is that we are all stakeholders in our nation's future—consumers and businesses alike. Our cities are a vital part of that future, and we must work together to ensure their health and prosperity." I couldn't have said it better.

In January 2003, the Laidlaw Foundation issued a report that reminded us, "the social health of urban communities is essential to the economic future of Canada." A few months later, a group of prominent Torontonians, the Toronto City Summit Alliance, put out a report that stated the problem very starkly: "Quite simply, Canadian federalism is not working for our large city regions." The Calgary-based Canada West Foundation was among the first to make the same point.

What does all that mean?

The City of Winnipeg's gross domestic product (GDP) accounts for two-thirds of Manitoba's economy; Calgary's and Edmonton's GDP is 64 per cent of Alberta's; Vancouver's GDP is 53 per cent of British Columbia's; Montreal's is half of Quebec's; and Toronto is responsible for 44 per cent of Ontario's GDP. The larger cities represent a considerable proportion of federal government revenues as well. The Greater Toronto Area (GTA) all by itself accounts for over one-fifth of Canada's entire GDP.

In Winnipeg in 2001, over 50 per cent of the taxes paid by residents went to the federal government, 43 per cent to the provincial government, and less than 7 per cent to the city government. In the GTA, residents' taxes resulted in a net contribution (that is, their tax revenue minus payments back to the city) of $17 billion to Ottawa and $3 billion to the province. The GTA municipal governments pay Ottawa about $100 million in GST, and they pay the province about $150 million in PST for the purchases they make.

These are a lot of numbers, but what they mean is this: Canada's cities generate enormous revenues for the federal and provincial governments. What the cities get in return is a pittance. Federal, provincial, and territorial governments control the spending of over 95 per cent of all tax dollars.

Municipalities control less than 5 per cent. Across Canada, about half of all municipalities' revenue comes from property tax. (In the U.S., it averages about one-fifth.) So let's look again at Winnipeg, whose revenues and expenses are fairly typical of Canadian cities. In 2001, 54 per cent of Winnipeg's municipal revenue came from property tax. User fees, licences, fines, utility bills, and other miscellaneous local revenues amounted to 30 per cent of the city's income. Grants from the federal and provincial governments provided only 16 per cent of Winnipeg's revenue. And Winnipeg is lucky! Manitoba's NDP government has been transferring fixed percentage points of income taxes collected to municipalities on a per capita basis, essentially sharing a little income tax revenue directly with the city.

Yet, over the past decade in particular, as they sought to balance their budgets and reduce their deficits, federal and provincial governments have been steadily downloading costs and services to municipalities—the level of government whose hands are most tied when it comes to collecting revenue from the economic activity that municipalities spawn. Because cities are creatures of the provinces, the provinces have traditionally limited the ways that municipalities can fund themselves. By law, with rare exceptions, cities don't have the authority to collect income taxes, fuel taxes, sales taxes, or most other kinds of tax except property tax. So when the federal government wants to wrestle the deficit to the ground, it does so by passing on costs to provinces, which pass some of them on to municipalities, the level of government with by far the least capacity to pass them on to anyone else—or to raise money to backfill the fiscal excavations. The result? More potholes. As MP Brian Masse, our federal caucus urban advocate, has been saying, higher property tax bears no resemblance whatsoever to a citizen's ability to pay. It would be no exaggeration to state that the corporate tax cuts implemented by Paul Martin were paid for in part by property tax increases on every homeowner, including retired people. Bad policy and unfair to boot.

Speaking to a symposium we organized at the FCM in 2002, former Ontario NDP premier Bob Rae said:

> The governments at the provincial and federal level have to be challenged: if you're not prepared to transfer the resources yourselves, then at least give us the financial room to make those decisions and let the local governments really decide. Governments are much better at downloading than at transferring resources. The only way the senior levels of government have been able to balance their books is by sabotaging other levels of government. What do you do about the services that have been underfed and starved? If you really want to discipline all levels of government, you have to make sure that the level of government that is actually delivering the service has the taxing authority and capacity to deliver that service.

The mayor of St. John's, Andy Wells, summed the problem up nicely: "We've got the responsibility, but we don't have the legislative authority and the fiscal tools." At FCM, we used to refer to the federal government's attitude toward cities as a "culture of non-recognition and neglect."

How has this downloading affected cities? Let me give some examples from my own city.

In the mid-1990s, the provincial government downloaded all the responsibility for affordable housing and 20 per cent of the responsibility for Family Benefits and Ontario Disability Support programs to municipal governments. They did this, of course, because they had promised to "lower taxes," but all they did was shift the burden to towns and cities. And how are the cities supposed to pay for this increase? As I've pointed out, about the only lever a municipality has is to increase property taxes. I can only speak directly for my own city, but there was certainly no money in the city's budget for new affordable housing, and little for the maintenance of the existing social housing stock.

Through the 1990s, government funding for the Toronto Transit Commission (TTC) was cut by $92 million, to less than twenty cents for each dollar spent. Because of this, more than 80 per cent of the TTC's funding comes from the public transit riders paying their fares. This is far below government support for public transit in any comparable urban centre in the world. As a result, the TTC is trapped in the bind of either increasing fares or reducing service—both of which inevitably result in lower ridership, exactly the wrong outcome for any sensible public policy.

In May 2003, in a speech to the FCM, the backbench MP for La Salle–Emard and Liberal leadership front-runner Paul Martin said he would give municipalities a share of the federal gasoline tax. Good news? Canadians have heard Martin on gas taxes before. In 1995, when he was finance minister, he increased the gas tax by 1.5 cents a litre. He said it was to help pay down the deficit. (Actually, it would help pay for the hefty corporate tax cuts that arrived five years later.) He emphasized at the time that this gas tax hike was temporary, and that, as soon as the deficit was eliminated, the gas tax hit would come off. But, even when the government began to run up huge surpluses, the increased gas tax stayed, and none of it went to municipalities. The surplus resulted in more tax cuts for the well-to-do—and swelled corporate bottom lines. The 2004 election featured more Martin promises of gas tax revenue. But, despite the cities' call for half of the gas tax, five cents per litre, the Martin proposition was only

1.5 cents per litre to start, and gradually increasing to five cents over a five-year period. This of course was the same 1.5 cents a litre he had promised to restore when the deficit had disappeared. All this was the backdrop to the NDP budget amendment that forced the Martin Liberals to accelerate the transfer of gas tax and to dedicate some of this to transit.

• • •

The Federation of Canadian Municipalities estimates that our towns and cities need about $60 billion for necessary repairs and maintenance on the existing urban infrastructure—our roads, public transit, waterworks and sewer systems, and housing. Under the current fiscal framework, it simply isn't possible for the cities to pay for all this. As the 2002 Toronto Dominion Bank report on cities pointed out, "Hit by the double-whammy of weak revenue growth and downloading of services, it is hardly surprising that municipal governments have had to run up debt, defer infrastructure projects, draw down reserves, sell assets and cut services in order to stay afloat."

Cities need a new deal. But, as the big-city mayors stated in their spring, 2005 report on the fiscal imbalance respecting large municipalities it has to be the real deal, with fundamental reorganization of federal and provincial financial arrangements concerning municipalities, giving access to growth based revenue sources to cities. Communities of all sizes need more tools to build healthy, workable, productive communities. And they need some share of the financial resources they produce plowed back into their productive processes.

We need a new urban vision, one that looks into the future with the benefit of hindsight. Let's consider just one key area of urban policy that we actually had right in Canada—then we watched it collapse before our eyes.

The Shame of Homelessness

Forgetting basic lessons about the need to invest in our communities can actually be fatal. The people who died in Walkerton from bad water are testimony. So is abandoning the idea of building some housing for those who cannot afford the rough-and-tumble world of free-enterprise home ownership. But that's exactly what our former national finance minister and former prime minister, did. Martin pushed his shortsighted policies, in my opinion, with impunity, and in the process perpretrated social injustices and disastrous results.

Why he's regarded as a "deficit-wrestling hero" escapes me. Especially after Eugene Upper died. One cold and snowy night—January 4, 1996, to be exact—Olivia and I were walking home around midnight from Metro Hall, up Spadina Avenue. Along the way we passed two homeless men huddled in their sleeping bags in doorways, the snow drifting up around them. We checked quietly on them, not to disturb them, but to see if they showed any obvious signs of trouble. They seemed okay.

Across the street, another person had sought refuge from the cold and snow in a TTC shelter. We didn't see him. All night long, Spadina buses passed him by every half hour, never stopping. No one's proud of it, but a homeless person tucked into a Toronto bus shelter is not an unusual sight.

Trudging on home, we wondered aloud what we'd do if we did meet someone who seemed to be in difficulty. Here we were, two experienced city councillors, and even we didn't know whom to call—911? Police? A hospital? The Salvation Army? We just didn't know.

We got home, glad to be out of the cold, glad to be in comfortable surroundings. It's something most of us take for granted.

Early the next morning, over coffee and the newspapers, we were both stopped in mid-thought by the CBC radio news: "Overnight, a man was found frozen to death in a bus shelter on Spadina Avenue," the announcer said. We knew immediately that we had walked right by him.

His name was soon released: Eugene Upper. He had died from the killer cold in the winter-moon shadows of the bank towers in the richest city in Canada. I felt sick that I hadn't done enough to prevent it—not only that night but in my job at city council. I should have been working to make sure there were more emergency services, more shelters, more housing, a hotline people could call. It is a tragedy and a disgrace that Eugene Upper died. Yet within a short period of time, two other Toronto men, Mirsalah-Aldin Kompani and Irwin Anderson, also froze to death. And the city finally took notice.

A few years later, I wrote a book called *Homelessness*, and I dedicated it to Eugene Upper, both as a tribute to the man whose horrible death galvanized us into action, and as a reminder that we must do so much more as a society to provide affordable housing and services for homeless people. That book describes in detail the plight and extent of homelessness and suggests solutions for Canada's housing crisis.

Canada is the only G8 country without a national housing program. We had one for a generation, forced into being in 1972 by NDP leader David Lewis on the minority government of Pierre Trudeau as a condition of his caucus's support for the Liberals. Hundreds of thousands of co-op and social-housing units were built for families, seniors, students, people with various challenges, and the general public. At its height, in the years between 1989 and 1993, an average of 12,675 new social-housing units were being built annually. I am one of the hundreds of thousands of Canadians who have lived in co-op housing. What makes co-op housing especially successful is that it brings together people who can afford to pay market rents, like me, with those who cannot. This ensures a vibrant mixed-income community that avoids the many problems created when low-income earners are "ghettoized." This mixed-income model was recognized globally as a "best practice" by the United Nations Habitat Program.

In 1993, when the Liberal government came into office again, Paul Martin became finance minister, and the number of social-housing units being built dropped, even as he instituted his $100-billion tax cuts. Mr. Martin simply axed the whole program. The Conservatives under Brian Mulroney had frozen it; Martin killed it. In the years 1994 to 1998, an annual average of only 4,450 units of new affordable housing were built, a drop of 65 per cent. Those that survived were projects where construction had already begun, and those were built by provinces, like Ontario, British Columbia, and Quebec—all with social democratic governments at the time.

In 1990, as a member of the opposition and when he was seeking votes for his Liberal leadership bid, Mr. Martin wrote the following: "[A]ll Canadians have the right to decent housing, in decent surroundings, at affordable prices.... Only the national government has the financial resources to address the full dimensions of the needs of this country." Were Canadians being sold a similar bill of goods when his government promised a new deal for cities?

Let's also recall Article 25 of the Universal Declaration of Human Rights, adopted by the United Nations in 1948 and ratified by Canada: "Everyone has the right to a standard of living adequate for the health and well-being of himself and of his family, including food, clothing, housing and medical care and necessary social services, and the right to security in the event of unemployment, sickness, disability, widowhood, old age or other lack of livelihood in circumstances beyond his control." Are those, too, just nice words, or do they represent a commitment? For the thousands of homeless people across Canada, they ring hollow when governments won't build housing.

In 1998, prompted by the Toronto Disaster Relief Committee, the mayors of Canada's largest cities declared homelessness a national disaster. Heroic street nurse Cathy Crowe and dedicated outreach worker Beric German had pulled together an extraordinary group of homeless people, along with others who believed in their cause, and insisted that we use the concept of disaster relief to address homelessness. As Crowe told me, as well as the city council committee charged with these issues, "I was getting ready to go help out during the ice storm in Quebec. They told me I'd be dealing with people in cramped quarters, on mats or cots, crammed in hostels, without their homes, coping with the effects of the cold. There will be hundreds of these people in many communities. I said, 'Wait a minute! This is what I do every day in Toronto, working with five thousand homeless people in our shelters and on our streets.' How come we react to an ice storm with the Canadian army and an army of volunteers, but we languish in the luxury of inaction and blame-the-victim rhetoric when faced with a similar situation arising from homelessness?"

These powerful sentiments and the effective pressure of grassroots organizations prompted me to work with a group of municipal representatives in the FCM to lay out a detailed national housing strategy. We said, "Let's put forward a plan designed to reduce homelessness by 50 per cent in ten years." (It also included a five-year plan to cut in half the number of households whose rent is more than half their income.) The essence of the plan was to supply 20,000 new affordable housing units and to rehabilitate 10,000 units every year for the next ten years. Thus, 30,000 housing units a year, which would have housed 60,000 to 65,000 additional people each year and a total of 600,000 to 650,000 over the next decade.

We envisioned what I like to call "Lilliputianism" at work—thousands of small local projects, maybe averaging one hundred units, developed and managed right there in the communities where they were being built, which collectively would produce giant results. This program would have created tens of thousands of jobs in planning and construction, provided an enormous stimulus to the economy, built new energy-efficient units, retrofitted older homes for greater efficiency, increased population density and reduced urban sprawl, and revitalized urban neighbourhoods. It would also have brought homeless people in from the cold.

Too many people think of social housing as a blight. On the contrary, it can be a real community builder. One of the best examples is right in my own backyard.

Remember those brownfields I wrote about earlier? The St. Lawrence community sits on once-polluted land from abandoned factories near Toronto's waterfront. Using funds resulting from NDP leader David Lewis's efforts in the early seventies, non-profit and co-op housing organizations worked together, and with the city transformed a dreary post-industrial neighbourhood into a wonderful blend of social, co-op, municipal non-profit (under the cozy-sounding moniker Cityhome), and market rental and condo housing. A whole neighbourhood sprang to life, creating a district not only with decent places to live but with arts and culture. Far from having driven down the value of land, the St. Lawrence community has increased property values and economic activity on surrounding lands. It's a thriving neighbourhood, located so close to the inner city that most residents can easily walk to work. (Walking to work—what a brilliant idea!) Across Canada, similar communities have been built and are flourishing They were a big part of the reason why urbanologists from all over the world trooped to Canada to study cities that worked. Such pilgrimages have largely stopped because our cities no longer work as they should.

The St. Lawrence community is an example of "smart growth," with increased density, mixed housing, access to public transit, job creation, cultural enhancement, and community participation. Everywhere in urban Canada, huge swaths of federally owned land languishes—vacant, under-used, often polluted, and tied up in skeins of red tape. Federal politicians occasionally float pet schemes with much fanfare, but that's usually where the story ends. Where is the sense of urgency? Where's the vision? You would think, especially with the housing crisis evident around us, that action would be the watchword.

With careful study of both the long-term demand and the immediate problem, the FCM estimated the federal costs for its proposed national housing program at $1.6 billion a year. To achieve the goals we set, these costs would ideally be matched by the provinces and the municipalities, each contributing $1.6 billion in land, old buildings, financial support, or other forms of assistance.

Spurred on by the national attention that homelessness was getting, Prime Minister Chrétien named his labour minister, Claudette Bradshaw, as the person responsible for the homelessness issue. Just before Christmas 1999, Bradshaw did indeed announce the National Homelessness Initiative, a three-year program "designed to support community efforts" against homelessness. About half the money went into the Residential Rehabilitation Assistance Program, some was directed specifically to worthy Aboriginal initiatives, and $305 million —over three years—went toward the new Supporting Community Partnership Initiative (SCPI). That $100 million a year wasn't much, but it was a start. That money could be put into emergency shelters (new and expanded), other support facilities, and food and furniture banks. What it did not do—what it explicitly could not be used for—was to build a single unit of housing.

In all, sixty-one communities designed programs that were funded in part by SCPI. (About 80 per cent of the funds went to the ten largest cities; the rest went to small programs in fifty-one other communities.) When the initial program ran out in 2003, the government extended it for another three years, with funding of $405 million.

In Halifax, which was one of the first cities to sign on to SCPI programs, sixteen agencies received funding in the first round. They included residential facilities, transitional houses for both men and women, a centre for immigrants and refugees, supportive housing for low-income people, and more. They even funded the Shining Lights Choir, made up of homeless people and service providers. (The choir gave people a real sense of pride, belonging, and self-confidence; choir members sang on CBC national radio.)

SCPI funding in Saskatoon helped the food bank purchase the building they're housed in, it paid for staff for a round-the-clock mobile crisis-intervention service, renovated the Salvation Army's men's hostel, supported programs for at-risk young people (including purchase of a ten-bed transitional house for youth), and helped furnish a housing facility for women survivors of childhood sexual abuse. That names just a few.

Dozens of other small and worthwhile programs like these—in many Canadian towns and cities—have received, or are still receiving, federal SCPI funding. I want to give credit where credit is due: Claudette Bradshaw personally stickhandled this through the Liberal cabinet and came up with money that funded some imaginative and necessary community efforts to ease the effects of homelessness. As far as it goes, it's a good program that relies mostly on local organizations to design programs that best meet their needs. It's a bottom-up approach, not a top-down one, and that's the way it should be.

But it didn't build any permanent housing. Communities across Canada, housing activists, the FCM, property developers, and the housing industry continued to draw attention to this huge and growing gap in Canadian public policy. The pressure was on. Finally, the Chrétien government cracked.

The spring 2001 federal budget included $680 million to be spent on housing over five years, subject to agreements with the provinces. The months that followed featured fierce negotiations between the federal and provincial governments. As president of FCM at the time, I had a chance to help achieve wording for a federal-provincial agreement that would allow enough flexibility to permit provinces to work on affordable housing in their own ways while, we thought, being true to the common goal of affordability.

Despite the feeling that the federal government was "invading" provincial jurisdiction, Quebec, ironically, was the province that moved the most quickly. The Parti Québécois government, realizing that the funds were essential to continue building affordable housing, designed a made-in-Quebec plan that produced new housing within months. That government even asked if it could spend its share of the five-year program funds in two years instead! Who says Quebec is the problem when it comes to federal-provincial relations?

However, several ultra-conservative provincial governments, led by Ontario's Mike Harris, sabotaged the programs in their provinces. Ideologically opposed to any social housing programs at all, they dragged their feet, refusing to invest any funds. Two and a half years later, there was barely a single housing unit funded and built in Ontario. The same happened in several other provinces. Where is the accountability to the public for promises made? Why didn't the federal government bypass, override, or cajole the reluctant provinces? Why didn't the federal government deal directly with the municipalities that were chafing at the bit to get going on housing construction?

The answer to these questions lies in the lack of political will of our national government. When the will is there, as it was in 1972 when the government had to act in order to ensure its survival, affordable housing solutions were put into place rapidly and effectively. We need to reconstruct that will to invest and build.

A final key idea: affordable housing is an investment, not just "an expense." Funds invested in the bricks and mortar of housing create an asset. The economy grows, and the asset becomes a basis for further growth. The embedded value of public and social housing could be capitalized to create more housing. This is out-of-the-box thinking—at least for government. The private sector has been capitalizing its assets since capitalism began. Why not do this in the public portion of the economy as well? Wouldn't Canadians be happier knowing that their future pensions were securely invested in providing housing for people in need, rather than gambled away on speculative stock schemes?

One example of a real estate company doing just this is Concert Properties in B.C. The company is entirely owned by twenty-one union and management pension funds, and their commitment is to work with communities to develop rental housing projects that are both good for people and good for the bottom line. In the past several years, they've contributed over $28 million back to their affiliated pension, health, and welfare plans. These pension funds are making money—and they're making a difference.

Housing investments also save taxpayers' money. The total cost of helping homeless people in our cities is at least four times more than the cost of providing affordable housing for them. Hostels, police, emergency rooms, and jails all cost money—lots of it. So why not save that money, create a more caring society, and make people happier and more productive all at the same time by investing in housing. A good idea whose time has come again.

One day, I got a call from a woman living in a family homeless shelter. She told me, amid angry tears, that her daughter was on the bed they shared in the tiny room, studying for college. She told me she thought she had made a terrible mistake. Her rent had come due at the same time that her daughter's tuition had to be paid. She was so proud of her daughter, who had worked so hard to get the grades to qualify for college. As a single mom with little support, she had to make a terrible choice—the tuition for her daughter or the rent to the landlord. She couldn't afford both. Because she wanted a better future for her daughter, she chose to pay the tuition and hoped that the landlord would give a few days' grace, that luck would somehow intervene. The landlord showed no mercy, and hence the call from the shelter. No Canadian should have to make a choice like that.

Transportation in Our Communities

Our cities need a cardiovascular workout. Witness our clogged arteries. Check out the traffic reports for varicose veins. Ever been a part of a metaphorical blood clot on a broken-down subway train?

The right fitness program would make our infrastructure healthy—and encourage sensible solutions to transportation challenges.

People sometimes ask me, "What exactly is municipal infrastructure?" In the metaphor of the human body, infrastructure is the system that moves the things we need to wherever we need them to be—oxygen and nutrients to where they are used, wastes from where they're produced to where they can be sent on their way. Let these systems atrophy, and the body will suffer. Ditto communities.

In recent years, we have taken these systems for granted. For example, we thought our transportation networks could get by as we loaded them up with more and more demands. Now look at rush-hour traffic in most urban areas. Public transit provides an efficient and effective way to avoid transportation blood clots. Yes, the solutions involve federal government reinvestment in mass transport, but this alone will not solve the problems we face. So let's look at other solutions.

Working with the B.C. provincial government when Mike Harcourt was the NDP premier, the Greater Vancouver Regional District put together the most advanced approach in Canada for tackling the long-term problems of congestion, sprawl, and smog reduction. With the help of community consultations, all the municipalities in the area identified green space they wanted to make immune from suburban sprawl or other development. (Future generations will be very thankful!) The communities could spell out how much development they would permit on the remaining lands. If they chose to allow higher density development, rapid transit lines would be developed to serve them. If not, then only minimal improvements in transportation would be provided. This produced an incentive to create new community growth in a way that encouraged transit use and reduced automobile travel. Sensible and efficient, and good for the environment, too.

The links between development patterns, intensity of development, and appropriate infrastructure are key to sustainable community planning. Vancouver has set a high benchmark.

- Number of G8 countries other than Canada with no national housing program: 0; with no national transportation program: 0

- Number of people killed a day in traffic accidents worldwide: 2,425

- Number of fatal jumbo jet crashes a day it would take to reach that number: 10

- Percentage of urban trips made by bike in the Netherlands: 30; in the U.S.: 1

- Number of bicycles in Copenhagen available for free public use: 2,300

Most often, new directions in urban public policy come from the grassroots. A terrific example is the burgeoning and immensely healthy phenomenon of bicycles in cities.

In Montreal, cyclists have led a veritable "vélolution" over the past quarter century. Travelling by bicycle produces no greenhouse gas emissions, and bikes use far less of our scarce urban land for storage. When hundreds or thousands of daily car trips are replaced by bike rides, pollution is reduced, and human health improves. Community bike advocates in Montreal have urged governments to mark off lanes on roads for bikes only. Gradually, a network has been created that allows people to move around many parts of the city, most of the year, by bike. Many other cities have since followed suit.

But the federal government has yet to come up with any substantial policy and funding to promote cycling. It's as though they think biking is a frill in the transportation matrix. It's time that attitude was changed. Federal invest-ments in cycling infrastructure could well be the least costly way to improve transportation. Why not reward people who use their bikes and who, by doing so, keep the air cleaner and the roads less congested? And cycling improves the urban cardiovascular systems and the human ones, too! Just as I will propose rebating the GST for advanced-technology, low-emission vehicles, I think we should consider all bikes advanced-technology vehicles themselves and rebate GST on every bicycle sold in Canada. Let's start rewarding good behaviour.

We should also be preserving rail services and railway lines and putting bike paths beside them. The abandonment of rail lines and their wanton auction to the highest bidder—usually the neighbouring landowners or speculators looking to subdivide—is blind stupidity. Once a rail line has been chopped up and sold off, there is no likelihood that it will ever be replaced. That's why the federal government should ensure that all rail lines, abandoned or not, are preserved as corridors in perpetuity, with federal laws and with appropri-ate financial arrangements for those who own them. Don't governments remember that they gave the railways the land on which those companies made enormous profits? Holding rail corridors in the public trust would allow future genera-tions to use them for all kinds of transportation needs. Recreational uses are obvious. But what if we do develop new technologies for easier and more environmentally advanced movement of people, goods, and services? They will likely need corridors. If we keep the rail corridors for future use, generations to come will thank us.

When it comes to sustainable infrastructure funding, Europeans can teach us a lot. The European Regional Development Fund (ERDF) is the main source of infrastruc-ture funding. They wisely plan for the long term, and the

2000–2006 ERDF budget is for 195 billion euros (approximately $300 billion Canadian). Half of the infrastructure budget in 2000 went for transportation—including both public transit and roads. About 30 per cent of the ERDF allocation is dedicated to environmental and water projects.

France has its own national Transport Contribution Tax (the Versement de Transport), which is levied on all employers with more than nine employees and fixed at 1.75 per cent of their payroll. The tax finances the investment and operation of urban public transportation in France's larger cities.

Even the United States has surpassed Canada by a long shot. Our policies should, I hate to admit it, emulate theirs—although with one proviso. Let's keep our systems public and not turn them over to the private sector in the fashion of our southern neighbour.

How do we pay for all this? Steady, step-by-step investment with long-term plans is far better than one-shot pre-election announcements for politically sexy projects of the moment. Boring? Yes. But like the daily turn on the exercise bike, it keeps the cardio ticking more happily and longer. It turns out that's the "real deal" training program for cities, too.

A case of empowerment: Hudson, Quebec

Even advanced policies from the federal government backed up by enhanced resources are not sufficient to chart the paths and achieve the most sustainable results for communities. People in our cities and towns need more democratic decision-making power to shape their future. Vibrant local democracies are the best course to follow to overcome democratic deficits.

A case in point. I am so proud of my little hometown of Hudson. When a small group of women in this little bedroom and farming community (between Montreal and Ottawa on the Ottawa River) came to the conclusion, in the early 1990s, that pesticides were one reason their kids were suffering from asthma, they decided to act locally. Their local actions have shaken up Canada's Constitution, rocked the massive chemical industry, and produced global implications—as well as fewer asthma attacks in Hudson. And hundreds of other communities are following this example.

After some Hudson residents collected signatures on a petition to ban pesticides in the town, the local council brought in a bylaw to do just that, except in situations where special permission was sought. The mighty global pesticide industry feared that should the Hudson precedent ever become popular across Canada, pesticide sales could drop dramatically. Corporate moguls decided that this clearly could not be permitted, so the industry weighed in behind two small local lawn-care companies and mounted a legal challenge to Hudson's right to adopt such a bylaw. They claimed it exceeded the authority of municipal governments, and off to court they went.

Round one went to the companies. The Quebec courts ruled that, yes indeed, the good burghers of Hudson had committed an act ultra vires: they had exceeded the authority granted to municipalities. The argument was—and it's been long-standing conventional wisdom in municipal government—that city and town councils can adopt only measures that they have been specifically authorized to adopt by the provincial governments that supervise their activities. This limit on democratically elected municipal councils has for years stood in the way of innovation at the local level, preventing Canadians' creativity from flourishing and holding citizens back. Hudson explored the idea of appealing this reversal of its pesticide law to the Supreme Court of Canada.

At the time, I was incoming president of the FCM. On behalf of the one thousand local governments that the FCM represents, we joined with Hudson to appeal. Environmental groups also came aboard.

Canada's Supreme Court heard the arguments and issued a historic ruling on behalf of local democracy and environmental sustainability. The learned justices concluded that not only did the town of Hudson, or any other municipal government, have the power to adopt such bylaws, but that they had better be considering the future health and well-being of their residents and adopt measures accordingly. Essentially, the Supreme Court changed the ossified interpretation of the Canadian Constitution that had hamstrung local democracies for over a century—liberating them and their citizens to take action to secure and enhance the health and safety of their citizens.

It was a clear case of empowerment of Canadian communities. Indeed, municipalities by the legion began to follow Hudson's lead. Halifax was one of the first big cities to severely limit the use of pesticides.

But the international headquarters of the pesticide manufacturers were determined that this ruling not be allowed to stand unchallenged. Corporate profits were at risk.

As a result, multinational pesticide manufacturers are attacking the Hudson initiative through world trade agreements, suggesting that controlling pesticide use is a restraint of trade! It remains to be seen if they will succeed.

Because the challenge takes place under the undemocratic structures of trade deals, there won't be the same opportunity to present the public-interest perspective as there was at the Canadian Supreme Court. No. By contrast, the global tribunals that will rule on the case will not have representations from Hudson, or other municipalities, or any other citizens' groups. They will hear from the corporations and from national governments, behind closed doors. They will make their decisions without accountability or democratic contexts. The considerations will be limited to the impact of the laws on the commercial interests of the firms involved.

This is the new global constitutional framework in action—a set of rules designed not to ensure people's rights but to protect investment rights against the decisions of democratically elected governments. If allowed to stand, this new world order will set back the struggles for democracy that have taken place over the past three hundred years.

That's why, in the spring of 2006, we brought forward legislation to ban the cosmetic use of pesticides across the country. That the Conservatives opposed it was no surprise, but what really shocked me was that Liberal MPs couldn't figure out where they stood on the issue. The Bloc decided to oppose the bill because they said there was already good pesticide control in Quebec and, in their myopic view, it's a provincial responsibility. How could the Bloc possibly feel that it's right to use their votes in the House to vote against something that would improve the health of children and adults across Canada? To me, it is blatantly irresponsible. Does the Bloc really believe that it's a bad idea to control pesticides in Ontario that otherwise would flow into the Great Lakes and then down the St. Lawrence River and into the bodies of Quebec kids? It's yet another indication of the narrow-mindedness that we increasingly see from the Bloc. Coming from Quebec, I know that Quebecers would want to be a part of helping the rest of Canada to wean themselves from their dependency on chemical biocides—chemicals that kill living organisms.

Sovereignty from the Ground Up

The Hudson case is about much more than pesticides. It's the story of people using the level of government closest to them to achieve their desired goals. I call it sovereignty from the ground up.

There's a saying that national governments are "too big to solve the small problems facing citizens and too small to solve the big ones alone." That sentiment recognizes that local governments are best positioned to deal with the "small problems" that become big issues in people's lives. It also reflects what's called "subsidiarity," the idea that, as an FCM report explains, "decisions should only be taken at a higher level of government when there are manifest reasons to do so." The principle recognizes that people get the best, and the cheapest, governance when services are delivered by the most local level of government that can afford to deliver them. Properly funded, either by revenues collected nationally or by their own authority, local governments are often the most imaginative and the best equipped to deal with social and economic issues. There is no one-size-fits-all solution, because everything is a different size.

Here's an example. The federal government designs labour-market training programs intended to provide people with skills to enter the workforce. But they take no account of the lack of child care or the availability of public transit, which can prevent the very people the program is designed for from taking advantage of it. Provincial governments might support clean air initiatives, but if they fail to give municipalities the powers to control urban sprawl or provide the funding necessary to operate public transit programs, the result will be increased air pollution. This lack of co-ordination and consultation with local governments undermines the good intentions of initiatives that provinces and the federal government sometimes put forward. Your local government, with the people of your community actively engaged in the process, plays—or should play—a very important role in shaping what goes on right around you.

Without being "told" to do so by the federal or provincial governments, the city of Calgary decided to build a wind turbine to generate the electricity to power its light-rail transit. (Are you thinking that cities can't do much about clean air? Studies show that half of a city's air pollution comes from cars and trucks in its own community.) Without the federal or provincial governments guiding it, Halifax decided to become a leader in waste management. Elsewhere, rent controls started locally. Settlement houses and immigration policy happened in cities first. Public potable-water networks and sewer systems are city creations. Municipal policies can support urban agriculture, promote green space, reduce sprawl, provide housing, put meals in schools, stimulate the arts, and yes, even eliminate pesticides—sovereignty from the ground up, or as they said when I was a young activist, power to the people.

To fulfill its responsibilities, cities urgently need a new fiscal framework. I've already pointed out the very considerable revenue that cities generate for the federal and provincial governments and the little that they get back. We cannot continue along this path or our cities will decay—they are already decaying—and if we allow that, the quality of people's lives will deteriorate along with them. Classrooms are overcrowded, local environments are suffering, public transit systems are being cut back, and sprawl is encouraging the Wal-Martization of our communities, just to name a few outcomes.

Ironically, Canadian cities used to be the shining North American urban success stories. Americans marvelled at our clean, safe, functioning cities, where people still live downtown and walk the streets at all hours of the night. (While not as safe as they once were, they're still much safer than our neighbour's cities are.) Yet these days, it's south of the border where urban investment and renewal are taking place. For example, Americans are putting public money into urban transportation at more than one hundred times the rate of Canadian governments. The waterfront in Baltimore, the area around the Rock and Roll Hall of Fame in Cleveland, downtown Philadelphia and Minneapolis–St. Paul, and many other American cities have all undergone wonderful renewal with considerable state and federal contributions.

In Canada, many towns and cities have been working hard to renew their infrastructure, improve their schools, and protect their environment, but they've been doing so with inadequate resources. Under our current system, even when cities do things to stimulate local economic activity, Ottawa benefits from it, and the cities end up with more costs. Here's one example.

Let's say you want to promote a successful tourist activity. I'll pick Caribana, one of the best and largest community festivals in Canada. Toronto has to give money to the event organizers to help make it happen. The city also has to hire extra police, put on more buses, hire the drivers, pay for extra fuel, and pay municipal workers to clean up after the fabulous, colourful parade. Okay. I support all that, because it's important to the community, and because it draws thousands of tourists to Toronto every summer. They eat in the city's restaurants, stay in the hotels, support local businesses, and stimulate the economy in countless other ways.

Economically, activities like Caribana are probably break-even operations for the city. For the federal and provincial governments, they're a bonus, as they collect tens of thousands of dollars in additional corporate tax, sales tax, and GST.

It's clear—not only to municipal governments and the FCM, but also to the chambers of commerce, the banks, and the social scientists and academics who study the situation—that cities need a new deal from the senior levels of government. They need a better division of existing revenue, and they need new opportunities to collect revenue.

Municipal governments are in a bind, as I've said, because they have very limited opportunities to collect revenue, apart from property tax. In Europe, transfers from senior governments account for 31 per cent of a city's revenues. In the U.S., it's 27 per cent. In Canada, it's less than 19 per cent. In the U.S., cities may legally charge sales tax, income tax—on both individuals and corporations—and business tax. In Canada, cities generally don't have this authority. American cities may also issue tax-exempt bonds, another major revenue source denied to Canadian cities. And as I've pointed out, municipal governments must also pay sales tax on their purchases to their provinces and GST on goods and services to the federal government.

Some provinces are beginning to earmark revenue to cities. In Alberta, the provincial government directs 1.2 cents a litre of the tax on gasoline sold in Edmonton and Calgary back to those cities. In British Columbia, the Greater Vancouver Transit Authority gets 11 cents a litre in gasoline tax for use in sustainable transportation. (Wisely, the province sets some laudable guidelines for how the funds can be used; it doesn't tell the city specifically how to use the money.) Manitoba gives a grant to municipalities equal to 2 percentage points of personal income tax and 1 percentage point of corporate income tax. Quebec also gives a portion of the gas or fuel tax to its cities. In a couple of other instances, cities have some other sources of tax revenue (in Quebec and Nova Scotia, they can levy a land transfer tax), but these exceptions are rare.

It's the federal government, which spends the greatest portion of Canadians' tax revenue, that should really be dedicating funds directly to municipalities. One incident sheds light on the issue.

As FCM president, I had the chance to introduce Finance Minister Paul Martin as a featured speaker at our convention on the fateful weekend when he lost his job in June 2002. A month earlier, and just by chance, I had met him on a plane. "The cities are tired and struggling, after being downloaded upon in federal budget after federal budget. You need to help fund municipalities of all sizes with a new deal," I urged. Martin replied, in a conspiratorial whisper—Allan Rock, then also a candidate for leader of the Liberal Party, was sitting a couple of seats behind!—that "the budget cycle won't allow me to make an announcement in June, and besides, you have to convince Number One [Prime Minister Chrétien] about this."

I found this "budget-cycle" excuse lame. He had told me and an entire assembly of big-city mayors a few months earlier that he did not agree with diverting the $4.5-billion gas tax toward sustainable urban transportation, as we had requested. "I don't agree with dedicated taxes," was the extent of his explanation at that time.

On the plane, I told him, "Well, I'll have the pen, so you'd best have the cheque."

A few weeks later, there we were at the FCM convention, me with my pen, and Paul without his cheque! On stage in front of hundreds of mayors and councillors from every town in Canada, I offered the pen. Martin laughed at what he considered a joke. Still, Finance Minister Martin let fly, for the first time, the revolutionary phrase "new deal." The place erupted like starving masses being thrown flyers with a promise of water and rice in the next truck. The reaction from Number One was swift. Martin was pulled out of our intimate post-speech lunch to be told, apparently, that he was about to lose his job. Number One had spoken! A little over a year later, Mr. Martin became Number One. But still municipalities waited. It wasn't until the spring of 2005 that the Martin Liberals—desperately seeking to avoid an election—agreed with a budget amendment put forward by the NDP caucus (see Chapter 8 for details). It took a minority government and a determined band of nineteen NDP MPs to begin putting an end to the unfairness of unbalanced finances in our nation. With that change, urban Canada began to experience an infusion of resources and allow the enormous potential of our cities to be unleashed.

It would be fair to ask: can a national focus on cities really turn around these revenue inequities? Sure. With the proper funding, our towns and cities will blossom, our infrastructure will be restored, and our communities will thrive. Consider these initiatives:

The Okanagan Valley in B.C.'s southern interior is using its wineries and tourism as a departure point for building a knowledge-based high-tech sector. Saskatoon has developed an innovative community program linking its large First Nations population with jobs and training in an Employer Circles Program. This provides skills and employment for young Aboriginal men and women, as well as training in cultural understanding for business owners and managers. Saskatoon also put in place an exciting program linking social housing to community economic development. Beauce, Quebec, is organizing to turn itself from small, localized production into a new "techno-region." Hamilton is undertaking a Vision 2020 plan. The City of Ottawa held a Smart Growth Summit as part of its planning initiative. Winnipeg embraced principles of sustainable development in its Homegrown Economic Development Strategy for Winnipeg. Dozens of bright ideas are turning into bright futures, where cities are thinking smart.

Watching Mr. Martin work his way through his first months as prime minister was eerily similar to observing his nine years as finance minister. Before assuming the new office, he spent much of 2003 talking about his much-hyped new deal for cities. But the deal became less and less ambitious the longer he was on the job. In his first month, Prime Minister Martin's priorities were a freeze on public spending, ballistic missile defence (BMD) talks with the U.S., and more corporate tax cuts. Indeed, he flatly refused to follow Ontario Premier Dalton McGuinty's lead and cancel corporate tax cuts. The new prime minister proceeded with further corporate tax reductions. Joining the Americans' dangerous BMD (or Star Wars) program could cost Canada $10 billion if we were told to contribute only 1 per cent of the cost (based on a complete cost of $1 trillion, according to the Center for Arms Control and Non-Proliferation).

These were significant choices with large impacts on government finances and our ability to help cities. But the most basic first step toward helping cities—sharing the gas tax—has gone from an inviolable commitment to something that might not have occurred at all. We were told that, instead of sharing the gas tax, municipalities may receive a bigger GST refund. This is good, in fact I proposed it when I represented the FCM in a hearing before the House of Commons finance committee in the spring of 2003, but it was not a panacea. It's actually just a proposal that the federal government not take as much money from cities as the federal government had done since the GST was imposed. No net change happens as a result of the GST per cent change. Still, it was certainly welcome when this this full rebate of the GST to municipalities was made into law as a part of the 2005 budget. It was a change that not even Stephen Harper's Conservatives could reverse. Canada's mayors would have been after his head had he tried, and he knew it.

While returning the GST to cities would be a start, it would not even begin to address the infrastructure crisis, let alone get rid of the infrastructure deficit. For example, in the nine years Mr. Martin was finance minister, the City of Toronto alone paid $500 million in GST. A full refund would have provide only about $49 million a year to Toronto, which meant that the infrastructure deficit would have continued to climb by $1.5 billion a year instead of $2 billion. This would leave the city's transit authority underfunded and would have done little to alleviate the housing crisis. Each Canadian city can tell its own tale of GST woe as its property taxes marched dutifully into the federal treasury. Celebrating a GST refund is akin to thanking a robber when he stops taking the cash he's been stealing from you for years, but not asking that what he's already stolen be returned.

During his two years as prime minister, Mr. Martin suggested transformative change—to quote one of his favourite phrases. Yet transformative change remains exactly what's needed.

A Real Deal for Canadian Communities

After spending years in municipal government, at the Federation of Canadian Municipalities, and now as leader of the New Democratic Party, I know we can do better. I call it a Real Deal for Canadian Communities.

First, municipalities should stop paying any GST. Second, the federal government should share half the federal gas tax as a dedicated transfer for sustainable transport such as public transit, cycling, pedestrian infrastructure, and rural roads. Sustainable transport is key to our economic health and central to fighting smog and climate change.

Ignore the nonsense we've heard from Ottawa that sharing the gas tax is somehow "complicated." It's not. Nothing prevents gas-tax revenue from being transferred immediately. Funds could be forwarded for the first year with a simple letter of transmittal. Here's a draft:

> *To the Premiers:*
> *As promised, this portion of the gas tax is being returned to your provinces and territories for distribution to municipal governments for sustainable transportation improvements. Please forward the funds to the cities and towns ASAP. Next year's installment will be sent after we have worked out a plan together that accomplishes national objectives concerning climate change and transportation while assuring maximum local flexibility.*
>

Yours sincerely,
Government of Canada
>

Immediately after this announcement, the government could then put together a high-level negotiating team to finalize a permanent arrangement with the provinces over the subsequent year. If the prime minister believes in cities, he must have faith in our mayors' ability to ensure that provincial governments extend the funding. I firmly believe that the way to a healthy federalism is to start with a little good faith.

It's not naive to believe that Mayor Sullivan of Vancouver or Mayor Tremblay of Montreal would make their premiers pay a heavy political price if the received federal gas-tax money was not passed on to municipalities. But it is naive to require provinces to match federal funds, since most provinces (unlike the federal government) are facing deficits. In fact, it would be unfair and bad public policy for the federal government to insist on this in these times. Demanding that cash-strapped provinces share the bill for cities is a delaying tactic that allowed Mr. Martin to take credit for trying while having an excuse to blame the provinces for failing. It's also hypocritical, given that Martin refused long-term investment plans when he was fighting deficits federally in the mid-1990s.

Third, a national affordable housing plan is needed in Canada. We know this is a good idea and works in Canada because we've done it before. Some 2.2 million people live in houses built by the housing program that NDP leader David Lewis began with Pierre Trudeau in the 1970s, during a rare period of federal minority government. Martin abolished it in the 1990s and then repeatedly refused to announce a significant new program, despite housing crises in our biggest cities and smallest First Nations communities.

Affordable housing is a real key to fighting child poverty, increasing disposable income, creating jobs, and finding new markets for our beleaguered softwood lumber industry. I propose that Canada launch a national project to reduce homelessness by building two hundred thousand new affordable homes and one hundred thousand renovated houses at reasonable rents over the next ten years. This would cut by half the affordable-housing-deficit number.

Canadians tell me that they want an end to homelessness and that we have a responsibility to provide decent, affordable housing to all. It's time to allow Canadians to mobilize home construction. The details of the plan have already been developed by the FCM. I know, because I was in charge of that project.

Fourth, instead of starving municipalities financially, give them a permanent infrastructure program. Starvation only forces a municipality either to privatize its public services, such as water, or sign deeply flawed public private partnerships (P3s) that actually cost taxpayers more in the long term and are profoundly unaccountable. An infrastructure program would help Canadians repair and upgrade their water and sewage systems, invest in green energy solutions, as well as improve their building infrastructure through energy conservation measures. And the program would create jobs, lots of jobs.

This plan costs money. But corporate tax cuts and weaponizing space cost money as well. I believe creating cities that work are of far more importance to our economy than helping the chartered banks record even larger profits. We should be also building affordable homes to cover our heads instead of building missile shields to cover our skies. Paul Martin was clear that he didn't agree. But, after a decade of his choices, Canadians began to disagree back. I believe that was one of the reasons why the Liberals were unsuccessful in achieving the majority government that Mr. Martin expected and so desperately craved in June 2004. Canadians were fed up with the smog, the traffic, and the housing crisis. That's why they elected a minority government, hoping that it would be prepared to make wiser choices and improve our cities, our economy, the natural environment, and our quality of life.

Revitalizing Local Democracy

There is a final and fundamental piece to this puzzle. We have to unleash our urban democracies from the bonds of archaic decision-making structures imposed long ago, when Canada was a predominatly rural country. We need to enhance local democracy by permitting flexibility and creativity so that communities can put our national financial resources to work to meet their local needs. They can do so while also helping achieve broad national goals—like a cleaner environment, more robust local economies, and greater equality for our citizens. The exciting community events and projects that bring people together and give them a chance to celebrate their collective achievements are often rooted in the processes of their local governments. It's time they were exalted, not demeaned.

Radical democratic reform really begins by engaging and involving people in the local governance of their communities. Stronger local democracies will help infuse the population with greater democratic culture and values. Want to increase voter turnout in elections? Think locally. Involve people directly, and in a meaningful way, through local democracies in their neighbourhoods and communities. This is more easily done when the resources are available to create, build, sustain, and nurture those communities. The healthiest communities are the ones with the greatest amount of local engagement.

Quebec City's stunning system of arrondissements, with community-based budgeting processes and real engagement of citizens, is the best of its class in Canada. Too bad so few in English-speaking Canada know anything about it. Other communities, like Banff, Alberta, have truly exciting plans afoot to achieve community sustainability through local involvement. Instead of fearing citizen involvement, effective local democracies reach out and embrace them, pulling them in to shoulder some of the responsibility and allowing their creativity and community spirit to flow.

There are countless success stories when Canadians focus on the hard but rewarding work of making their communities better places to live, for everyone. The FCM's Sustainable Communities program, accessible through its website at www.fcm.ca, provides a treasure trove of optimistic and successful stories from our municipal grassroots. It's diffficult to find examples of successful federal policies and programs that engage people as directly and positively. So let's turn government on its head and use our federal government to raise the funds that can be funnelled back into dynamic local community efforts.

A new national policy is needed, one that focuses on nurturing our economic and community roots. A spirit of co-operation and collaboration between Ottawa and the provinces has always been important and now is more essential than ever. What's required is a serious commitment to engage local energy and enthusiasm through municipal democracies, through our cities and towns, to achieve the dreams we have for our communities. This is how our sovereignty and our democracy can best be preserved and enhanced. Think nationally, act locally.

[CHAPTER 6]

Building the New Prosperity

It's time to put our hands on the tiller of our economy once again. After more than twenty years of being told first by Conservative and then Liberal governments that we must abandon the ship we call Canada to the winds of the global corporate marketplace, Canadians need to take charge once again. We have done this before with powerful and long-lasting results. Over the years, Canadians have invented fiscal and social infrastructure for our own advancement. The National Dream became a railway that tied a countrywide economy together. The Bank of Canada provided a financial framework for building and rebuilding our country through measured and strategic investment in the public interest. This allowed growth and fiscal prudence to be pursued simultaneously, especially during the reconstruction period following the Second World War. The Canadian Broadcasting Corporation/Radio-Canada was created so that our voices, and subsequently our images, could be transmitted to one another across the land. The CBC has been critically important, allowing Canadians to gain an appreciation of both our unity and our diversity. In the process, the CBC and Radio-Canada laid a foundation for the now vibrant Canadian communications industry. In its original format, the unemployment insurance system provided stable financial assistance for citizens who found themselves out of work. But Canada's public health-care system is perhaps the nation's best example of Canadians taking action on behalf of all, to ensure our individual and collective physical well-being—the foundation of a flourishing economy, society, community.

Engaging in a proactive economic agenda again would mean a considerable shift away from Canadian policies of the past two decades. We have experienced almost a generation of economic policies calling for the reduction of public services, rampant privatization, and the removal of regulations and protections. As we look around, we have begun to see the consequences: homelessness, increased smog and pollution, record student and personal debt, have-not provinces that can't balance their budgets, cities and towns forced to cut basic services, health-care systems unable to cope, and more than one million children in poverty, despite the statistical affluence.

Simple laissez-faire economics does not serve the public good. Individual enterprise is essential, but dynamic economic development requires it to be complemented with national goals and clearly articulated strategies for achieving those goals. We need to create a system within which enterprise can flourish and be sustained so that long-term jobs are created and the country's tremendous talents and possibilities can be harnessed and focused to achieve all their potential. Lately, the very idea of collective public effort has been rejected in favour of unbridled corporatism. The result is a vacuum, rather than the substantive support provided by a nation-building program.

When he was seeking to replace Prime Minister Chrétien, Paul Martin was touted as a miracle worker because of his success as finance minister from 1993 until 2002. He had presided over an economic recovery program while at the same time ridding the nation of chronic deficits. At least, that's how the Liberals were spinning the Martin saga, aided and abetted by his coterie of advisers at Earnscliffe, a powerful Ottawa-based lobby firm.

But is that what really happened during Martin's tenure at the till? First, revenue savings realized from the draconian cuts to health and education funding were subsequently given away in tax cuts that primarily benefited the corporate sector and the highest-income earners. But those cuts were not responsible for eliminating chronic deficits. What worked was the decision by the Bank of Canada, finally responding to pressure that it lower interest rates dramatically over time. While this decision put downward pressure on the Canadian dollar it also unleashed a flow of economic growth that produced nearly $100 billion in surpluses between 1997 to 2003. This economic growth didn't help most working families. Between 1993 and 2002, average weekly earnings grew by 16.8 per cent while the consumer price Index (CPI) rose by 16.9 per cent. Wages had stagnated, and income inequality was growing by leaps and bounds. Corporate pre-tax profits tripled, and the top 20 per cent of Canadians increased their incomes significantly.

Mr. Martin's policies did little for most Canadians and even less for creating a healthy economy. Let's look at some of the key indicators. In the absence of industrial strategies or policies, the productivity gap between Canadian and American industry continued to widen. Wages and salaries increased only slightly, and there was also an increasing discrepancy between high-paid and low-paid work. Canada attracts less foreign investment per capita than the U.S., but most foreign direct investment in our country goes to purchase existing firms, such as the recent purchase of the Hudson's Bay Company by an American company. These acquistions create nothing new in the form of economic activity except to drive up the value of the dollar and increase the lilkelihood of job losses in the export-focused sectors.

What would a nation-building economic policy look like? It would focus on the domestic economy first by creating the conditions for strong local and regional economies across the country. This would mean a shift away from what has become an overly exclusive focus on international trade.

Because successive governments have preached the mantra about the importance of trade, it astonishes most Canadians to learn that trade actually accounts for less than 20 per cent of our total economic output. Canadian policies of the past twenty years were designed to place trade considerations first, but ended up benefiting a relatively small number of Canadian businesses. Four per cent of all exporting firms accounted for 82 per cent of the total value of all merchandise exports. Of course, 20 per cent still represents millions of jobs and is absolutely vital to the economy. And, by incorporating trade into a broad, nation-building strategy, we will help guarantee more value added to our resources before they are traded away, and that would fundamentally strengthen our position in the global economy.

Four out of five businesses in Canada do not sell outside the country. A nation-building policy would pay more attention to the needs of these enterprises, which, after all, tend to create most of the jobs. How do we strengthen the domestic economy? We do it by investing in infrastructure throughout Canada and accepting that cities are vital economic engines. We do it by exploring strategies to create higher-paying jobs—the ones most in danger today. Creating those higher-wage positions drives spending, generates tax revenues, and helps foster a new prosperity.

Such a nation-building concept would create, and then invest in, industrial strategies that target the technologies of the future, especially leading-edge renewable energy and energy conservation sectors. But such a strategy would also create value added for our natural resources. Every time a truckload of raw British Columbia logs crosses the border to Washington State to be turned into two-by-four studs, Canadian jobs go with those logs. It's high time that restrictions were put in place to prohibit raw log exports and keep those jobs here.

Nation building needs minds, well developed and well trained. Education is a fundamental economic and social foundation. That's why investment in our public schools, universities, training centres, and Canadian cultural industries is crucial. Modern economic growth will flow from nurturing good ideas. Indeed, the idea sectors of the economy, such as the arts, have proven themselves to have the highest impact on job creation.

The tight money policies of the Bank of Canada—particularly in the early 1990s—hurt job creation by restricting the building process. Healthy economic growth returned only after the reins were loosened a little. Current low interest rates have helped stimulate our economy. Among the challenges facing the Canadian economy today is the size of the U.S. deficit. The U.S. deficit has shot up alarmingly, exacerbated, in part, by the tax writeoffs and deductions signed off by the Bush administraton that went to the largest American businesses and to the country's wealthiest citizens. But it was made much worse by the money expended to fight the war on terrorism and the war in Iraq. The U.S. deficit has reached historic proportions and shows no sign of receding given the president's dogged commitment to "stay the course." The impact of this high deficit is to devalue the American currency, making the value of the Canadian dollar higher. Because the vast majority of our exports go directly to the United States, this higher Canadian dollar makes our exports more expensive. Consequently, the Americans buy less, putting Canadian manufacturing plants and the employees who work in them at risk. This is a perverse example of how deficit spending and war in one country can cause unemployment and reduced productivity in another.

In 2004, Paul Martin's new minority government was apparently guided by the same principles as the Chrétien Liberal regime, the one where Mr. Martin held the purse

strings for nine years. As we've seen, he was doggedly determined to eliminate the deficit and pay down the national
debt, even at the cost of many important social programs.
The by-products of these policies included higher unemployment, reduced public services, increased poverty and
homelessness, and higher rates of pollution. Going from that
string of dubious successes, as prime minister, he proposed
to establish a national goal—a debt-to-GDP ratio of 25 per
cent. What harm could it do to have such a target?

To understand why it was harmful, I always suggest that
people consider the analogy of owning a house with a mortgage. It's great to be able to pay down a mortgage faster than
the scheduled payment plan. But should that be a family's priority under all circumstances? What if the roof leaked,
Grandma was sick, or a teenager needed money for post-
secondary tuition? I don't know any family member who would
say: "Sorry, we can't afford to do anything about those problems because we're going to use our extra funds this month,
and every month from now on, to pay down the mortgage."

Our country cannot build if we are totally fixated on paying down the national debt. We should use any surpluses to
invest, thereby stimulating the economy and creating jobs,
while at the same time providing essential services like
health care, education, housing, and transportation. Such
new activities strengthen the domestic economy as the wages
and salaries of a more robust workforce are injected into
local community businesses. And when the economy is
strengthened, gross domestic product increases and the
debt-to-GDP ratio falls as a result.

In the 2004 election the NDP asked Canadians to imagine
what a national childcare program could do, arguing that it
could create tens of thousands of jobs and contribute to the
well-being of the workforce of the future. When we had the
opportunity, in the minority government that followed that

election, we insisted that the Liberals implement such a plan. Surely this was more important than accelerating the paying down of our national mortgage. In fact, such an investment in human potential improves our capacity to retire the already shrinking debt. This kind of economic thinking allows the building process to flourish. Although people are a country's constant resource, every new generation must be nurtured afresh. That's why a reliable continuum of funding for child care and education ensures ongoing, stable productivity. Just paying down the debt faster than we have to, when it impoverishes such programs, is short-sighted. We simply can't afford not to invest continuously in the future.

But our critics say: "That's all just tax and spend and we'll eventually end up with another deficit and bigger debt." Not at all.

Having served two decades on Toronto City Council, I learned to live comfortably with balanced budgets. Every time you propose an idea, you have to identify a source of funding. Sometimes you can find money by saving in other programs or by financing through efficiencies. Other times, you have to argue that the policy you are advocating deserves a higher priority than an existing one and hope you can persuade a majority of your colleagues to support you. In the days before federal and provincial government downloading became an annual tradition that mopped up any surpluses, the city council would have some new funds each year at its disposal, as a result of growth in the property tax revenue. As well, council would be prepared to enact a small tax increase to keep up with inflationary costs, for example, or to backfill where downloading had left an unacceptable hole. In my time in municipal government, I learned always to think about the tax dollar as something precious. When you consider the work that someone had to do to create that tax resource, it takes on real meaning. Knowing my constituents in Riverdale and the work they do daily, I think of them flipping burgers, teaching students, making films, working on a factory floor, or running a small business. With a piece of their paycheque being deducted for government's use, I always felt as if I were holding a specific individual's tax dollar in my hand and making choices with it that I should be able to explain and defend when asked. And in local government, you're asked, believe me! It comes up all the time on the street corner, in the coffee shop or pub. That's accountability. It's also one of the reasons I'm always on the lookout for municipal councillors to run for the federal Parliament. They get it. They have held that tax dollar in their hands and made difficult choices as to how best it should be spent. It's a lot like meeting a payroll—a similar sense of responsibility flows from the experience.

When governments run deficits, they are essentially deferring the inevitable. Banks and investors benefit because they will collect the interest. That's why it's always better to pay as you go, rather than chalk up a shortfall. Not that you can always predict these things perfectly. Unusual events such as SARS, mad cow disease, forest fires, and international peacekeeping missions can strike, sometimes all at once, as they did in 2003. Major recessions can suck the economic wind out of all the sails at once. At one time or another, combined blows to communities and the economy have left all provinces struggling to maintain a balanced budget. Most people understand that, in emergencies, you have no choice but to dig deep. But as an operating principle, the annual balancing of current budgets is a very sound one.

The huge surpluses that the government of Canada has posted in the past few years, and that are projected to be collected in future, mean that we can initiate important nation-building projects on many fronts without having to worry about running a deficit. This would also require that governments not give away those surpluses by reducing taxes. Such reductions always reward higher income earners most. While everyone would love a tax cut, most would not call for one if they felt confident that the money would be responsibly used to tackle pressing needs. The notoriety around federal scandals shook what little remaining trust citizens had that the government could be entrusted to spend their hard-earned tax money wisely. That's one of the tragic impacts of the sponsorship debacle.

Balancing budgets while investing in the future also requires that we stop the rush to pay down the debt faster than we need to when we have a range of social, economic, and infrastructure programs requiring urgent and immediate attention. Because the federal debt is shrinking so rapidly as a ratio of the GDP, interest payments are shrinking right along with it. This opens up additional spending room annually without having to incur deficits or raise taxes. According to Canadian Auto Worker economist Jim Stanford, when Paul Martin was minister of finance he allocated between 80 and 90 per cent of all surplus money to tax cuts and debt repayment. With this preoccupation on reducing the debt as quickly as possible, the percentage share of federal money for social policies and programs fell to its lowest level since the end of the Second World War. The point is that it is possible to reinvest in good social programs without increasing overall taxes. Intelligent and well-crafted sustainable strategies for the economy, combined with smart policy levers, would reopen the door for Canadians to build.

While it is not the intention of this book to lay out an industrial strategy for Canada, I would like to give an example of how one could be constructed from my own experience dealing with a large power corporation, Ontario Hydro.

I love those eureka moments when a good idea crystallizes, and on this occasion a light went off, not on. Suddenly, I could see a way to create jobs, reduce costs, improve economic efficiency, and cut smog—all at the same time. The setting was the office building of Canada's largest electricity company. It was over a decade ago, and I was one of a small group of sustainable-energy enthusiasts who had gathered to talk with senior engineers at Ontario Hydro about saving energy.

The venue for the briefing was a boardroom located high up in the Hydro building, facing south toward Lake Ontario on a wonderful, bright, sunny afternoon. The window blinds were closed against the natural light abundantly available outside. White fluorescent fixtures flooded the room. As we began the meeting, it was easy to see by their body language that the engineers and Hydro officials in the room were more than a little skeptical about our ideas for practical, grassroots energy reduction in Ontario. What could we know about the high-technology business of energy production and distribution? Why on earth would they want to reduce electricity consumption? By doing that they would sell less energy and make less money. This was not going to be an easy crowd to convince. Then it hit me.

I got up, turned off the fluorescent lights, and opened the blinds. Sunlight filled the room. I said, "How about that? We're saving energy right now. At the same time we have prevented some coal from being burned to produce electricity, reduced pollution a little, and saved money for Ontario Hydro's ratepayers; that means all of us. Win-win. Imagine if we made it possible for millions of similar modest win-win situations to happen over and over again by retrofitting thousands of buildings with high-efficiency lights, motion detector light switches, more insulation, draft proofing, better control systems and motors, new windows that lost less heat, and more?" Thus was born Toronto's Better Buildings Partnership.

Years later, the Big Blackout of August 2003 across much of eastern North America focused our minds once again on conservation. The blackout demonstrated that the solution to daily energy needs was best met by conservation and self-sufficiency. We were reminded that massive energy production from a small number of plants on a single grid could not guarantee our power supply.

Around the world, people have no shortage of bright ideas that would be good for the environment, good for the economy, and good for people. What we too often lack is the will. What often holds us back is bureaucratic lethargy in government and private-sector organizations alike and, to put it bluntly, short-sighted greed.

It's time to open the blinds.

Energy for a New Prosperity

Everything we do requires energy, from the food we eat, to the electronic equipment we use, to the vehicles we drive, to the products we build, to the buildings we live in. The types of energy we use, the ways in which we transport it (electrical grids, natural gas pipes, gas stations, and so on), and the levels of energy use all contribute to drive our economy. For over a century now we've been largely completely reliant on hydroelectric power and fossil fuel. Since the 1950s, some Canadian provinces have also developed nuclear power. In all the industrialized countries, this type of power production has evolved into a highly centralized system in which multinational corporations wield enormous economic and political influence. Oil-producing regions, particularly in the Middle East, have become powder kegs; and nuclear power plants around the world remain potential targets for terrorists. In short, our current energy system is not only fundamentally undemocratic and environmentally unsustainable, it is a security threat.

The solution to the biggest environmental problem facing our generation is also a way to ensure new prosperity for future generations of Canadians. We now have a unique and historic opportunity to be held hostage no longer to this system and to replace it with a new system of renewable energy resources.

Imagine a Canada where we are the recognized world leader in developing the most innovative and sustainable economy in the world. Imagine a Canada where over three million new person years of jobs have been created to build this new economy. Imagine a healthier Canada that practises conservation and energy efficiency with a growing range of more livable buildings and factories powered by electricity generated without creating the smog that kills thousands prematurely every year. Imagine a Canada where there are no nuclear power stations or coal-fired generating stations.

Impossible, you might say; it would cost too much money and create too many economic hardships for Canadians. The fact is this new prosperity is not only imaginable, the way to make it a reality has already been outlined by some of the most innovative minds in Canada. At a minimum, it wouldn't cost us any more money than we are currently spending. In the longer run, it could even save us substantial funds as health-care, pollution, and climate-change remediation costs decline.

How do we get there? Let me outline key elements of a green energy plan that, if implemented, would usher in a new prosperity for Canada, the likes of which we have never seen. Much of the thinking in the next few pages is reflected in the detailed programs that are part of the NDP Kyoto Plan. Which means many of the ideas that follow are ready to be implemented immediately. All they require is political will. I have drawn on a number of sources, but in particular, the 2002 report for the Suzuki Foundation by Ralph Torrie, one of Canada's foremost energy consultants.

We all live and work in buildings. Bad insulation, leaky doors and windows, old and inefficient furnaces and air conditioners mean many of our buildings use much more energy than they otherwise would. By increasing insulation and installing state-of-the-art windows, doors, furnaces, and air conditioners, building owners can cut energy use, save money, and help create a large amount of economic activity. In order to make this happen, we need a national energy retrofit program for residential, institutional, commercial, and industrial buildings. I know this will work because a smaller version of it has already proven to be a big success. In Chapter 2, I described the highly successful Better Buildings Partnership (BBP) in the City of Toronto. To date, the BBP has retrofitted 39 million square feet of space in 433 buildings, creating 3,850 person years of employment, with a local economic impact of $132 million. At the same time, the owners of those buildings (private and public) reduced their annual operating costs by $16 million and cut carbon dioxide emissions by 172,000 tonnes a year.

In June 2002, I asked one of the foremost energy retrofit entrepreneurs in Canada to outline the details of a national program for the industrial, commercial, and institutional (ICI) sector.

Here are the details:
- **Number of square feet covered by program: 631 million**
- **Average reduction in greenhouse gas (GHG) emissions: 20 per cent**
- **Average annual energy savings from retrofits: $7 billion**

- Average payback period for retrofit investment: 6 years
- Direct employment from program: 839,000 person years
- Indirect employment from program: 2,097,300 person years
- Overall investment in retrofit program: $41 billion
- Estimated tax revenues to provincial and federal governments from program: $4.1 billion

This is a fairly conservative plan, based on data collected in the late 1990s. The plan does envisage taking full advantage of all the existing technology and savings. So the real numbers are probably better. But even so, a conservatively calculated national retrofit program for just the ICI sector would create just under 300,000 permanent jobs for ten years running, put over $7 billion per year in the pockets of building owners after six years of no price increases, reduce GHG emissions by 20 per cent, and generate $4 billion of tax revenue. And all of this could be financed through a revolving loan fund, just like we did in Toronto.

Once we begin bringing the residential sector into the picture, we get even more exciting results, because there are around fourteen million households in Canada that can be retrofitted. But a residential retrofit program does much more than create new jobs and reduce our energy costs. It also improves the livability of our homes with state-of-the-art, energy-efficient windows and high-efficiency furnaces. Winter drafts that plague many of our homes disappear.

We also need to make sure all new buildings meet the highest energy-efficiency building code standards. As I outlined in Chapter 2, energy-efficient buildings can be cost competitive. As Greg Allen, one of the most innovative engineer/architects in Canada, has often said, building state-of-the-art, energy-efficient buildings won't raise construction costs. It's time that energy efficiency standards become the law for new building construction. This won't cost a penny more to build and will save everyone money in the long run.

Next, we need to make sure that all the machines, appliances, electronics, and motors in Canadian buildings are energy-efficient. Right now, when consumers go to buy appliances and electronics, only a handful of models have an Energy Star rating (which means models meet or surpass existing energy-efficiency standards). It's time all appliances, electronics, machines, and motors meet efficiency standards.

And why not have these electronics and appliances built here in Canada? Canada used to have a much larger appliance manufacturing industry, which was decimated when we entered into the free trade agreement with the U.S. I believe it's time the federal government shifted the tax structure and created a policy framework to assist appliance manufacturers to build energy-efficient products in Canada. Think about the number of new jobs that would be created.

We need to think innovatively in all sectors. While I was a city councillor, I learned firsthand about some innovative ways to reduce traffic congestion on the busiest highway in Canada—the infamous 401. One is to increase rail freight transportation in a way that helps trucking companies, is safer, preserves highways, and reduces smog. It could be accomplished by puttling the semi-trailers directly onto the flatbed cars and moving the truck trailers on a train track instead of a highway. These systems are already in place elsewhere and they do work. But they tend to be at a competitive disadvantage because governments subsidize highway construction, which, in turn brings down the cost of trucks using highways.

While highways should remain public, continuously building more public highways is not the answer. As anyone who has tried to travel in downtown Vancouver or southern

Ontario knows firsthand, traffic congestion is getting worse. It makes little sense to focus heavy spending on highway expansion for goods movement, except where that is the only practical option, where bottlenecks are problems, such as at key border crossings, or where safety considerations drive the agenda, such as twinning the Trans-Canada. Rather, let's invest in innovative freight transportation systems. Fewer trucks on the road means less congestion and greater safety for other vehicle users, less pollution, and cost savings for businesses of all sizes, including, of course, the agricultural sector. It's time the federal government reinvested in rail freight transportation. It's win-win-win.

Another element of a green energy strategy is improving the energy efficiency of the industrial sector. Like building owners, many industries could save substantially by switching to more energy-efficient equipment. The federal government should set robust targets for each energy subsector and provide companies with incentives, which could be paid back over time from realized energy savings.

Another industrial strategy focuses on industries that burn fossil fuels as part of their production process. This often creates large amounts of so-called waste heat. Most companies just dump this waste heat into the atmosphere or a nearby body of water. They don't realize that waste heat can actually make them money and help Canada reduce greenhouse gas emissions. How? By using it to turn turbines that create electricity. Called "cogeneration," this method turns industries into small-scale power producers. So instead of building more large fossil fuel electrical power generating stations, the federal government could provide incentives for industrial companies to become small-scale electrical generators. When I helped lead "energy tours" of Scandinavia over the years, municipal leaders who joined me to see district energy in action marvelled at the efficiency and the economic development that flows from these integrated energy strategies. We also saw how countries like Denmark and Germany fostered remarkable export industries in insulated-pipe and cogeneration technologies, just as they did in the wind turbine sector.

Just as the cold water in Lake Ontario can be harnessed to provide green power, the wind across Canada can be harnessed. This would not only bring significant environmental benefits, it would create a significant number of jobs as well as sustainable economic activity. The Canadian Wind Energy Association (CanWEA) has calculated that there is enough wind in Canada to supply 20 per cent of our electricity needs (about 36,000 megawatts). That's enough to power almost all of the 14 million typical households in Canada. Currently, Canadian wind turbines generate enough electricity to power 126,000 typical households. CanWEA has challenged Canadians to achieve what they call the ten-by-ten goal: install 10,000 megawatts of wind power by 2010. This would supply almost four million households with green power, contribute 5 per cent of all our electricity needs, create between 80,000 and 160,000 permanent jobs by 2010, and generate between $10 and $20 billion worth of economic activity. And it would reduce greenhouse gas emissions by 15 to 25 million tonnes per year. Currently, we must rely on foreign companies to supply most of the components for building wind turbines. I think it's time Canadian workers started building these turbines in Canadian factories, not only to supply the Canadian market but to export to the rest of North America.

I want to be absolutely clear: this plan doesn't cost Canadian taxpayers one more penny. The beauty of sustainable energy is that it can be entirely funded by reallocating existing federal government and consumer spending to new priorities. Let me illustrate:

It may come as a surprise to most people that the federal government subsidizes the fossil fuel and nuclear industries to the tune of about $1.4 billion a year. These subsidies might have made sense before we knew about the environmental threats posed by climate change and nuclear waste; before we knew of the tens of billions of dollars in economic and health-care costs associated with smog-related illnesses and deaths; and before the security concerns resulting from the tragic events of September 11, 2001. But the world has changed. It's time to re-examine how government tax dollars are spent. I propose fully phasing in, over four years, a tax-shifting regime to transform incentives, subsidies, and investment programs from supporting energy sources that contribute to climate change or produce toxic residue, to those that focus on green energy sources, including wind, solar, and tidal power, as well as on transitional technologies.

Doing this would obviously have ramifications for the national economy as well as regional economies. That's why implementation of this plan must be fully sensitive to, and include, negotiated adjustments for regional economic impacts, maturity of sectors, and establishment of compensating strategies. Let's also make sure that we use the federal revenues from such a tax-shifting plan to ensure the most negatively affected regions are the first places where new green energy jobs are created.

An even bigger source of funding for the green energy strategy would come from revenues generated by a new market mechanism that has emerged as a crucial policy tool for countries interested in fighting climate change: a domestic emissions trading (DET) system. Essentially, emissions trading is a way for companies to trade permits that give them the right to release greenhouse gas emissions (one permit typically allows a company to release one tonne of carbon dioxide or an equivalent greenhouse gas). For example, let's say Company A releases thirty tonnes of GHG emissions every year making widgets. Under an emissions trading system, the company must have thirty permits, one for each tonne it releases. But let's assume the company decides to invest in energy efficiency measures that reduce the actual emissions to twenty-five tonnes. The company can now sell its extra five permits at an agreed-upon price to another company that needs them. Meanwhile, Company B thought it needed only twenty permits but because of higher demand for its products needs an additional five, so it decides to purchase the five permits from Company A.

Emissions trading systems can involve trades among companies in one country as well as among companies on opposite ends of the planet. While all emissions trading systems rest on the principle that allows a company to make investment decisions in either energy efficiency or GHG permits based on market conditions, not all systems achieve the same positive environmental results. To date, the federal government is advocating a system that will effectively give away 85 per cent of the allowable permits that companies want. And there will be no cap on the number of available permits. This system has the potential of actually undermining the goal of reducing emissions. Giving away most of the permits means there is almost no financial incentive for companies to reduce their emissions. And without a cap on the number of permits issued, it is difficult to understand how actual emissions will be reduced.

That's why I'm proposing what is called a "cap and trade" system, based on the auctioning of permits. Under this system, there is an absolute cap on the number of permits available to companies. Over time, the cap is reduced, resulting in a steady decline in emissions from all companies. Unlike the proposed federal government system, under cap and trade, companies emitting carbon dioxide must purchase their permits from an auction held by the federal government. The proceeds of this auction are collected by the government.

Interestingly, in spring 2002, the government released a report called "A Discussion Paper on Canada's Contribution to Addressing Climate Change." The report offered four possible options for meeting the Kyoto commitment, and noted that an emissions trading system that auctioned all the permits would be the most economically beneficial option for Canada According to the report, auctioning permits would raise about $4.5 billion annually, which could then be reinvested in the economy! As the report indicated, electricity prices would rise by 6 per cent, and the price of gasoline and natural gas would go up by about 2 per cent, which is much less than the average weekly fluctuation at the pumps. But the report does not say that overall energy costs to consumers would likely fall, as well, because we would be using less energy. Overall, the report concludes that the most economically beneficial way for Canada to meet its Kyoto commitments is by implementing an emissions trading system where permits are auctioned. But, sadly, the Liberal government decided not to pursue this option. It's hard to understand, except that the carbon cabal of combustion multinationals has blocked such a move politically every step of the way. This, even though a trading permit system was proven to work two decades ago, when Canadian campaigners successfully convinced Canada and the U.S. to implement emissions trading for sulphur-dioxide emissions as a way to combat acid rain. Fortunately, the Doer government of Manitoba is developing a carbon emissions trading system, hoping to be ready when good sense befalls Canadian and American policy-makers. The Manitoba leadership is currently provided by the minister responsible, the fervent Tim Sale.

Canada also needs an integrated energy grid to connect the sources of the most efficient, clean, and green power to the places where power needs are greatest. The winds of

Alberta, Saskatchewan, and Manitoba must be able to deliver power to southern Ontario, not only for sustainability but also for security. During the summer 2003 blackout, most Canadians noticed the bizarre news accounts of a darkened Parliament Hill illuminated by the bright lights of the city of Gatineau (formerly Hull) just across the river. Cars were crossing the Ottawa River that evening, but not electricity. This is absurd. A pan-Canadian energy grid would be a project for our economy today, a modern national dream akin to the great railway construction projects of the past centuries. It would be best accomplished as a partnership, the federal government working with the network of public energy companies in the provinces and cities. Indeed, the provincial ministers of energy proposed the creation of such a grid to the federal Liberal government in the mid-1990s. The idea went nowhere. It would be hard to find a more important element in an industrial strategy for Canada than a public green power grid. Quebeckers know this well. That's why, under the leadership of a young René Lévesque, then Liberal energy minister, Hydro-Québec was created by nationalizing private energy companies. In this bold move, a product of the Quiet Revolution, Quebec was duplicating one made in Ontario two generations before, when Sir Adam Beck created Ontario Hydro, under a Conservative administration. A move by the Mike Harris Conservatives to privatize Hydro One (part of their reorganization of Ontario Hydro) was rejected soundly by voters after a brilliant campaign by the unions, environmentalists, consumer groups, and the Ontario NDP led by Howard Hampton. The defeat of this privatization plan paves the way for the trans-Canada power grid as the next great sustainable industrial development project.

To recap: by phasing in a tax-shifting regime and by auctioning permits, the federal government would have $5.5

billion each year available to finance the green energy plan outlined above. Over ten years, this would mean investing $55 billion in green economic activity that would:

- potentially create more than 3 million new person years of work—that's 300,000 new jobs for 10 years straight;
- develop a brand-new green power industry with possible sales of over $20 billion;
- dramatically cut Canada's greenhouse gas emissions and put us on the path to cutting emissions by 50 per cent by 2030;
- reduce smog emissions, which currently cost Canadians billions of dollars a year in health-care costs and lost economic productivity;
- reduce overall energy costs for all Canadians, including businesses, by providing incentives and programs to invest in energy efficiency;
- not require any tax increases.

As we saw in the debate around Kyoto, the fossil fuel industry will undoubtedly claim that such a plan would bring economic ruin to Canada. As many studies show, the fossil fuel industry is wrong. For example, the Canadian Wind Energy Association estimates that every $1 million invested in wind turbines creates eight permanent jobs. Contrast that projection with international estimates that $1 million invested in oil exploration creates only 1.5 jobs. With the help of a just transition strategy for workers and communities, as outlined in Chapter 2, the federal government could ensure a smooth transition to sustainable jobs. And the federal government can target the establishment of new green power industries and activities in provinces that currently rely heavily on the fossil fuel industry.

An Industrial Strategy for Green Cars

Canadians have always been at their best when they provoke their governments to pursue bold and strategic plans to build for the future: building a national railway, creating public energy companies like Ontario Hydro and Hydro-Québec, or even massive social projects like public medicare. In the early twenty-first century, our plans should focus on key economic sectors and be rooted in the concept of sustainability. Let's take our massive automobile manufacturing sector as a starting point.

With some 150,000 Canadians directly employed assembling vehicles and making parts for them, the automobile manufacturing sector is essential to our economy. Its extensive use of robotics and computerization also makes the auto sector one of the most high-tech industries in the country.

And for every auto assembly or in-house parts production job in Canada, there are approximately 6.5 more related jobs in manufacturing, transportation, and the after-market service industry. Canadian auto workers alone pay over $2 billion in personal income taxes, and the GST and PST on automobile sales generate $7 billion in government revenue. The steel and rubber industries, in particular, are highly dependent on the vitality of the auto industry. On top of that, the auto industry is an important source of export earnings for Canada in the global economy.

So, as much as I'm interested in reducing the negative impacts of our "car culture," we need to do so in ways that continue to assure employment and economic growth in Canada. Having a healthy automotive industry is crucial to our economy; making it healthier for the environment is crucial to our well-being. That's why I was delighted when Buzz Hargrove, president of the Canadian Auto Workers (CAW) union, Peter Tabuns, then executive director of Greenpeace and later a member of my staff, and Joe Comartin, MP from Windsor–Tecumseh and our caucus lead on sustainability, met with me in the summer of 2003 to announce our joint commitment to a new green car industrial strategy. It's a concept and strategy that protects both jobs and the environment.

At our news conference unveiling this proposal, Buzz Hargrove said, "If you think about the future of the industry, any automotive policy, any automotive strategy, must include vehicles that are going to be environmentally friendly. We believe that is going to be the wave of the future."

How different a view that is from the auto manufacturers themselves, who are looking to earn greater profits by selling larger vehicles that consume more fuel. Too often, the latest vehicles off the assembly line are bigger, heavier vehicles with even larger engines—gas guzzlers. And despite Canada's commitments under the Kyoto Protocol, Ottawa hasn't done anything substantive to insist on improved fuel efficiency and lower sulphur levels from the manufacturers, or to make it easier for consumers to buy alternative-fuel vehicles that reduce greenhouse gas emissions.

The green car industrial strategy we have proposed is based on the idea that the national government should shape our economic development with proactive strategies. We should jump in with both feet to create jobs, improve the environment, and allow the auto industry and other businesses to make money responsibly. Of course, this is directly contrary to the let-the-market rule philosophy of the Liberals and the Conservatives. We need to challenge the view that we should sit back and let industrialists decide our future— with no guidance, incentive, or requirements from society as a whole. If that had been the philosophy years ago, we would never have developed the national railway system, the national health-care program, the St. Lawrence Seaway, and much more. So what sort of proactive industrial strategy would be best for the auto sector? After all, Canada wouldn't have an auto industry today were it not for similar efforts in the past—like the Auto Pact, which required companies to invest here in return for granting tariff-free access to our market. How can we use similar far-sighted policies to stimulate made-in-Canada investment and employment in crucial high-tech industries like auto manufacturing?

It's frustrating for conscientous consumers who want to do the right thing to discover that it will cost them more to purchase a vehicle that produces less pollution. That higher price means they also pay more in the GST and the PST to governments, further punishment for trying to do the right thing. And then they factor in that their purchase hasn't likely created jobs in Canada because the vast majority of hybrids and other advanced vehicles sold here are produced elsewhere.

Back in the mid-1970s, after the first oil crisis, my dad and brother Rob, both engineers with an outside-the-box approach to innovation, worked with another specialist to develop what is now referred to as a hybrid car. Years ahead of its time, this one, just like today's hybrids, used both a gasoline and an electric engine; the electric engine helped conserve gas and reduce emissions. It was energy efficient and sophisticated. They never went into production with it because there was no Canadian strategy at that time to encourage innovation that benefited the environment. And the big-three auto companies certainly had no interest in developing the concept car into mass production. Today, the crisis of global climate change has created a new awakening, or at least a possibility of one.

Why shouldn't Canada be the epicentre of advanced-technology auto manufacturing in the Americas? This could help revitalize our auto sector and restore a sense of confidence in our capabilities to create work and clean the environment at the same time.

The federal government should insist that by 2010, auto manufacturers in this country develop and build vehicles with at least a 25 per cent improvement in the average fuel efficiency compared with today's new vehicles. (Automakers in Japan and Europe have already agreed to similar goals.) But Canada should find partners. Our government could work with American and Mexican authorities to develop a North American approacch. Massachusetts and New York have already begun to move in this regulatory direction. California's rules have helped create markets for low or zero emissions (LEV/ZEV vehicles). If Canada joined forces with those states, we would create a market of more than eighty million people for environmentally advanced vehicles—a force that could reshape the entire North American auto sector.

Canada should encourage consumers to buy new, cleaner cars. Combined with regulations that would make a greater number of cleaner cars available (and thus less expensive), incentives would let consumers pay less for fuel-efficient vehicles. The NDP, CAW, and Greenpeace are suggesting that the federal government offer Canadian buyers a GST rebate of between $2,500 and $5,000, depending on the technology used, when they purchase an alternative-fuel vehicle (AFV). AFVs include vehicles that run on compressed natural gas, hybrid power systems, ethanol blends, or hydrogen fuel cells. If provincial governments offered similar sales tax rebates on these types of vehicles, production would really take off. Of course, smog would be reduced, with all the attendant health benefits and cost savings.

To make more of these alternative-fuel vehicles available, Ottawa should enact a market-share schedule that would grow over time, steadily increasing the proportion of AFVs in the total new-car market, beginning with 5 per cent in 2010.

Ottawa should use its own purchasing power to set an example and expand the market. Every year, the federal government spends about $80 million to buy roughly three thousand new vehicles, only three per cent of which are currently AFVs. Imagine if we set as our goal for 2010 that, if appropriate models were available, all federal light-duty vehicle purchases would be AFVs. The federal government should establish an AFV procurement purchasing agency, and work with provincial, territorial, and municipal governments—and the broader public sector—to demonstrate its commitment to this goal. If we pooled purchasing decisions and telegraphed well in advance the new performance directions we wanted, it would send a strong signal to industry, and that would help ensure that we could meet, and even exceed, our Kyoto targets. We have it in our power to move the industry toward the manufacture of cleaner cars, and assure automakers of a market for AFVs during a period when people would become more familiar and comfortable with these new technologies. This is how we could make the new prosperity a reality.

The Catalytic Approach to Transforming Markets Works

I was vice chair for many years of the publicly owned energy company Toronto Hydro. During that time we introduced ethanol-based fuels into the mix for a significant part of our vehicle fleet. The results exceeded all the projections. And the public liked knowing that their hydro trucks were powered, in part, by soybeans! The move also helped this type of fuel take hold, encouraging markets to grow, which stimulated production. Now, we see governments beginning to require small proportions of these biofuels to be included in products sold to the public.

Think about it: our powerful auto sector grew dramatically during a time when we had a proactive national auto strategy—the Auto Pact, negotiated in 1965. What a terrific example of Canadian bargaining savvy and strategic intervention in the marketplace. Thousands of working families and whole communities benefited because our nation was proactive.

The Auto Pact was killed in 2001 by a ruling of the unelected and unaccountable World Trade Organization. Since then, the federal government has abdicated any role it had in a national strategy for one of the most important sectors of the economy. These days, the bottom-line corporate interests of the auto manufacturers determine whether they will keep investing in Canada. If they decide they can make more profit elsewhere, they leave. In the past few years, more than seven thousand Canadian auto assembly jobs have disappeared—most of them to northern Mexico and the southern United States. Now, these same multinationals are starting to shift production to China and India, where even lower wages and virtually no benefits like pensions for workers are in place.

Once again, we need a made-in-Canada strategy for the application of new technologies in the auto sector. Despite the expertise and ingenuity of our own scientists, and the demonstrated technical capacity of Canadians in these areas, virtually none of the manufacturing and production of these new systems takes place here. This poses a great risk to the Canadian industry, especially at a time when we need to be shifting gears.

Existing federal policies could be expanded so that government participation can stimulate investment and production in new high-tech sectors. For example, the Technology Partnerships Canada program could be extended to include strategic investments in the development and production of AFVs, and the existing Research and Development Tax Credit could also be expanded to encourage innovation in this area. We should make sure that Canada's auto industry—and the men and women who make the vehicles—benefit from the development and production of new technology.

Assuring Our Economic Independence

Building a sustainable economy, expanding community economic development, and assuring people an adequate income through living wages, unemployment insurance, and public pensions—all these depend on having the tools we require as a country to maintain our economic independence. Canadians wouldn't willingly give away our democratic rights and we shouldn't willingly give away our economic rights, either. The extent of corporate takeovers in Canada, and the provisions we've signed in international trade agreements, do just that.

In *The Vanishing Country*, Mel Hurtig quotes Alberta's former premier Peter Lougheed, a Conservative free trade advocate, who said in 1999, "I know people will fall from their chairs to hear me say this, but maybe right now we need to return to the Foreign Investment Review Agency. We need to be more interventionist. The passive approach isn't working. If [the present trend] continues, we are going to look at our country in about three years and say: What have we got left?"

The three years are up, and the rate of takeovers has only increased. Mr. Hurtig points out that "in 2000 there was a new record of 509 Canadian firms taken over by foreign non-residents. The value of these takeovers, according to [Industry Canada's] Investment Review Division, was a startling $81.8 billion. The previous record, set the year before, was $18.1 billion."

And, as Mr. Hurtig says, "No one has any idea as to how much of the takeover of Canada is being financed with our own money." That's because former Liberal industry minister John Manley approved the elimination of many of the requirements that foreign corporations once had to report on their financial activities in Canada.

Corporate takeovers export profits as well as well-paying executive jobs from Canada. They also remove key decision-making, research and development, and strategic thinking from Canadian industry. Takeovers make jobs in Canada dependent on doing what's best for American shareholders, and that isn't always going to be in our national interest.

Canadians have a right to know when investment is or isn't in our country's interest. We should also have the right to retaliate when the country's national interest is harmed by the actions of any corporation, including a foreign-owned one. In the early 1980s, I studied efforts by the Canadian government, through the Foreign Investment Review Agency, to screen the takeovers that were threatening Canadian economic independence at that time. My research found that the review agency had relatively little impact, with the exception of protecting some cultural sectors from accelerating foreign takeover. I also showed that if present trends continued, Canada would experience continuing deindustrialization and high unemployment levels. Actually, I hate it when predictions like this come true. But that's exactly what happened. Data from the 1990s reveal overall continued high unemployment levels relative to the United States and financial hardships for too many families. I also predicted that lack of concrete action "will strip Canada's political independence beyond the point where Canadians can have any say whatsoever over the direction of their own affairs." We have now seen early signs of that prediction coming to pass, with trade deals overriding our ability to make democratic decisions such as controlling which toxic substances can be sold in our country.

Of course, our concern over the takeover of Canadian industry is only one, albeit an important and vital piece of the economic sovereignty puzzle. The larger context is the international trade agreements we've already entered into, and any future trade deals.

Canada's Free Trade Agreement (FTA) with the United States came into effect in 1989, and the North American Free Trade Agreement (NAFTA), which includes Mexico, in 1994. We are also party to the World Trade Organization (WTO), which was formed in 1995, replacing the General Agreement on Tariffs and Trade (GATT). The unelected and unaccountable WTO is the only international body dealing with the rules of trade among nations. The negotiations that led to the creation of the WTO are conveniently recorded on 22,000 pages in volumes weighing 385 pounds—a formidable obstacle to anyone who would seek to question the organization. Successive Canadian governments have also tried to negotiate other major international agreements like these—more initials in the alphabet soup of trade deals.

Despite the "free trade" guarantees of these deals, the United States has felt free to impose tariffs on the import of softwood lumber, Canadian wheat, and other products. Such American import duties have seriously affected these industries and caused thousands of layoffs of Canadian workers.

Under the provisions of these treaties, the Canadian government has willingly signed away some of our rights, and we stand poised to give away more. Trade is obviously important to our economy, but not at the expense of trading off our rights to determine our economic and environmental future. Others have written extensively on the various effects of the trade deals that we have embarked on. Let's consider how our right to control the use of our water resources may be affected.

NAFTA defines water as a commercial "good." It defines water's delivery to people as a "service," and a corporation's involvement as an "investment." This includes the water that flows from your tap. Goods, services, and investments are all subject to NAFTA restrictions. NAFTA says that no country can favour its own private sector over a corporation in another NAFTA country when it comes to the commercial use of water resources. As Maude Barlow explains, "If a Canadian company, for instance, gained the right to export Canadian water, American transnationals would have the right to help themselves to as much Canadian water as they wished."

NAFTA's infamous Chapter 11 gives a foreign corporation the right to sue the government of a NAFTA country when the corporation feels that a government has "expropriated" the corporation's future profit by denying it the opportunity to make money from providing a good or service, or engaging in an investment, where a Canadian firm, or even a Canadian government, provides it on a non-profit basis. An important distinction: domestic companies don't have this right—just foreign companies. And it's happened. In 1991, the NDP government of British Columbia thankfully and wisely banned the export of bulk water. In 1998, Sun Belt Water Inc. of Santa Barbara, California, sued the Canadian government for U.S. $10 billion because the company lost a contract to export water. This is just one example, and the outcome is still pending. At a minimum, however, it is costing B.C. taxpayers many thousands of dollars in legal fees, just to protect our right to pass our own laws.

When it comes to controlling our energy, the FTA and NAFTA also tie our hands. For example, if Canada should conclude that we are running out of oil or natural gas, we certainly couldn't turn off the tap to the United States. Under the terms of the FTA, we would still have to continue selling a proportionate share of our resources to the U.S, and we don't have the right to charge higher prices for this non-renewable resource in the U.S. than we charge at home.

About 90 per cent of the trade in energy between our two countries flows in ony one direction: south. Over half of all the primary energy now produced in Canada goes to U.S. customers. We are America's largest supplier. Alberta has agreed to new coal-fired power plants that will export electricity to the U.S.—pollution here, power there. Nova Scotia is exporting its offshore, clean-burning natural gas to the U.S. but has to import American and other foreign coal to burn for its own electricity. We pollute; they get cleaner energy. Canadians have every right to wonder what our governments are doing when they agree to trade deals like these.

During the 1993 election campaign following the signing of NAFTA, Liberal leader Jean Chrétien promised electors that he would renegotiate the treaty before it came into effect. Once he became prime minister, that never happened. But if we are to regain our sovereignty over the environment and have more control over our economy, the renegotiation of trade deals will simply have to be done. How? By supporting the world's new superpower.

Since the collapse of the Soviet Union, people are fond of saying that there remains only one world superpower—the United States. Well, that's not quite right. There's another superpower emerging. We can call it the power of the world's peoples. Awakening slowly, coalescing in new ways, as in the antiglobalization movement, it's another energy source we need to tap into more fully. It's a movement dedicated to building international solidarity while respecting the rights of independent nations to chart their own future.

The trade deals of the WTO are squarely in the sights of this newborn superpower. How is Canada to participate in this exciting process? Shall we oppose the growth of a movement for fair trade, human rights, peace, and the environment? Will we be a junior partner in the sale of our own destiny? For me, the choice is quite clear and very important. We should work with new social democratic governments in the Americas and with labour, environmental, and development organizations to create democratic trade agreements based on the principles of fair trade. These new treaties must ensure that environmental, social, and labour rights take precedence over the trade in goods and services. Canada's goal must be to promote fair trade deals that go hand-in-hand with sustainable environment and strengthening our economy. As Ed Broadbent said recently, "As we did years ago with democratic states, it's time to ensure that human rights have the same global reach as the rights of property. Until this happens, there can be no global democracy."

Insuring Your Employment

Sometimes good ideas wilt. Years ago, Canadians developed an idea that was working well—an insurance program to help you out if you lost your job. That's why we called it Unemployment Insurance (UI). Working people and their employers paid for the plan, and the program worked well for a number of years, giving workers somewhere to turn in times of need. That good idea isn't working anymore.

A few years ago I was having a meal in a Toronto hotel restaurant and started talking with the server, a cheerful, middle-aged Filipino man.

"How's it going?" I asked him.

"Not bad," he said.

"But with rents as they are, going up all the time, it's got to be tough," I prompted.

"Oh, not really," he said, really quite pleased with the explanation he was about to offer. "My forty hours a week here pays for the entire rent for me and my family, and my other job covers most of the other costs!"

He was proud that he was providing for his family, and you can't blame him, but it turned out that he was working seventy-six hours a week!

Is this the prospect that we offer our working families? Is this the promise we hold out to immigrants to Canada? Holding down two full-time jobs, just to make ends meet? He hadn't had a significant raise in years. The hotel always said they couldn't afford it. For too many Canadians, this is the new reality.

Very shortly after we'd had this conversation, the ownership sold the hotel to the University of Toronto for use as a student residence. More than two hundred employees were laid off, including that hard-working waiter. To make matters worse, in the aftermath of SARS and the downturn in Toronto's hospitality sector, there was little prospect of jobs elsewhere in the industry. With as many as thirty thousand working people laid off in the hotel, restaurant, and entertainment business, it was tough competing for the few employment opportunities that did exist. And, to add insult to injury, many laid-off waiters and hotel workers were not able to collect what the Liberals had renamed Employment Insurance (EI).

When the Liberal government came into office in 1993, about 74 per cent of Canadians who paid into UI were eligible to receive benefits when they applied. When the Liberals had finished changing UI to EI and toughening the rules for eligibility, more than 60 per cent of Canadians who applied for benefits under the revised system failed to qualify. Even when they did qualify, benefits were reduced, as well as the length of time they could receive them. The number of unemployed Canadians who had paid into the EI plan but who were not eligible to receive benefits topped eight hundred thousand.

Because of the regulations and the nature of employment in sectors dominated by women—especially those sectors with more part-time work—women are particularly discriminated against in qualifying for EI. Only about one-third of unemployed women receive EI benefits. What good is an insurance plan that you are compelled to pay into but that refuses benefits to almost two-thirds of those who need them?

As finance minister, Paul Martin led the dismantling of Canada's unemployment insurance system and hijacked the EI fund to eliminate the deficit. The EI fund is generated by contributions from workers and employers. The government doesn't pay a dime. By cutting off a great number of unemployed workers and sharply reducing the benefits to those who were eligible, the Liberal government built up a surplus in the EI account that, by the time they left office, had surpassed $45 billion. This represents the cumulative difference between the money Ottawa has collected from workers and their employers and what they've paid out in benefits to the unemployed during the Liberals' twelve years in office. Roughly speaking, Ottawa was collecting about $19 billion a year in premiums but paid out only $10 to $11 billion in benefits. Finance Minister Martin built his budget surplus and eliminated the deficit, in large part, on the backs of unemployed Canadians.

NDP MP Yvon Godin has spent a great deal of time studying unemployment insurance since he was elected in New Brunswick in 1997. In 2003, he introduced a comprehensive bill to bring justice to unemployed workers under the EI system. His bill would have eliminated the two-week waiting period, reduced the hours needed to qualify for EI, and increased the benefits paid to workers who lose their jobs. It would also have created a trust account where all EI funds would go, so the government of the day could not use the money to pay down the debt, as the Liberals did. Yvon's bill was defeated by the Liberals and the Alliance (led by Stephen Harper).

Increasing numbers of Canadians today are self-employed. They are running small businesses, taking risks, and creating jobs. Yet, although they are required to pay into the EI plan on behalf of their workers, they cannot pay into the plan for themselves. So, naturally they aren't eligible to collect benefits if their business fails. And once more, women are discriminated against. That's because those who run their own businesses, unlike their female employees, aren't eligible for paid maternity leave should they decide to have a baby or adopt a child. What in the world would prevent Canada from creating a program to provide insurance for self-employed women, which they would pay into, in order that they too can take some time out and raise a child and collect maternity leave benefits while doing so?

Training should be another crucial element of an unemployment insurance program, especially in an era when new technologies are rapidly being introduced into our workplaces. Workers ought to be eligible for an EI training benefit by taking compensated education or training leave, with a right to return to their jobs. Across the country (but unfortunately primarily only in cities), community organizations and numerous schools offer English-as-a-second-language (ESL) courses; community colleges run training, retraining, and apprenticeship programs; private companies provide various technical learning programmes. In some cases, costs for these programs are covered by EI, but many are not.

Ten years ago, people were concerned that the fragmentation of Canada's approach to training would put us at a competitive disadvantage in the new economy. The Liberals in power, with Paul Martin leading the charge, responded by taking the government of Canada out of the training business—and turning a problem into a crisis.

Minority governments can correct the unfairness of the Employment Insurance system. One of the first acts of the 2004 Parliament was the adoption of a set of motions put forward by the three Opposition party leaders as an amendment to the Speech from the Throne. One of those motions called for a reform of the Employment Insurance system.

Yvon Godin once again took the lead and worked tirelessly with labour groups and social justice advocates on three fronts. He worked through a parliamentary committee to build political support for the changes he'd been advocating. He again introduced legislation to improve the system. And, in June 2005, he introduced a motion in the House of Commons aimed at changing the EI system to help the unemployed in areas of Canada with high levels of unemployment. Unfortunately, both the Harper Conservatives and the Martin Liberals ensured this motion was defeated. In spite of the rhetoric from both Martin and Harper, when it came to actually helping unemployed Canadians, only the NDP was willing to act.

Sharing Pensions in the New Prosperity

In Canada, one of the wealthiest nations in the world, about half the single elderly women live in poverty. Search as I might, I can find no excuse for it. And it's not as if single, older men fare much better—about a third of them are poor, too. Their labour made us rich and, by way of thank you, we cast them aside. That's nothing to be proud of.

Our public pension system was supposed to ensure that all elderly people have enough resources to live in dignity, regardless of their income during their working years. It was also designed to assure people that their living standard would not decline significantly at retirement. These guarantees have expired.

Public pensions in Canada take several forms. We have the Canada and Quebec Pension Plans (CPP and QPP), which are income-related and paid to all former workers. Then there are Old Age Security (OAS) and the Guaranteed Income Supplement (GIS), which are paid to eligible residents of Canada sixty-five years of age or over. Most provinces and territories also have smaller supplemental programs. These plans are the bedrock of income security for retired Canadians. Women sixty-five and up receive, on average, about 60 per cent of their income from these public pensions and other government transfers.

For several reasons, CPP or QPP benefits paid to women are significantly lower than those paid to men. First, women in the paid labour force have traditionally earned less than men—as much as 27 per cent less on average—in spite of equal-pay legislation. Second, women are much more likely to work in sectors of the economy where part-time jobs are predominant. This reduces their pension plan contributions and benefits. Also, women frequently leave the paid workforce temporarily to bear and raise children, and there's no government contribution to their pension for this work. While CPP rules ensure that women who "drop out" of the workforce to have a child or raise children don't pay a penalty for the time away from paid work, nothing compensates for the lost opportunity to improve their incomes. In addition, women still do much more unpaid labour than men. The year-by-year impact of such subtle but real discrimination leaves the vast majority of women at retirement age receiving lower pension benefits than men. The average monthly CPP retirement benefit for new retirees aged sixty-five in September 2003 was $597 for men and just $362 for women.

The Old Age Security program is available to most residents of Canada over sixty-five, whether or not they ever paid into the Canada or Quebec Pension Plans. The average monthly

OAS payment at the end of 2003 was $441.43. The Guaranteed Income Supplement is needs-based and paid to eligible low-income seniors on application. In 2003, the average monthly payment for a single person receiving GIS was $371.17.

In recent years, our public pensions have come under attack. In his 1995 budget speech, Finance Minister Paul Martin raised the spectre of what critics called a "demographic time bomb." The minister proposed that when the bulk of Canada's baby boom generation reached retirement age, the CPP would be unable to support them. He warned that, without changes, the cost of the CPP/QPP, OAS, and GIS would "jump" from 5.3 to 8 per cent of gross domestic product by 2030. It's important to point out however that, in the same year Mr. Martin was fretting about this, the average pension cost amongst all the countries in the Organization for Economic Co-operation and Development (OECD) was already 9 per cent higher than its GDP. The arguments behind this ticking "time bomb" scenario have since been defused, but nevertheless, Mr. Martin instituted changes to the CPP that, just like changes to unemployment insurance, resulted in higher contributions and lower benefits.

The finance minister was aided by predictable right-wing pressure—the corporate and financial establishment, the Reform/Alliance Party and its research arm the Fraser Institute, and others. They argued that either our system of pensions should be privatized, or individuals should have the right to opt out of CPP in favour of their own private pensions.

Canadians have to understand that public pensions are more than just retirement plans. They are a broad-based, universal social-insurance plan. The CPP provides disability, survivor, and maternity benefits, and benefits to dependent children. It provides protection for people who can't contribute to the plan temporarily—because they leave the workforce to raise children or because they become disabled.

And the CPP is there to provide the benefits that you are entitled to beginning at age sixty. Those on the right arguing to
privatize pensions don't seem to see the virtue in pooling
risk, or in accepting collective social responsibility.

When Margaret Thatcher's government allowed people in
Great Britain to opt out of the public pension plan, insurance companies rushed in and persuaded people to put their
money into private plans. Not surprisingly, the end result was
lower benefits. The unscrupulous companies made enormous profits and were later fined an estimated £11 billion.
On top of that, one study showed that fees and commissions
from the private money managers consumed 40 to 45 per
cent of the revenue. By comparison, administrative costs for
our CPP are about 1.3 per cent.

No wonder greedy Canadian stockbrokers want as much
of this pie as they can stuff into their investment portfolios.
Canadians must resist these siren calls—that only the private
sector can lead the way in pension reform—by extending
confidence in our capacities to invest our collective savings
through public processes. In a January 2002 speech, Monica
Townson, a Canadian pension expert, described the pitfalls
of privatizing public pensions: "It would do away with the
collective responsibility for and to our older citizens, which
has been the fundamental basis for Canada's social programs." She's right.

Now is the time for all Canadians to decide what a fair
guaranteed annual income for senior citizens should be. It's
clearly inadequate and not guaranteed in any way at the
moment. A cross-country discussion would produce a basic
consensus, just as it has on the funding of health care. Then,
a step-by-step strategy to achieve that fair, sustainable pension level needs to be put in place. Making it a success will
have a lot to do with how we manage our public pensions
and how we invest both private and public pension funds.

While we need to protect the public pension system for all, private pensions can provide additional income security. But only about 30 per cent of private-sector workers have a private pension plan. On the other hand, about 85 per cent of government employees are members of private plans. With people shifting employment more often, we need laws to guarantee better portability of pensions. As well, the NDP recognized the need for laws and backup insurance plans to be put in place to protect workers' pensions in the event of bankruptcy of or refinancing by their employer. We argued that, since private pensions are a form of deferred wages, workers should be the preferred creditors in the event their company goes broke.

Pensions as Community Investments

One of the most exciting but controversial ideas about pension funds involves putting them to work by investing in our communities and helping create needed infrastructure. The patient, relatively low but steady rates of return sought by pension funds are ideal for investing in longer-term projects such as affordable housing, water- and sewage-treatment plants, transit systems, or sustainable energy development projects.

What about the idea of giving Canadians the option to invest in their country, not just on the stock market? One consequence of turning Canadian debt and pensions over to the private sector—instead of holding it in public bonds or Bank of Canada instruments—is that the interest is paid to others, generally not the citizens of this country. Another is that the savings of Canadians are less available to invest in the future they want to see for their children. During the Second World War, we called on Canadians to invest their savings here at home in the form of war bonds. Those who did were paid interest, and the money collected from war bonds drives created the wherewithal to help defeat the Nazis. The system worked, although in the intervening sixty years, Canada has largely forgotten or given up on that economic toolbox. The relentless drive to reduce debt continues, causing us to limit investment needed in our cities, environment, new industries, education, training, health, and culture. This is false economy. It's like deciding not to put the necessary money in to maintain a key piece of machinery. Without such maintenance the machine will begin to fail. Instead of waiting for the inevitable failure, let's establish a massive campaign to mobilize our pensions and personal savings in an invest-in-Canada's-future project. We're talking here about investing, not spending. And it's no different than any other successful business venture. By bringing our savings back home, so to speak, we'd have the money to be able to build the affordable homes, successful industries, liveable communities. In short, we'd be building the society that we dream about.

I know it works because it's been done before. A British Columbia pension fund group is building affordable rental housing in that province. Some of us persuaded their team to join with the Ontario Municipal Employees' Retirement System (OMERS) to build similar housing in Ontario. OMERS has also invested in the project to cool Toronto's downtown office high-rises with cold water from Lake Ontario, rather than continue to use outdated and polluting air conditioners. It is projects like these that prove that pension funds can be invested—safely and profitably—in projects that improve our collective well-being as a community.

Canada Needs a Raise

According to the latest available figures, the top 10 per cent of the population holds 53 per cent of the wealth. The bottom 50 per cent own less than 6 per cent of Canada's wealth. The people in the bottom 10 per cent actually owe about $2,100 per capita more than they own. And not only are the rich getting richer and the poor getting poorer, but immigrants and families raising children, in particular, are much worse off than they were a generation ago.

Our distribution of income is similarly skewed in favour of the rich—and is only getting worse. Since 1995, we've seen the most rapid increase in the inequality of incomes among Canadians since we've kept track of these records, and this has been allowed to occur at a time when the economy has been growing significantly.

I've already demonstrated how the unequal distribution of wealth adversely affects people's health. In terms of building a productive economy, and in terms of human decency, the degree to which wealth is fairly distributed in a society is a mark of success in that society. Bringing poor people out of poverty does more than improve their living circumstances and their health, it actually improves the foundation of the entire economy.

On January 1, 1995, Ontario's minimum wage was $6.85 an hour. In their eight years in office, the Conservative governments of Mike Harris and Ernie Eves never raised it a dime. Over those eight years, inflation ate up about 20 per cent of that minimum wage. That pushed the estimated three hundred thousand Ontario workers earning minimum wage even further below the poverty line. And, once more, it's women who have borne the brunt of this economic inequality 61 per cent of minimum wage earners in Ontario are women.

In booming Alberta, the minimum wage is so low that many workers holding down full-time jobs can't afford to rent an apartment and are forced into homeless shelters. In British Columbia, the former NDP government raised the minimum wage to $8.00 an hour, but when the Liberals came to office in 2000, they introduced a new entry-level wage of $6.oo for people with no job experience. Aside from the United States, which is even worse, compared with the rest of the industrialized world, our minimum wages are appallingly low.

Lest one thinks that minimum wage laws are mostly for high-school students looking for some pocket money, the majority of minimum wage workers in Canada are adults. Furthermore, 40 per cent of them work full time. Many of them work at more than one job, and they still live in poverty.

But instead of giving poor people real assistance to break the poverty trap, too many provincial governments have cut off their social assistance and driven poor people further into despair. To be sure, the federal government did its share of the damage. It cut access to unemployment insurance, reduced transfer payments to the provinces, and eliminated the national standards that provinces used to follow in their income support programs. Some provinces took a bad situation and made it worse by cutting social assistance, freezing shelter allowances, and downloading services to cash-strapped municipalities. Some provinces, like British Columbia, even imposed limits on the length of time an individual could receive social assistance and then cut them off any aid. Other provinces, including Ontario and Alberta, instituted punitive "workfare" programs that compelled social assistance recipients to find employment without providing them with the necessary social supports such as child care or public transit passes that would make it possible for them to hold a job successfully.

Yet, as governments have been failing Canadians, communities across the country are running innovative, visionary, and helpful programs that provide people with support. These programs give training that enhances skills and instills confidence in individuals and helps return them to the world of work. Many of these programs fall under the umbrella of community economic development (CED), which also aptly sums up the goal—community, economy, and development.

The broad range of CED projects falls into five main categories. The first is employment, helping marginalized people back into the job market, as well as helping those currently in dead-end jobs to find more meaningful careers. These programs take a variety of forms. Normally, they involve personal-development sessions in groups, including interviewing techniques and personal skills. They often include hands-on training in a particular field, sometimes in connection with a community college or private training institute.

The second category is geared to self-employment. A program in this category helps people acquire skills and knowledge to assist them in opening their own small businesses. This program has been extremely successful as thousands of people have become entrepreneurs, and countless small companies have started up with the help of CED training.

The third category offers access to credit. Under this program, small start-up loans are provided to allow people to open up a shop and purchase basic tools and equipment. The loans may also pay for some formal education or provide the security and damage deposit an individual would need to rent an apartment. CED organizations frequently require loan recipients to take some credit counselling and money-management sessions before the funds are advanced.

Neighbourhood revitalization programs are the fourth category. This initiative is an attempt to bring people together in a community to work collectively. Frequently the purpose here is to find local volunteers willing to work together to improve the quality of their neighbourhoods. This might involve setting up a community garden or operating a community kitchen. It might mean revitalizing a business district or developing a farmer's market. In these

latter examples, people would be trying to create an incubator for business.

Broader capacity-building is the fifth and final category.
Programs in this category also help people build confidence
and self-esteem. But they go beyond personal development
to community action. That is accomplished by encouraging
people to become involved, developing local leadership, creating directories of community assets and resources, and
forcing governments to listen.

The oldest formal CED program in Canada is called New
Dawn, located in Cape Breton, Nova Scotia. It was inspired
by the famous Antigonish Movement, led by Father Jimmy
Tompkins, who founded the People's School at St. Francis
Xavier University in 1921. The People's School brought in students to learn leadership skills and to inspire others to
"become masters of their own destiny." Today, the New Dawn
program still follows that tradition. Incorporated in 1976, it
now employs more than 175 people from the Cape Breton
community. Its wide variety of programs and services involves
six hundred Cape Bretoners every day. Their oldest venture is
the Cape Breton Association for Housing Development, a
real-estate company providing affordable housing. New Dawn
also manages a host of other projects. These include a home-
care company, a private career college that provides industrial
and occupational education and training, a thirty-bed resi-
dential-care facility, a seniors' home, living centre and a
residential apartment building. New Dawn also co-ordinates a
volunteer resource centre and publishes an island magazine.

In Calgary, the year-round Fair Gains program is run by
MCC Employment Development, another CED organization.
This helps people living in poverty to save money toward
acquiring an asset. Most of the participants in the program
are working poor, and they come together twice a month to
learn how to save and manage their income. The money they

bank is matched—three to one—by the CED organization. This helps them build up not only their resources, but their confidence as well. "Working toward an asset transforms not only their situation," explains veteran CED co-ordinator Lisa Caton, "but it changes people's minds because it changes how they think about themselves." These assets may be for capitalizing a small business, for their own education, for opening a Registered Educational Savings Plan (RESP) for a child, or for another worthwhile goal. If participants are interested in saving for home ownership, they can sign up for a second year. At this level, they learn basic repair skills and how to manage household finances; they also learn about home insurance and real estate. Though the program has been running for only a few years, several Fair Gains graduates have inded managed to buy their own homes.

In Winnipeg, experienced CED activists brought together community leaders to form the North End Community Renewal Corporation. The goals of the corporation are to promote locally owned businesses, better housing, and a safe, clean neighbourhood in Winnipeg's North End. The group, now with more than ninety participating organizations, received long-term operational financing from the NDP provincial government, an experienced business development officer, and space donated by the Mennonite Central Committee. In 2001, the North End Community Renewal Corporation had an annual budget of $500,000, with nine employees and two hundred volunteers. They have successfully revitalized two commercial districts, established a training and employment centre serving more than five hundrred people, and designed a program to renovate more than four hundred houses over a five-year period. They have also put in place a school literacy program, provided Internet access for North End residents, and held summer festivals centred on community diversity.

• • •

Another bright idea was hatched by the Pakistan Canada Association of Edmonton, which formed a seniors' group in 1995 and brought together older women who loved to sew. They started producing ethnic dolls, clothing, and multi-purpose bags. Quickly, they decided to reach out to other cultural groups by offering other products. Before long, with help from a CED project, they opened the Handicraft Production Centre and commenced working with women from Bosnia, Cambodia, Vietnam, China, and several Arab nations, producing marketable cloth bags for conferences. As well, this centre offers courses in sewing and cooking and also helps participants overcome the isolation often experienced by older women living at home.

The non-profit Highbanks Society in Calgary bought the building that housed the nostalgic but trendy Dairy Lane Diner. Above the diner, Highbanks renovated four apartments and decided that they should be occupied by teenage moms. These young women gain work experience in the diner, while providing mutual support to one another.

A group of women in the Niagara district of Ontario turned to a CED organization to help them organize and manage their network of micro entrepreneurs, each of whom produces her own local specialty food products. Now they operate a commercial incubator kitchen, a retail showroom, plus a marketing and distribution service.

As all these examples show, CED organizations have stepped in to fill a real social and economic need. They have recognized the importance of personal development, skills training, financial assistance, mutual support, and community relationships. They have rolled them all into one coherent package, designed to meet individual and local needs. And they've been much more creative and responsive than most government programs in helping people find jobs and keep them.

Some critics point out that CEDs are small and don't reach enough people. Both of these are true, but neither is a problem.

About 97 per cent of businesses in Canada employ fewer than five people. In total, small business—understood as having fewer than fifty workers—employ over one-third of all Canadian workers. In fact, most new jobs are created by small businesses, so CED projects involving a small number of participants are part of the mainstream of economic development. And they should be encouraged to reach more people. Their model ought to be made more widely available, to open up CED-sponsored programs to a much greater number of people. Certainly there's no question that CEDs are a valuable tool in building the new prosperity—from the ground up.

> - **Corporate tax revenues as a percentage of total federal government revenues in the 1960s: 19.0; in the 1990s: 10.8**
> - **Personal income tax revenues as a percentage of total federal government revenues in the 1960s: 32.2; in the 1990s: 46.9**
> - **Estimated number of jobs created by a tax cut of $1 billion: 9,000**
> - **Estimated number of jobs created by spending $1 billion on roads and hospitals: 25,000**

Measuring the New Prosperity

The way economists look at it, the 1998 ice storm, Nova Scotia's encounter with Hurricane Juan, and British Columbia's forest fires and floods of 2003 were all good for the economy.

How's that? Because they all caused hundreds of millions of dollars of damage that needed to be repaired. They forced both governments and the private sector to spend money creating direct jobs. Those events resulted in a building boom. Stimulus! Spending! That has to be good.

Of course, they were absolutley horrible events for the people who had their homes destroyed, who went without electrical power for a month or more, or who were forced into temporary shelters—to say nothing about the people who died or the grieving families left behind. But, on the economic ledger, they went down on the plus 'side. They were good for the economy because they created demand. Such ledger-keeping also shows why the way in which we measure the economy is nuts!

Automobile accidents stimulate the economy because they result in consumer spending on repairs or a new car plus higher insurance premiums. Crime stimulates the economy because we pay more salaries for police officers and those who work in the criminal justice system. Divorce stimulates the economy because people set up separate homes and buy more stuff. Spraying more pesticides on lawns is good for the economy, because people are buying and spending. If this produces increased health costs later, as far as our economic measurements go, so much the better. The absurdities go on and on.

Our common measure of economic activity is the gross domestic product (GDP). It simply adds up the total market value of goods and services produced in Canada. It attaches no value whatsoever to whether we actually want to be spending that money in the ways that we do. It draws no distinction between money spent on commodities that improve our well-being and those that diminish it. And, since the GDP measures only economic activity, where money changes hands, it leaves out everything to which no dollar value is attached.

The time you spend raising your family? Not measured. The contribution you make volunteering in your community? No value. If you spend $30 on a junk-food dinner in a fast-food restaurant, it's worth $10 more to the GDP than the $20 you might spend cooking a healthy meal at home.

And then there are all those detrimental items the GDP doesn't count at all. Damage to the environment? Not counted. Depletion of our natural resources? Not included. The GDP has no measure for strategies that might save the earth's ozone layer and protect us from damaging ultraviolet radiation. In fact, if suntan lotion and hat sales go up as a result, the economists are smiling. And, should you walk to work instead of taking the car, that's a negative, because you are not spending money on fuel, or on the wear and tear on your vehicle. Help Canada's economy—don't walk when you could drive!

Using the GDP as our sole economic measure gives us a completely false impression of the real costs and benefits of economic and social activity. It leads us to think that the economy is doing well, when what we're really doing is perpetuating costly mistakes. We need a different measure, one that acknowledges quadruple bottom line thinking and that measures our progress toward achieving the new prosperity.

One exciting idea being developed, largely in Canada, attempts to change these calculations so that they make more sense. Some economists are starting to use what they call the Genuine Progress Indicator (GPI). The GPI takes account of both plus and minus costs, and includes factors for which we've previously never assigned an economic value. In addition to personal consumption, it takes into account income distribution in a society, unemployment rates, and net capital investment. It factors in social costs, like family breakdown, and the contributions made by unpaid housework and child care. It takes away value for time spent commuting to work, for loss of farmland, wet-lands, and forests, and for loss of leisure time.

Canadians need to introduce new measurement tech-niques like GPI so we can honestly measure the new prosperity. The GPI adds value when we make improvements to those things that are good for our society and subtracts when we have lost things of value. If we switched to the GPI and away from the GDP, Canadians would have a better idea of what was actually going on around us, and we could help shape our economy in ways that recognize the interconnec-tions between the economy, the environment, and ourselves.

[CHAPTER 7]

Building a Just Society

Pierre Trudeau coined the phrase "the Just Society" in the late sixties. I was captivated—so much so, that I organized an early version of Rock the Vote at the Fairview Mall on Montreal's west island, all a part of Trudeaumania. In my late teens, in the era of Woodstock, I was caught up, as so many young people were, by the purity and the idealism of his political rallying cry. Human rights, equality, justice for all!

These were values that Canadians, young and old alike, wanted their country to fully embrace. At the same time, multiculturalism—the great Canadian welcome for immigrants from around the world—was the watchword. So was another Trudeau phrase: "participatory democracy." Trudeau himself abandoned many of these principles during his years as prime minister. Whether it was the War Measures Act or imposing the repatriation of the Canadian Constitution without the consent of Quebec, the policies of the Liberal governments he led betrayed his original idealism. Over the twenty-plus years of Mulroney–Chrétien–Martin governments that succeeded the Trudeau era, such high ideals have faded from national discourse. The focus became what's-in-it-for-me economics, tax and program cutting, scandals, and security above all else.

There was a time when Canada was known as a world leader in human rights. John Peters Humphrey, a native of New Brunswick, was the principal author of the *Universal Declaration of Human Rights*, proclaimed in 1948, which has arguably become one of the most important human rights documents ever. This UN document and two others, the associated *Covenant on Civil and Political Rights* and the

Covenant on Economic, Social and Cultural Rights, establish a just framework for human affairs that goes well beyond narrow concepts of civil or property rights to embrace the full spectrum of human needs. Canadians have long recognized the importance of understanding the connection between rights, equality, social justice, and democracy itself. As Frank Scott, distinguished McGill legal scholar, poet, social reformer, and one of the original founders of the CCF/NDP, put it, "The trappings of democracy hang loosely on an emaciated body politic."

Canada now has its own Charter of Rights and Freedoms, and a body of legal reform is emerging through laws and court decisions that is slowly expanding human rights.

Canada has taken a leadership role in other ways too. We were a world leader in advancing gay and lesbian rights, evident as early as 1967 in Trudeau's vanguard legislation as justice minister and in his famous pronouncement that "the state has no place in the bedrooms of the nation." I was glad to play a modest role in continuing the Canadian human rights tradition with our NDP caucus in September 2003 when we played an instrumental role in defeating an Alliance Party motion (a motion that was supported as well by fifty-three Liberal MPs) that would have denied same-sex marriage under Canadian law.

In this chapter, I will touch on some of the elements of the broad understanding of human rights, equality, and democracy—all of which could help define a more just society. Many eminent scholars, legal experts, and passionate advocates have tackled these issues, and whole sections of libraries are devoted to them, so don't expect an encyclopedia here. When it comes to a just society, the truth is, we can achieve much more than we are currently achieving. We can reverse the backsliding and, once again, be an example to the world. Let's consider some ideas about how to do just that.

Democracy and Civil Society

The most profound transformation needed to create a vibrant democracy involves what is called "civil society." Civil society encompasses all the ways in which people can be engaged in shaping their world outside the formal political process. A broad understanding of civil society takes in the thousands of groupings of Canadians who work away, on a daily basis, trying to make one or another aspect of their community better. It could be environmentalists, volunteers at a local homeless shelter, peace symposium organizers, workers advocating for improved safety in the workplace—the list is endless. But our formal political system doesn't include mechanisms for local organizations and the movements behind them to actually shape and affect public policy.

Within the NDP, there is a strong consensus that we should open ourselves up to working with groups in civil society. It's not that the social movements should be absorbed by a political party or even encouraged to advocate on behalf of a political party. It's actually very important that these movements retain their independent voices and their capacity to be critical. But on the other hand, there are distinct advantages to working with such groups on common projects. We should seek to benefit from their front-line experience and the depth of their knowledge and try to co-ordinate some of their efforts to have a greater effect on the direction of public policy in Canada.

Ultimately, we have to find ways to connect the delicious turmoil of citizen engagement and activism more frequently and effectively within government processes in general. One of the best models is found in Brazil, where thousands of citizens are drawn into the process of setting the budget for the nation. Some Canadian cities are starting to try this kind of participatory democracy. As a very modest experiment, I held budget hearings in the winter of 2004 with MPs Libby Davies in Vancouver, Alexa McDonough in Halifax, and Judy Wasylycia-Leis in Toronto, as well as one in Montreal. We also had a special consultation with national women's organizations in Ottawa. We asked community members and organizational representatives how they would rather have spent the billions of dollars in tax breaks Paul Martin gave to corporations in January 2004. Of course, this is only a beginning—we have a long way to go.

The Electoral System

To build a more democratic society, we need to change our electoral system. We need to ensure that all Canadians have a more equal voice at the ballot box, and that the people elected to the House are a more true reflection of the country than currently exists. Just because all citizens of voting age have the right to vote doesn't mean that their voices are equally represented.

The ten federal elections we've had since 1968 have produced eight majority governments. But in only one of those elections—1984—did the governing party actually receive more than 50 per cent of all the votes cast. in seven of these elections, a minority of votes produced a majority of seats for one party.

Of nearly eighty democracies in the world, only two rely solely on the first-past-the-post, winner-take-all system— Canada and the U.S. All the others have some form of proportional representation (PR), which means that the parties receive a share of seats in Parliament more proportional to the number of votes that they get. (Many of our largest cities used to have systems of PR. In fact, Calgary and Winnipeg used the system into the 1950s and 1960s. Some twenty cities—including Edmonton, Vancouver, and Regina—once had elections based on PR.)

The details of the systems vary greatly from country to country, but in every case their elected governments are much more representative of the voice of the people. In Canada, such a system would also ensure that Parliament would have members from all parties, from all regions of the country— improving representation and reducing geographic alienation. All views would be represented, as they should be. PR would create a more responsive government, one better equipped to listen to and meet the needs of the people. I like the look of the approach taken in New Zealand, which recently trans- formed its voting system from the type Canada has always had—known as the "single member plurality" or "first past the post"—to PR. Essentially, such a system for Canada would have voters choose their local MPs just as they do now. With that, however, would be additional seats in the House of Commons that would be awarded to each party whose per- centage of MPs elected under the single-member plurality fell short of the party's percentage of the popular vote. Who would fill those PR seats? These additional MPs would be selected from a list each political party would publish in advance of the election date. Local representation would be maintained, which is also important in a country as large and diverse as Canada. But with a system of PR, a party that received 25 per cent of the popular vote on election day would have 25 per cent of the seats in the House.

Depending on which variation of PR was chosen, such a system could also significantly improve the number of women and minorities in elected office.

Of course, in order to get more women and other affirmative-action candidates elected under the current sys- tem, more of them must run for nomination and be successful. In the NDP, our first step toward achieving this goal has been to adopt policies ensuring that affirmative- action candidates, including women, are recruited and given training and assistance to become candidates. Thanks to these policies, the NDP consistently has had a higher percentage of women MPs in the parliamentary caucus than have other parties. There are many barriers confronting women who consider running for political office. To help lower those barriers, the federal NDP requires riding associations to demonstrate that they have made significant outreach efforts to recruit at least one affirmative-action candidate before a nomination meeting is authorized to proceed. Although the significant breakthrough of women elected by the NDP in the 2006 election begins to approach gender equality in our caucus, we may still have to consider other processes. We want—and all other parties should want—to help women and other affirmative-action candidates overcome obstacles to being candidates, whether they be financial, cultural, or social. I think that real change in this area will come only with a great many more women's voices in Parliament, and I believe PR is a key to that change.

Proportional representation would revitalize the voting process itself. People would know that even if their individual candidate lost locally, their ballot would still count toward the overall strength of the party they supported in the election. Instead of the current situation, which is all too often people voting against one or another party or candidate, under a system of PR, people would always have something to vote for. This would improve voter turnout and make for a healthier, more inclusive democracy.

In the 2004 federal election, just over 61 per cent of eligible voters did so, and it was the lowest turnout in our history. (Compare that with recent turnouts of 93 per cent in Belgium, or 86 per cent in Austria and Sweden.) Elections Canada estimates that less than 40 per cent of young voters (under the age of twenty-four) cast a ballot in the 2000 election.

In the fall of 2003, Lorne Nystrom, an NDP MP from Saskatchewan, introduced a resolution in the House of Commons calling on the Canadian government to consult its citizens in a referendum about modernizing our democracy with a system of proportional representation. It was the first opportunity to consider PR that Parliament had been given since 1923. The Liberals and the Alliance, however, voted down the idea of even asking Canadians for their opinions.

In this chamber, sir, one's stature is measured from the shoulders up. —TOMMY DOUGLAS, RESPONDING TO AN MP'S QUIP ABOUT HIS DIMINUTIVE FRAME.

Elections that are more democratic would also help address the arrogance that can, and has, set in as governments begin to see themselves as invincible. As a result of our archaic voting system, invented long before the telephone, our governments learn that they can win elections even when most Canadians oppose their policies. "Majority" governments become high-handed and inattentive to the public good. Abuse of power can follow, making politics susceptible to scandal.

The media tend to treat scandals as one-off affairs, a few politicians getting too close to their corporate friends. This ignores the systemic nature of corporate scandals, which, sadly, are as old as Canada itself. Even our first prime minister, Sir John A. Macdonald, was embroiled in scandal in the 1870s over railway contracts to his corporate friends. Prime Minister Paul Martin must have realized that the root of the sponsorship scandal, which came to a head with the auditor general's report in early 2004, was not a few rogue Liberals or bureaucrats but rather too many Liberals, including Liberal MPs who had become so comfortable that they believed they could do whatever they wished. The arrogance is ironic, given that all three Liberal "majorities"—1993, 1997, and

2000—were not elected with 50 per cent approval from the voters. But our current system is a winner-takes-all system. The winning party takes it all and then shares the spoils amongst its friends. In countries with effective PR systems, parties that have to interact with others to pass legislation tend to be somewhat more humble and accountable.

A fundamental principle of a just and democratic society is empowering its people and engaging them as active players in their economy and society. Ensuring that all our citizens— native-born or new to Canada—are equipped to participate fully must be a cornerstone on which Canada is built. And revitalizing our democracy—through proportional represen- tation and by encouraging people to participate directly in their own communities—must also be our goal.

The Gender Gap

What if a group of women had written the Canadian Constitution, instead of a group of men? What would they have done differently? What guarantees do you think they would have assured all men, women, children, and the elderly in our society?

Everyone knows that there's an enormous ideological gen- der gap. Every poll verifies that. Women are much more inclined than men to support programs of economic and social justice—and to support the redistribution of wealth. That stands to reason: these attitudes reflect the reality of most women's experiences.

So the point is not really what a constitution written by women might look like. The important thing to acknowledge is that women, by and large, have different experiences, different priorities, and different visions than men. Yet most of our social and economic structures have been designed almost exclusively by men. As such, they tend to reflect a male point of view.

We've already gone over some of the territory of women's inequality in Canada. Women receive seventy-three cents for every dollar that men earn. Too often they're destined for low-wage and minimum-wage, service-sector jobs. They take years out of the workforce to raise children or care for elderly relatives, which diminishes their pensions, making them susceptible to poverty later on. And that only names a few inequities. Systemic and institutional discrimination can be addressed in law and with better social programs, but that requires a political vision different from the one that has dominated politics in Canada so far.

In our culture, women still assume the primary responsibility for raising families. They are the unpaid caregivers, the "shock absorbers" in the system, as one report puts it. Often they juggle all these responsibilities while they continue to work. Here is just one statistic. In Ontario, about 95 per cent of single parents receiving family benefits are women. Yet our governments design punitive social programs that fail to acknowledge this reality. Wholly inadequate social assistance condemns women and children to lives of poverty when the children are young, while miserly public pensions force a disproportionate share of women into poverty in their senior years. A society that truly values families and understands and accepts the family responsibilities that women assume would reward these duties accordingly. Workplace laws, social assistance, and pension legislation designed by women or at least with the real world of women in mind— would look much different than the current legislation.

We also need to acknowledge the special forms of discrimination confronted by women of colour, women with disabilities, and Aboriginal women. Their multiple barriers to equality are almost always extremely difficult to overcome.

The past few decades however have been marked by a vibrant, energetic, and progressive women's movement in

Canada. Thanks to their activism, we have a better understanding of what the real issues for women are and what will
make a real difference in their lives. Change has happened
slowly, but we can point to some improvements.

Not so long ago, we didn't even have a name for sexual
harassment. Now most men are finally beginning to understand what it is and why it's so wrong. Laws and workplace
codes have begun to address that.

We know affirmative-action programs can address
inequalities of race and gender, and we know these programs
can work. It's no longer inconceiveable to think about a
female judge, prime minister, pipefitter, firefighter, doctor, or
CEO. Attitudes toward women and their capabilities in the
workplace are starting to change.

As recently as the 1970s, abortion was still a shocking or,
at best, an impolite word—an operation, though common
enough, then taking place in back rooms, at great risk to
women's health and lives, and without public acknowledgement. Laws restricting the procedure were eventually
abandoned and attitudes readjusted, all as a result of an
arduous struggle by a determined, dynamic women's movement. Though access to reproductive choice remains a
divisive issue, our legislation and courts have, at least, recognized a woman's right to choose—and have publicly funded
women's clinics. A full range of reproductive health services
is slowly becoming a reality.

Pay-equity legislation and related court challenges are other
breakthroughs. The most significant settlements were
achieved after long battles by women employees, their unions,
and pay-equity advocates. Although the issue has been technically "won" in legislatures and courts across the country,
employers continue to drag their feet on implementation. This
forces women to have to fight again and again for the pay they
deserve. And still women receive only three-quarters of what

men do and, on top of that, there are even indications of back-sliding. Economic equality requires constant vigilance.

Nowhere do we see this backsliding more than in relation to child poverty. As we dig beneath the surface, we find the deeper phenomenon of women's poverty. Canada has piously expressed its hope for a new prosperity for Canada's children. Have we delivered? At the United Nations World Summit for Children in 1990, Canada, along with many other countries, signed a statement that read, in part, "The growing minds and bodies of children should have a first call on our societies, and children should be able to depend upon that commitment in good times and bad." Just the year before, Parliament had approved federal NDP Leader Ed Broadbent's resolution calling for an end to child poverty in Canada by 2000.

The year 2000 has come and gone—and Y2K got a lot more attention than the children. Nice words didn't feed children, house them, provide them with an education. 1.2 million children live in poverty in 2005 —about one in every six children—with a substantial increase since that resolution. What does that mean? It means that in an "average" elementary school classroom of thirty kids, five live in poverty. In Canada, that's appalling, and shameful. Meanwhile, social assistance benefits to poor families, most led by women, have declined by about 20 per cent, and the total number of visits to food banks has gone up about 90 per cent. We're told that children make up about 40 per cent of food bank recipients.

This came about at a time when the Canadian economy was growing steadily. Even the federal finance department bragged about the fact that among all OECD (Organization for Economic Co-operation and Development) countries, Canada has had the sharpest drop in program spending since 1997—and that spending is at its lowest level since the 1940s. Should this actually be a point of pride and something to brag about?

Ideologically conservative provincial government—particularly in Ontario, Alberta, and British Columbia, which altogether are home to two-thirds of Canada's young people—are greatly to blame for the current plight of children and families, particularly mothers. But once again, the federal government must take responsibility for its failure to fund social programs adequately. It failed miserably to implement pan-Canadian programs (for example, child care), or to provide any affordable housing for low-income families. The Liberal government eliminated the Canada Assistance Plan (CAP) in 1995. Who knew what the CAP was, anyway? With a mere "doff of the CAP," the national government could claim victory over deficits while silently and simultaneously abdicating its role in meeting the needs of Canada's children and their families. Then the other shoe dropped: Ottawa's financial mandarins reduced federal funding to the provinces by about $12 billion under the Canada Health and Social Transfer. Most provinces in turn reduced their financial and program supports for children and their families, and downloaded services, and their costs, to municipalities. Municipal governments are the least able to respond to such demands because of their limited ability to collect taxes. So the downward spiral finally hit families, and more families were plunged into poverty while those already living in poverty found it even harder to climb out.

Harkening back to the UN's statement that children should have "first call" on our societies, Toronto launched a pilot project called First Duty. This was the title of the first report of the child advocate, a new position on city council developed by Olivia Chow with her dynamic advisory committee on Children and Youth. This positive notion of "advocates"—not "critics"—I am now using in our federal caucus.

Toronto's Children's Services worked together with the school board and the charitable Atkinson Foundation to design the program and identify five pilot project locations, which have guaranteed funding for three years. In the pilot project locations, individual elementary schools have combined with community centres and local agencies to administer multi-dimensional and comprehensive services to children and families. Inevitably, governments complain that they can't afford programs like these, but once again, initial investments save much more money later, and people receive valuable services and experience improved lifestyles.

Combining the recommendation in the Romanow Report about health-care delivery in community clinics with a broad range of seamless, community-based childcare services integrated into the school system makes sense. Such a coordinated approach would also help translate into action the values we share as inhabitants of a country filled with communities that believe in caring for one another.

Advancements—on these and other issues—have been made, but there have been other instances of serious slippage. For the past hundred years, Canadian women have shown tremendous energy and commitment to build a more just and equitable society. Undoubtedly they will continue that struggle. For my part, I commit the New Democratic Party to working alongside progressive women in their efforts.

In speaking out about the environment, the economy, and our cities, I've mentioned many times that workable, practical solutions are available, and I've stressed that a key to imagining solutions is to understand the interconnectedness of the issues. The same thinking applies to efforts to overcome the systemic discrimination that creates women's inequality.

The struggle takes place on many fronts—in workplaces, in legislatures, in courts of law, and in the community. Without having to be forced by laws to take action, the private sector needs to address women's inequality by providing all private-sector workers with decent pay and benefits, and by recognizing and respecting talent in women as well as in men. Much greater equality would also come about if employers and governments removed the obstacles they throw up to union organizing. It's a responsibility of government to be aware of the barriers that deny women access to choices and equality. And government must play a major role in providing programs designed to overcome those barriers.

One exciting idea that reflected an understanding of this interconnectedness was adopted by the former NDP provincial government in British Columbia, which established a Ministry of Women's Equality, designed to infuse the perspective of women into all aspects of government decision-making. It acted like an internal audit system, to ensure that the prevalent tendencies to reproduce existing inequalities were challenged and checked. It was smart, and it worked. In fact, it was such a good idea that the incoming Liberal premier, Gordon Campbell, eliminated the ministry at his earliest opportunity. His government also quickly did away with the B.C. Human Rights Commission, which also had worked to address equality for women and other equity-seeking groups.

Instead of just one ministry dedicated to keeping an eye on issues of particular concern to women (which, frankly, could be rendered quite powerless), think of the impact women's perspectives would have if they were completely integrated into the decision-making of all institutions, whether the House of Commons, government departments, or major corporations. Imagine what society would look like if the decisions about priority spending and program design, for example, all had to run through the filter of "How will this affect women?" Then the systemic discrimination that women face would begin to get the attention needed for real change to happen. That's why a standing committee of the House of Commons on women's issues was a key proposal that New Democrat MPs raised successfully. Such a focus for discussion of women's inequality and how to eliminate it could help tackle a real democratic deficit.

Men's violence against women would certainly rate a higher priority in our national government's agenda if this kind of attention to women's concerns were in place. I know that some people are uncomfortable calling this injustice "men's violence against women." I remember having to push hard, even at the Board of Health in Toronto, to have the term accepted, rather than the more neutral "family violence."

For me, the penny dropped with the Montreal Massacre in 1989. The moment I learned of that horrific attack and the murder of fourteen women engineering students, I reacted the way many other men did—by assuming it was the expression of just one man's hatred, one man's difficulty with women. As the months passed, it was as though women in many corners of my life concluded that I just didn't get it. And although it was often extremely painful for them, they took the time to tell me about their personal stories. I was one of those guys who didn't doubt the statistics about the high percentage of girls and women who had experienced men's violence. It's just that I didn't seem to know any of the women who had had such a horrible experience! (Actually, I did know one: Jane Doe, attacked by the balcony rapist in my ward. In 2003 her book, *The Story of Jane Doe: A Book about Rape*, was published, and it's now the subject of a Gemini Award winning docudrama.) One by one, over a period of months, women told me their stories. Finally, as yet another woman friend in my life took me to that terrifying emotional place in her history, I said to myself: I don't think I know any woman who has not experienced some sort of violence from a man!

Most men are not violent. But I had to confess that most men, including me, were not speaking out about the issue. By remaining silent, we were in a very real sense complicit.

Women's groups had been working for decades, creating shelters, sounding the alarm, calling for changes to the justice system, and much more. But where were the men's voices? That conclusion led me to work with a group of men to kick-start the White Ribbon Campaign. Wearing a white ribbon would be easy for men—we wouldn't even have to say anything, tongue-tied as we so often are.

After an awkward start (White Ribbon men drew attention away from women's voices in the media around the December 6 commemoration, which rightly angered some women's groups), we invited a group of wise women to advise us. At that meeting, a long-time worker at the Rape Crisis Centre made a summary comment: "The way you guys started White Ribbon really made me angry. The only thing that would make me angrier is if you stopped. Just get it right next time."

Working with women's groups over the years, White Ribbon became a modest but useful expression of men's opposition to violence against women. It now exists in more twenty-five countries, and it continues to grow. However, the sad reality is that violence against women is still increasing worldwide. So much more needs to be done.

If women's priorities are not reflected in every government in Canada, the funding of shelters and clinics, improvements to the justice system, policies to reduce women's poverty, and many other needed initiatives will continue to get short shrift. The backsliding of the past decade will continue, and that's not fair, healthy, or acceptable.

Education and Equality

By any standard, we are a rich country. But Canada's greatest asset is our people, and we can do a much better job of seeing to it that they have equal opportunities to be equipped to participate more fully in our economy, our society, and our democracy. As I've pointed out, there is no shortage of good ideas, only a shortage of willingness to try them. We have to be prepared to think outside the box.

Two pivotal factors affect people's ability to use their talents. The first is to make sure that our citizens are well educated and trained. The second is to make sure that the people who arrive in Canada already skilled are encouraged to put their abilities to work.

Just about everyone agrees that the key to success—for each individual and for the country as a whole—is education. That begins with early childhood education and care, which sets the foundation for lifelong learning and healthy human development, and continues through post-secondary education and ongoing skills training. Like so many other issues, our education policies need to be better integrated, and we need to remove barriers to education at every level.

In the 1980s and 1990s, progressive governments around the world developed early childhood education and care systems. Canada was an exception, lagging behind other industrialized nations. In the 2003 Canadian budget, for example, the federal and provincial governments agreed to a Multilateral Framework on Early Learning and Care, but funds allocated to this program were very limited, and there were no targets or timetables for implementation. Today, in most of continental Europe (France, Italy, Spain, Belgium, Denmark), virtually all children start publicly funded programs sometime between their second and third birthdays, whether the mother is in the labour force or not. These services are largely free, with parents paying some fees for publicly funded infant/toddler programs and "top-up" portions of the day that accommodate parents' work hours.

Wendy Lill, our NDP MP and critic on disability issues, has frequently pointed to the broad agreement that early childhood programs should include all children—whether their families are poor, wealthy, or middle class, whether the mother is in the workforce or not, whether they're able or disabled, and whether they live in a big city or in a remote rural community—that is, they should be universal.

Quebec was the only province in Canada to adopt a universal childcare program. In 1997 the province launched a $5-a-day program as part of a new family care policy. Phased in by 2000, the childcare program was available to all children under five years old, regardless of whether the parent worked. Through to 2001, the Quebec government steadily increased the childcare budget, ensuring more spaces and better wages for staff. By 2003 more than 150,000 spaces had been created. But, with the election of the Charest Liberals in April 2003, this unique program was threatened. By late 2003, the Charest government had announced it would cut $25 million in funding from publicly funded daycare centres and increase the fees to between $7 and $10 a day. Ignoring all protest, the Quebec Liberals planned to open new spaces to the private sector, further undermining the universality of the system. More backsliding, but Quebec citizens rose up to prevent the move.

When a low-income mother is provided with childcare services, she is able to go to work, replacing social assistance costs and generating taxes. At the same time, her child receives the opportunity for social and educational development and preparation for the schooling to follow. Making sure that expectant mothers get nutritional advice and proper diets also saves the rest of us money: Health Canada estimates that the cost of neonatal intensive care for each premature infant ranges from $32,000 to $52,000. Low-birth-weight babies (under 2.5 kilograms) are at much greater risk of death, disease, and disability than infants of normal weight. Cerebral palsy, learning disabilities, and visual and respiratory problems can affect these babies for their entire lives. Though low-birth-weight babies are, fortunately, relatively uncommon, women living in poverty—and teenagers, with little or no prenatal care skills—are more likely to deliver them.

About three-quarters of mothers of young children in Canada are part of the paid workforce. Their children need child care—not just so their mothers can hold down jobs, but also so their mothers themselves can take part in training and lifelong education. Our schools need to provide children with nutritious meals (a healthy diet is a key to the ability to learn) and to maintain good health in kids with regular physical education. Schools need to be able to reach young people of many different linguistic backgrounds, with English-as-a-second-language (ESL) training and other cultural programs. Schools also have to ensure that they are equipped to provide initial skills training to prepare students for today's world. And, let's not forget, schools must give students the opportunities to express themselves in a wide range of creative arts.

- **Percentage of Canadian families with children headed by sole-support mothers who were poor in 1967: 52; in 2001: 56**
- **Percentage cost of living increase, 1995 to 2002: 12.8**
- **Chances in 1967 that an unattached woman over 65 lived in poverty: 1 in 2; in 1997: 1 in 2**
- **Average income of men with disabilities, aged 35 to 54: $31,000**
- **Of women with disabilities, aged 35 to 54: $17,000**

It's surprisingly difficult to measure the rate at which young people drop out of high school. (There are complex reasons for different grade requirements in different provinces, and the fact that many people return to school later.) However, between 15 and 20 per cent of young Canadians leave school without receiving a diploma. They drop out for many reasons—often because they are poor and need to find a job—but whatever the cause, high school dropouts are usually doomed to low-paying, low-skilled jobs. Since a lot of kids are living in poverty when they quit school to earn income, their leaving often unfortunately perpetuates the cycle of poverty. Better income-support programs would help them stay in school, get their diplomas, and be equipped to hold more meaningful, better-paying jobs later on. That's an investment well worth making.

Generally, we are a well-educated people. Nearly half of Canada's adult population has post-secondary education. But access to college and university is getting more difficult—and not because we've raised the requirements. We've raised the fees.

At the beginning of the 1990s, tuition and other student fees accounted for an average of 18 per cent of a college or university's operating budget. But through that decade, as governments cut back their funding of post-secondary institutions, revenue from students increased. It now amounts to about 32 per cent of a school's budget. Tuition itself went up by over 125 per cent through the 1990s—six times the rate of inflation. And while tuition and other fees were going up, scholarships and grants were being reduced or eliminated altogether, forcing more and more students to depend on loans. The Canadian Federation of Students estimates that by the time someone graduates from college or university, he or she is saddled with a debt of $25,000. Young Canadians graduate indentured with a mortgage—but they have no house!

Here's a twisted irony. As finance minister and then prime minister, Paul Martin wanted to reduce the debt of the country, but he saw no problem with students having to go further into debt. His first Throne Speech even offered permission for student debt limits to be increased! National borrowing happens at a low interest rate. Students pay higher interest rates on their debts. Who benefits from this shifting of debt directly on the shoulders of students'? The banks, of course. They pick up the extra interest. No wonder that, in 2003, the banks were making record profits and donating "liberally" to the governing party.

At the same time, Canada's affordable housing construction programs have been axed, so we haven't seen very many student residences built, or co-ops where students could find low-rent housing.

For many students, these extra financial burdens make post-secondary education simply unaffordable. A study at the University of Western Ontario showed that the participation rate from low-income families has been reduced by half as tuition increased. When the tuition at UWO's medical school jumped from $4,844 in 1998 to $10,000 in 2000, the average income of the families of first-year medical students rose from $80,000 to $140,000.

Inequality with respect to education is growing. We're shutting the door to thousands of potential college and university students, despite the fact that everyone—advocates for the poor, the chambers of commerce, the Conference Board of Canada, right-wing think tanks—says that a competitive economy depends on a well-trained and well-educated workforce. By excluding tens of thousands of families from participating in post-secondary education, we are also shrinking the pool from which we will be drawing our "best" students. Natural systems decline when gene pools shrink. So do societies and economies.

A 1999 survey of Ontario college graduates showed that two years after graduation, 97 per cent were employed, and 81 per cent were in work directly related to their education.

Employers are always on the hunt for well-trained applicants, and many businesses say that finding skilled employees is their biggest challenge and most important requirement.

So why are we slamming the door in the face of so many potential students? As a country, can't we afford to lower fees?

Sweden, Finland, Norway, Denmark, the Netherlands, Austria, and Greece have no tuition fees for students from their own countries. Most of these nations cover significant living costs too. In Germany, not only is there no tuition for German students, there's no tuition for international students. French students at public universities pay a registration fee of under $100. In England, families with incomes under £20,000 (approximately $45,000 Canadian) can send their children to university without paying tuition. For the most part, Canada is headed in the opposite direction.

Some provinces have recognized the importance of keeping fees low to ensure access for as many students as possible. Quebec froze university tuition for fifteen of the twenty years prior to 2001, and college admission is free. B.C.'s NDP government froze tuition for 5 years, and cut it by 5 per cent in 2000. Manitoba froze tuition for two years and in 2000 came through with a 10 per cent reduction. Memorial University in Newfoundland reduced its tuition in 2001 and promised a 25 per cent cut over three years.

But elsewhere, the story is very different. At the three universities where I have taught in Toronto, average tuition since 1995 has gone up by more than 50 per cent, and now Ontario's funding is the lowest per student in the country. In 2002, Ontario's colleges were teaching thirty-five thousand more full-time students than they were ten years previously, but doing so with $79 million less in public funding. One result is that my students had to sit on windowsills or stairs to take notes. Alberta and Nova Scotia also increased tuition significantly.

The effects of this transformation have been evident in my own classes. Having taught for most of the past thirty years, I have watched the physical facilities deteriorate and the class-rooms become more crowded. When I began teaching, most students could be fully involved in the educational commu-nity. They had time after class for clubs, sports, student associations, and study groups. There was time to work in the library and for enthusiastic discussions with professors and other students outside of class hours. In those early days, few of my students had significant employment outside school.

I saw the fatigue in their faces as they struggled to keep their eyes open. And before someone says it, it's not because my lectures are more boring than those I gave thirty years ago! Students are tired because in addition to their classes, they are working twenty-hours a week or more to help pay for their classes. Some work even longer hours. They have no choice. Tuition, books, supplies, food, and housing costs have escalated. It doesn't help that in most parts of Canada, the minimum wage has lagged, been frozen, or even reduced—as happened in British Columbia. Some lucky students have parents picking up all the costs and can still experience the diversity of university or college life. But most endure as best they can. Four-year degrees take five. Debt limits further study. Too many drop out, wasting their precious time and our collective investments. In the end, the educational system suffers from inefficiency and quality concerns.

Training, apprenticeship programs, and lifelong learning also need to be priorities. Skilled labour draws industry, pro-vides better wages for workers, and reduces inequality all at the same time. Trained and employed Canadians pay taxes that help the whole system be adequately financed—another form of investment that's key to our long-term economic sustainability and human well-being.

The steady decline of our commitment to post-secondary education and to training in general is one of those social phenomena the effects of which are not immediately apparent. The process brings to mind the story of frogs placed in water that is slowly heated to the boiling point. They are unable to detect the slow changes in temperature, and even though they might jump out, they let themselves get boiled to death because they never realize what is happening to them. The signs of deterioration in our education system are evident. Let's do something about it. We need to invest in our education system, steadily targeting the best practices of European countries rather than copying the income-segregated educational tendencies of our U.S. neighbours. At the same time, we need to insist that international trade agreements protect our public and more egalitarian approach to post-secondary and trades training from intrusion by corporate, profit-making models.

Welcome to Canada?

Our other great untapped energy source is the skills that immigrants bring to our shores. Members of the Toronto City Summit Alliance, among many other groups, recognized the importance of newcomers' talents. The Alliance group wrote: "The large number of immigrants in our region are an unparalleled competitive advantage in today's global economy." No kidding. Like our citizens, over half of the newcomers to Canada also have some form of post-secondary education. In 1999, for instance, 25 per cent of immigrants from South Asia had been professionals in their home country, but only half could find work in their field in Toronto. The Conference Board of Canada estimates that "if all immigrants were employed to the level of their qualifications, it would generate roughly an additional $4 billion of wages across the country."

Immigrants bring specific skills and trades that are greatly in demand in Canada. Yet we put up barriers, and newcomers commonly find it hard to get Canadian work experience, employment-relevant language training, recognition of their credentials, or even information about employment in their own trades or professions. Our programs to aid immigrants are fragmented among levels of government and dozens of private and voluntary organizations.

The average age of skilled trades workers in Canada is about forty-eight. In the next seven to ten years, most of these people will retire. The community colleges (and CEGEPs in Quebec) have about nine hundred thousand full-time and 1.5 million part-time students, and they are doing a great job of training them. But even this influx of graduates will not fill the gap. We will need the skills that immigrants bring to Canada. For the sake of these newcomers and our economic growth and competitiveness, we need to ease the way and smooth the transition for their deeper entry into the Canadian labour force.

Our colleges are creating imaginative ways to do this, and rather than cut their funding, we need to let them improve their ability to train both Canadian-born and foreign-born students. Since the federal government is responsible for having both an immigration policy and a labour market strategy, Ottawa can—and must—play a role in skills development through the college and CEGEP system.

Canadian colleges already run programs and facilities all over the world. As one example, Centennial College in Scarborough, Ontario, provides training in the Middle East, Kazakhstan, Brazil, Sri Lanka, India, and China. These international connections are typical among our national network of colleges, and they represent a fabulous resource and link to people all around the world.

A number of colleges have presented the federal government with a proposal to reach out to potential immigrants even before they leave their country. People who want to immigrate to Canada can go to a local Canadian embassy or consulate and get information about the services Canadian colleges offer. They'd get a prior assessment of their own credentials, which would be matched against Canadian requirements, and they'd be told what they need so they can work in their field in Canada. The colleges would develop the capacity to provide potential immigrants with a program (or part of a program) to fill the gap—and could even link these newcomers with potential employers. As well, programs could be designed to provide immigrants with co-op work experience while they study in Canada, completing their application for immigrant status while they're here. Instead of being stuck for years driving cabs or waiting on tables, they'd get the right credentials to secure the right job and be able to contribute their skills in Canada. Plus, they'd be on a much faster track to earning the wages they're entitled to. The federal government is still studying the proposal. They should go for it. Both Canada and the people who could take advantage of it would be better off.

In the fall of 2003, a commitment made by the Toronto City Summit Alliance came into being, when the new Toronto Region Immigrant Employment Council launched two pilot programs. One provides internships for immigrants in finance, manufacturing, technology, and other industries. The other is a program where professional employees of the City of Toronto—including accountants, engineers, information technology specialists and others—act as mentors to new immigrants in those fields. This idea was promoted by Toronto's new mayor, David Miller, when he was chair of the city's Working Group on Immigration and Refugee Issues, and it has great potential.

On Canada Day, 2003, I was invited to a Muslim community celebration of our country's birthday. In a modest backyard, several dozen families had gathered. The mood was upbeat. The host led us in singing "O Canada" with gusto. In the conversation afterwards, one of his friends, an electrical engineer, told me that he had been encouraged to come to Canada because the immigration officer had assigned him high points on a scale that measures professional training and experience. In his country of origin, he told me, many of his professors and most of his engineering texts were British. "Obviously, Canada wanted people like me, with my skills and training," he said, "because they gave me many points specifically because of my background." He became angry as he went on: "But I found out the Canadian government was lying to me! Since I came here, I have been unable to find work in my field, even though they say there is a shortage. They won't accept my credentials. Why did they give me points if they wouldn't accept my credentials? I brought my family here for a better life. I have ended up driving a taxi for eighteen years, twelve hours a day, for six or seven days a week. I'm trapped. I've been cheated."

Then his friends started sharing their stories—a dentist, an accountant, a medical technician, a surgeon, all driving cabs or working in cleaning or security jobs. The most successful one had a small cleaning business with five employees, all of whom had professional backgrounds. "What a waste of talent," he said. "What kind of society lets perfectly good talent like that go unused?"

These stories hit close to home, right in my own family. Olivia's mother and father were both professionals in Hong Kong in 1970 when they decided to come to Canada "to make a better life for our daughter." Wai Sun Chow, her father, was a baritone in the Hong Kong opera, a biologist, and a school superintendent. Ho Sze Chow, Olivia's mother, was an elementary school teacher. On arriving in Toronto, they tried to find work in the educational system, which was expanding rapidly at the time. Qualification issues stood in their way, but they had to earn a living. Dad struggled through various jobs from heavy labour to service work and was unable to find a long-term fit despite repeated efforts. Mom landed a job cleaning rooms and working in the steamy basement laundry of a downtown hotel. She brought home the bacon that way for thirty years. Their combined talents were never able to benefit their adopted country as they could, and should, have done. But as they would point out, they did make a good life for their daughter—now perhaps the best-known elected voice of the Chinese community in Toronto. (They also used their considerable teaching skills to introduce me to speaking Cantonese.)

In 2003, the president of the Canadian Council on Social Development, Marcel Lauzière, wrote an article for the *Globe and Mail* called "Welcome to Canada. We lied about the opportunities." He showed how immigrants aren't getting ahead, despite their qualifications and willingness for hard work. Programs like those I've described would go a long way to making the opportunities we've offered genuine and achieveable.

September 11, 2001, took a terrible toll on human life immediately and in its long and continuing aftermath. But in Canada, 9/11 also added an insidious new dimension to the diverse communities we live in: fear, and the racism that flows from it. Arab, South Asian, and Muslim families have told me their stories. In the immediate aftermath, Alexa McDonough, NDP leader at the time and now foreign affairs critic, told the story in the House of Commons about the children with names like Osama being attacked in Canadian schoolyards. These children would angrily ask their parents why they had been given such names! One parent told me of her child wanting to change the colour of his skin.

Discrimination raised its ugly head in many ways, showing how easily our comfortable veneer of tolerance can be pierced when we live in a culture of fear. At the border, Canadian citizenship lost its meaning as Maher Arar was stolen from his family and shipped to a Syrian prison for a year of horrifying torture. Many young Arabs have told me how this has affected them. A young journalism student at Ryerson, brimming with wide-eyed energy and enthusiasm, for sure on her way to a funky new-wave newsroom somewhere in Canada, told me that she felt she could not travel to the United States or even through the U.S. because of her fear of treatment similar to that experienced by Arar. She did at the same time share her pride in the strength exhibited by Arar's wife, Monia Mazigh, as she mounted a courageous and single-minded campaign, first to free her husband and then to ensure that such a fate never befalls another.

From the insidious and growing practice of racial profiling to racial discrimination in the workplace, inequality based on race, culture, and religion is severely tarnishing Canada's former reputation as an open society that celebrates diversity. That's why, in our caucus on Parliament Hill, we created a Diversity Advocacy Team to work with groups across the country to break down barriers, to make racial profiling illegal, to broaden the possibilities for families to reunite here in Canada, and to support immigrant settlement services. As Canada becomes more and more diverse, we need to reform our laws, policies, practices, and programs to reflect and enhance this basic fact of Canadian life.

Let's realize the potential of all our people. It's not only a matter of justice and equality—it would also be good for our whole society, in every way.

[CHAPTER 8]

A Call to Action

Ominous Beginnings

One would have expected that, in a minority government, the prime minister would have been anxious to open doors to discussions with Opposition parties concerning the budget.

"What would the key budget items be for the NDP?" would have been the question posed in a discussion between the Liberals and our party, for example. "Are there budget initiatives on which we could agree?" No such questions were asked. The Martin Liberals seemed intent on governing as though they had a majority government.

It was an arrogant attitude that led to their relatively quick demise. Pretending that the Canadian people actually wanted the Liberals to continue governing as if they had a majority was not only an inaccurate reflection of the June 2004 vote, it also reinforced the notion that the Liberals were, once again, taking Canadians for granted.

I had hoped that the election of a minority government would produced a House of Commons with a chastened Liberal Party and one that was ready to work, to adopt a new approach. I imagined that they would try to work closely with the Opposition parties to find workable coalitions around key votes. Obviously, the yearly budget vote is one of the most important events on the parliamentary calendar. In both parliamentary and Canadian tradition, budget votes are matters of confidence. If a majority of MPs in the House votes against the budget, the government falls. Knowing this, I fully expected that the Liberals would send out envoys to open channels and begin to establish links and discussions. None of this had happened by January 2005, one month before the budget was to be presented to the House.

So we began to prepare our own budget priority plan, based on widespread consultations of our own. Such a plan had to adhere strictly to the new approach we were taking in the NDP. All budgets were to be balanced. No artificicial debt reduction targets, like the prime minister had set. No spending sprees that could not be covered by revenues during the fiscal year.

Our plan was to propose a new energy strategy as the heart of our budget proposal. We were looking to ensure a plan was implemented that would begin to deal with the air-pollution and climate-change problems. So many people were telling us that they wanted Canada to be a leader in the environmental challenges faced by the world, and they wanted clean air to breathe at home.

We also put investing in ourselves and our communities as a top priority, together with lowering the costs for post-secondary education, community environmental infrastructure, affordable housing, and child development across Canada.

Our budget proposals were proactive and sweeping, designed to kick-start change because we knew that—on all these fronts—there was no time to waste. We worked to develop public support so that we could insist on some of these directions finding their way into a reluctant Liberal budget plan. Of course when the finance minister introduced his 2005 budget, it contained the $4.6 billion to reduce corporate income taxes. This was certainly something that Prime Minister Martin had not hinted at during the election, nor did it spring from any wellspring of common values between his party and ours. With the Conservatives beside themselves with glee that their corporate friends were getting another tax break, they certainly weren't going to vote against the budget. That looked to be the end of any possible NDP involvement in the 2005 budget, but then the hearings into the sponsorship scandal began, and that changed everything.

The Challenge of Canada's Beautiful Mosaic

Canadian society is an immigrant one, made up of people who have come to these shores from all parts of the world, from all cultures and civilizations and linguistic origins. Aboriginal societies in Canada have roots that go back thousands of years before the modern waves of immigration. Thus, Aboriginal peoples have a unique place in this country and unique claims upon it.

I doubt I'd be here today had it not been for the hospitality of Aboriginal peoples. My family on my mother's side arrived on the distinctly inhospitable shores of what we now call New Brunswick in 1765, in a small sailing ship packed with several other homeless German families. They were looking for safe sanctuary, where their religious beliefs could be nurtured in freedom and where they could build a community. It had been a tough journey; their chances of surviving the oncoming Canadian winter were bleak. Thankfully for the family, there were already people on these shores who welcomed them and helped them recover their health after the disease and hunger of the journey—the people we now know as the Mi'kmaq. The Steif family, now known as the Steeves, based in Hillsborough, near Moncton, numbers in the hundreds of thousands across North America. I'm named after Jack Steeves, my grandfather, who grew up in Hillsborough.

The treatment of Aboriginal peoples in Canada has been nothing short of disgraceful. Denied respect, denied the benefits and riches of the resources that were theirs, denied even the provisions guaranteed under treaties signed by the

Queen, the First Nations have been driven into desperate living conditions on reserves, in remote communities, even in
urban areas. International organizations have rightly con-
demned Canada for its treatment of the original inhabitants
of these lands.

It is now time to treat Aboriginal peoples as full and
respected partners in the evolution of Canada. The excellent
1996 report of the Royal Commission on Aboriginal Peoples
continues to offer a guide. By forming partnerships with
grassroots organizations, we can put the report's recommendations into action. Witness, for example, the collaboration
between the NDP, particularly MP Pat Martin, and First
Nations organizations in the summer of 2003 to filibuster and
ultimately defeat the patronizing First Nations Governance
legislation, Bill C-7.

In recent years, New Democratic governments have made
great strides toward settling outstanding claims and finding
new ways to work with First Nations. Recent land agreements, such as those reached with the Nisga'a and Sechelt
peoples, are particularly significant, but there are many other
achievements that should be acknowledged. Participants in
the NDP's Yukon round table a few years back, for example,
were proud of the partnerships that Aboriginal, municipal,
and territorial governments have developed. Svend Robinson
often reminded me that the 1982 Constitutional package recognized Aboriginal rights only because the federal NDP
caucus, led by Ed Broadbent, succeeded in insisting that
Aboriginal rights had to be included.

The true heroes, however, are First Nations leaders and
communities. Like Barrière Lake Reserve Chief Harry
Wawatie, whose community of four hundred people live in
sixty decrepit houses in abject poverty while resource-
extracting firms and tourism companies suck the enormous
economic wealth out of the lands that should provide the

community with sustenance. Courage and wise determination are what you see in the chief's eyes, along with deep sadness as he watches an affluent nation systematically deny basic human rights and security to the next generation of his community.

In most immigrant cultures, there is a convergence around one common language for public discourse. In the United States, this is English; in Argentina, it's Spanish. In Canada we find not one but two such languages of convergence: French and English. Essentially, there are two immigrant foundations in this country—two dominant, coexisting foundations that have been enriched and strengthened by several waves of immigration from all corners of the globe.

Aboriginal peoples are in an important sense part of this duality, in that their societies were forced by circumstance or coercion to choose English or French as the language used to interact with public institutions. The most brutal instance of imposed acculturation was the re-education of Aboriginal children in residential schools.

French and English each have their areas of geographic strength. Acadians in the Maritimes are a key francophone component, as are significant communities in Ontario and Manitoba, but the centre of Canada's French-speaking immigrant society is clearly the province of Quebec—dynamic, varied, multicultural. As the heart of Canada's francophone population—a diverse one comprising several Aboriginal groups and people from all parts of the world—Quebec has responsibilities and challenges unlike those of any other province.

Quebec is the vibrant, distinct society it is today primarily as the result of its policies since the Quiet Revolution, which began with the election of the Liberals under Jean Lesage in June 1960. I grew up in the midst of this transformation from hidebound conservative traditionalism to the inspired reform of economic, social, and cultural institutions. Debates were passionate, and there were deep disagreements and crises in Quebec at the time. Still, the policies that prevailed and allowed Quebec to flourish were frequently based on the values of social democracy. Indeed, the province's progressive agenda in the latter part of the century influenced policy-making in Canada as a whole.

I find it tragic that language and culture continue to divide Canada into two solitudes. One key reason I decided to seek the leadership of the NDP was to see if I could somehow assist in making a bridge between the social democratic impulses of Quebec and those found elsewhere in Canada. I believe that the NDP, a social democratic party, could be the ideal means to accomplish this, but we have a great distance to go. And we have had to revise our traditional, rather centrist, approach to a relationship with Quebec. We need to assist in the evolution of a flexible federalism that allows Quebec to achieve its goals within a Canadian nation-state.

I witnessed the possibilities for flexible federalism up close when I was involved in trying to bring the federal government and the provinces toward an agreement on a new, affordable, social housing construction program. As a vice-president of the Federation of Canadian Municipalities at the time, I was charged with working with the federal minister of public works, the singularly unhelpful Alfonso Gagliano, and the provincial ministers responsible for housing. Fortunately, the lead ministers were Tim Sale of Manitoba and Louise Harel of Quebec. Flexibility in our approach ensured that Quebec could pursue its social housing program the way it wanted to—essentially elaborating on the excellent initiatives that it had under way. In fact, the Quebec approach was the best in the whole of Canada. It was beautifully ironic, I thought. Here was Quebec, the most likely to object to federal dollars being devoted to a policy field that was being actively pursued by the Quebec National

Assembly, and yet Quebec was the most effective at achieving the affordable housing goals with dedicated federal dollars. It put other provinces to shame, particularly those like Ontario that refused to match the federal funds and thus left the homeless in that province out in the cold.

Prior to my becoming leader, the NDP began work on a framework for flexible, asymmetrical federalism structured around co-operative decision-making, respectful of the jurisdictions that have been established in our Constitution, to achieve the goals that Canadians agree on. This practical concept of managing the relationships of Canadian federalism has a lot of appeal. Hard work? Yes. But worth the effort, certainly. In the process, I am extending my hand to today's Quebeckers with an invitation to help build a coast-to-coast-to-coast social democratic movement to serve as a real, viable, and exciting alternative to the corporate drift we see in the two old-line parties, the Liberals and the Conservatives.

Elsewhere, relationships in our Canadian federation are terribly strained. Years of neglect and even disdain at the hands of a remote and uninterested national government have left deep scars in western Canada. And those wounds have been reopened with the inadequate response to years of inadequate incomes for western farmers, a cautious financial response to offset the devastation of closed borders after mad cow disease (BSE) was discovered in one Alberta cow, no retaliation against killer U.S. agricultural subsidies making it almost impossible for our farmers to sell some commodities profitably, punishing softwood lumber tariffs, and federal fishery management ineptitude. The lists of grievances are long and detailed.

I've learned a lot about the realities faced by western Canadian communities from my years building the national movement of communities of all sizes through the Federation of Canadian Municipalities.

I've also learned about the grievances in eastern Canada. Population flows out to central Canada like a hemorrhage. Especially of young people. No wonder communities lose hope. As laissez-faire economics took hold, central Canadian corporate interests have shifted investment in ways that leave communities struggling. A clear case in point is the Saint John shipyards. Once a source of secure, well-paid jobs, these operations have been closed down following decisions by international firms to build ships where cheap labour is plentiful—firms like Canada Steamship Lines, which used to build ships in Canada and now uses low-paid workers in the shipyards of China. Or the coal-mining community of Sydney on Cape Breton Island, where unemployed coal miners watch ships roll into the harbour to unload Venezuelan coal. The polluting coal dust floats over the community and into the lungs of the residents of Whitney Pier, while coal of equivalent quality lies in closed mines underneath their feet and Cape Breton families struggle to survive. No wonder the East feels left out of the so-called national equation.

Canada's North raises similar concerns. Climate change will have the most dramatic effects in the North, yet Canada is not leading the way to respond to the crisis. Northern health needs tend to be forgotten. When the provincial premiers met in 2003 to hammer out some modest federal funding, for instance, the northern territories were completely forgotten. NDP health advocate Svend Robinson made a trip to the North to collect evidence, and only then was there a response from the governing Liberals. Ottawa loves to exploit the image of the exotic North but does not give a considered response to its needs.

Over the years, I've learned how diverse groups can pull together in support of one another to secure federal attention and support. At the FCM, I argued that the neglected needs of all our communities should be presented as one.

That's why the FCM created the Rural Caucus to represent northern and remote communities. Their voices were added to the Big-City Mayors' Caucus, and the unified message was irresistible. The call for federal investment of the gas tax in community transportation for cities, towns, and rural areas across all of Canada was an example of the approach I recommended. At first, Paul Martin completely rejected the idea. "I don't believe in dedicated taxes!" he told me. But once he began to hear from a thousand democratically elected community governments, all with the same message, he could not continue to resist the demand for action.

That's why we need to build united voices around the full range of community concerns in this country. There's only one way to cure alienation: we must control the situation through united action. Westerners, easterners, Quebeckers, northerners, and central Canadians with common values have to come together to support one another in the effort to meet essential needs.

The fact is, Canadians have a basic instinct to do just that. I remember discussing the reaction in drought-ridden Saskatchewan when eastern Ontario farmers got together with big-city politicians like Ottawa City Councillor Clive Doucet in Ottawa and with me in Toronto and pushed bumper-crop surplus hay into western Canada to feed starving animals. People simply couldn't believe it. They were surprised that anyone east of Kenora cared. Well, I know that Canadians do care about each other. It's the federal government that too often doesn't care. That's what has to change.

Our relationships with each other within Canada need some work, but we all know how important they are. And what ties us together in our astounding diversity is the idea that we share sufficient core values to allow us to work together, in our different ways, on our common project— building the country that captures our hopes for the future.

Issues North and South

Is this an approach that should guide our relationships with those outside our own borders? I think so. Let's consider our history. Canada has long championed multilateralism—the idea that many ethnic groups should work together to achieve security and improve the well-being of the human family. It is a logical position for us, politically situated as we are between Europe and the United States. Canada has played an important role in building and supporting multilateral institutions such as the United Nations. In general, Canada has been a voice for peace over aggression.

We saw this most recently with the outburst of opposition by Canadians to the invasion of Iraq by George W. Bush, armed with his new unilateral doctrine of the pre-emptive strike. As the newly elected leader of our party in January 2003, I found myself at the centre of the debate in Canada about what we should do. The NDP took the position that Canada should not participate in the invasion and should instead support the work of the United Nations arms-control inspectors who were slowly making their way through Iraq, searching for weapons of mass destruction. We urged our government to take a strong stand too. I and other NDP MPs spoke at rallies in the freezing cold all over Canada. We mounted petitions and websites. At first, things did not look good. Jean Chrétien ridiculed the NDP in the House, saying, "They think a good singsong would solve all the problems."

But we formed alliances with the broadly based movements that were working for peace. This created a positive process of connecting with Canadians across the land who felt strongly about an issue and were organizing on the ground to make their views known. And it produced powerful results: the most memorable moment for me was when

Prime Minister Chrétien rose in the House on the eve of the invasion to announce that Canada would not participate.

Then, much to my dismay, Liberal leadership candidate Paul Martin was quoted on the front page of a national newspaper suggesting that the decision not to go to war might have compromised our relationship with the Bush administration, and that to set things back on track we should initiate talks with U.S. officials concerning Canadian participation in "National Missile Defence." At first, the Chrétien cabinet balked at this idea, but it did not take long for the Martin forces in the cabinet to prevail, and talks were initiated.

The whole concept of a missile shield is the antithesis of multilateral action to accomplish greater human security. The Bush government has laid out a plan ultimately to involve land-based, sea-based, and space-based interceptor missiles. The idea is to erect the equivalent of a fence of weapons around America to block incoming warheads. Not only has the system never been successfully tested, it is also monstrously expensive and will certainly provoke a new arms race around the entire planet. After all, the mere deployment of the first phase of a scheme involving land-based missiles required the U.S. government to tear up its Anti-Ballistic Missile Treaty with Russia. As though to underline the dangers of this strategy, the Russians publicized their successful test of a new rocket that could be guided away from missile interceptors as it manoeuvred toward its target. This development effectively makes obsolete Bush's Star Wars II before it has even been built. The Russians rightly fear that the American initiative will provoke powers like China to develop more sophisticated weapons in greater numbers. All in all, a new arms race is effectively under way.

So what did Canada do? In 2004, we were told by Prime Minister Martin's government that we had to "be at the table" to influence the program. His officials even suggested that by being at the table we could help convince the Pentagon not to put weapons in space. Piously, Martin rose in the House to say that the National Missile Defence system did not involve weapons in space and that the Canadian government would never support weapons in space. I was criticized by Liberal MPs for scaremongering.

There was only one thing to do. I went to Washington to meet with members of Congress, to get the facts. The congressmen and congresswomen I met with were incredulous that a Canadian prime minister could be suggesting the plan did not involve the weaponization of space. Everyone in Washington, they said, knew what the program was about. The land-based missiles were only the first step. They showed me Defense Department budget submissions, clearly indicating the funds that were being requested for the development of more than three hundred space-based interceptors by the latter part of this decade. A study by the American Physical Society—the physicists—showed that a land-based interceptor system could not, even in theory, be effective. I was told that more than one hundred members of Congress had voted against these appropriations because of their fears of a new arms race.

This meeting made it clear that opposition to Bush's absurd plan was strong both in Canada and the United States. In Canada, Alexa McDonough, MP from Halifax and NDP peace advocate, had been spearheading a caucus effort to work with peace and security groups to ensure Canadians opposed to the Bush Star Wars plan had a voice in Parliament. Since spring 2003, she had been working closely with civil society groups like the Polaris Institute to keep pressure on the government. As I travelled cross the country that year and in early 2004, it became clear to me how widespread Canadians' opposition was to this absurd plan by Mr. Bush and to our government's involvement in it.

In early April 2004, a poll done by Ipsos-Reid found that 69 per cent of Canadians were against Canada joining the Bush administration's National Missile Defence plan. Yet not three weeks later, we found out the Martin government had been engaged in secret negotiations with the Bush administration and was on track to sign an agreement sealing Canada's participation in the National Missile Defence system. And we found out the Martin Liberals were planning on delaying any announcement of this secret agreement until after an election, which everyone expected to be called late that spring.

Not surprisingly, during the spring 2004 election, Mr. Martin chose to say little about the National Missile Defence system. Canadians, however, chose to elect a minority Parliament and take away the right of the Liberals to ignore their wishes.

When the new Parliament convened in the fall of 2004, Mr. Martin continued his convoluted argument that the Liberals would not support the weaponization of space but would continue negotiating with the United States on Canada's involvement in the National Missile Defence system. Ignoring the facts, Mr. Martin continued the fiction that Bush's missile defence shield would somehow not lead to the weaponization of space.

All of this came to a head in late November 2004, when President Bush made his first official state visit to Canada since Paul Martin became prime minister. The National Missile Defence system was not on the official agenda, nor was there an expectation that the topic would be raised in any signficant way when the two heads of state met. One of the perks of being a party leader is that you get invited to state dinners for visiting heads of state. The evening of President Bush's arrival, I attended the state dinner for him and had the opportunity to briefly chat with him. I asked the president whether his missile defence plan involved putting weapons in space. He said yes.

The next day the president gave a keynote speech in Halifax and urged Canada to sign on to his national missile defence plan. What was to have been a fairly straightfoward state visit that allowed Mr. Martin to show Canadians his good relations with President Bush turned into a political crisis. On one hand, the president was looking for the prime minister's support. On the other hand, there was now clear evidence that this support would mean undermining the Liberal government's assertion that such support would not to involve Canada in a program that would lead to the weaponization of space.

As was often the case with the former Liberal government, it was the author of its own crisis. The simple solution would have been to listen to Canadians and announce publicly that Canada would not participate in the U.S. national missile defence plan. Alternatively, Mr. Martin could have immediately called for the issue to be debated and voted on in the House of Commons. Instead, the prime minister once again dithered and let the Christmas season come and go.

One of my most memorable days in politics came on February 24, 2005, when Prime Minister Martin finally did the right thing and announced Canada would not participate in Bush's missile defence plan. While most Canadians were celebrating the decision, I was also celebrating the huge effort of countless Canadians who forced the Martin government to reverse its stance. And I was celebrating the fact that my party had shown how we can do politics differently in this country by working closely with civil society groups on issues that matter.

Where does this leave us? Canada has said no to formal participation. However, questions remain whether there is still informal participation going on and whether the Harper government will reopen this issue. If Prime Minister Harper chooses to reopen discussions on Canada's involvement in the National Missile Defence system, it will send out a message to the world. The message will be that Canada believes this is an idea worth pursuing. Such a message will undermine any credibility we may have gained through our decision not to support the invasion of Iraq. We will not be seen as an effective, independent, sovereign voice on the world stage. Our historic role as advocate for peace will be abandoned. We will have instead become a lapdog, a bit player in the Bush initiative.

Is the NDP stance anti-American? Absolutely not. In my first year as leader, I met with members of Congress on two trips to the U.S. capital. They included John Tierney from Massachusetts, Rush Holt from New Jersey, and Bernie Sanders from Vermont. I also encountered many Americans who, like me and my party, often disagree with President Bush's policies but who, like me and my party, have a deep respect and affinity for America.

Sometimes our countries agree—on fighting acid rain, on the Second World War, on Korea, and on Kosovo. And sometimes we disagree—on the Iraq and Vietnam wars, on our relationship with Cuba, on the International Criminal Court, on the Kyoto Protocol. Though our values are similar enough to us to be good friends, they are different enough for us to disagree, respectfully. Though our Canadian system of universal medicare is not perfect, it is fundamentally more equitable and efficient than the system found in the United States, a health-care system that many Canadians find offensive—one designed to exclude those who cannot buy their way in. We share a continent, but we do not always share the same values. When we do have common goals, we do not necessarily use the same means to achieve them.

Like Canada, Mexico is sometimes moved to disagree with American policy. We need to look no further than the chilling of relations between Mexico's President Vicente Fox and President Bush after Mexico took a far more public stand against the Iraq War than did Canada, given that Mexico sat on the UN Security Council at that critical time.

It is time for a different view of Canada-U.S. relations that enables us to co-operate, on the one hand, and respectfully disagree, when necessary, on the other. Canada is not a neutral nation, nor are we a pacifist one. We have unequivocally taken sides in some of the world's great choices and fought for freedom. In fact, some argue, Canada became an international citizen through the world wars of the twentieth century. Those wars shaped the world, and in their aftermath, Canada and the United States joined to find ways to co-operate with other nations to try to prevent future wars, most notably through the creation of the United Nations. Whatever its faults, and there are many, the UN represents a very Canadian world view.

For a country like ours, multilateralism allows us to play an effective role in solving global problems such as the environment, arms proliferation, AIDS in Africa, or grinding poverty in developing countries. It also allows us to effectively contribute military resources to crises, working with like-minded nations in peacekeeping or peacemaking.

Canadians are justifiably proud of our historic role in the world and justifiably proud of the successes of multilateralism—from the Montreal Protocol on the ozone layer, to helping rid the world of the scourge of land mines, to creating the treaties now used to dampen the nuclear escalation between India and Pakistan. This is not to say the model is perfect. Given recent atrocities in Rwanda, the world's failure to respond to the emerging crisis of climate change, and our complacent acceptance of trading models that cement fundamental global inequalities, we clearly have much work to do.

Prime Minister Paul Martin once quoted rock star Bono: "The world needs more Canadas." And Bono was correct, even if Martin's policies were by and large not. The world does need more nations working together on common concerns—in other words, multilateralism. President Bush recognized this, too, given that he was so anxious to portray the Iraq War as a coalition rather than a unilateral American war. I'm still not certain what the Solomon Islands or Micronesia contributed to the effort, but at least Bush recognized that despite being the world's last superpower, America could not be seen to be acting alone.

The world does not become safer because a superpower decides to launch a new weapons system. Nor is America's growing deficit helped by spending upward of $1 trillion to weaponize space. Furthermore, the United States does not strengthen its positioin in the world by undermining arms control agreements such as the Anti-Ballistic Missile Treaty and the comprehensive test ban treaty. Nor would Canada's position in the world be helped should we become involved in these U.S. policies.

Inevitably, the credibility of American foreign policy has suffered significantly. The White House is the symbol of Western values to much of the world. If it resolutely espouses unilateralism, it does us all a disservice, the U.S. included. America needs allies with credibility. That makes American insistence that Canada join in their National Missile Defence system doubly dangerous. Multilateral arms control and weapons reduction require rules that are made by all, applicable to all, and protective of all—America included.

Fortunately, many Americans are joining what I call a new superpower, one proposing just such a vision—that is, the gathering strength of citizens around the world. We saw it in the streets in Canada, in the United States, and, indeed, in most countries during the Iraq War. I believe fundamentally that citizens can create the political impetus that requires governments to respond. I know this because I've seen it in action. In Canada, as we were deciding our role in the war, the public voice for peace played a role in the decision not to join President Bush in Iraq.

Yet in Canada, the new prevailing view in our government is that questioning Bush's policies is dangerous, while obeying them is safer; thus, we consign Canadian values and those of millions of Americans to irrelevance. I do not believe in the false choice between foreign policy obedience and economic success. We need to recognize that there are ways in which we can co-operate that reflect our values, respect our security, and reward our economy. History does not justify the fear-mongering theory that Canada must blindly go along with our biggest trading partner on foreign policy so economic growth will flow automatically. During the Vietnam War, Lester Pearson stayed out of the conflict yet simultaneously negotiated the Auto Pact, perhaps Canada's best trade deal ever. In Afghanistan, Jean Chrétien joined the American effort but received no consideration or assistance in correcting the unjust U.S. softwood lumber surcharges that have thrown thousands of Canadian workers onto unemployment lines.

In U.S.-Canadian relations, one area badly in need of significant improvement is trade. Workers on both sides of the border are hurt by the current NAFTA model, as corporations move jobs to countries whose workers are paid lower wages. In addition, Americans and Canadians are disadvantaged by the Bush administration's punishing duties on softwood lumber, which eliminate employment opportunities in both countries and notably affect American families who rely on our lumber for construction jobs and affordable homes. With an economy in trouble, the U.S. should build homes *with* our lumber, not build walls *against* it.

The American Congress needs to understand it cannot selectively penalize Canadian resource industries, all the while benefiting from safe, affordable energy from Canada. This means putting all issues on the table when we negotiate. If President Bush wishes to ignore NAFTA as it affects lumber, there is no reason Canada should not ignore NAFTA as it affects energy.

When Prime Minister Harper sold out the Canadian forest industry in his rush to please George W. Bush, he had no mandate to do so. Only Parliament can decide such matters, a fact that Mr. Harper may not like, but must accept. Rather than threaten an election on the matter, he should reach out to the Opposition parties and work with us to find a softwood sector solution that respects Canadian soveriegnty and provides real relief to besieged forest sector communities.

Canada and the United States can work toward common ends, even if the means differ. Certainly this is true on environmental issues, as we share the airspace and watersheds of a single continent. President John F. Kennedy once said, "The deepest common thing in us is that we live on the same small planet. We breathe the same air. We all care about the future of our children and we are all mortal beings." This is true now more than ever before. Canada, which nominally supports the Kyoto Protocol, receives smog from the U.S., which does not support Kyoto. And my son ends up in an emergency room with asthma. And American sons end up in emergency wards with asthma as a result of pollution from our coal-burning plants. No gasping children care if their government supports Kyoto, but every parent who's stood by as a child struggles to breathe wants clean air.

And so, although I hope America finally joins the world's only climate-change treaty and I hope Canada finally honours it, I say, "Let's work outside Kyoto for the benefit of both." Canada should join with progressive American states such as California, Massachusetts, and perhaps New York to create larger markets for cleaner cars. California and Canada together represent a market of almost sixty-five million people, and such a market gives manufacturers a powerful financial incentive to build cleaner cars in greater numbers. If treaties alone are unappealing, we can use market mechanisms as well. Because, make no mistake, no politician's legacy can match that of helping arrest climate change. If humanity's going to Mars, let's do it as explorers, not refugees. When Stephen Hawking says, as he did in the spring of 2006 because of impending catastrophes, that we have to prepare to leave the planet, let's prove him wrong.

I say to our American friends, let's share each other's technologies and ideas—from our deep-lakewater cooling in Toronto to your massive wind farms in Texas, from our fuel-cell technology to Iowa's program that gives farm families money in exchange for wind turbines on their fields. As inhabitants of the continent, we've all seen floods, forest fires, and droughts. Melting ice caps are yet to come. It's time for North Americans of good faith to use our ideas and pocketbooks to shame our timid leaders and show the world how it's done.

Let's also recognize that our militaries should co-operate. NDP MP Peter Stoffer made arrangements for me to have tea in the home of Rear Admiral Glen Davidson, commander of the Canadian East Coast fleet. Admiral Davidson told me of some of the rescue missions Canada has carried out at sea, thanks to American satellite data from the air. This joint effort saved distressed sailors from countries near and far in a spirit of true co-operation. Our militaries have often worked together in a troubled world. Our diplomats should collaborate, too, to create tools to improve conditions for the international populace. Nobody can be proud of the way member nations of the United Nations have responded to crisis. From Kosovo to Rwanda to the Congo, the world has watched as millions were slaughtered.

We must establish a United Nations rapid deployment capacity in order to intervene in a timely way during crises. Days of delay meant the loss of thousands of lives in Rwanda. Months of delay meant the wrath of ancient hatreds unleashed in Kosovo. And, since no country is perfect and all have their prejudices, we need a neutral force ready and willing to react. Democracy doesn't develop during strife. Though American sensibilities may be bruised by following the orders of a military with UN blue helmets, American self-interest dictates that a multilateral response force be ready and willing. We must implement, globally, a vision based on practical co-operation and multilateral response. To draw from Noam Chomsky, the choice between multilateral versus unilateral responses amounts to a choice between hegemony and survival.

To be clear, I do not wish for continental security perimeters or a joint Canada-U.S. command, or even a massive increase in defence spending. Nor do I support draconian anti-terrorism or security laws like those that have already ensnared hundreds in the American prison at Guantanamo Bay, detained without access to justice.

Canada's next federal election will determine whether we pursue integration with the United States on security, economic, and environmental issues. As with the last such debate, in the 1988 federal election, I believe the choices will be clear and the debate invigorating. Over the past century of Canadian politics, we have had three prime ministers who are fundamentally integrationist: Wilfrid Laurier, Brian Mulroney, and Paul Martin. Laurier was defeated over integrationist policies in 1911. Mulroney was indeed re-elected on those policies in 1988, thanks to an out-of-date voting system, but as the impact of those policies became clear, his party suffered the worst possible defeat in the following election. History shows Martin entered dangerous territory in aggressively pursuing integrationist policies immediately before an election—and immediately after several decisions by the Bush administration that were deeply unpopular in Canada, the Iraq War and the U.S. decision not to ratify the Kyoto Protocol being chief among them. Now Mr. Martin is out and Stephen Harper is the prime minister. Canadians will learn over the life of this new minority government how closely the Canadian and U.S. administrations will choose to work together.

I've travelled to many parts of the United States and Canada over the course of my life, and I've never heard anyone say, "You know, I don't mind my son being in the emergency ward, choking on smog-related asthma, because I got a tax cut today." Or, "I'm really happy we're investing billions in Star Wars because I'm worried about a rogue state launching an intercontinental ballistic missile attack tomorrow." Since North Korea's missile launches I hear Canadians being stronger in their commitment not to jump on board George Bush's new arms race, the weaponization of space.

What I do hear is people saying they're concerned about being able to afford university tuition for their children, or they're anxious about health care for their families, or they're worried about the future of the family farm, or they're nervous about the security of their pension plan. Though Canadians and Americans do in fact differ on some values, on essential issues we agree. And so while relations between our two governments can chill, the bonds among citizens across the border are far from severed.

Canadians have a unique contribution to make, to the neighbourhood of our continent, to the rest of the hemisphere, and to the wider world. The values on which we propose to build a better society in our own complex and extraordinary country are values that serve us well in our relations with the rest of world. They are the values on which Lloyd Axworthy draws when he speaks of "human security," the values that motivate Stephen Lewis when he urges us to adopt proposals to save millions of lives by eradicating AIDS and tackling poverty in Africa. We have the opportunity to reject policies of fear and to embrace initiatives of hope. At home and abroad, let's make that choice.

[CHAPTER 9]

Two Seats Short

After the dust had settled from the June 28, 2004 election, it was as though Paul Martin and his Liberal team failed to understand or accept the fact that they no longer had a majority in the House of Commons. Canadians had issued a rather stern rebuke to the Liberals, a party that only a few short months before had been widely expected to sail back to power with another comfortable majority under Mr. Martin, their new white knight. What happened? I believe that the revelations of the auditor general concerning the sponsorship scandals hit hard, and voters were not about to reward a party that had been accused of such outrageous mismanagement of their money. Anger was the operative emotion as the campaign began, and Stephen Harper's Conservatives capitalized on the mood to surge forward in the polls. A little premature Conservative arrogance about the likely election outcome, including speculation about Stephen Harper becoming prime minister, allowed the Liberals to ramp up a brilliant fear-based campaign in the last ten days before the election. Liberal strategists constructed messages that appealed directly to NDP voters and urged them to help stop the Conservatives by switching their vote to the Liberals. Unfortunately for the NDP, too many Canadians bought into that strategy. As a result, our two Saskatchewan incumbents, Lorne Nystrom and Dick Proctor, both lost, ironically to the Conservatives. In other ridings, this last-minute Liberal strategy had an impact on the NDP team—Nettie Wiebe and Dennis Gruending in Saskatchewan, Olivia Chow and Peggy Nash in Toronto, David Turner and Catherine Bell on Vancouver Island, and

Dennis Bevington in the Western Arctic all suffered narrow defeats. Chow, Nash, Bell and Bovington all won their seats in the House 18 months later in the 2006 election.

I hadn't helped matters with my ineffective inaugural performance in the leaders' debates. I didn't like what I had to do during the debates, which was to interrupt and try to wedge my way in. For me, those debates were the political equivalent of a mud-wrestling match, rather than a debate about serious issues. Going into those debates, the NDP was regarded as a fringe party—not real players, a party largely relegated to the sidelines over the past decade. We were perceived as just hoping to be noticed, with no possibility of winning the big victory—government. Looking back, I must confess that I helped fulfill these prophesies, as I tried to jump into the debate without a scrap of subtlety in the free-for-all exchanges. In my own defense, the format negotiated by the parties and the television networks was simply atrocious. After introductory exchanges there were to be a total of four seven-minute virtual mud-wrestling matches. This meant that whichever one of us could claw his or her way to a position of prominence— usually by out-shouting the others—got to speak. Whether any of us was heard however was another matter. The mean-spirited, constant interrupting and downright rudeness turned many people off the political process altogether.

Important national elections shouldn't be determined on the basis of which leader is most effective in elbowing his opponent aside. I swore that I would never agree to such a format again. The American presidential debate a few months later, with George W. Bush debating John Kerry, was far more civilized. On this score, the Americans had a better approach, and our party insisted that there be significant changes to the debate format in the future.

As for the rest of my first campaign as national leader of the NDP, I really liked the optimistic tone and hopeful message we conveyed throughout. It fit well with my own deep feelings about what politics could and should be about, namely an optimistic call for Canada to achieve its potential. We called for "a green and prosperous Canada where no one's left behind." We also had a strong program to back up the optimism. It was particularly gratifying that two major national environmental organizations, Greenpeace and the Sierra Club of Canada, determined that our platform document was the "greenest" of all the parties, even out-greening the Greens.

The Liberals, too, started their re-election campaign with a hopeful appeal to Canadians for the future. But the negative message of Stephen Harper gained more traction for the Conservatives in the early weeks of the election campaign. The voters were grumpy, anger was growing, and the Conservatives were the main beneficiaries. By the mid-point of the election the disaffection for the Liberals peaked and, at that point, our internal polling showed us winning a number of seats currently held by Liberals. "Anger has trumped hope," my communications director, Jamey Heath, told me as we struggled on the campaign plane to try to figure out what was happening.

After the leaders' debates, though, the Liberals smartly switched gears. They chose to mount a campaign of fear at the prospect of a Conservative government. Playing directly to NDP supporters, Mr. Martin's campaign launched a week-long blitz appealing to the real fears of progressive Canadians about the potential impact of a Harper government. The Liberals asked the electorate to just imagine what the Conservatives would do to human rights, the environment, our health-care system, and our foreign policy! The campaign was skillfully put together and targeted with precision, and fear trumped anger and the Liberals rebounded to eke out a minority and, in the process, took back seats from the NDP that it had appeared we were about to win. Frustrating? That's for sure.

We had asked Canadians to give New Democrats a "significant role" in the new House of Commons so that we could work on behalf of people and the environment. It was a thinly veiled call for Canadians to elect a minority government, although I was careful never to say so explicitly. Perhaps, in retrospect, I should have been more direct. Canadians however seemed to hear the message nonetheless. So on June 28, 2004, Canadian voters built a minority House consisting of 135 Liberals, 99 Conservatives, 54 Bloc, 19 New Democrats, and one Independent.

In retrospect, despite the fact that they were twenty seats short of a majority, I think Paul Martin and his Liberals simply saw themselves as having regained unconditional power. With their come-from-behind, last-minute surge, they had pulled the rabbit out of the hat. As a result, I don't think it ever sunk in to this party—so long accustomed to power—that, while they'd won the most seats, they no longer had a majority. And, without a majority, they no longer had the authority to govern alone.

At our first NDP caucus meeting we agreed that we would do our best to produce some positive results from this minority Parliament. No party received what it really wanted in the election. The Liberals won a minority; the Conservatives won only a handful of new seats; the Bloc won more seats but were chagrined they hadn't done even better. For our part, we would certainly have been happier with more seats—just two more and we could have negotiated with the Liberals from a position of strength. And it was irritating in the extreme to know that more than 2.1 million Canadians had voted for NDP candidates but had translated into only nineteen seats. Ed Broadbent—a colleague in caucus, which was a thrill in itself—tried to assuage the deep disappointment at the inequity of the results. He reminded us that, when he had led the NDP to its best performance ever in 1988, his team hadn't received that many more votes than we had, yet it had translated into forty-three seats. There was the additional frustration of looking over at the fifty-three-member Bloc Québécois caucus and knowing full well that the Bloc had received half a-million fewer votes than the New Democrats had, but because of their vote concentration in our first-past-the-post system, they had elected thirty-four more MPs than the NDP had. Ed suggested that our caucus should make democratic and electoral reform a priority, advice that we took to heart.

Our fresh-faced and enthusiastic new nineteen-member caucus assembled in July 2004 and immediately focused on opportunities that would achieve the commitments we'd set out in the campaign:

1. create opportunities in a green and prosperous economy;
2. improve public health care through innovation, not privatization;
3. invest in cities and communities to produce safe drinking water, more affordable housing, and better public transit;
4. expand access to post-secondary education and training;
5. make life more affordable, starting with expanding child care, removing the GST from family essentials, and protecting pensions;
6. strengthen Canada's independent voice for peace, human rights, and fair trade on the world stage;
7. restore integrity and accountability in government; and
8. balance the budget.

We were able to convert most of these commitments into positive results through our budget amendment and other initiatives during this minority House. But things didn't start well.

Statistics buffs might find the following facts remarkable: in the 2004 election, the Bloc Québécois elected one MP for every 31,000 votes cast for their party; the Liberals chalked up an MP for each 37,000 votes; the Conservatives needed 40,000 to capture each seat; while the NDP—always having to try harder—needed 110,000 votes to elect one MP! But before we start feeling sorry for ourselves, it has to be said that the Greens received 500,000 votes, but no seats.

As to how we might start to try to make a difference, I asked each caucus member to be in touch with the cabinet minister who corresponded to his or her critic areas (subjects or policy areas I assign to each MP). We wanted to offer to each minister the opportunity to work together on issues of common concern. I was sure that we could find a number of areas of common ground. The response from the cabinet ministers however was deeply disappointing—a virtual silence. Only two of the almost three dozen cabinet ministers bothered to respond at all—Immigration Minister Judy Sgro and the minister responsible for implementing the child-care program, Ken Dryden. The prime minister, despite what I took to be a friendly election-night call, did not agree to meet with me until two full months after the election. To be fair, I hadn't pressed too hard for an immediate meeting with him. Even so, the delay seemed a trifle odd, given the election outcome and the uncertainty in the air.

The afternoon finally arrived, in late August 2004, when I was scheduled to meet with Prime Minister Martin for the first time. I was both hopeful and optimistic that, despite the significant differences between Liberals and New Democrats, we would be able to reach agreement on a priority package of legislation to help Canadian families in a number of different areas.

After all, former Liberal leader Lester B. Pearson and his successor, Pierre Elliott Trudeau, had led minority governments where, with the pushing and prodding, suggestions and demands, help and encouragement of NDP leaders and their caucus, good policies and programs were put in place that improved the lives of Canadian families. I pictured Tommy Douglas preparing to sit down with Mr. Pearson and his key advisers following the 1965 general election. Mr. Douglas found Mr. Pearson affable but indecisive, and the Liberals were told by pollsters to try to work with Mr. Douglas since Liberal polling indicated that 83 per cent of Canadians had positive comments about Mr. Douglas. The two men would certainly have talked about the urgent need for a Canada Pension Plan and how Saskatchewan's successful medicare program—pioneered by Douglas and his successor, Woodrow Lloyd—could become a national program. Although not nearly enough Canadians know their history, medicare wasn't always available for Canadian families. It didn't just fall from the sky to land on Canada but not the United States. Canada's public health-care system was negotiated by Tommy Douglas and his NDP caucus after the 1965 federal election. Now, it's true that in the 1965 election, the Liberals had promised to introduce medicare. But nobody believed them because the Liberals had made that promise in every election since 1919!

I also thought about Tommy Douglas's successor, David Lewis, and envisaged him sitting down with Mr. Trudeau in the fall of 1972, after the Liberals had been reduced to just two more seats than the Progressive Conservatives. As NDP-CCF historian Alan Whitehorn noted: "...Many Canadians consider the 1972–1974 minority Parliament to have been one of the most productive and progressive in recent Canadian history." That minority resulted from what Paul Martin Senior described as "one of the greatest election campaigns of all time." In the election, NDP Leader David Lewis mounted his campaign against the "corporate welfare bums."

On October 30, 1972, Canadians gave Mr. Trudeau's Liberals 109 seats, the Conservatives under Robert Stanfield 107, and the NDP 31. For David and the NDP it was a 41 per cent increase in seats and, with that increase, the balance of power in a minority government. What was important about the result in 1972 was that there was never any rest for the Liberal or NDP MPs—they had to work day-in and day-out, negotiating amongst themselves how best to get real results for Canadians. There were no laurels to rest upon! Exhausting. This, in fact, *was* good for democracy in Canada. No guarantee of a relaxed four years for the MPs. Instead, constant insecurity—would the government fall? When? How? More important, a constant discussion in and out of Parliament about what was best for the country.

Agreement: not often, but often enough.

Accomplishments: many.

• • •

The achievements of that earlier minority Parliament helped Canadians from coast to coast to coast and resonated for a generation. My favourite was the national affordable housing construction program. Hundreds of thousands of seniors, low-income families and people on welfare live in housing built at that time with funds approved by that minority Parliament. Ed Broadbent, then the young housing critic for the NDP, worked with the co-op and non-profit housing advocates across the land, and his proposals struck a chord with the Liberal cabinet ministers. The result was a plan to build affordable homes across the land. Twenty years later, that plan was recognized by the United Nations as the best affordable housing program in the world. In 1995, Finance Minister

Paul Martin killed the entire program. And, just as night follows day, within a couple of years, homelessness was on the rise and with it a new housing crisis in Canada. It would require huge community pressure over the next decade, and another minority government, to get affordable housing construction back on track in Canada.

All this weighed on my mind in August 2004 as I readied myself to meet the prime minister and imagined the possibilities of a minority parliament To learn more about those possibilities, I'd spoken at some length with Ed Broadbent, who had been NDP caucus chair in that 1972 minority. In addition to social housing units, Canadians had seen improvements to old-age pensions and the establishment of a Food Prices Review Board. The NDP caucus had also forced amendments to the Election Expenses Act, allowing a large portion of donations made to federal political parties to be deducted from personal income tax. But the crown jewel for Canadians was undoubtedly the creation of a national energy Crown corporation—Petro-Canada. Ed explained his own role in that accomplishment: "It was one of those survival votes that always seemed to take place in those days just before Christmas, and the issue was the creation of Petro-Canada. I remember delivering the message to Allistair Gillespie, who was the minister responsible. I said, if the Liberals don't create Petro-Canada, the NDP would defeat the government. So, lo and behold, they publicly committed themselves to create Petro Canada."

The energy company was originally established as a national energy Crown corporation, owned by the Canadian people at a time when our non-renewable resources were being gobbled up by foreign investors—mostly American multinationals—at a furious rate. The company ceased to be a Crown corporation in the early 1980s and was eventually sold off in a two-stage process by prime ministers Brian

Mulroney and Jean Chrétien. Still, both the national energy company and the affordable housing program survived for a generation, and left a lasting and positive impact.

Now, here I was, leading a nineteen-member NDP caucus in a new minority Parliament, scheduled to meet a Liberal prime minister and anxious to move forward on a series of initiatives to benefit today's working families. I was particularly aware of the real possibilities that existed because, after all, that's why we were here. At least, that's what I thought. As I would hear over the next hour, and amplified over the next several months, this however was not a Liberal prime minister or a Liberal Party prepared—or even inclined—to work with New Democrats in the way prime ministers Pearson and Trudeau had.

I arrived at 24 Sussex Drive and was shown into a large living room to await Mr. Martin's arrival. The room, with its open, airy decor, wood floors, and panelling, commanded a stunning view of the Ottawa River and put me in mind of a large stone cottage—one in need of an extensive energy retrofit. I was reminded of something else. I was thinking about the many times my father had been in the same room meeting with another prime minister, Brian Mulroney. For most of the nine years Mr. Mulroney was prime minister—from 1984 to 1993—my dad chaired the Wednesday morning Progressive Conservative caucus meetings. Before each meeting, Robert Layton would sit down with the prime minister at 24 Sussex and advise him of any issues within the caucus that he felt the leader needed to know about; he also reported on the general mood of the MPs. Many of those PC MPs would say later that Mr. Mulroney's strongest leadership characteristic was his ability to unite disparate MPs during those closed-door caucus meetings. The polls could be terrible for the government; there could be nasty divisions between their western and Quebec members; the Opposition parties and media might all be gunning for them; and scandal might be in the air. Yet, week in and week out, those Conservative MPs would emerge from their Wednesday caucus, buoyed up by their leader, ready to take on anyone and everyone.

Now it was my turn to be served coffee at the PM's residence. As Mr. Martin welcomed me into the living room I mentioned that Olivia and I were in the process of completing an energy retrofit at our Toronto home, and that it looked to me like 24 Sussex Drive would be a candidate for one as well. The prime minister readily agreed, stating the residence hadn't been upgraded in more than twenty years. He said it was because none of the previous long-term residents—Mr. Trudeau, Mr. Mulroney, or Mr. Chrétien—had been prepared to face the public's wrath for extensive—and expensive—renovations. I indicated that such thinking was penny-wise and pound foolish. After all, a good energy retrofit will last a half century and, from the energy savings alone, completely pay for itself in just a few years. The prime minister motioned to the windows overlooking the river on the north side to show where they put plastic over them in the fall to try to reduce wintry drafts. (Canadians would later see Mr. Martin and comedian Rick Mercer on national television purchasing plastic window material at a Canadian Tire store then applying it with a hair dryer.) I recommended that solar panels would be an appropriate way to conserve and store energy. (I later delivered a solar panel to him in the House of Commons. No news on whether he installed it.)

We then discussed what had transpired in the June election, and I talked about the priorities the NDP caucus had identified earlier in the summer.

I said our caucus members had been asked to contact cabinet ministers and were ready to work on a package of progressive issues. I expressed the hope that we could work together for the benefit of Canadians. The prime minister responded cautiously, saying that, while we could expect to see movement on some of these issues, it was unlikely the NDP caucus would be fully satisfied with the results. He joked that the "wellspring of common values between Liberals and New Democrats" that he'd so successfully exploited in the campaign "might run dry pretty quickly!"

We agreed to stay in touch, and the prime minister assured me that, yes indeed, we all wanted this Parliament to work well for Canadians. In any event, he said, most of the business of the House would be worked out between the government House leader, Tony Valeri, and his Opposition counterparts, including Libby Davies of the NDP.

"Is that all there is?" was the refrain rolling around in my mind as I left the residence. I was surprised that there was not more of an agenda or formal outcome. Perhaps, I thought, that would come in future work together. As it turned out, it would be six months before the two of us would have another meaningful conversation, and—once again—I had to instigate it.

From the prime minister's viewpoint, the biggest stumbling block to working together was undoubtedly that our caucus wasn't large enough. The government needed 155 votes in order to control the House and pass bills. Our 19 votes weren't enough. He refrained from saying at this first meeting: "Jack, you're two seats short." (Although he would use those exact words later.) By the spring of 2005, however, with his government on the ropes, the actual number of seats we had in the House was of far less concern to Mr. Martin. Grasping as though for yet aother coil of a precious lifeline, he would take every vote we had.

Ed Broadbent had also told me about his invitation to meet with Prime Minister Trudeau shortly after the 1980 election. Mr. Trudeau had been brought out of retirement for that winter campaign and promptly returned the Liberals to a majority government. Despite this majority, the Liberals had been virtually shut out in the West, winning only two seats—both in Manitoba. Mr. Trudeau's main purpose in requesting a meeting with Ed was to see whether the NDP leader, with several other NDP MPs, would agree to sit in a coalition Cabinet. Mr. Trudeau explained that having Ed and some western MPs in Cabinet would give the government more credibility for legislation he intended to introduce.

While Ed declined the prime minister's offer very quickly, I found the history fascinating. Here was one Liberal prime minister who had proposed a coalition with the NDP, even though he already had a majority, while the current prime minister—with a narrow minority—didn't seem to have any ideas, or apparently much interest, in how we could work together. Clearly, the backdrop of successful relationships in minority governments had been lost in the collective memory of the Canadian political system, and there seemed to be no discernable sign of collaboration from the Liberals anywhere on the horizon.

Paul Martin strikes me as someone who has a large presence. This is not a criticism but, when he enters a room, he automatically takes up a lot of space. This ability undoubtedly comes from that kind of innate confidence possessed by a few, usually those individuals who have been in powerful positions for protracted periods of time. Mr. Martin was a CEO of a shipping company, a powerful minister of finance for a decade, and now the prime minister. While I respected all of that, I certainly wasn't in awe of any of it. But, in the initial meeting and the handful of meetings we would have together, I always found it difficult to have a "let's get down to business" kind of conversation with him. His subtle condescension, bred of accustomed power, seemed to get in the way.

As I reflected on our inability to put together any common agenda for the fall session, I concluded that election results for the Liberals and undoubtedly the Conservatives are all about identifying political winners and losers. Who's in, who's out? Who has power? Our view is best summed up by Alexa McDonough, MP for Halifax: "While the NDP has never made government in Canada, we've always made a difference for Canadians."

There is no doubt in my mind that now, however, the NDP is ready to make government in Canada with ideas that make Canadians the winners.

Still, whether it was Douglas, Lewis, or Broadbent at the NDP helm, this was the approach and attitude the NDP always brought to minority Parliaments. Our party assumed then, and assumes now, the most important goal is to generate positive results for Canadians, and it certainly was not about to be any different this time with this leader.

One of the realities of minority government is that if one side isn't interested in working with you, other arrangements are possible. I began to think about a new and different approach. Specifically, what could happen if the three Opposition parties co-operated and came up with some reforms and initiatives and then brought them to the floor of the House for action? Through a series of exploratory individual conversations, then brief joint meetings, which included tabling of proposals, Stephen Harper, Gilles Duceppe, and I were moving toward an agreement to bring forward changes to the House of Commons rules to increase the impact of all Opposition parties in the decision-making process. Our first key element was the requirement that treaties and troop deployments would have to be debated in the House. Each of the three Opposition parties wanted this proposal because we all firmly believed that there should be a vote in Parliament to decide whether the country would participate in George Bush's missile defense program. Of course, each of us had our own reasons for wanting the changes. Mr. Harper wanted a recorded vote to demonstrate his party's support for Bush's foreign policy. Mr. Duceppe and I had precisely the opposite intent, because the U.S. "Star Wars" program, as we labelled it over the objections of the Liberals, did include the weaponization of space and was a kick-start to a new arms race. Both the NDP and the Bloc wanted to force the Liberals into a vote on missile defense because we were convinced that a majority of Canadians agreed with us.

We also found common ground on the proposal advanced by the NDP Women's Caucus to create a permanent Standing Committee on the Status of Women. To be honest, I was pleasantly surprised at Mr. Harper's quick acceptance of this proposal, although I remain puzzled by it.

Another change, important to First Nations, came when our Aboriginal affairs critic Pat Martin convinced me that Aboriginal affairs was too important to continue to be lumped in with natural resources and should have its own standing committee. Similar thinking was emerging in other parties, so this too was included in the package of reforms.

Another important reform was to ensure that, when committees of the House tabled their reports, they would then have the assurance of a debate and vote in the House. In the past, committees of the House would toil away, gathering information and hearing from Canadians who could have been forgiven for thinking that their input might actually produce results. The committee's report would be produced, tabled in the House, but then simply languish forever, without a vote, unless the governing party decided to bring it forward for debate. It seemed to too many MPs that a lot of their hard work was for nought. Naturally, this created frustrations for MPs who, after all, had worked hard on these studies and assumed their recommendations would be addressed by the executive branch of government—the Cabinet. It's my firm conviction that the vast majority of those who stand for election do so because they have a cause or causes they want to work toward improving.

Canadians, whose knowledge of the House of Commons is limited to the theatrics of question period, would be surprised to find MPs from all parties working together on committees that actually produce positive results. Frequently, these committees even reach unanimous recommendations as to how specific issues should be addressed. Moreover, in this minority Parliament, the three Opposition leaders could see real advantages to having committee reports debated and voted upon in the House, since the three parties combined enjoyed a majority on all committees and in the House of Commons. This would enable us to force votes, ensuring the majority will in the House was being expressed, regardless whether that conflicted with Liberal policies.

While this change had the potential to reshape the way in which the House operated, it didn't happen. The House voted to adopt this change, but the Liberals simply ignored the change whenever it suited them. The most startling example took place after Alexa McDonough convinced the Standing Committee on Foreign Affairs that the Canadian government should support the worldwide call of the Make Poverty History Campaign. Specifically, the campaign called for first-world countries like Canada to increase support for international development and assistance to 0.7 per cent of our GDP by the year 2015. Under the revised rules, this recommendation came to the House of Commons and was adopted. Nonetheless, Paul Martin rejected the House of Commons motion when he represented Canada at a subsequent G8 meeting in Scotland. In so doing, he thumbed his nose at a motion that represented the majority opinion of those MPs elected by Canadians and countless Canadians involved in the Live8 concerts and the Make Poverty History Campaign. While the Liberal prime minister was certainly prepared to make long-term commitments for tax cuts to business, such largesse did not extend to helping the world's poorest peoples.

I believe these parliamentary reforms will eventually have value, but will ultimately require a deeper democratic reform so that a future prime minister cannot ignore the expressed will of the House with such apparent ease.

The "Three Amigos," as the media dubbed us, worked on other reforms as well. Gilles Duceppe wanted all the changes we had agreed upon to be put forward in an amendment to the Speech from the Throne. As the most experienced Opposition leader, he clearly wanted to move into the driver's seat, and successfully did so for the first couple of meetings. Forcing the Liberals to accept our recommendations as an amendment to the speech from the throne amounted to a game of parliamentary "chicken." If the government refused, Mr. Duceppe pointed out, the three parties had enough votes to ensure its defeat. Waiting outside Mr. Harper's office for our meeting to begin, I asked Mr. Duceppe what he thought would happen if the prime minister refused to accept such an ultimatum. He replied that a government defeat so soon after a general election meant the Governor General would then have to turn "to one of us" to form a government. We both knew that meant Stephen Harper and his Conservatives. I asked Mr. Duceppe if he could accept such an eventuality. He was not only clear that he could, but he would.

Stephen Harper, while less inclined to brinksmanship, nevertheless warmed to the seduction of Mr. Duceppe's strategy. Under this scenario, Mr. Harper would become prime minister in an informal alliance with the Bloc. Unthinkable? Not to either Mr. Harper or Mr. Duceppe. The Bloc leader was willing to strategize for Stephen Harper to become prime minister, despite the Conservatives' many negative policies— policies completely contrary to the desires and values of most Quebecers. While shocked, I could not say I was surprised.

Mr. Duceppe and the Bloc would have been key players in any Harper coalition, demanding significant dismantling of our collective capacities as Canadians as the price for his support. That dismantling was something that would coincide nicely with Mr. Harper's ideological and visceral distaste for any federal government oversight or ability to intervene in any social or economic programs administered by the provinces but utilizing federal tax dollars.

Realizing immediately the full magnitude of what was at stake, I knew I had to walk away. I was not about to participate in any scheme cooked up by the Bloc and the Conservatives that would put the country in the hands of Stephen Harper. It was clear from the election results just three months earlier that Canadians were not ready to elect Mr. Harper as prime minister. In fact, judging from the results, Canadians were not particularly keen on any one of us being in control. None of the four parties in the House had succeeded in receiving the support of even two of every five voters. My decision made, I informed the other Opposition party leaders that I was withdrawing from the talks. The Three Amigos were down to two.

The other two Opposition parties made it clear that, with my withdrawal, the NDP had lost any bargaining leverage. But, as it turned out, the NDP proposals were included in the package of amendments. It's just that we didn't secure any credit for the effort. So be it.

In my judgement, shared by the NDP caucus, it was far more important to respect the wishes of Canadians. Namely, that the minority House constructed by the voters in that peculiar collective wisdom that unfolded on election day be respected and given a chance to show what it could do. And it was even more important that my party not participate in any plot to turn over the country to a difficult and potentially devastating marriage of the Conservatives and the Bloc.

Instead, we decided to work to try and make Parliament work, ignoring the insults and derisive jeers hurled by the other two Opposition parties, as well as the dismissive media reaction to our first parliamentary gambit. In times like this, it's comforting to remember the old adage that you can get a lot done if you don't have to take credit for it!

As it turned out, our most significant opportunity to make Parliament work and deliver results for people would come several months later, when we were able to reshape the budget as the House teetered on the edge of collapse—and on the edge of an election that few Canadians seemed to want. There is more on that dramatic spring dynamic later. But talking with lots of folks in dozens of communities in the months that followed, it was clear that our positive approach to the parliamentary process was well received.

The most significant event in the 2004 fall sitting of Parliament was the visit of newly re-elected U.S. President George W. Bush. He was here on a mission—to bring Canada into his National Missile Defence program (NMD). In the House and throughout the public discussion of this latest kick-start toward a global arms race, we referred to this dangerous initiative as "Star Wars." Ridiculed by Liberals for suggesting that the initiative would ever involve weapons in space, our MPs, especially foreign affairs critic Alexa McDonough, held fast to the terminology because we were convinced it was true.

Peace and disarmament groups across Canada did remarkable work to raise the public awareness, and Mel Hurtig produced an excellent book on the subject in record time. My earlier visit to Washington to meet experts in the field confirmed that, while Liberals in Canada pooh-poohed it, Americans were under no illusion—NMD did involve placing weapons technology in space. Liberals were either in complete denial, or deliberately misleading Canadians. At every opportunity, they tried to convince people that NMD was a rather innocuous land-based defense system that would proceed regardless, that it had potential benefits for Canada, and that our country should therefore have a "place at the table."

From an NDP perspective, we had tried to make the debate about Canadian foreign policy a key issue in the 2004 election to create the conditions where simply falling into line with Bush policies like NMD would be difficult or impossible for which ever party won. Throughout the televised leaders' debates and during early election campaigning, the Liberals continued to claim that NMD did not involve placing weapons in space. Their message: why worry about NMD? Still, despite the government assurances, it was clear that voters were very concerned about this possibility. Before the campaign ended, Mr. Martin was forced to indicate that, as prime minister, he would not approve of any participation in the weaponization of space, all the while maintaining that the American plan didn't call for it in any event.

Following the election, it became clear that there would soon have to be a decision by the Canadian government on NMD. The U.S. wanted the system to become operational within months. In August 2004, the prime minister called each of the Opposition party leaders to indicate that he was authorizing what he described to me as a modest adjustment to NORAD to permit data collected in Canada to be also made available to the United States. He indicated that this was only a minor change and would certainly not lock us into NMD. I expressed my grave concern about the move and reminded him privately, and then publicly, of the need for a full parliamentary debate.

With the House in session however and no government announcement forthcoming on NMD, our caucus began to seek answers. Typically, when I raised the issue in question period, Conservatives and Liberals alike would join in a display of heckling and abuse. Frankly, I could barely hear myself asking the question, the racket was so loud. I'd experienced wild debates in Toronto City Council over the years. But nothing in that forum remotely compared to the basic lack of respect, the shouts and insults, all designed to intimidate MPs from raising a subject even when they had been recognized by Mr. Speaker. The cacophony was especially intense whenever I used the words "President Bush." The mere mention seemed to touch a raw nerve, especially from the back rows of the Conservative benches.

I was trying to seek assurances from the prime minister that Canada would reject the Bush plan for NMD on several grounds. The NMD plan would reduce the security of the world by launching a new arms race. It would also threaten our national security by making us a more likely target of attack. It would divert already scarce funds from international aid, and, of course, it would place weapons hardware into the last global frontier—space. We continued however to receive dismissive answers from the prime minister and assorted cabinet ministers.

So, with the news that the American president was headed north on a state visit, I elected to try to ask President Bush about NMD directly. This would, initially at least, prove to be a challenge. Through the Prime Minister's Office, we requested an opportunity to meet the president on his official visit to Ottawa, but failed to receive a positive response. This was somewhat surprising since, just a few weeks earlier, a positive precedent had been set when the president of Mexico was on a state visit. On that occasion, all Opposition party leaders were given an opportunity to meet privately with Vincente Fox.

Asked about this on CBC's national radio show, *The Current*, on the morning of President Bush's arrival, I replied that our request for a meeting had not been granted. Within half an hour, U.S. Ambassador to Canada Paul Cellucci called me on my cellphone and offered an opportunity for me to meet the president prior to the state dinner.

When the brief meeting finally took place, it occurred in the presence of the U.S. ambassador and Paul Martin. I simply told President Bush that a great many Canadians were opposed to his missile defense initiative. I asked him whether he could, at a minimum, guarantee to Canadians that his NMD system would never involve placing weaponry into space. "We'll do whatever it takes to defend our people," declared the president.

These chillingly clear words confirmed my fears and those of so many Canadians. They also put to rest any Liberal claim that Canada could somehow participate in NMD without becoming involved in the ultimate weaponization of space.

The outgoing secretary of state, Colin Powell, was even more explicit in my conversation with him. Without batting an eye, he explained, in his warm, soothing baritone voice, that Canadians didn't need to worry about the weaponization of space because "we'll be there to make sure that no other country is there." His characterization of the program reflected the blunt language of the U.S. military leadership of "dominance in the space war theatre!"

Assertions by Mr. Cellucci, in a book he published later, that I couldn't possibly have had a conversation with Mr. Powell that evening are simply wrong. When I spoke with Mr. Powell, the U.S. ambassador was nowhere nearby. Mr. Powell was actually standing alone near the escalators that we would all take down to the state dinner. Remember, it was Condoleezza Rice who had just been named to succeed Mr. Powell as U.S. secretary of state. Consequently, she was much more in demand that evening than Mr. Powell. Besides, throughout the entire reception, the American ambassador was virtually attached to the elbows of the president and Prime Minister Paul Martin. Snatches of conversations were audible, I recall. Manitoba

Premier Gary Doer used virtually every second of his time with the president to press for a solution to the Devils Lake diversion, which simultaneously threatened the Lake Winnipeg watershed and the work of the International Joint Commission. Gilles Duceppe engaged the president with his excellent knowledge of baseball. So, there was simply no way Ambassador Cellucci could have known that Colin Powell and I even said hello that evening, let alone what we discussed.

My last conversation during the Bush reception on NMD was with Ms. Rice. I asked her to comment on any weaponization of space involved with the NMD program. She pointed out that, of course, there was no weaponization of space in the current initiative. I suggested that U.S. military budgets submitted for approval included funds for a "test bed" of kinetic interceptors (weapons in space that could destroy other weapons through kinetic energy, combining motion and mass). She acknowledged that these funds had been requested from Congress and pointed out that "one always had to be testing for future phases."

It was clear from my direct exchanges with President Bush, his current secretary of state, and his incoming secretary of state that none of them had denied that weapons could be deployed in space as a result of their NMD program. The prime minister and his officials had been maintaining for months—in public and in the House of Commons—that there would be no weapons placed in space through NMD. They were flat wrong.

When New Democrats and disarmament advocates had spoken earlier about opposition to "Star Wars" they were not misleading Canadians at all. Even some Liberal backbench MPs were pressing Mr. Martin to reject the idea.

President Bush left Canada without securing Canada's engagement in the next phase of the arms race, and a few weeks later, the Canadian government announced its decision not to participate in NMD.

347

What had happened here? In my view, grassroots Canada had spoken, and that loud voice, combined with the wise decision by Canadians to send a minority government to the House of Commons, had ultimately forced the Martin Liberals to back out of the NMD project. This reversal was the first major accomplishment of the minority Parliament.

There was a deeper lesson here as well. Canada has been without a vision for its foreign policy for too long. The Liberals, in power for eleven years, were adrift on this file. Decisions were being made ad hoc or not at all. What was required was a clear framework for our relations with others. This framework needed to include the enhancement of our sovereignty and the pursuit of human security against threats such as the effects of climate change or the spread of diseases borne of poverty. That would be a foreign policy that would give effect to Canada's values.

• • •

Since being elected, I'm sometimes asked what working in a minority Parliament is like. I've learned that, for NDP MPs, it's like dancing on a knife edge. It can be done, but a slip-up can be dangerous, if not fatal. Despite the dangers, however, the dance is worth the effort. Because good things come from minority Parliaments—in fact, as we've seen, some of Canada's best ideas have occurred when Canadians elect a minority government.

"You're two votes short!" That's what Paul Martin said to me in January 2005, bluntly rationalizing why he and his Cabinet had refused to work with our party at all during the first six months of the minority Parliament.

My caucus members had made contact with their respective ministers, offering to work on whatever common ideas could be found. The silence was almost deafening and completely different to the early months of minority governments in the 1960s and in 1972–1973, when the NDP had played a significant role in shaping important policy for the nation. In those earlier instances, there had been regular discussions between NDP representatives and Liberal counterparts.

With the Martin Liberals, there was none of this. No discussion, in fact virtually no contact, aside from the formal posturing in question period. In this cone of silence, I requested a meeting with the prime minister to have a frank discussion about the next phase of this minority government. I reminded him of the positive results of previous minorities, adding that I thought that we were squandering valuable opportunities.

That's when he shot back with the "you're two votes short" remark. I was saddened by this attitude because it seemed to me to reflect a degree of arrogance. It was as though the NDP had nothing to offer in helping to shape policy because we couldn't guarantee power to the Liberals. Yes, we were two votes short of being able to provide such a guarantee. Still, it seemed blindingly obvious to me that the Liberals would be a lot closer to winning critical votes on the budget, and other important measures, if they had our support than without it.

Undaunted by the prime minister's response, I pressed my argument. I said there should be some sharing of ideas about the budget. And we should work to make the House of Commons a more respectful place. I told him I was shocked, like a lot of Canadians, about the deterioration of debate in the House and of the decline in political discourse in general. Mr. Martin agreed with me on this point and said, "Yes, we should work to improve the tone in the House of Commons and, by the way, isn't it terrible the way the Conservatives are behaving?" Here I was urging that we should all work to improve decorum in the House, and his response was to single out the Conservatives with no acknowledgement of his own offending benches or real recognition of the responsibility we all shared to make Canadians proud rather than disgusted by what they saw and heard during question period

On the budget, he agreed to have Finance Minister Ralph Goodale meet with the NDP finance critic, Judy Wasylycia-Leis, to learn about our ideas for the 2005–2006 budget. We had conducted public consultations across the country to determine some priorities for the budget. From those meetings we knew that Canadians wanted another balanced budget. We agreed. They wanted investment in key areas according to what was affordable. We agreed.

Judy presented our ideas to Minister Goodale. We were certainly not expecting that all our proposals would be adopted, but actually thought there was a reasonable chance that some would be. I thought that, just maybe, we'd turned an important corner, and that the creative juices of this minority Parliament were about to flow. Little did I know that a quite different and cynical plot had already been hatched. Our lack of votes, coupled with the fact that the Bloc Québécois would never support a Liberal budget, meant there was only one place for Paul Martin to turn—to the Conservatives!

How could this be? Paul Martin and his Liberal campaign team had created such fear of the Harper Conservatives during the election campaign. Martin had appealed to NDP supporters to switch to the Liberals in order to prevent the Conservatives from winning. Surely he couldn't now, in good conscience, turn to the Conservatives—that party that behaved so badly in the House—to support the most important government legislation—the budget. Yes, he could, and conscience, I realized, had absolutely nothing to do with it.

Size does matter. It was, after all, about raw power and the numbers to back it up. In order to assure Conservative support for the budget, Paul Martin and Ralph Goodale included a line item on a $4.6 billion tax cut for the corporate sector while ignoring completely many commitments made barely weeks before to help with funding for aboriginals, affordable housing, education, and foreign aid. Stephen Harper was beside himself. He declared victory within moments of the budget speech. It was a "Conservative budget," he purred, and he assured Canadians that his party had no intention of defeating the government over it. As it happened, his MPs simply abstained on the budget vote, assuring the Liberals the support they needed to stay in power. All this came as an out-of-the-blue gift to the corporate sector, which had, just five years earlier, seen its tax rate drop from 29 to 21 per cent.

Where did the Liberals get the money for this huge unexpected tax cut? Hadn't they already told Canadians that there was no money to help students suffering from rapidly rising tuition fees and crushing student debt? Yes, they had, despite the fact that the prime minister promised funding on national TV in the "Great Canadian Job Interview" televised debate with me in the early days of the election. In this budget, not a penny for post-secondary students!

The Liberals also told Canadians that there was no new money in the budget to clean up smog by siphoning more of the gas tax to public transit. The country also couldn't afford to build new affordable housing, despite a growing need. Nor could we apparently afford to meet our international commitments to help the poorest countries of the world. Instead, Canada would stay at the back of the pack, rather than move toward honouring the United Nations goal for developed countries to devote 0.7 per cent of their GDP to overseas development aid.

No, despite Liberal election promises of additional funds in all these areas, there was no new money in the budget to address any of these issues. But somehow the Finance

Department had managed to scrape together $4.6 billion in corporate tax cuts—something the Liberals never hinted at during the election. Yes, of course, working Canadian families, whose real incomes hadn't risen in a decade, would be happy to see their taxes going to help the nation's biggest corporations with another multi-billion-dollar tax break. And the Conservatives agreed.

This was outrageous. Canadians had been betrayed once again. The values on which the Liberals had campaigned had been tossed out the window for rank political expediency. I admit, I never saw it coming. The significant role we'd hoped we could play in helping shape the budget appeared to be dead.

Naturally, the NDP voted against the budget, and we were joined by the Bloc. The Liberals supported it, and the Conservatives abstained. It was only first reading, but the die had been cast. There was no reason to think that second and third reading debates and votes on the budget would be any different from the first vote. Oh, but they were!

Judge Gomery was at work. As the budget debates played out on Parliament Hill, the judge was hearing testimony in Montreal about the "Sponsorship Scandal." "Dirty deeds, done dirt cheap," if I may borrow from rockers AC/DC. Except the deeds were an attempt by the Liberals to buy the support of Quebecers for Canada and federalism with their own tax dollars. The dirty deeds included kickbacks to Liberals and their friends. Québécois TV viewers, and there were millions of them, were glued to their sets as the testimony played out over weeks and months. English Canadian viewers got a taste of it in their nightly news coverage, but Quebecers got the real stuff through wall-to-wall daily coverage, repeat broadcasts, and analysis. Stories of Canadians' hard-earned tax dollars being passed across restaurant tables in brown envelopes erupted into media headlines. The Liberals fell like a stone in public opinion polls. In Quebec, the Bloc could sense an electoral sweep while, in the rest of Canada, the Conservatives sensed an opportunity for victory.

Given the tectonic shifts at play, electoral war drums began to beat, and a non-confidence motion seemed inevitable. Such a motion could be presented on one of the Opposition Days each party is granted in the parliamentary calendar. These Opposition Days are designated to occur regularly throughout the House of Commons schedule, and whichever party has the designated day moves a motion for debate. There is nothing in the rules that prevents such a motion from being one of non-confidence, which, if passed by a majority of MPs, would precipitate an immediate election.

"Let the political games begin!" yelled the pundits and strategists.

There was just one problem: when was the next Opposition Day scheduled? The Liberals, desperately playing for time, sent out revised schedules for House business. All remaining Opposition Days had been shoved to the last days of the session, which meant they wouldn't occur until just prior to the summer break. The Liberals obviously believed this would prevent the Opposition parties from pulling the plug on Parliament, because no party would want to be accused of causing an election over the summer holidays.

It's safe to say that Mr. Harper was not amused by these abrupt changes to the parliamentary calendar. He had Brian Mulroney and friends all lined up to create a Conservative transition team once the Liberals were disposed of in the election. The Conservatives immediately withdrew their support for the budget.

Stuck, Paul Martin appealed to Canadians through a live TV broadcast: "I will call an election within thirty days following the release of Judge Gomery's report," he promised. After

Stephen Harper and Gilles Duceppe took the microphone and blasted the Liberals for causing the scandal, it was my turn.

I said it was time to put the interests of Canadians ahead of the interests of political parties. I said that if Paul Martin was willing to change his budget and transfer the $4.6 billion corporate tax cut to key investments that Canadians had been promised in the election, then the NDP would be willing to consider working to have such a "better balanced budget for people and the environment" passed through the House.

When the Liberals were on the brink of collapse, the fact that we were "two votes short" seemed far less important to Liberal strategists than it had for the first ten months of the Parliament. The phone rang. When could I meet with the prime minister?

We were ready for the meeting, ready to "get results for people." We had crafted a proposal that would shift the $4.6 billion in corporate tax cuts toward investments in key areas that we had promised Canadians we would work to deliver. Included in our eight campaign commitments was a balanced budget every year. Our plan had to be completely consistent with this. We proposed shifting the funds from the tax cuts scheduled for years 4 and 5 of the budget to expenditures in years 1 and 2 of the budget as follows: post-secondary education and training, including for Aboriginals; environment through accelerating 1 cent per litre of the gas tax to be invested in transit and through a housing retrofit program for people with low incomes; construction of affordable housing, including for Aboriginals, an increase in foreign aid: and a protection fund for workers who lost their jobs because their employer declared bankruptcy. We also proposed that Employment Insurance reforms be considered. Such reforms had solid support from all sides in the House, as represented by a unanimous report from a standing committee.

I took our proposal to a Sunday night meeting in April with Paul Martin. I was joined by NDP House leader Libby Davies and our new chief of staff, Bob Gallagher, while Paul Martin had with him government House leader Tony Valeri and the head of the PMO, Tim Murphy.

It was a short meeting in a Toronto hotel room. I presented our proposal and said we would need a response by Tuesday morning. If the government would agree to accept our proposal as an amendment to its budget, the NDP would oppose all non-confidence motions until the budget amendment became law.

Except for the proposal to reform EI, the Liberal team accepted our package. The lack of an agreement on EI was particularly disappointing for Yvon Godin, our MP who championed the need for EI reform so eloquently. Yvon represented the Acadie–Bathurst riding in New Brunswick, where seasonal unemployment continued to be devastating. Our team had to decide whether to proceed on the basis of what had been negotiated or to walk away. We had obtained an agreement to shift $4.6 billion in proposed corporate income tax cuts to key investments that would educate and train many, house thousands, including Aboriginals living in squalor, reduce killer smog, protect workers, and help tackle global poverty. I decided that we should proceed. It was far from a perfect budget, but it was a "better, balanced budget for people and the environment." I held a news conference Tuesday afternoon announcing that our proposals had been largely accepted and that we would support the government in exchange for their support for our budget amendment.

The reaction was fast and furious. "How could you get into bed with those corrupt Liberals?" Calls flooded our message board, especially from our supporters. Talk radio went to town condemning the so-called death-bed alliance. In fact, there were far too many bed-related metaphors for my taste!

As the days passed, however, incredulity turned to reflection. Many Canadians apparently realized that, by acting in the way it had, the NDP caucus had tried to put people ahead of politics. After all, with the Liberals as low as they were in the polls, and falling even further, we could probably have picked up seats at their expense. Instead of the possibility of short-term electoral gains, we had decided to deliver actual results to Canadians.

John Ibbitson, *Globe and Mail* columnist, captured the emerging characterization of our efforts: "The NDP, a party that knows what it wants. A party that gets things done."

Still, the first NDP budget in Canadian history was not law yet. There was still the dicey matter of the two-vote gap to bridge. Drama was building as the vote approached. Some Conservative MPs were seriously ill, making their attendance uncertain for the too-close-to-call vote. Still, it didn't look good for either the Liberal minority or the NDP budget amendment. Then Belinda Stronach announced she was crossing the floor from her Conservative front-bench seat to become a Liberal Cabinet minister.

This dramatic announcement was followed quickly by Conservative MP Gurmant Grewal's claim that he had taped conversations between himself, Liberal Health Minister Ujjal Dossanjh, and Tim Murphy, Paul Martin's chief of staff. The meeting apparently broached shady topics, including the possibility of an offer of government posts for Mr. Grewal and for his wife, Nina, also a Member of Parliament.

"There is a real concern amongst Canadians about this taped conversation. It has placed the entire House under a real cloud," I said. I did feel that the political shenanigans, name-calling, and brinksmanship were turning Canadians off. Disgust at all the participants seemed to be the most common reaction to the sordid Grewal affair.

As we prepared for the motion of non-confidence we also

had to be ready for the eventuality that our budget amendment would not pass. A defeat would clearly demonstrate
lack of confidence in the government on a money bill and
precipitate a general election. An NDP campaign plane had to
be booked. A campaign team had to be assembled and made
ready to start campaigning the morning after the vote.
Literature and signs had to be printed and sent out to candidates across the country. All this was done. Team members
had relocated to their temporary quarters in Ottawa. All was
ready and, as Canadians awaited the vote, there was tangible
tension and palpable excitement in our party's campaign
offices on Bank Street, just a few blocks from the House.

As the bells rang to summon MPs to the House for the vote
on our budget amendment, one Independent MP's courage to
return to the House—despite being gravely ill—stood out.
Chuck Cadman was fighting cancer and, at the same time,
grappling with his conscience. Mostly, though, he had listened
to his constituents and was ready to do his duty. On the night
of the key vote, he calmly waited in his House of Commons
backbench seat, chewing gum and awaiting his turn to vote.
No one knew how he intended to vote. As I passed his chair in
the House, I simply said: "You have an important decision rest-
ing on your shoulders, Chuck. Best wishes."

A few minutes later, he stood and voted for the NDP budget
amendments. Cheers and a standing ovation erupted from our
corner. His vote had created a tie in the House. The Speaker,
honouring tradition, cast his vote in favour of our amendment.
This meant there would be no summer election, and the first-
ever federal NDP budget bill passed in Canadian history.

I want to pay tribute and acknowledge my sincere thanks
for Chuck Cadman's principled decision. His death just a
few weeks later touched us all because he had always been a
principled parliamentarian, someone who made Canadians
proud. With Chuck's decisive vote, I was satisfied that our

terrific caucus had indeed made a positive difference. We celebrated rather late that night.

The next morning, I headed to our campaign office to thank the team for having been so well prepared for the election that did not happen. I thought they would all be pleased at what we'd accomplished. The mood was not at all upbeat, however. Dejected faces and a sombre mood greeted me as I hopped off the elevator. I didn't get it at first. Then the penny dropped. These committed, dedicated New Democrats had been entirely keyed up and ready to give their all in an election. They were like racers poised for the starter's gun—a pistol that hadn't fired.

I needed to help them understand the magnitude of what we had achieved. First I talked about the housing funds. The $1.6 billion to be invested in new affordable housing would create communities that would put a roof over the heads of thousands of people. The $1 billion for environment would mean that some families wouldn't have to rush a family member to the emergency ward, unable to breathe from asthma. Funds for more affordable post-secondary education and training would mean that young people would be deciding to pursue their dreams. International aid increases would save lives far from our shores. Our work would have tangible results, and so we shouldn't be disappointed about an election that didn't happen. We should be thankful instead that we had the opportunity to put some of our ideas into practice for a change, instead of just talking about them.

[CHAPTER 10]

Working Hard
for Working Families

There's no doubt that the gung-ho approach, backed up with
hard work by all in our nineteen-member caucus, laid the
foundation for the growth in popular support for the NDP that
was to come that was to come in the 2006 election. From the
get-go, we took the position that we were there to try to
accomplish things for people and make their lives better. Our
MPs understood the concept of teamwork and respect for one
another. We looked forward to caucus meetings because of
the positive discussion that was going to take place. It could
be heated. It could be energetic. But there was always a powerful energy that radiated from that caucus.

So, despite being two seats short, we had successes and
surprised a lot of people in the process. The highlight was, of
course, the NDP's first-ever budget amendment. Besides
achieving tangible results for working families, we also
gained enhanced public recognition and credibility that the
NDP caucus was working hard to get results in Parliament.
That was also important when we had to go back to the electorate a few months later.

The spring agreement between the government and our
caucus to work together to revise the budget not only helped
avert an early election call, it also allowed Parliament to continue working into the summer. One of the most important
legislative items that we dealt with was the emotional issue
of same-sex marriage. Had our budget agreement not stipu-
lated that we would continue to work with the government

on legislation to see it through the House, including royal assent, the same-sex marriage legislation would never have been debated. Because Parliament was still in session, we had the opportunity to debate and pass a bill that provided for the recognition of same-sex marriages, while still permitting those religious institutions that did not choose or sanction same-sex marriage the freedom not to have such ceremonies performed on their premises.

I saw this debate as, fundamentally, a human rights issue for many Canadians. This was both a historic and a very moving moment for me personally. When Olivia and I were married in 1989, we had so many gay couples attend our ceremony. These were personal friends who were in long-standing relationships, just as loving as ours. But, these dear friends could not do what we were able to do. The law at that time did not permit them to draw the community together around their expression of love for each other and have it recognized by society. To highlight this difference at our marriage ceremony, we asked Toronto School Trustee John Campey, one of our gay friends to speak on our behalf to express our hope that, one day, it would be possible for same-sex couples, including those in attendance, to be recognized by society for the love that they so clearly had for one another.

My awareness of same-sex relationships had been underlined in the early days of the AIDS crisis, when I'd seen the deepest love and affection that I'd ever witnessed in long-standing relationships. As a city councillor in downtown Toronto and as chair of the city's Board of Health, I saw many couples totally devastated as one of the partners became ill and died because the AIDS medications at that time were not able to prolong life very long at all, unlike today. The depth of love that I saw between those couples at that time equalled and maybe exceeded the depth of love I'd witnessed in any heterosexual relationships. So, from that personal history, to have the opportunity to stand in the House of Commons and give effect to those hopes that Olivia and I had shared at our wedding ceremony was the most moving experience I've had since being elected to Parliament.

One of the clouds hanging over Parliament as we prepare to return for the fall session of 2006 is the revisiting of equality rights sanctioning the marriage of same-sex couples, adopted previously by both Parliament and the courts. Prime Minister Harper says he intends to re-open the debate by holding a free vote on the matter. This is both unfortunate and deeply troubling. When a society recognizes basic equality, and then threatens a short while later to remove that equality, it leaves people stranded in a netherworld of illegitimacy. So many couples all over Canada have approached me quietly to show me their rings. Their proud faces as they introduce each other to me speak louder than words about pleased they are that they have been able to marry. It's meant so much to them, and it would be a tragedy to go back. I hope it won't happen. Our twenty-nine-member NDP caucus will be totally united in opposing any attempt to re-open this issue.

It was also a delight to watch Alexa McDonough work with the other three parties and obtain their agreements for a substantial increase in Canada's overseas development assistance. She provides constant positive support and is a superbly effective parliamentarian, seasoned enough to be totally undeterred from any concerns that, as a member of the fourth party in the House, she wouldn't have much clout in Parliament.

She manoeuvred through that spring session of 2005 to obtain the signatures of all three Opposition party leaders recommending an increase in foreign aid and saw that it was presented to prime minister Martin before the 2005 federal budget was introduced. She and I were in regular contact with UN AIDS advocate Stephen Lewis, who was calling urgently for wealthy nations such as Canada to increase foreign aid significantly, and thus quickly control the spread of the pandemic. We all wanted to see Canada reach the UN target of 0.7 per cent of our gross domestic product, a commitment our nation had made years earlier. Alexa persuaded the foreign affairs committee to adopt the target, and the committee's recommendation was accepted by the House of Commons without dissent. Alexa is successful because she is totally engaged and in synch with what is required. She was able to persuade the foreign affairs committee to hear Jeffrey Sachs describe his findings in his powerful book, *The End of Poverty*. The result of all this hard work by Alexa and her team was a brand new commitment from the foreign affairs committee. Unlike previous approaches, which all too often had been to dispense foreign aid that primarily benefited Canadian companies and our own economy, our nation's new approach would focus on alleviating poverty and truly assisting humanitarian efforts in third-world countries.

In addition to her dogged determination, Alexa has the ability to accomplish things on the Hill because she remains constantly in touch and working with groups in civil society. These non-governmental organizations, more often than not, have such little political clout that they truly need an ally to shepherd their concerns and give them a voice in Parliament. Alexa is that ally and voice, a parliamentarian who is able to turn today's fears into genuine hope for tomorrow. Her ability to accomplish amazing results is also due to her effectiveness and ability to work collegially with MPs from other parties. As a result, Alexa's overall impact and effectiveness in the House of Commons is truly remarkable. In caucus and in the House I was proud to give tribute to an Alexa McDonough milestone: twenty-five years of elected public service to her home province, Nova Scotia, and to Canada.

Following the summer 2005 recess, we returned to the House, pleased with what we had been able to accomplish during the spring session, but anxious and eager to move forward on new initiatives. We were optimistic, in spite of the fact that Prime Minister Martin had already put an end date on the life of this Parliament. He had made a commitment on national television to dissolve Parliament and call a general election within thirty days of the tabling of Justice John Gomery's final report. Justice Gomery had been appointed to investigate the extent of involvement and corruption in the Liberal Party from an advertising scandal in Quebec that had occurred in the late 1990s. This decision by Paul Martin was a grave political error that proved fatal. He would have been wiser to say to Canadians that once Justice Gomery produced his report, he would take the time implement the recommendations of the Gomery Commission, whatever they might be and no matter how many Liberals might be implicated, showing that he meant business. Martin should have insisted that he needed the time to institute the reforms suggested by Gomrey and rapidly brought them before the House, challenging the other parties to support Gomery's agenda. Instead, he locked himself into an early termination of the minority parliament, one that had just shown that it could deliver results for people when parties worked towards that goal. This deadline gave no opportunity for Martin to deliver on the Gomery agenda, to produce and implement a plan for accountable government. Instead, he guaranteed that the election itself would focus on accountability and the failures of the Liberal administration identified by the judicial inquiry. Why did he do this? I believe that Paul Martin felt that he could successfully convince Canadians that he was distinct from the Chretien Liberals and able to chart a new course. He believed that, at root, Canadians wanted the Liberal Party to successfully prove itself and then continue to govern. Martin's misjudgement stemmed from a fatal flaw: swallowing hook, line and sinker the old idea that the

Liberals were the "natural governing party" and that, whenever the election took place, Canadians would rally in sufficient numbers around their big red logo to secure power once again. Martin was wrong. Wrong for the Liberals and wrong for the country.

Against the backdrop of this pivotal decision by the prime minister and heading into the fall 2005 session, everyone was fully aware that an election was just around the corner and its essential subject matter would be ethics in government. Nevertheless, the foremost question in the NDP caucus remained: "What can we accomplish during this session that will achieve some positive results for Canadians?" That was always our watchword and, because we weren't receiving any messages from the Martin Liberals, we decided to set out some ourselves.

We set them out in a speech I made to the Ottawa chapter of the Canadian Club. We offered quite a broad menu. We said we were willing to work on a number of key issues. We weren't terribly precise. Our goal was to try to give the government as much flexibility as we could, while getting useful things done. We certainly didn't want to simply sit in the House twiddling our thumbs and collecting our salaries while we waited for the election.

So far as our caucus was concerned, the single most important political event that had happened over the summer of 2006 was the court decision in the Dr. Jacques Chaoulli case in Quebec—a decision with earth-shattering consequences for the future of public health care in Canada. Based on the Quebec Charter of Rights, the Supreme Court had ruled that the province of Quebec had an obligation to ensure that medical services were provided to patients within a reasonable time period. This obviously could have ramifications in all other provinces and would open up several doors in the growth of for-profit medicine throughout Canada.

There is nothing New Democrats believe in more strongly than preserving our public medicare system. Yet, weeks after the Supreme Court released its ruling on Chaoulli, Canadians were still waiting to hear what the federal government thought of the court's decision and how it intended to react. From our point of view, there was no doubt the judgement could threaten the very foundation of medicare—namely, the single-payer system. This view was shared by such broad-based citizens organizations as the Canadian Health Coalition, with whom we worked closely.

I told the Canadian Club that the NDP wanted to see legislation introduced that would assert Canada's interest "to protect single-payer medicare and hold all provinces to meaningful standards. If Canada doesn't stand for Canada's interest, nobody will."

I made sure that the Martin government knew of the contents of this speech and what we wanted to achieve. Privately, we told the government that, in exchange for them closing the door to further privatization of our health-care system, we would give unconditional support to the government until the pre-determined election date, roughly six months later. We would do this—despite any interim findings from Justice Gomery. In other words, slamming the door shut on further health-care privatization would result in an NDP commitment to accept the election timetable set out months earlier by Mr. Martin.

We also said that some willingness on the government's part to take significant action on pollution would be an extremely positive signal. We were specifically seeking support from them on a motion to crack down on the country's biggest polluters. We had introduced a motion in the House to this effect, but it was opposed by both the Liberals and the Conservatives. As a young boy, my son Mike had to be rushed to emergency to combat his asthmatic condition. Now I had reason to be scared all over again. Olivia was diagnosed with cancer of the thyroid gland. The cancer had gone undiagnosed for some time. I noticed that lumps on my wife's neck were becoming quite large. She hadn't really noticed them at all and went off to have them checked, confident they were benign. They weren't. Let there be no doubt, it was a terrifying moment, as it is in any family when a loved one is diagnosed with cancer. It's in those instances that you turn to your friends for support and, fortunately for us, that support was everywhere. A combination of successful treatments by our wonderful public health-care system plus Olivia's upbeat, positive approach to life carried her—and me—through the crisis successfully.

Because she was a high-profile Toronto city councillor, there was a lot of publicity about her thyroid cancer, the treatment, and her recovery. She was invited to speak about it in various Ontario cities. One of her appearances was in Windsor, directly across the river from Detroit, Michigan. Windsor happens to have the highest incidence of thyroid cancer in the country. Olivia's invitation to speak in Windsor was a graphic reminder of my many visits to that city. I'd be at events with our two MPs "the twinsors," as one caucus wag dubbed Joe Comartin and Brian Masse. The three of us would be at a Tim Hortons, talking to people on the streets or at a community meeting, and the number of people we met with family members who'd either recently died or just been diagnosed with cancer was absolutely shocking.

Olivia's scare with cancer and the alarming cancer statistics in a city like Windsor serve to underline the intensity of pollution levels experienced and endured in too many Canadian communities. Such events and statistics serve to remind us that we must combat pollution. Rick Smith, executive director of Environmental Defence, worked with environmental groups in the United States to complete a series of studies in which family members and individuals have their bodies analyzed to ascertain what toxic pollutants reside there. The studies reveal a shocking accumulation of poisons in the bodies of most people in our communities. Smith invited me and other elected representatives to participate by having my own blood tested in the summer of 2006, results to be available for consideration by Canadians and by Parliament. I agreed. At time of writing, the findings are pending but I have little doubt that I'll be found to be loaded up with toxins from the flame retardants used in computers, televisions, mattresses and children's clothing, to the stain repellents and non-stick chemicals used in carpets, furniture and non-stick pans, or the grease repellents preventing grease from leaking through microwave popcorn bags and fast food packaging, or the mercury found in contaminated fish or air polluted by coal power plants, perhaps including lead found in the dust of older homes from the days when lead paint was popular or from industrial air pollution.

Maybe all of the above.

A graphic example of this phenomenon of human body contamination was provided on March 5, 2006, when well-known CBC-TV news reporter and anchor Wendy Mesley read her blood results during a thirty-minute documentary called *Chasing the Cancer Scare*. Ms. Mesley was diagnosed with breast cancer in 2004. She was tested for fifty-seven carcinogens, and forty-five of them were found in her body. As stark as those numbers are, Ms. Mesley concluded that the cocktail of cancer-causing poisons in her body is about average for North America.

"Cancer is multiple exposures to multiple risk factors over a period of time. I'm contaminated and I'm sure everyone else who grew up in North America is too. Now, our kids are starting out contaminated and that's the really depressing thing."

According to her documentary, it's through ignorance, neglect, misplaced trust, and cynicism that we are allowing ourselves to be poisoned with commonly used legal carcinogens and, even worse, condemning an alarming number of children to the same fate. In light of all this, we worked with environmental experts to prepare proposals to ban and control pollutants in Canada.

We added still more policy issues to the list of initiatives we were prepared to explore with the government. By the time we were through we had a virtual buffet of possibilities from which the Liberals could choose to work with us.

We put our wide-ranging suggestions on protecting health care and reducing pollution in a letter to the prime minister. We made the letter public so that all could see that our efforts to find common ground were genuine and specific.

I met him on October 25, once again at 24 Sussex Drive. I went through a menu of possibilities, providing plenty of details. I wanted to open the door as wide as possible to cooperation that would achieve concrete results in the few months remaining in this minority parliament. At the end of the meeting, it was agreed that Jean Crowder, our health critic, would follow up with Health Minister Ujjal Dosanjh. The prime minister, while noncommittal, didn't give a flat no. Instead he said: "Well, why don't you run it by Mr. Dosanjh and we'll see where it goes."

Still, I left the meeting not feeling in my gut any enormous amount of enthusiasm about the likelihood of action. The meeting did not have the same "feel" as the budget negotiations I had had with Mr. Martin only six months before. It did not seem to me that Martin felt anywhere near the same need to work with us on solutions as he had earlier. Maybe he had come to the conclusion that it was time to have a showdown with the Opposition parties. Maybe he had a sense that it was time for him to show that he could force the Opposition to defeat his government and triumph at the polls.

Despite these instinctive misgivings, I asked Jean to follow through with the letter to the health minister in the hopes that, just maybe, there would be a significant and positive response. We knew that achieving a positive outcome on health care was far more important than playing politics. When the health minister eventually responded, he did so in a way that accepted only one piece of our proposal. He agreed that medical doctors would not be permitted to work both inside and outside the public health system at the same time. Regrettably however Mr. Dosanjh rejected several other elements, including the key one, to preserve the single-payer system: ensuring that people would use their health card, not their credit card, to get health care. He also disagreed with our proposal to it was time for the federal government to act, not just talk, by insisting that future transfer of federal funds to the provinces would be conditional on provinces ensuring that public money could not go increasingly to for-profit medicine.

Looking back, I can only assume that the Liberals were so preoccupied with the next election that they were unable to respond in a significant way to the issues we had placed in front of them. It seemed to me, given the mocking, provocative behaviour they were exhibiting in the House toward all three Opposition parties, the Liberals indeed secretly relished the prospect of an election. Whatever the reason, and despite what I truly believe to have been our best efforts to make parliament work, the Liberals would accept no basis on which we could collaborate to get results, and our caucus had to grapple with what to do next. Our MPs were surprised at the Liberals' inability or unwillingness to work with us. Frankly, we thought the proposals we'd made would have been far easier for the cabinet to accept than the budget amendment we'd negotiated in the spring. Still, we had our answer. We knew that our job was not to prop up any party that refused to work together to get things done for Canadians while insisting on its own pre-determined election timetable. Our job in Parliament was to work, not twiddle our thumbs while the clock kept ticking on the health of Canadians. And, if nothing was getting done, then it was not possible to simply vote confidence in the government with no justification.

In light of these developments, I decided to sit down again with Bloc Leader Gilles Duceppe and Conservative Leader Stephen Harper. It was immediately clear that both of them couldn't wait for an election and were perfectly ready to pull the election trigger almost immediately upon the release of Judge Gomery's first report. I said no, despite the pressure cooker of a non-confidence vote, our caucus still wants to try to get something done. Before we took a non-confidence vote, I urged that our three parties agree to push some legislation through the House. I suggested we take a handful of bills that had already been introduced by the government itself and work together to see them passed. These were bills that all parties essentially agreed with, even though each of us might have some quibbles on the details. Since each of them would benefit Canadian families, I suggested they be brought forward and rapidly pushed through Parliament before the government would be put to the test of a confidence vote.

I found it more straightforward to discuss issues with Stephen Harper than with Paul Martin. Our meetings were rather matter-of-fact. Harper understood specific points where he and I were going to disagree. He didn't try to argue them with me. It was just clear that there would be fundamental points of departure between us on specific policy matters.

I had also had frequent and cordial relations with Gilles Duceppe. He was a little more inclined to reveal himself emotionally, especially when I didn't go along with him and Mr. Harper, as happened in October 2004. When I refused to be part of their scheme to bring down the Martin government within days of Parliament coming into session, Mr. Duceppe claimed I was breaking faith. His language could be intemperate, but, on occasions when I need to talk with Mr. Duceppe about a piece of legislation, he could be smart, clear, and accommodating. That was certainly true when we talked about the precise steps needed to ensure all the bills passed both the House and Senate before the government fell on the motion of non-confidence.

In fact, at those meetings in the fall of 2005, both he and Mr. Harper were fully accommodating. The three of us worked hard to reach agreement, and I was adamant that the timing of a non-confidence motion had to be such that we could get these bills passed before the government fell. That way, we couldn't be accused of doing nothing and standing in the way of good ideas—in fact, we would be ensuring the passage of legislation that was good for Canadians.

The three of us talked it all through on a Sunday afternoon in Mr. Harper's panelled fourth-floor boardroom in Centre Block. We took a break or two to consult privately with key advisers and we eventually reached an agreement. I said, "Look, we've got to produce some positive results for Canadians out of this Parliament before it collapses." The other two were willing to work together on that, even though there were aspects of each of those bills they didn't particularly like. They took a deep breath—we all did—and supported the proposed legislation.

There were four bills, and we informed the government that all three Opposition leaders were urging they be passed quickly—through both the House and Senate—before the government fell on a motion of non-confidence.

- **Bill C-53 was a bill placing the onus on organized criminals to prove that property in their possession had not been obtained illegally;**
- **Bill C-54 was an act allowing First Nations to manage and regulate oil and gas currently being managed on their behalf by the federal government;**
- **Bill C-55 was an act ensuring that workers employed by bankrupt companies would not lose the wages owed to them;**
- **Bill C-66 was an act giving home-heating rebates to seniors and low-income Canadians, as well as providing additional funds for energy retrofits and locking in money for public transit.**

We made certain that all non-confidence motions were placed on Thursdays, which meant that the actual votes didn't happen until the following Tuesdays. As Harper and Duceppe were bursting at the seams to place their confidence motions, I insisted on a full week between the first and second non-confidence votes to maximize and stretch parliamentary procedure to the limit, in order that there was sufficient time to have the four key bills passed.

Certainly, there was a lot of pressure on our caucus from interest groups to see the bills passed, and undoubtedly the Liberals were working actively behind the scenes to ensure such pressure happened. Once they realized we were serious about joining the other parties to vote non-confidence, cabinet ministers began telling interest groups and non-governmental organizations that a non-confidence vote could result in no money for their group. I can only assume that Liberals hoped one of two things might result. Either these groups would exert so much pressure on the NDP caucus that we'd get cold feet and reconsider our decision, or voter backlash for causing an election to be waged over Christmas and New Year's would force us to back off.

There was one other important item to be factored in to our tight timetable, an item that had nothing to do with legislation but which had enormous significance for Aboriginals in Canada and for all Canadians. A summit involving First Nations people, the federal government, the provinces, and the territories, had been planned for late November in British Columbia. If the federal government were to fall before the scheduled dates, the Kelowna Summit, as it became known, would be cancelled. That was yet another reason I insisted on extending the timelines, to ensure that a vote of non-confidence wouldn't pass until after the First Nations summit, leading to the signing of the Kelowna Accord, took place.

There was a lot of nervousness on all sides about whether the government would fall before all the pieces of legislation passed and the First Nations summit was held. But it all worked out. Each of the four bills was adopted in the House and passed in the Senate. The First Nations summit meeting produced its landmark accord. Days later, we stood in the House of Commons and voted non-confidence in the Liberal minority government of Paul Martin. The government had lasted just seventeen months.

Despite this success, plus our earlier budget amendment, our caucus was under no illusions. We knew there would be criticism for foisting a winter election on the Canadian public and we were prepared for that and ready to defend ourselves.

Throughout the fall of 2005, NDP MPs had had plenty of opportunities at our weekly caucus meetings to discuss forcing an election versus no real movement from the Liberals. All viewpoints from all MPs were put on the table and discussed thoroughly. The timing turned out to be extremely positive because it allowed us to think carefully through our options.

We knew intuitively that we weren't there to just take up space. We were there to encourage the government to take positive steps and, when they weren't doing that, it was our job to call them to account. Overall, the NDP caucus strongly supported our recommendations to pass the four bills and then vote non-confidence. Our MPs were convinced that we were being fair and reasonable and that we had clearly laid out the areas where we thought we parliament make progress for people.

The inescapable conclusion was the Liberals were playing games with Canadians. They were simply biding their time with no real legislative agenda. It wasn't until it became clear that the government was going to fall that, suddenly, they produced legislative proposals and made a string of announcements. All this last-minute frenetic activity on their part was to try to give them have a head start on the election by laying out virtually everything they intended to announce.

Meanwhile, the Conservatives and others had been saying to us: "How can you possibly work with a corrupt party like that? Haven't you read Justice Gomery's first report?" We said that if the government produces results for Canadians, we would support them. If not, we wouldn't. In the end, the Liberals showed, once again, that they were a little bit too comfortable. In the House their attitude was almost like the old school yard taunt, "Come and get us." The Liberals were ahead in the polls before the election, so perhaps they thought they could ride out the storm. Canadians however didn't appreciate that kind of guff. The voters wanted a bit of humility from those they elected, but saw precious little of it from the Liberals. The NDP caucus saw that the government had become so arrogant it was not prepared to work with any

other party in the House. In a minority situation such an attitude made it impossible to accomplish anything. To extend
the life of the government, we first had to be able to show
Canadians that their interests were being well served in
Parliament. We simply couldn't do that.

As the date for a non-confidence motion loomed larger,
the discussion of whether an election was going to interrupt
the Christmas holidays was often in the news. The NDP proposed—and worked with the other Opposition parties—to lay
out a scenario by which Parliament would carry on until mid-
December—or about another three weeks. We did this in
order to try to get additional work done. This would then
allow for the election to start in early January, with election-
day in mid-February. Incidentally, had this plan been
accepted, it would have placed the election period in virtually
the identical time frame that Mr. Martin initially proposed to
Canadians, back in the spring when he had suggested that
Justice Gomrey would report his recommendations by mid
December. We saw it as a creative approach. It's too bad the
Liberals couldn't see their way to show any flexibility on this.
Here we had three Opposition party leaders—representing a
majority of Canadians' votes and seats —proposing a format
to ensure that the election would start after Christmas, not
before. But, as they'd done throughout most of this minority,
the Liberals seemed to search for every excuse not to try
something new, useful, and sensible.

Whether the election date was in late January, mid-
February, or early April, there was a strong sense that a change
was coming in Ottawa. I do not believe for a minute that an
alternate timing of the election would have produced a different result. I know that Liberals like to suggest that given that
little bit of extra time, their government could have been re-
elected. But why? The Liberals had been judged by Judge
Gomery, and Canadians had lost faith in them. Afterall, most

Canadians had not voted for the Liberals in 2004, and those people never did have confidence in them. But even among their bedrock supporters, Liberal confidence was waning. In the 2006 election, Mr. Martin failed to offer a vision forward for the country. I think it was simply because the Liberals had lost their way. They had betrayed the confidence of Canadians, and the electorate was ready to pass judgement. On January 23, 2006, NDP support went up. Conservative support went up. Liberal support went down.

The Conservatives ran a well-executed campaign but, despite the attitude Canadians had toward the Liberals and despite all the gaffes the Liberals made during the election, Mr. Harper's party was still only able to eke out a razor-thin minority government, winning 123 seats. Since this minority Conservative government was sworn in, some rightly expressed fears about the future of many social programs. Many Canadians have been justified in worrying. Liberals had gone further by saying: "We're losing childcare program at the hands of Stephen Harper all because of the NDP." But Liberals, better than anyone, knew their twelve-year promise of a national childcare program was betrayed again and again. They know that it was implemented in any meaningful way only after they found themselves in a minority government facing strident demands from NDP MPs to proceed immediately and depended upon the support of the NDP caucus which voted in favour of the budget that contained the financial commitment, allowing it to pass.

Our party advocated for child care for many decades, and we shared with many Canadians the great disappointment they felt when Stephen Harper tore up the flimsy agreement that the Liberals had with the provinces to establish childcare funding across the country. If the Liberals had listened to New Democrats, if Social Services Minister Ken Dryden had accepted the effective arguments from Tony Martin (MP for Sault Ste. Marie) in the thirty-eighth Parliament that child care should be enshrined in a national act just like the Health Care Act, then Mr. Harper would have been unable to tear up those agreements unilaterally. We pleaded with Mr. Dryden and with the Martin government to ensure a universal high-quality, non-profit, publicly administered childcare program that drew on the excellent leadership model to be found in Quebec.

After Prime Minister Harper announced that he would not respect the childcare deal, Olivia Chow, NDP child and youth critic, worked with Denise Savoie, MP from Victoria, who brought forward her private member's bill to do what the Liberals refused to do. It will be voted on in the fall 2006 session. It is called the Canada Childcare Act and, just like the Canada Health Act, if it passes, it will put in place a childcare system across the country. As the prime minister has so amply proven, it isn't until Canada actually has a national childcare act that Canadians can be certain of an ongoing federal commitment to the funding of child care.

Mr. Harper's plan to give $100 a month per child to qualifying families is a sham of a childcare program. It doesn't qualify in any way to be called a universal childcare program, although what makes it doubly insidious is that Mr. Harper uses that kind of language to describe the initiative.

Olivia Chow held a press conference at which she piled up $1,200 in the form of five-dollar bills and then began taking off what governments—federal and provincial—intended to tax and claw back. With the exception of one-income families where one spouse is able to stay at home, virtually everyone would see a major chunk of money clawed back. In fact, low-income working families would be left with just pennies per day—not enough to buy diapers, let alone pay for childcare. Olivia and Denise made their points so effectively that Mr. Harper was forced to back off and cancel some of the clawbacks, but only some. The result is that several hundreds of millions of dollars that were to have been clawed back under Harper's initial scheme will now go to qualifying families—the ones with the more modest means. Once again, the NDP honoured its commitment to work for working families. This achievement didn't get a lot of publicity—perhaps none, come to think of it, but we were happy to have made the Conservative plan a little less unfair.

Canadians know the NDP didn't cause the Liberals' electoral defeat. They know that it was the Liberals themselves who caused their own defeat. How do Canadians know this? They are the ones who cast the votes! The Liberals lost, in large part, by virtue of their culture of entitlement, or, as Justice Gomery put it, their sense of "*tout m'est du*" (all is owed to me). As damning as the Gomery Report was for the Liberals, their mediocre re-election campaign offered nothing to encourage Canadians to keep this crowd in government. I'm sure I was no different than other Canadians in never knowing what to expect next from the Liberal campaign. Their commitments and promises veered wildly off track with random, disconnected policy pronouncements that seemed to be made up totally on the fly. In addition, there was a series of embarrassing leaked blogs written by prominent Liberals, and their paid advertising insulted many.

For us, the 2006 election campaign was very different from 2004 for several key reasons. We knew it was coming with greater certainty and so we'd been preparing for it for some time. There had been that false start in May 2005 when we'd all been on the starting line in the crouch position with the starter's pistol raised. We knew the election could begin no later than early March 2006. The prime minister had said so.

Also, our candidates were a lot more engaged and excited in 2006. Going from forty-four seats in 1988 to just nine in the

1993 election had been a devastating setback for the NDP. The party had fought to regain official party status in 1997 and delighted itself with a big breakthrough in Atlantic Canada and twenty-one seats. In 2000, however, we slid backwards again, winning but thirteen seats and barely qualifying as an official party. In such lean times, it hadn't been easy to line up candidates early in every riding. In fact, in some ridings, NDP candidates had been nominated pretty much at the deadline. By fall 2005, however, our candidates were nominated and ready to go. Many had been canvassing door-to-door for months. They were keen and enthusiastic, in part because we'd held a very exciting conference in Ottawa in September. We called it the Breakthrough Conference and we had all our candidates there. There were great discussions and wonderful speeches from some of our truly inspirational leaders. Ed Broadbent, who'd already announced he wasn't going to re-offer in Ottawa Centre in order that he could care for his dear Lucille, made a marvellous speech to New Democrats who were thrilled to meet him and savour the words of someone they truly loved. Another highlight of the conference was the after-dinner speech by Shirley Douglas. She just had the four hundred of us entranced as she spoke about her father, Tommy, and provided recollections of her life on Parliament Hill as a young girl between 1935 and 1944 when Tommy was an MP. For so many of the young people there, learning about our roots and why we were doing what we were doing, plus hearing it from one of the most authoritative sources in the party, was simply amazing. Shirley's magnificent way of communicating with her dramatic Shakespearian pauses at just the right moment had us roaring with laughter, tears, passion, and on-your-feet applause. She had us hanging on her every word—it was just incredible. Our candidates felt as if they were ten feet off the floor and couldn't wait to take on the world to make it a better place.

We also went into the campaign with the same team that had prepared for a spring election. We had been able to recruit the best of the best for our election planning committee, under the capable direction and co-chairing of Brian Topp and Sue Milling. As a result, our team just hummed like a well-tuned clock and delivered the campaign with fewer errors than in 2004. In 2004, we did find ourselves stepping in a few potholes along the way, which was unsettling. We found ourselves having to respond to internal disagreements on topics such as the Clarity Act, gun control, and estate taxes.

It's true. In 2004, I had suffered from the occasional bout of a disease that can afflict those in public life—allowing the foot to get too close to the mouth! But in the 2005–2006 election, for the most part I had learned to control that reflex tendency. We also had a better idea of how we wanted to speak to Canadians, louder than before, about what we had to offer—namely, that you can trust the NDP to stand up for you, and here's the proof. We were able to run on our record—specifically our budget amendment. And it seemed to meet the "nod test. The "nod test" is met when people take in what you are saying with that little instinctive nod that lets you know that whatever you have said makes sense to the listener. Here's the most common example: when I'd go on a radio talk show, for instance, to talk about our $4.6 billion budget amendment for people and the environment, it would most often be recalled and recognized by the radio audience, sometimes before I had even had a chance to raise it. Chances were that either the host or a caller would even remember the details. Frequently people could cite our budget number to the decimal point.

We also decided to focus on a straightforward appeal to Canadians that went back to something Ed Broadbent had done extremely well during his fourteen years as NDP leader. Ed always talked about "ordinary Canadians" and it was no accident that, in the four elections Ed waged as leader, more and more ordinary Canadians voted NDP. We tweaked the phrase, choosing instead to talk about "working families." Talking about issues that working families faced allowed us also to talk about issues of concern to seniors and young people. I knew we were onto something because I could see the resonance and response the phrase received during the campaign. When I used a phrase like, "working families and seniors...the people who built this country," I could see some people's eyes begin to get shiny from the emotion of it. This was especially so for the seniors in the crowd. The response was quite incredible. When you think about it, virtually all of us—regardless of our situation—tend to think of ourselves as being part of a family. Single folks might think of their parents or siblings as their family, while couples without any children of their own might identify with the previous generation. Whatever the personal story, people wanted someone, some party, to speak out loudly for them, raising their concerns, putting their hopes and dreams into the national debate.

Another reason I think we touched a chord was the fact that, while we are an aging society, we had a national government without any plan whatsoever to assist more and more of our senior citizens who were facing a financial crunch. This is especially true of many older women on the verge of falling into abject poverty and who would be absolutely the last people on earth to complain about their plight. But many of today's working families know only too well the struggle their elderly parents are facing. These working families are out there on the front line, coping with parents as they move into that phase of their lives while, at the same time struggling to save money for their own children's education.

Aware that our audiences were hearing and reacting to our election messages, we began promoting the essential core recommendations from the Roy Romanow Royal Commission on Health Care, specifically for a new essential service—home and long-term care. We also promised one other recommendation from Mr. Romanow's report, the establishment of a pharmacare program to reduce the soaring price of drugs. We pointed out that cheaper drug costs together with the freeing up of health and hospital budgets, via home and long-term care, would dramatically reduce waiting lists.

Our second major theme was about young people. We talked about an OECD (Organization for Economic Co-operation and Development) study done in Canada that found, outside Quebec, there had been no significant expansion of public child care in a decade. Despite the agreements with the provinces, we said the Liberals continued to fail Canadians by allowing federal tax dollars to be diverted to profit for commercial childcare companies. Our policy called for the introduction of a National Child Care Act to establish a framework for a national childcare and early learning system with a permanent role for the federal government. Our plan would establish standards for a network of high-quality, licensed, non-profit care for our children. Our call for a childcare act was necessary to avoid seeing the program quashed after a party that didn't believe in it won 37 per cent of the popular vote and became the government. If the Liberals had done this, it would have made it impossible for the Conservatives to try to renege on the federal government's five-year signed agreements with all ten provinces, as they announced they would do in the wake of winning their minority.

We also spent a lot of time talking about young people wanting to pursue their education. Our key campaign promise was to make it more affordable so the young student could acquire a strong post-secondary education or solid apprenticeship training without either students or their parents having to borrow huge amounts of money.

Overall, I felt really comfortable with the core messages of our campaign, and we received a lot of positive feedback from Canadians. It especially struck a chord with folks caught in the sandwich generation. I'm biased, being in the sandwich myself.

The great fear for our party following a minority government is to be squeezed out in the next election as voters begin to think about which party they want to govern and whether they want to hand that party a majority. New Democrats are still haunted by what happened to David Lewis and the NDP following the 1972–1974 Trudeau minority. Despite all the good legislation that occurred at that time, the NDP did not benefit politically. In the summer election of 1974, the NDP received 246,000 fewer votes than the previous election only two years before. The leader lost his seat, and the number of MPs was cut in half, from thirty-one to sixteen.

In 2006, however, it was interesting that the idea that a majority government would be good for the country never really took hold. People certainly weren't about to hand the Liberals a majority. In fact, the voters could hardly wait to send an opposite message—that the Liberals had become too comfortable in office and abused their power. Canadians were ready for change.

On the other hand, by an almost two-to-one count in the election, Canadians expressed their dissatisfaction with the Conservatives' approach. For New Democrats, it was critical throughout the campaign to try to make sure that people would keep us in mind on election day, and to avoid being relegated to the sidelines. That meant we had to be focused and disciplined with a constant message. We said we were offering a third option, one that would speak up in Parliament for working families.

Following the election, I heard criticism that our campaign hadn't been hard enough on the Conservatives, but I simply fail to understand the basis for it.

I've gone back and studied what I said, day-in and day-out. In my speeches, I spoke consistently about how the Conservatives were wrong on the issues, while pointing out the Liberals had not earned people's support. To my way of thinking, criticizing the Conservatives in that way was even stronger than the words we chose to use against the Liberals. The Liberals, I said, didn't deserve people's support because they had promised a certain direction in the 2004 campaign and, after winning a minority government, reverted back to their same old practices. They had promised to reduce pollution by twenty per cent, but pollution had gone up by 20 per cent. They promised democratic reform and then claimed the timelines for implementing it were unrealistic. They promised to protect our health-care system, and Canadians witnessed the privatization of health services and for-profit medicine growing more quickly than it ever had since the creation of our public health-care system.

Canadians were fed up with the Liberals, and the NDP campaign said "enough is enough."

At the same time, we pointed out that the Conservatives were simply wrong on so many of the issues. We said they were wrong for working families, as we're already beginning to see. We specifically warned that the Conservative plan to scrap the childcare agreements with the provinces and instead give all families—regardless of income—$100 a month for each child under the age of six was not the way to go. In fact, it would be a huge mistake. At the local level, we ran hard against all our opponents and had success in defeating several Conservative incumbent MPs. There's no question we were critical of what the Conservatives stood for and the failures of the Liberals for the past thirteen years, so I just don't accept that it's accurate to say that the NDP somehow let the Conservatives off the hook.

One item that did garner plenty of attention throughout the 2006 campaign was statements by Buzz Hargrove, president of the Canadian Auto Workers, urging Canadians to vote strategically. At the outset of the election, Mr. Hargrove advanced the position, adopted by his organization, that the NDP only had a realistic chance of winning forty-two ridings. He urged people living in those ridings to vote for our candidates. In the rest of the country, the CAW president encouraged the electorate to defeat Conservative candidates by voting for the Bloc in Quebec or Liberals everywhere else.

It must have been especially tough for the 266 NDP candidates and their teams of supporters to learn that a high-profile New Democrat was recommending that electors should vote for their opponents. I felt badly for them. Being a candidate is tough enough, even at the best of times. You put your name and reputation on the line. Your whole family becomes engaged and involved in what you're doing. You commandeer friends and try to coax various groups to become involved in your campaign. And you become excited about your possibilities on election day. Then you read in the newspaper that another New Democrat is urging voters to support one of your opponents.

That kind of tactic is hard to square with the notion of teamwork. To me, teamwork and solidarity mean working on each other's issues and supporting one another through thick and thin. Historically, the roots in both the labour movement and social democracy in Canada developed from social injustice and unrest—and in spite of unfair laws and unsafe working conditions and vociferous opposition from mainstream thinking. In such an environment, the need to stand united and stick together has always been paramount. It's like being a player on a team. As long as you're on a team, you play with and for the team. You might have disagreements in the locker room but, when the game starts, you're all skating in the same direction. You don't try to score in your own net.

Since Mr. Hargrove made the CAW position known on "strategic voting" in the first week of the campaign, the topic was revisited almost daily. Instead of seeking details on how NDP policies would help working families, journalists asked: "Jack, how come the labour movement is abandoning the NDP?" I was able to point out that ninety-nine out of a hundred labour leaders were actively supporting the NDP, but that did not always do the trick.

Certainly, we were ecstatic to see Peggy Nash, one of Mr. Hargrove's most senior staff, elected as Member of Parliament for Parkdale–High Park. Still, against the backdrop of the controversy, it must have been particularly tough for her to be knocking on doors every day in a riding we'd never won before. She was running on the need to invest in cities and communities, because the Liberals—despite all their talk over so many years—had utterly failed Canadians on this promise. This inaction meant there were an awful lot of low-income people living in tough times in this west-end Toronto riding, as well as plenty of other Canadian communities.

At various campaign stops around the country, hardworking NDP activists told me that arguments around strategic voting were short-sighted. They argued the rationale that to stop the Conservatives one had to vote Liberal or Bloc was not only illogical, but actually harmful to working families because it nelected Conservatives who would have been defeated by the NDP. In the auto worker city of Oshawa, for instance, strategic voting resulted in the defeat of Syd Ryan—a strong New Democrat and trade unionist—to a Conservative. While there's no question that Oshawa was one of the ridings where Mr. Hargrove strongly encouraged residents to vote NDP, the vast majority of electors simply didn't make the distinction. What they heard, and absorbed, were media reports stating that Mr. Hargrove had abandoned the NDP in favour of the Liberals. A lot of our people concluded that, while dissent and discussion were important and healthy, coming together around a common cause at election time was vital.

Among the vast majority of labour leaders who worked hard for NDP candidates were plenty of CAW members themselves. The controversy may result in positives for the future. For instance, many union members have been working for years—but only quietly—on behalf of the NDP. In addition, changes made in 2004 as to how political parties can be financed effectively prohibit national unions and their locals from donating money. In the 2006 election, I detected a conscious effort by the leadership in a number of trade unions—especially the United Steelworkers of America, United Food and Commercial Workers, Communications Energy and Paperworkers, Canadian Union of Public Employees, National Union of Public and General Employees, and the International Association of Machinists—to look at new ways to activate and involve their members in the electoral process. These trade unions were saying: "Let's really involve our rank-and-file members, the people that work on the shop floor, in a mine or factory or office, a daycare or health-care centre. Let's talk with them much more directly than we have previously about the political issues of the day."

The Canadian Labour Congress led by example with CLC president Ken Georgetti and secretary-treasurer Hassan Yusseff campaigning hard for all our candidates. Their physical presence on the campaign trail, together with the CLC's Better Choice Campaign, sent out a strong message to CLC members that set the stage for change to focus on workers' issues. In turn, our commitment to improve life for working families in Canada resonated with organized labour and the trade union leadership. In the long run, this whole episode of strategic voting may turn out to have had more positives than negatives.

This issue was a bump in the road that any organization goes through, particularly when it's becoming more successful and taking itself more seriously, as we certainly are. In March 2006, the Ontario NDP Council voted 90 per cent in favour of suspending Mr. Hargrove's NDP membership in that province. While my personal preference might have been to move on and build for the future, it was obviously not the feeling of most other party members. After some soul-searching, I concluded that when you're given leadership responsibility in an organization, you have a duty and obligation to be in tune with, respect, and reflect how your team is feeling across the country.

We're certainly going to continue to work alongside the CAW, which is one of Canada's most progressive organizations representing a lot of workers who are very much under threat in Canada. We'll work very closely with Mr. Hargrove and his team to ensure that auto plants and other industries employing CAW members don't see these plants move offshore. One of the pressing issues for Canada and the Canadian auto industry certainly is the need to encourage plans to build hybrid cars and other twenty-first-century vehicles here. Our very survival depends on continuing to move people and goods, but in new ways that will dramatically reduce greenhouse gases and other pollutants. I'm sure the CAW bargaining team were as disappointed as I was that the 2005 negotiated contract settlements between the CAW and Ford, General Motors, and DaimlerChrysler did not contain any specific commitments for a green car strategy in Canada. But it's encouraging to hear that Ford Canada may be looking at a hybrid initiative. Such a development would be exciting, and something Canadians could all celebrate.

Overall, our 2006 campaign was more carefully and effectively crafted than the previous one, and we deliberately tried to chart a steady course that avoided tacking this way and that in response to shifting winds. Another facet of the 2006 campaign that I was much more comfortable with was the leaders' debates. The 2004 debates were a nightmare and pushed me to violate everything my mother and father had taught me about being respectful toward others. It was a terrible experience for me and, totally exasperated, I told staff members afterwards that, unless changes were made for the future, I wouldn't participate. So I was very happy that a new leaders' debate format was arranged for 2006. A few journalists reported the debates were dull, but most Canadians thought they were a marked improvement over 2004. And, contrary to most recent general elections, voter turnout actually went up slightly. Now, it couldn't have been solely because of the debates. There had to be other reasons, and we could speculate what they were. Also, I thought having two rounds of debates in 2006 was a plus.

Another personal plus for me in the 2006 election was the thrill of having my son Mike with me throughout. On the morning the election was called, he had just turned in his thesis on environmental studies at York University. While he still had to defend his thesis, that wouldn't come until after the election was over. It meant Mike was able to travel with me and help me throughout the campaign. It was a special treat—father and son travelling, experiencing and learning together—and the personal support he provided to me was enormous. Meanwhile, my daughter Sarah, who had always been a little shy about canvassing, was out door-knocking virtually every day with her partner and Mike's partner. Together with Olivia, they tramped up and down the highrises in Trinity–Spadina delivering the NDP's message to the electors. Of course, we were all desperately hoping to avoid the big disappointment we experienced in 2004. For me, the most disappointing aspect of 2004 was that Olivia didn't win and wasn't able to join me right from the start in the House of Commons. So 2006 was certainly a thrilling result. As someone said when we were thanking all the 1,496 volunteers in the Trinity–Spadina NDP campaign: "Each of you has been involved and engaged in an important family reunification project!" But there was much more for New Democrats to celebrate on election night than simply winning that riding. We had set an objective in 2006 of having far more women elected. The NDP has always led the other parties in seeking out and encouraging women candidates to run for us. Our party believes strongly that the House of Commons should mirror and reflect the composition of the country. To try to reach that goal, local candidate search committees have followed our party's policy to follow affirmative action guidelines and attract and recruit candidates who normally don't run for political office. We want more women, people of colour, people with disabilities, gay men, and lesbian women to seek an NDP nomination. After the 2004 election, only 21 per cent of all the seats in the House of Commons were occupied by women. We led the way with 26 per cent but our goal remained 50 per cent. In past elections we attracted many women candidates to run for us, but they often weren't nominated in ridings where we had a reasonable chance of winning. So leading up to the 2006 election, we put specific emphasis on recruiting women and other affirmative-action candidates to ridings where the NDP had a reasonable chance of success. I really salute our caucus chair Judy Wasylycia-Leis for all the work she's done over three decades to recruit more women to seek elected office in our party. Jean Crowder was the chair of our women's caucus and also worked hard on this file, with Tara Peel, a determined young recruiter at the federal office. I met with them regularly to ensure that we had a slate of excellent women candidates in winnable ridings, and those efforts paid off. Eight of the eleven new seats won by New Democrats in 2006 went to women. Of our twenty-nine MPs, eleven are women. That's 41 per cent. That's the highest proportion of women ever elected to the Canadian Parliament by any officially recognized caucus. (A caucus must have twelve MPs to be officially recognized.)

Seeing the expression on Alexa McDonough's face when she walked into that first meeting and saw a caucus approaching gender parity was truly something. After a quarter century of effort, she had a mile-wide grin on her face that was wonderful to behold. I know Alexa must have been remembering her first day in the Nova Scotia legislature. Not only was she the first female provincial NDP leader—with no caucus members—she was the only woman in the Nova Scotia legislature.

Another big lift on election night 2006 was that all our incumbent MPs were re-elected, and we were the only party that could make that claim. Ed Broadbent had retired, but Paul Dewar retained Ottawa Centre. New Democrats won a total of five new urban Ontario ridings, in Hamilton, Toronto, and London, to go with the seven we already held. We doubled our seats in British Columbia, picking up two new seats on Vancouver Island, two more on the lower mainland, and one in the southern interior. These five new seats gave us a strong contingent of ten B.C. MPs. Dennis Bevington rebounded from a forty-seven-vote loss in 2004 to win the Western Arctic seat for the NDP.

In addition to the eleven new ridings held by the NDP, we made good progress on other fronts, as well. The 17.5 per cent of the popular vote was the sixth highest ever for us, and our best overall percentage since the Bloc Québécois was founded in the early 1990s. More than 2.5 million Canadians voted for NDP candidates, a total exceeded only once previously—in 1988 when Ed Broadbent led the NDP to 43 seats and 2.68 million votes.

My sense overall is that the federal New Democratic Party is in a step-by-step building process, and that what happened in 2006 was a consolidation of gains made in 2004. Many more Canadians are taking a serious look at us now, and the question we need to answer is, "What do we have to do to open the door wide so that a lot more Canadians can join with us?" Starting at the general level, we have to learn how to be even more effective in getting our message out that working families have not only a trustworthy ally in the NDP, but also a team that is really read to work for them in the House of Commons. We have to take that message door-to-door right across the country. In 2006 we had some really exciting people step forward to run for us. Reading their biographies and learning about their previous accomplishments was a real eye-opener. Even though many were unsuccessful in 2006, we must encourage those candidates to stay active and run again for us. By remaining involved, they'll become even better known in their communities. That's going to be very important because, in the next election, I know that progressive Canadians are going to react very negatively to what Stephen Harper and his government has been bringing forward, and they will be looking for a choice next time that will work much better for them—a choice consistent with their values, that and a choice that delivers the goods.

As always, the biggest challenge for New Democrats will be to show the way for a great many Canadians to move past their traditional default position—which is to support Liberals. This is something the Canadians must do if they are to take the bold step to pull away from the kind of politics represented by George W. Bush and the rush to unbridled individualism while turning our back on collective responsibilities and opportunities to build Canada together.

In Quebec, I think the recent election results reveal a real breakdown in traditional voting patterns. Going into the 2004 election, the NDP had a base in Quebec of less than 2 per cent. We doubled it in 2004 and redoubled it in 2006. More than 276,000 Quebeckers voted NDP in 2006, but, victim once again of that perversion of democracy known as the single-member-plurality system of voting, those tens of thousands of NDP voters in Quebec did not end up with an NDP MP in Quebec. Still, we now see a lot of Quebeckers believing in the NDP. That's progress and, if we are able to double it once or twice more, we'll be significant political players and winning seats in Quebec. Still, even now when I rise in the House of Commons to speak against the Afghanistan war or in favour of taking action on Kyoto or childcare, I know I am speaking for over a quarter million Quebecois. Having been born and raised there, it is truly an honour to do so.

In Nova Scotia, we had a higher percentage of the popular vote than in any other province—nearly 30 per cent. Yet, in spite of this strong showing, we were unable to win any new seats. Alexa McDonough and Peter Stoffer were re-elected.

Clearly, when our party polls more than 2.5 million votes but wins only 29 seats, there's something that is preventing us from having the number of voices in the House of Commons that Canadians, by their support, want us to have. And that something is, of course, our antiquated, outdated, first-past-the-post system of determining who wins and who loses. In 2004, the NDP had 15.7 per cent of the popular vote but captured only 6 per cent of the seats in the House of Commons. In 2006, we did better, winning 29 seats with 17.5 per cent. But the fact remains that, under a system of proportional representation, New Democrats would occupy 17 per cent of the seats (about 55 of 308).

It was, however, Stephen Harper's Conservatives, with 127 seats, who were called upon to form a minority government. I thought Mr. Harper's approach to the election was clever and at the same time dangerous to the Canada we hold dear. Doing the wrong things well, as Mr. Harper strives to do, does not lesson the damage done. He picked up on the public's anger at how the Liberals had misspent their tax dollars, and he tapped into that reservoir of sentiment that Canadians could put those dollars to better use themselves. He clearly recognized that Canadians were out there working for a living, toughing it out, and that most times it was not easy for lots of them. The voters were looking for someone who understood that. His approach of cutting taxes here and there—just about everywhere actually—appealed to that reality. What the Conservatives did effectively was to attach a tax-cut promise to daily real-life situations that people were dealing with—taking kids to hockey, job training, or taking the bus to work. It was effective and, while I can't swear to it, I think Mr. Harper even used the term "working class" in the campaign. Coming from a Conservative, this was an interesting recognition that the people who go to work every day are the key constituents of the country.

Or it might also be nothing more than a ploy by the Canadian Conservative Party to borrow the language of their friends in the U.S. Republican Party and play on hot-button issues. Tactics by the Republicans have dramatically transformed voting patters in several American states. This is documented in an informative book entitled *What's The Matter with Kansas*. Not long ago, Kansas was one of the most progressive states in the U.S. Kansans traditionally elected Democrats to the state legislature and the U.S. Congress. Today, however, Kansans vote hard right and overwhelmingly support Republican candidates dedicated to increasing the power and influence of a small elite at the expense of the vast number of Kansans. As a result, many Kansans find themselves the working poor, held back, in large part, by right-wing legislation including regressive right-to-work laws that make it virtually impossible for workers to join a union and bargain collectively. What has happened in Kansas and a few other Midwestern states is really a remarkable deception as to the real needs of working families.

In Canada, I believe we have the possibility of nipping that trend in the bud. But it does send a sharp signal to those of us on the left. Perhaps we aren't tied in closely enough with working people and their day-to-day concerns. As we've reached out to attract others to join with us, perhaps we've unintentionally distanced ourselves from workers and the trade unions and associations that represent them. It's something we must guard against, although in the 2006 campaign, I'm fully confident that we identified with working families and their specific concerns.

From my meetings and observations of Mr. Harper while he and I were in Opposition, I believe this prime minister is someone who thinks carefully. But there can be little doubt that he's on a mission to take Canada—in a policy sense—to a very different place than most Canadians want to go, and certainly to a different place than it would be desirable for Canada to go. His policies won't help working people. I've never seen a tax cut yet that hired a nurse or a childcare worker, cared for a senior or made childcare spaces available. But, while New Democrats strongly believe Conservative policies are the wrong way to go, Mr. Harper clearly recognized there was a thirst in the electorate for someone to recognize their struggles and address them during the election.

One of the often repeated criticisms of New Democrats by our political opponents is that we've never met a subsidy we didn't like. Our right-wing opponents say: "New Democrats are nothing but tax and spenders," and they say a lot of other nonsense. But the facts speak otherwise. In both the 2004 and 2006 campaigns, federal New Democrats ran on a platform of balancing the books. In 2006, we pledged no new tax increases, and our total platform promises were more modest than those of either the Conservatives or the Liberals. There were no new taxes in the NDP budget amendment of June 2005. The $4.6-billion amounted to transferring money out of a budget line that would have given Canada's largest corporations tax reductions they didn't need and using that money instead for health care, childcare, energy retrofits, and public transit.

Reviewing how various political budgets have managed the books when they've been in government at the provincial level over the past twenty-five years is also revealing. A study shows that provincial NDP governments ran deficits 59 per cent of the time. But that was better than the Conservatives when in power provincially or federally, at 69 per cent, and much better than the Liberals, at 83 per cent. Still, whenever New Democrats ask questions about the wisdom of cutting corporate taxes or reducing the debt faster, the lecture commences on our lack of fiscal responsibility. These are diatribes from right-wing spokespeople whose parties have a demonstrably worse track record than ours.

Saskatchewan provides a good, historical example of one political party that balanced the books and one that didn't. In 1944, Premier Tommy Douglas took a province reeling from the ravages of the Great Depression and, while making huge advances in social programs, also balanced the books for seventeen years in a row. Between 1971 and 1982, NDP Premier Allan Blakeney balanced the books each and every year. And, from 1991 to 2000, NDP Premier Roy Romanow was equally prudent, with nine consecutive balanced budgets. Between 1982 and 1991, however, a Conservative government, led by Grant Devine, ran Saskatchewan—into the ground, many would say, leaving a province of one million people with a debt of $14.8 billion. If the Devine government wasn't the worst provincial government in Canadian history, it was certainly the most corrupt. Fifteen Saskatchewan cabinet ministers were convicted of fraud and four served jail time. The Devine administration drove Saskatchewan's assets into junk-bond status before Mr. Romanow and his successor, NDP premier Lorne Calvert, took over and began systematically paying down the enormous debt left behind by the Conservatives. In fact, the stench from the Devine era was so bad the Conservatives' provincial executive put the party into mothballs for a decade, and perhaps much longer.

At the federal level, Canada's national debt is decreasing in both relative and actual terms. It stands at about 44 per cent of our gross domestic product, with $52 billion paid off by the Liberal governments of Jean Chrétien and Paul Martin. But because—year in and year out—the Liberals consistently low-balled the size of the government's annual surplus, it was impossible to have any kind of meaningful debate as to how and where those surpluses should be allocated. Like clockwork at the end of each fiscal year, the Liberal finance minister would announce that Canada had a large "unexpected" surplus and then plunk all of it down on debt repayment. The reality today is that, even without any direct payments against the debt, the nation's continued economic growth ensures that our debt-to-GDP ratio will continue to decline. Most Canadians also don't realize that this total preoccupation with debt reduction has driven federal spending on social programs to its lowest percentage in more than half a century. Make no mistake, federal New Democrats are firmly committed to annual balanced budgets. But we also know debt reduction will occur as our national economy grows. Therefore, when it comes to immediate priorities, we want to see money invested in the priorities of Canadians—investment long overdue.

From conversations with Mr. Harper, I know he believes that politics in Canada ought to be based on competing sets of ideas, competing visions of the country. I remember him saying to me at one of our early meetings after the 2004 election: "You know, politics really should be about the clash of ideas—your party and its ideas and my party and our ideas." Let there be no doubt, however, that his objectives and those of the NDP are completely different indeed.

One area where I was hoping he would do the right thing was the whole question of ethics in government. Mr. Harper spoke a great deal in the 2006 election about the need for greater accountability, higher ethical standards, and an end to the culture of entitlement. As a result, most Canadians were prepared to give him the benefit of the doubt that significant changes around issues of ethics would be pursued vigorously by a Harper administration. That was until we witnessed the astounding decision to violate—completely and rapidly—the very commitments on ethics he'd made so forcefully during the campaign. He appointed one of his campaign managers, Michael Fortier, to the Senate in order to make him minister of public works. This totally contradicted and violated two major planks of Harper's ethics package platform. First, he said that he wanted to elect senators, instead of having them appointed. Second, he said that, in order to serve in cabinet, a person first had to be elected. Yet, at the cabinet swearing-in ceremony two weeks to the day after the federal election, there was Mr. Harper introducing a man who hadn't even run in the election as a future senator and a minister.

But, as mind-boggling as Mr. Fortier's appointment was, it paled in comparison with the swearing in of David Emerson. In contrast to Mr. Fortier, it must be acknowledged that Mr. Emerson had indeed been elected. It's just that he was elected on January 23 as a Liberal in Vancouver–Kingsway, and two weeks later was appointed by Mr. Harper as a Conservative cabinet minister.

During the first set of leaders' debates, we had all been asked our position on floor crossing. Mr. Harper indicated that he was opposed in principle to the concept. In the wake of Conservative Belinda Stronach's defection to the Liberals, the NDP had introduced an Opposition Day motion in the House to indicate our strong objections to this practice. We said that floor crossing should be eliminated and that any elected member who chose to leave one caucus for another should resign their seat and run in a by-election. This would ensure that their electors approved of the MP's decision. Peter Stoffer, our MP from Nova Scotia's Sackville–Eastern Shore, led the fight against this party-hopping practice since he was first elected in 1997.

Mr. Harper's position throughout the election campaign that he disagreed in principle with floor crossing meant sweet nothing, however, when he abruptly appointed the Honourable Mr. Emerson to his Conservative cabinet. During the campaign, Mr. Emerson, the Liberal candidate in Vancouver–Kingsway, had promised to be Mr. Harper's worst enemy. On that point, it seems Mr. Emerson will be proven right, as the fallout from the appointment was the biggest story following the election. It was to be followed later by another betrayal of the communities and workers that David Emerson had said he would defend, only then to turn around and shepherd the Harper administration's sell out to the Bush administration concerning the softwood lumber controversy.

There's no question that these flip-flops by Mr. Harper reflect a pursuit of power at any and all costs and an ability to ignore ethical commitments made in the election. The timing and cynicism behind David Emerson's appointment disturbed most Canadians and clearly shocked the voters in

Vancouver–Kingsway. I was positively astounded by the energy exhibited by the people in the constituency, who demonstrated their opposition to the Emerson appointment. From the public meeting I attended, my sense was there were a great number of people in attendance who were not normally engaged in partisan politics. They indicated, in no uncertain terms, that they had been betrayed by the Emerson-Harper sleight-of-hand, with the result that their vote—which was obviously very precious to them—had been rendered worthless.

The Emerson appointment may reveal a different side of the new prime minister. A profoundly worrisome side that wants to ensure his specific agenda is adopted, regardless of the cost. He knows that his ambitious plan to restructure the country cannot be implemented with only 124 MPs. In order to have a hard-right Conservative agenda adopted, he needs a majority government. To try to achieve that, securing another seat by enticing an Opposition MP to join his cabinet is more important to Mr. Harper than abiding by the ethical principles he set out and insisted were desperately needed. It's all deeply disturbing and downright foreboding. Mr. Harper appealed to Canadians to vote for him so he could make the kind of changes he says need to be made around government ethics. Mr. Harper can speak the same language Ed Broadbent used—reform the system to make politics more civil, more ethical, and less cynical. But Mr. Harper's appointment of Mr. Emerson and Mr. Fortier belie his words. While Mr. Harper will be working to build a majority for next time, our caucus will be doing our utmost to ensure that it never happens.

Despite our gains in Quebec in the 2006 election, reflection suggests that the Conservatives were the major beneficiaries of the electoral shifts that took place with the remnants of their once historic organization in Quebec mobilized to defeat the Liberals. In fact, the Conservatives were able to rebuild to a surprising degree in the province. Although I was pleased with the policies we had in Quebec, those policies didn't catch the attention of the voters. Obviously the Conservatives' message did, in large part because Mr. Harper was seen as a strong contender to become prime minister. I talked about the need for reconciliation in Quebec, an end to the corruption and the game playing. I said that Ottawa needed to ensure Quebec people received the services they paid for —health care, aid for seniors, child care. We in the rest of Canada had to respect fully the unique nature of Quebec—not just mouth the words but really mean it. I said if we did all that, we would "create the winning conditions for Canada in Quebec" so Quebeckers would want to remain in Canada. The cherry on top would be to find a way for Quebec's National Assembly to ratify the Canadian Constitution. There's no doubt in my mind that if we do these things carefully, thoughtfully and well, a solid majority of Quebeckers would want to remain an integral part of Canada for a long time to come.

While the growth in NDP support in Quebec was encouraging in 2006, there were some lessons to be learned. In spite of the increase in popular support to 8.6 per cent overall, including 18.6 per cent in the riding of Outremont, my sense was that we failed to capitalize fully on our potential in Quebec. It was clearly an area where we would have to do more work, and the timing could be favourable. Federal-provincial relations appear to be changing in Quebec with the "national question" moving to a new stage. We've seen the establishment of an interesting and important new left-wing party, Québec Solidaire, headed by Francoise David and Amir Khadir—two individuals with whom I've had a warm, cordial relationship. It has become evident that there's a dynamic in Quebec politics that has moved a considerable distance in the past twenty-four months. I detected a seismic shift beginning to happen that might open the door for the advancement of social democratic politics at both the federal and provincial levels. I have also come to believe that with the fallout from the sponsorship scandal, as well as the insufferable paternalistic approach the federal Liberals bring to Quebec, it's going to be some time before we see Quebeckers moving back to the Liberals in a big way. That would also mean real opportunities for a major realignment in Canadian politics, and it would help open the door to democratic socialism. Any shift to the NDP, with the growth of Québec Solidaire taking on the Parti Québécois and its new leader, André Boisclair, could really shake up the political dynamic in Quebec.

The reality for such a long time in Quebec has been a bipolar political system between the Liberals and the Bloc Québécois. Such a system meant that other ideas—good ideas—about what we might be able to do together simply suffocated. Around 2002 or 2003, it began to look as if the Bloc had peaked and that this rivalry was beginning to fade slightly. Some pollsters were predicting the Bloc wouldn't win more than thirty seats in the future. Others wondered whether the Bloc even had a future. Then, almost overnight, there was this huge sea change in the province with the full revelation and gory details of sordid events of the sponsorship scandal—wrongdoing that had happened primarily in the late 1990s. Quebec's reaction was outrage—an outpouring of anger and resentment against the federal Liberals. It brought to the surface everything Quebeckers had been so upset about for so long—a fundamental lack of respect from the government in Ottawa. It was as though a wound was finally beginning to heal but then somebody tore off the scab and poured vinegar on it. Since old habits die hard, the natural beneficiary of this anger was the Bloc, and they jumped from thirty-eight to fifty-four seats in the 2004 election, all coming at the expense of the Liberals. After their success in that campaign, Bloc Leader Gilles Duceppe was keen to have another election as quickly as possible. He was convinced his party could win even more seats and boasted openly that his party would certainly defeat high-profile cabinet ministers Lisa Frulla and Pierre Pettigrew. (Ms. Frulla and Mr. Pettigrew did lose in 2006, but so did a number of Bloc MPs.) The Conservatives came from nowhere to win ten seats in Quebec. Overall, the Bloc lost three seats and there was a drop in their percentage of the vote.

What a difference one election makes! In the current parliament, instead of chomping at the bit for another election immediately, the Bloc appears to be shifting gears, saying they prepared to support the new Harper government for "a good long while." When reflecting on early unconditional capitulation from the Bloc, I am disappointed, but not surprised. I always thought that would be the likely scenario in any minority Parliament headed by the Conservatives: a Conservative minority, with a contingent of Bloc MPs, joining forces to dismantle and diminish federal capacities. In this minority situation, Mr. Duceppe's approach is to transfer as much power and funding to Quebec as quickly as possible. Of course, Mr. Harper and his party also fundamentally believe in much greater decentralization of federal powers and responsibilities. (It's not by accident that Prime Minister Harper had three separate meetings with Quebec Premier Jean Charest within a month of being sworn in.) This decentralization helps circumvent key pan-Canadian goals in vital areas where we need to work together. The net effect will be that those who believe in greater privatization, those who want collective national institutions to whither, will be in a better position to begin picking off provinces one by one. So, I'm very concerned about the way this informal alliance between the Bloc and the Conservatives is shaping up, and it's certainly not going to give Canadian working families what they need—especially seniors and young people. It is also a direction that betrays the Bloc's claims to be a progressive social force. The evidence is strong, and to the contrary.

A powerful example of how disconnected the Bloc has become from those who want to see progressive results was its opposition to the NDP proposal to ban pesticides for cosmetic use for lawns and flower gardens in Canada. Quebec has been a leader in this area, with strong laws in place. We wanted similar legislation for the whole country. No surprise that the Conservatives opposed the measure. The Bloc claimed that Quebec's laws were stronger so we did not need another law. The Bloc also made an uttlerly false accusation that the proposal infringed on provincial jurisdiction. In voting against other parts of Canada having laws similar to the Quebec initiative, the Bloc effectively used its votes in the House to deny better health for people elsewhere in Canada. When it came to the health of Quebec residents, did the Bloc believe that pesticides on Toronto lawns would not eventually find their way into Lake Ontario and down the river into the drinking water of Quebec children? Absurd. The bottom line was that Quebec just didn't want a "Canadian" anti-pollution measure to work. I do not for a minute believe that the Quebec people believe that this is the right way to use votes in the House of Commons.

Unlike the Conservatives and the Bloc, New Democrats want to see a level of equality as well as an informed discussion about how best to create and deliver quality social programs to all Canadians. We want to help them cope with the issues they face—whether it's child care, health care, or the environment. The Bloc firmly believes that all these issues and many more would be best handled if the programs and the funding were simply transferred to the provincial national assembly in Quebec City. I believe significant flexibility should be given to the national assembly and that their constitutional responsibilities should be fully respected. But that certainly shouldn't prevent us from trying—as one country—to do some things together.

As far as the federal Liberals are concerned, they are down at the moment, but political adversaries count them out at their peril. They have a strong presence and a strong organization virtually everywhere outside Quebec. They've always had plenty of hard-working volunteers in ridings across Canada. With Paul Martin stepping back after his party's defeat in January 2006, there are question marks about the future direction of the Liberal Party. Although a number of high-profile Liberals said they weren't interested in seeking the leadership, many subsequently threw their hats into the ring for the December 2006 leadership convention.

In the spring of 2006, as the Liberal backroom players planned for their leadership convention, the Liberal caucus appeared ready to sit back and enjoy the spectacle in the Commons. Their interim leader Bill Graham brought forward their big idea for the spring session: blaming the NDP for anything the Harper government did that was distasteful. I always have to remind myself how the Liberals have been formidable opponents, in part because they are willing to say just about anything, and in many cases to believe it, and then immediately abandon what they've said when circumstances change. A good friend, a self-deprecating Liberal, used to say to me: "Jack, what do you mean we don't have principles? We have principles! And if you don't like them, we have these other principles over here!" We've seen the seductive self-delusion of Liberals often. They will point to initiatives that go back decades—like medicare—and argue that it was actually their party that was responsible for its inception.

On child care, Mr. Harper served notice that he intended to cancel the five-year funding agreements. These agreements were put in place by the Liberals and all ten provinces and three territories, all with strong NDP support and encouragement. Mr. Harper's plan, now in place, is to cancel all agreements to fund childcare spaces after two years which had already been committed and instead give $100 a month to parents of young children, regardless of household income. Such a plan can be referred to in a number of ways, but the one thing it can't be called is a childcare program.

Liberal MPs response to this has been to flood the airwaves and blogsphere saying: "Because the NDP forced the election, they alone are responsible for any changes the Conservatives make to child care."

The NDP responded to the Conservatives' backward move with proposition, not just opposition. First, we worked with community organizations to crafting legislation to create a pan-Canadian childcare programme. This is because payments of modest sums to parents will not create childcare spaces for the parents on waiting lists, those in need. Harper's $100 cannot purchase child care that is not available! We submitted the bill to the House of Commons to become the law of the land, something no prime minister could tear up without full parliamentary approval. Second, we exposed the cruel clawing back of federal funds and credits to moderate- and low-income families that Harper had planned for his $100 monthly cheque, a claw back that would leave little in parents' hands after all was said and done. As a result, some of the clawing back was cancelled.

The different responses of the two national Opposition parties to the situation confronting child care indicates a fundamental difference in the approach of the Liberals and the NDP to the work facing parliamentarians. More illustrations of these differences in approach to parliament were to come as the spring session unfolded. They culminated in the shocking duplicity of the Liberals' claim to oppose the military adventurism of George Bush, yet ensuring that Stephen Harper had enough Liberal support to commit Canadian troops for a lengthy mission in Afghanistan.

I'm not convinced that a new leader can bring any fundamental change of character to the Liberal Party: a party so focused on power that it whichever leader is chosen will most likely continue to say one thing and do another in order to attain it. Doesn't such duplicity leave disillusion and disappointment in its wake? Is it not time for something better, for some authentic politics?

The New Democratic Party is a political party that focuses on ideas and a way forwards. Initially, I had high hopes that we could work with the new Conservative government on electoral reform. Canada badly needs to change its antiquated system of electing all MPs by our winner-take-all system and introduce an element of proportional representation.

I've spoken with Mr. Harper and I know that he has written positively about the need for proportional representation (PR) in Canada. We are one of the few democratic countries in the world that does not have some element of PR in its electoral system. The United States is another, but in an essentially two-party country such as the U.S., with its "red" and "blue" states, a system of PR is far less important than in Canada, where there are currently four officially recognized parties represented in the House of Commons, and many other parties working to have members elected. The disparities abound for all to see. Canadians talk rhetorically about "majority" governments, but only twice in the past fifty years has a political party obtained a majority by winning more than 50 per cent of the popular vote. Mr. Diefenbaker did it in 1958, followed by Mr. Mulroney in 1984.

Mr. Chrétien won three "majority" governments between 1993 and 2000, but his percentage of the popular vote hovered around 40 per cent every time. The "majority" only occurred because our first-past-the-post electoral system gave his Liberal Party about 60 per cent of the seats in the House of Commons. Any reasonable definition of democracy starts from the premise that the popular vote received by each party should be reflected in the actual distribution of seats in the House. Such a system would ensure that parties in the House reflect accurately the national point of view as expressed by the voters on election day. In the 2006 election, the Conservatives won 124 seats with 37 per cent of the vote. While it was not a majority government, Canadians "elected" one party to govern when more than 60 per cent of Canadians voted for other parties. This doesn't match any standard of democracy available anywhere.

With a system of PR, the 308 seats in the 2006 election would have been divided approximately as follows: Conservatives, 113 (they have 124); Liberals, 95 (they have 103); Bloc, 32 (they have 51); NDP, 55 (we have 29), and Greens, 12 (they have 0). It's obvious that, under a PR system, majority governments would be the exception, not the rule. I have no doubt this would force parties to work through the issues of the day together and would be a big improvement over the current system, where the government proposes legislation and the Opposition parties tend it oppose it. Proportional representation could also help alleviate regional tensions, something I've spoken with Ed Broadbent about. In his first year of political science at the University of Toronto, Ed presented a paper advocating proportional representation to highly regarded professor Paul Fox.

"Professor Fox was a great teacher and he gave me an A for my paper. But his written comments were bang on for the time. After reading my proposal for proportional representation in Canada, Professor Fox wrote 'ingenious but ingenuous.' I wrote that paper more than fifty years ago. Talk about the slow emergence of ideas," Ed said.

Broadbent also raised the issue of PR with Prime Minister Trudeau when the two leaders met following the 1980 election. Broadbent pointed out that one of the problems the Liberals had, despite their majority government, was the lack of proportionality from the electoral system. In the 1980 election, the Liberals won only two seats west of Ontario. Despite his majority, Trudeau certainly didn't have a representative caucus. According to Broadbent, based on the Liberals' percentage of popular vote in the west, Trudeau should have had at least twenty-five MPs from western Canada.

"And I believe, of course, that if Trudeau had won twenty-five seats in the West, some of the most objectionable features of the National Energy Program, which the Liberals introduced in that period, would probably never have emerged," Ed told me.

But even when a party doesn't win the most seats, proportional representation would be beneficial in reducing regional tensions. For instance, Reform Party Leader Preston Manning won 20 per cent of the vote in Ontario in the 1997 election, but secured no seats. As Broadbent said: "If we'd had PR, we wouldn't have had to listen to all these stories about Reform being shut out in eastern Canada. Voters did not shut out them out. The electoral system did. "

I spoke about the need for democratic reform with Prime Minister Martin and made it a condition of our support that the 2004 throne speech would contain a reference to democratic reform. The standing committee was established through the party leaders, and Broadbent took a huge leadership role in that committee; NDP MP Joe Comartin was also very active on it. The committee looked at electoral systems all around the world and came back with the recommendation that Canada should move in the direction of proportional representation. This was the first time a parliamentary committee had pushed fixing our electoral system this far. It's also perhaps significant that both Mr. Harper and I have written and talked about the notion that introducing proportional representation to Canada would be an important step forward in democratic reform. Of course, the Canadian Law Commission recommended it a few years ago, while the House of Commons Standing Committee on Democratic Reform recommended it in 2005 with a timetable for study. The timelines were put in by Broadbent, our representative on the committee, who was in close contact with Mauril Belanger, the minister responsible. Belanger advised that the dates would work but was later forced to tell Broadbent that, while the Liberals approved of the report and the recommendations, the government concluded the time frame was too short. Broadbent was not convinced. He said, "I really believe that it was deep-sixed, either by the Prime Minister's Office or the cabinet itself." The scheduled date to launch the study was October 1, 2005. And the part that was going to be public consultation—the citizenship engagement process—was to be completed by January 31, 2006. If it had been launched on October 1, it would have become a public document in early 2006 with recommendations about the principles that Canadians wanted to see in their electoral system. Do Canadians want a mixture of first-past-the-post and PR? Do they want pure PR? Do they want a system that would help ensure more women are elected and greater gender balance attained in the House?

Although we were disappointed that the Liberals killed this initiative, there is nothing to prevent it from being brought back in the new Parliament. In fact, in a brief reference to democratic reform contained in the Harper government's first speech from the throne, I was—a least initially—tremendously encouraged to hear Governor General Michaëlle Jean use phraseology almost the same as that used by Ed Broadbent and me when discussing proportional representation. The Governor General said these words: "Building on the work begun in the last Parliament, this government will seek to involve parliamentarians and citizens in examining the challenges facing Canada's electoral system and democratic institutions."

These words suggested that the work initiated by Broadbent, when he was on the Standing Committee on Democratic Reform in the thirty-eighth Parliament, would not be lost in the thirty-ninth. By talking about the need to work with Parliament, I thought the new government was sending a strong signal of its intention to work with the Opposition parties on advancing this concept. But the sad fact is that after the throne speech, parliamentarians and Canadians have heard nothing about PR from the government, and no amount of prodding has produced movement forward on this key issue.

In fact, it appears that Harper has abandoned any idea of moving forward on democratic reform, with the exception of talking about fixed terms for Senate appointments. For those of us serious about meaningful democratic reform, that is hardly a creative approach or a significant step forward. In fact, it inserts into the Canadian political dialogue the notion that the Senate has some degree of legitimacy and that the problem with the Senate is the term of appointment. The problem isn't the term. The problem is that appointments to the Senate are—in the vast majority of cases—patronage appointments. As a result, the unelected Senate has no legitimacy in twenty-first century Canada, we don't need it, and I believe the unacceptable anomaly of the unelected Senate and the basic question of why we need an "upper chamber" at all must become the central issues of debate.

For me, one of the real litmus tests of the new Parliament will be whether we can move on democratic reform. It's vitally needed. What a step forward it would be for our country if we were actually able to bring about significant electoral reform. With several provinces looking at PR and both the Law Commission and the House committee on democratic reform recommending it, surely this is the time to finally make it happen.

I took some encouragement on election night when I heard prime minister-designate Stephen Harper state in his victory speech: "Tonight, although Canadians have voted for change, they have not given any one party in the House of Commons a majority. They have called for us to co-operate— to work together and to get on with tackling the real concerns of ordinary working people and their families. I look forward to working with all of the parties and all of the Members of Parliament to build consensus and move this country forward."

"Co-operate," "working together," and "tackling the concerns of ordinary working families" were words right out of the NDP playbook. There was an initial optimistic flurry of activity and separate meetings between the prime minister and Opposition leaders, including me, and the new prime minister. But about two weeks before the March throne speech, phone calls and messages to and from the PMO abruptly ceased.

As the Harper administration was finalizing its first throne speech, the NDP caucus was deciding that the very first item of business in the upcoming session must be an in-depth debate about Canadian involvement in Afghanistan, specifically the war in Kandahar and southern Afghanistan. Before Parliament convened, we put forward to the Speaker's office a request for an emergency debate on this issue. We laid out our reasons, concentrating on the fact that the focus of the mission had changed dramatically since its inception. When the Liberals first committed Canada to dispatch troops to

Afghanistan, as an appeasement to U.S. President George Bush after rebuffing him on Canadian troops for Iraq, it was understood by Canadians that our modest contingent of men and women would be concentrating on the so-called 3Ds in Afghanistan—the interconnected goals of diplomacy, development, and defense—and that the three would be approximately in equal balance, with defence making diplomacy and development possible. In the Kabul area, for instance, work was being done to reconstruct institutions as well as social and economic systems and infrastructure, including educational infrastructure. Since those early days, however, there had been a very dramatic change to the purpose of Canadian troops in Afghanistan, and this change had never been discussed by Parliament. First, there had there been a change authorized by the Liberals to send Canadian troops to the south of Afghanistan to fight the forces of the Taliban. This was done in the midst of an election campaign and ran contrary to what the Liberals were suggesting a Canadian foreign policy would look like under their direction. Then there was the expansion of the commitment by Mr. Harper in his first days as prime minister. Neither of these changes had been debated by Members of Parliament. The NDP caucus felt it was critical that these matters be debated. There's no doubt that Canadians have always supported our troops, but Canadians have also strongly supported the concept that Parliament should debate how those troops are deployed. Canadians have insisted, and rightly so, that the men and women they elect to the House of Commons should carefully consider any deployment of personnel abroad. The elected members should have a thorough and comprehensive understanding of the nature of the mission, its decision-making structures, the ability to measure success—how else will we know if we're making progress or just becoming involved in a quagmire? Members' understanding should even contain the broad parameters for an exit strategy—not specifics of course but a general understanding of how and when we would judge an exit to be appropriate.

All of these questions had actually been asked previously in the House of Commons, not only by NDP members but also by then defence critic for the Conservatives, now Minister of National Defence Gordon O'Connor.

We called for an emergency debate believing that there was really no more important issue before Parliament than discussing how two-thousand-plus Canadian young people and officers were going to be deployed and placed in harm's way in a mission that was understood by very few Canadians.

Our request for an emergency debate was rejected and, in fact, some people suggested that just calling for a debate was somehow unpatriotic and exhibited a lack of support for our troops. That kind of jingoistic jumping to simplistic conclusions is the kind of thing you expect to hear from the Bush administration, not here in Canada. On the other hand, some commentators and editorials agreed with us and said: "Wait a minute, Parliament should be able to debate these matters."

We went further than just wanting a debate in the House by indicating that there should be a vote. There is nothing in the House of Commons more meaningless than having a debate on an issue but without a vote at its conclusion. Our request for a vote on troop deployment to Afghanistan was based on a position taken by the three Opposition leaders about eighteen months before. Conservative, NDP, and Bloc leaders put forward such a proposal during the Martin minority government, stating that the government should agree that there would be votes in the House of Commons on treaties and on deployment of troops. However, when we first proposed that there should be a vote on the Afghanistan mission, both the Liberals and the Bloc decided to hide behind a technicality. They concluded that, since the mission involved an extension by two years of a commitment already made by Canada that this was not technically a new deployment, and therefore there didn't need to be a vote. This was an absurd position. Not only was a two year extension of our commitment involved, the initiative authorized by Harper involved doubling of the size of our contingent and shifting the mission objectives away from defence in aid of peacekeeping and reconstruction efforts to war-fighting as an integral part of the American-led Operation Enduring Freedom against the Taliban. The House of Commons was only about two or three weeks into the session when the Bloc suddenly began to change its tune and said a vote on this issue might be appropriate after all. I told my caucus, "Something's changing here and we're no longer alone in calling for a vote." Claude Bachand, the Bloc national defence critic who had spoken forcefully in favour of troop deployment in Kandahar, was suddenly dispatched to Afghanistan, and it was Bloc leader Gilles Duceppe who took the lead in Bachand's absence. Duceppe was much more critical of the government's position. The backdrop for this change, I suspect, was the realization that the Quebec citizenry was strongly opposed to Canada's increasing proximity to George Bush foreign policies which included the new Canadian role in Afgthanistan as a part of the Bush effort to fight the Taliban.

At the same time, we had newly elected MP and Liberal leadership candidate Michael Ignatieff indicating that Canada should be supporting the extended engagement and preparing, along with his supporters in the Liberal caucus, to support the Harper initiative if it came to a vote. Harper also had the support of Bill Graham, who had been the defence minister when Canada first deployed troops to Afghanistan and was now interim leader of the Liberals. There were other Liberal MPs suggesting that we shouldn't be extending the mission. In all, there was confusion in the Liberal ranks, a 180-degree switch going on in the Bloc. The NDP call for a debate and a vote, initially dismissed by all and sundry, was suddenly beginning to have a lot more relevance.

It was at this point that Prime Minister Harper came forward with his surprise announcement that he was going to call for an immediate, brief debate and vote but allow for no amendments. That meant it would be impossible to fine-tune the mission's goals and objectives. As Mr. Harper and his spin doctors put it: "You're either for our troops or against them. You're either for ensuring that millions of Afghani girls go to school—helped by Canadian troops—or you're against it." A stark kind of picture, which reminded me of the movie *Wag the Dog*, was being painted by the government.

Not surprisingly, we protested very loudly on the manner in which the debate and vote were to unfold. At a minimum, we felt that there should be a hearing in front of the standing committee on national defence where chief of national defence Rick Hillier and other military staff could come and explain to Canadians what was going on. In addition, we could have heard from other expert witnesses with different viewpoints from the military brass. Such an informed debate was impossible given the way the Conservatives insisted the debate and vote be conducted. I have no doubt that the Harper team wanted it that way. This debate was not, in their eyes, to be based on reason or information, but was to be positioned exclusively on misinformation combined with emotion—fear of terrorism mixed with patriotism. This potent mix was drawn from the George W. Bush school of issue management. Mr. Harper's problem? In the end, Canadians will not buy this approach because it clashes with their deeply held values as citizens who value peace and cherish Canada's role on the international stage as a voice of moderation and as a facilitator of mediation.

In my wide-ranging consultations leading up to the vote, I talked with Darrell Dexter, NDP leader and respected Leader of the Opposition in Nova Scotia, whom I knew had been trained in the military. He said: "Every military officer is taught that time spent on reconnaissance is never wasted. Mention that in your speech, and every military person watching is going to know exactly what you're talking about because the one thing military personnel and their families are most concerned about is getting home safely."

Darrell was saying that one doesn't go into a dangerous situation without having seriously questioned, researched, and examined every way—up and down—what one eventuality might meet. His advice reminded me of whitewater canoeing, where instructors teach that you never go into a set of rapids without having studied absolutely every dimension of it. Not doing so could be fatal. You'll never know with 100 per cent certainty what's going to happen, but you certainly want to have first questioned every possible option and subjected it to detailed scrutiny and debate, because there's danger out there. It's exactly the same understanding required for Canada's mission to Afghanistan—only it affects many more lives. So, in the final analysis, it is the responsibility of Parliament—which is charged with the profound responsibility of deciding whether to send Canadian troops into harm's way.

Canadian troops are absolutely loyal to their country and will do whatever their country asks. That is their obligation to us, and why we value their willingness to sacrifice. But, by the same token, we have an obligation to them. The Canadian government and all parliamentarians had better be sure that what is being asked of the troops is the right thing. And uppermost in our decision-making should be the need to bring them home alive.

We obviously felt that the way the debate was being forced—a constrained time frame, with no opportunity for asking and answering important questions related to the mission—was simply wrong. Nevertheless, we had the debate, and our party unanimously—with all twenty-nine members present—voted against the continuation of the mission to Afghanistan.

In the days leading up to the vote, everyone could see it was going to be extremely close. I don't think Mr. Harper had any better idea than the rest of us exactly what was going to happen. So the PM stood in the House during his contribution to the debate and stated that if the MPs voted against the two-year extension of the mission in Afghanistan, he would proceed with a one-year extension regardless, and then seek the support of Canadians in a general election for a further extension. Government by ultimatum had begun!

This was a blatant example of arrogance on the part of Stephen Harper. He stood ready to bypass the will of the House of Commons if it voted against his proposed military mission, thumbing his nose and saying: "It doesn't matter if the House votes against this extension, I'm going ahead with one anyway."

What struck me was this was exactly the attitude that Mr. Harper used to rail about when Paul Martin said: "I don't care if the House of Commons wants an Air India inquiry, I'm not going there. I don't care if the House of Commons has voted against a patronage appointment of mine, I'm going ahead with it anyway."

What we see in this strategy of dealing with the minority parliament is a glimpse of a "culture of entitlement" almost before there had been time for such a culture to grow! It is quite revealing, profoundly disturbing and, in contrast to his words to the nation on election night, provides a real glimpse of the kind of government Stephen Harper intends to pursue.

The second most disturbing aspect of the debate and vote was to watch twenty-four Liberals support the motion and give

Mr. Harper a narrow win on the vote to extend the Canadian mission to Afghanistan for another two years. Even worse, the Liberals somehow managed to have more than 10 per cent of their caucus members stay away from this crucial vote.

I can't imagine a more important vote in the House of Commons than whether Canada is going to war. Even though Mr. Harper continues to refuse to use the word, there's no question that we are at war. How did this happen? Two factors combined. The prime minister decided that he would take us into protracted war in Afghanistan irrespective of the will of the House. Then an opposition party, the Liberals—by virtue of their shameful eleven absentees and twenty-four MPs voting in favour—gave the prime minister the authorization he needed by a mere four votes!

Reprehensible or tragic? Likely both.

After the debate and vote, Alexa McDonough reported that many military families had phoned her office to thank the NDP for the position we had taken. Even as they share the pride in our service personnel that so many of us do, military families are profoundly and daily worried about what could happen in Afghanistan, and their fears and concerns have been unabated since that vote.

It's very clear that Canadians are generally uncomfortable with the role that Canadian troops are playing in Afghanistan, and with the idea that our officials are apparently actively seeking to lead the war effort in Afghanistan profoundly disturbs them. Canadians want us to lead the war on dangerous climate change, not on insurrection in southern Afghanistan. After years of conflict in Afghanistan, it is time for a comprehensive peace process. Canada should play a role to bring such a process into being. Of necessity, such a process must involve many parties, including states such as Pakistan and those involved in the conflict itself. To effect such an initiative, Canada cannot at the same time be engaged in the active fighting on the front as it is doing at the moment. It is time for a new role for Canada in Afghanistan, one that builds on our tradition of acting as a catalyst in forming paths to peace and draws on the global respect for our mediation skills as well as the balance, care and independence on which we have traditionally constructed our foreign policy. Key to this new role for Canada will be the withdrawal of troops from the current mission.

NORAD

In the middle of the spring session, the Conservatives suddenly announced a proposal to extend the NORAD (North American Aerospace Defence System) agreement with the U.S. But, in reality, it was much worse than an extension. Normally these agreements are extended for five years, but in this case the proposal was for "an unlimited extension." The NORAD agreement was initially developed at the height of the Cold War—several decades ago—when our concern was that bombers or missiles might attack North America from the Soviet Union. But what Parliament was being asked to do this time was to amend and extend—indefinitely—our commitment to NORAD. This amounted to a major step in the deeper integration of the Canadian with the U.S. military and Canadian sovereignty being further eroded into the United States ambit.

The NORAD initiative was moved forward rapidly by the Harper administration during the spring session. The Liberals had been developing the NORAD agreement—the preliminary work had been done entirely under the Liberals, but they knew it was a political time bomb and held back because of of the impending election in which they would not want to be tarred with a proximity to George W. Bush and his administration. The Conservatives, however, jumped on it right away.

(The Harper PMO does possess the ability for swift surgical strikes, and they introduced NORAD quickly as a proposal containing much more than just a simple five-year extension of the NORAD agreement. The Harper administration is doing so many things that are wrong, but unlike the Liberals, the Conservatives did at least bring it to the House of Commons for a debate and vote. It used to be that NORAD extensions were agreed to without any vote in the House. So the Conservatives at least honoured the principle that a treaty extension should be approved in Parliament. However, they didn't permit any meaningful debate on the matter. They didn't permit a parliamentary investigation into the details of the extension. They simply said it's going to be voted on, yes or no, with no amendments, no finessing, no fine-tuning. We desperately wanted to make amendments because the extension contained some very worrisome elements.

Dawn Black (NDP, New Westminster–Coquitlam) asked the minister of national defence why sharing intelligence information with the United States included matters pertaining to shipping within Canadian waters, including the Northwest Passage. Dawn had carefully read the entire agreement and concluded that it went way beyond simple air defence to include maritime and inland waters.

Her concerns were initially dismissed by Minister O'Connor, but four days later he was forced to admit that the agreement to extend NORAD would include sharing information with the U.S. government on shipping in the "Arctic archipelago." The minister was admitting to a major change regarding Canadian sovereignty. Does anyone think for a nanosecond that the United States will be sharing with Canadian officials U.S. boating and shipping information on their inland waterways? This was all deeply offensive and, in addition, there was no provision for Parliament ever to review this, because the proposal was for an indefinite extension. What if this agreement was not working? What if it was compromising our independence in ways that were unacceptable, as we fully expected? How could it be undone or even reviewed systematically by Canadians? There were no effective provisions to address these key questions. When it came to the vote, the Liberals and the Bloc both voted with the Conservatives. The NDP was the only party to stand for Canadian sovereignty and vote against.

In the wake of the January 2006 election, Olivia, Trinity-Spadina, and I managed to escape for a few precious days to go snorkeling off the Bahamas. A new book entitled *The Weather Makers* had just been published by Australian writer Tim Flannery. It's all about how, over the past century, the human species has begun to transform the weather and the earth's climate in very dramatic ways, and I made this book my reading over the time we spent on a tiny island—an island close to sea level. There was something quite striking about imagining this chain of tiny islands under water which, if the scientific projections are accurate, could occur within the lifetime of my descendants. Flannery's book really confirmed once again for me the profound and massive impact that humanity is having on the planet. When I returned to Ottawa, I decided to offer the prime minister a copy of *The Weather Makers*. A few weeks later, when Mr. Flannery spoke in Toronto, I had the opportunity to introduce him, and his speech rammed home the powerful nature of the transformation that we are in the process of creating here on the planet.

Flannery told his Toronto audience that he was disappointed with recent developments in Canada on climate change. He said that, prior to the election of the Harper government, Canada had—at least on paper—been a leader in calling for action on climate change. Although Canada had not yet taken steps to reduce pollution and greenhouse gases, the fact that we had signed on to Kyoto had helped bring the Kyoto Protocol into force, and our presence had encouraged a number of other countries to sign on. Mr. Flannery said he was completely flummoxed to realize that a country like Canada would back off such an international commitment and, by its action, create a potential unravelling of the first global commitment to do something to begin to reverse the weather-making transformation we are causing on the planet.

When I met a second time with the prime minister in his Centre Block office, I noticed Mr. Flannery's book on his desk and asked if he'd had a chance to read it. He said not yet, and I replied: "I hope you will for the sake of our children and their children."

By his comments and the regressive steps of his government on this file in the first session of the thirty-ninth Parliament, I can only conclude that not only has the prime minister not yet read the book, he doesn't think climate change is a serious issue.

When the House of Commons resumed in March 2006, we began to focus on driving the climate change issue to the forefront of Canadian public debate. It became clear from our persistent questioning of the prime minister that a very cynical decision had been made within the PMO and by the business interests that are so strongly supporting the Harper government—the oil cartel. These decision-makers want to ensure that the oil industry and the biggest oil companies in the world continue to enjoy $1.5 billion annually in tax subsidies from the Canadian people, even as Canadians are being gouged daily at the pumps as the bloated industry rakes in obscene profits.

At the same time, Mr. Harper abruptly cancelled the funding of programs to finance wind turbines and wind farms, solar panels, and retrofitting of low-income housing so that people who earned less could pay less. His government was dismantling the few meagre initiatives put in place in the previous minority Parliament. He also cancelled some long-standing initiatives, including the Renewal Environmental Development Initiative (REDI). If that wasn't bad enough, he then had the temerity to suggest that pollution and the health problems it causes is what's of interest to him, not climate change. As if pollution and climate change are somehow different.

I believe there's a real misrepresentation underway in the Canadian public policy debate. I think the oil companies and the PMO have decided to try to create a wedge between people's concerns about clean air and the burning of fossil fuels. They want to try to shift the debate to say climate change is not the major concern, it's pollution that causes health problems. In reply to a question from me, Prime Minister Harper said: "The climate change agenda is principally about carbon dioxide, which is not a pollutant. This government is also concerned with pollutants such as nitrous oxides, sulphur dioxides, and other organic compounds, so there are differences and that is a difference." But there's no difference at all, because right alongside the five other greenhouse gases listed on the government's own website is nitrous oxide. Global climate change, record temperatures, hurricane and gale-force winds, floods, droughts, and the escalating number and ferocity of forest fires are all strong contributors to smog, pollution, and health problems.

Our caucus, environmentalists, and concerned Canadians are all going to have to work extra hard to make sure that Mr. Harper will not be successful in perpetuating some kind of hocus-pocus that pollution is what we should be concerned about and that greenhouse gas emissions are not a problem.

The government of Canada had been designated to chair a major international conference on climate change in Bonn, Germany. The purpose of the two-week conference was to try to figure out how targets could be set for the second phase of the Framework Agreement on Climate Change. Canada was represented by its environment minister, Rona Ambrose, who was to be the conference chair. Instead of presiding over the two-week conference, Ms. Ambrose chose to spend less than two days in attendance, effectively snubbing the international community. She was playing hooky from a role the world had asked Canada to play. Worse yet, she indicated that Canada was not fully committed to achieving its Kyoto targets and stated that, in fact, she didn't think Canada could meet its commitments. She didn't seem at all troubled by that.

Ms. Ambrose may not be troubled but, judging from the reaction, a lot of Canadians were troubled and across the country there was a visceral reaction against the minister's irresponsible, arrogant attitude. More and more Canadians began asking: "Where did Mr. Harper and his government get the mandate to walk away from this kind of international commitment?"

Canadians were already frustrated about Canada's role on climate change. They knew that Canada was a signatory to Kyoto, but they also knew that the Liberals hadn't delivered on any plan to reduce our greenhouse gas emissions. In fact, our emissions were up dramatically—well over 20 per cent from our 1990 levels, and more than 30 per cent from where we were supposed to be, to meet our Kyoto targets. Canadians had a clear sense that the Liberal government hadn't done nearly enough, and now we had Mr. Harper essentially throwing up his hands in surrender.

The NDP caucus decided that we had an obligation to go beyond simply opposing the government's inaction and propose some alternatives. We laid out a five-point plan called "A Greener Canada and a Greener World." The plan included some of the best ideas available from across the country and around the world. At the same time, the House of Commons was considering a motion to endorse the Kyoto targets, and the House passed that motion. Mr. Harper, who used to be highly critical of the Liberals for ignoring the will of the House, simply turned around and committed the same parliamentary sin. Just like prime ministers Chrétien and Martin before him, Mr. Harper simply ignored the wishes of a majority of MPs in the House.

It was clear that we had to hold Mr. Harper to account on Kyoto, so we began asking more questions in the House. We then laid out some alternatives showing how Canada could actually reach its Kyoto target date of 2010–2012 with the reduction of 207 megatonnes of emissions. This would not only reduce pollution, it would create tens of thousands of new jobs in the green transport sector, the public transit sector, and the energy retrofit sector—the retrofitting of buildings that creates employment while reducing energy consumption. With government purchases of green energy, we could stimulate that whole sector and create jobs by ensuring that some of the wind turbines and the solar panels were built and manufactured in Canada.

The simmering dispute between the NDP caucus and Mr. Harper on climate change all came to a head when, after weeks of demanding some semblance of a climate-change plan from Stephen Harper and Rona Ambrose, we had no choice but to put forward a motion demanding the resignation of Ms. Ambrose. This wasn't done lightly. We did this after an entire session of calling on the government to bring forward some sort of a plan on climate change. Canadians had heard the Conservatives in Opposition saying they had a made-in-Canada plan for reducing greenhouse gas emissions. Yet they only produced two slightly progressive proposals— re-announcing transit money that had been in our amended NDP budget in 2005, offering a tax credit for transit passes, and a modest gasoline blend of 5 per cent ethanol, one-half of what the NDP had proposed in its platform.

Under no definition could this be defined as a plan. It turned out they weren't telling the truth when they stated they had a made-in-Canada plan. The plan didn't exist. The result has left Canada wasting a whole year with galloping emission levels, and wasting that kind of time is something we can't afford to do. Dangerous climate change has been hurting working families all over Canada and around the world. The spring of 2006 saw three times more forest fires than in 2005 in North America, and 2005 was considered a bad year for forest fires. The people who rely on the forests for work have seen their livelihood jeopardized. Dangerous droughts have been forecast for western Canada, and these droughts have already threatened the livelihood of farmers. We have had prematurely warming on the ice roads in the far North; the warming has already claimed the lives of drivers whose trucks have plunged through the ice. Due to failures in ice roads, more goods have to be shipped by plane in the north, using more fuel and accelerating greenhouse gas emissions, making matters worse.

I accepted the opportunity to see widespread climate-change damage in our country when I was able to fly over the great pine forest of interior British Columbia in the early summer of 2006. I learned that once a pine tree began to turn red from pine beetle infestation, it had stopped living. The tree was no longer taking up water from its roots, taking in carbon dioxide from the atmosphere or producing oxygen. The forest I saw as we headed out from Quesnel, is a forest now rapidly turning red, then grey as the death wrought by climate change through the warming that has liberated the pine beetle to attack the trees. When winters were colder, the beetles were killed over the winter and could not infest freely. Then, as I left and flew on a clear day hundreds of kilometres down the mighty Fraser Valley, I saw tens of thousands of square kilometres of red forest, as far as the eye could see. And ecosystem collapse was taking place. As B.C. NDP MLA Bob Simpson told me, "if this devastation were happening in the form of one massive forest fire, we would have every major media outlet in world reporting on the crisis. But it's like a forest fire in slow motion!" Well through their massive meal in British Columbia, the bugs and their killing ways have crossed the mountains to the east and are headed for the great Boreal forest, one of the most important "lungs" we have on the planet.

Wasting a year doing nothing about climate change was a moral failure, and proposing the resignation of the minister of the environment was our way of trying to express the concern of our party, of Canadians and, we hoped, of Parliament, that the government was headed in the wrong direction. It was our way to try to force Mr. Harper to say: "All right, I recognize that you have lost confidence in the minister and I will put in a new minister and we will work with other parties to try and find a way forward." That's how I think a leader should act in a minority Parliament. Instead, what Mr. Harper did was to say: "I'll treat this motion as a motion of non-confidence in the government. If it passes there'll be an election." It was the bluster of a schoolyard bully. Government by ultimatum, once again. The NDP proposal was to have the motion introduced to the environment committee by our critic, Nathan Cullen. If it passed there in June, it would have come to the House of Commons for a vote in the fall. That would have allowed for a serious debate—one that could have engaged Canadians over the long, hot summer.

But following Mr. Harper's petulant outburst, the Standing committee on the environment—led by the Conservative MPs—said the motion was out of order. With the timid Liberals backing the Conservatives, the motion wasn't moved in committee. Ironically, this is the same committee that had been asking the minister of the environment to appear before the committee all spring to answer questions, and had been rebuffed by her at every turn.

I sincerely hope that climate change is an issue that Canadians will drive to the front of the parade of issues that confront parliament. Our NDP caucus decided to make the summer and fall of 2006 a campaign around climate change because we see climate change as one of the major dynamics of Canadian politics. Perhaps, with Al Gore and his film about the inconvenient truths concerning climate change having an impact on the millions worldwide who view it, there is some hope that Canadians can take this issue and put it on the top of the political agenda, where it belongs.

• • •

Canadians knew if there was one topic that was a major thread running through the 2006 election it was accountability, cleaning up corruption, opening up government, and trying to transform Canadian politics into something more ethical.

Stephen Harper and the Conservatives brought forward a major piece of legislation to deal with accountability, ethics, and openness, and when we saw it we were frankly disappointed. It didn't open up the doors of government to public scrutiny through freedom of information the way it should have. There was nothing on democratic reform, or the way in which we elect our representatives. It contained some further controls on election spending, which we were perfectly happy to support. But the bill in its initial form had major deficiencies.

Our caucus approached this issue in a spirit of getting something done because we knew, after the abject mess the Liberals had made of accountability and ethics, that Canadians wanted to see significant changes and improvements. Led by our ethics critic, Pat Martin, and by Paul Dewar, MP for Ottawa Centre, we put forward twenty amendments to the bill. These included opening up freedom of information for the media and the public, establishing an appointments commission with a process for selecting the commissioners, and closing some of the loopholes that had allowed Liberal leadership candidate Joe Volpe to receive $5,400 in donations from several children under the age of fourteen.

We brought these amendments forward and indicated that we were prepared to support the bill if those amendments passed. Liberals and some others suggested that the NDP was in bed with the Conservatives. That's ridiculous. The NDP was doing exactly what we said we would do when we asked Canadians for their votes. We said we wanted to try to make Parliament work for them. And we used as a guiding document the ethics package of reforms that Ed Broadbent had provided for us in the previous Parliament and that we had presented to the voters in the 2006 election. We were pleased when the Accountability Act passed through the House. Yes, it was a bill proposed by the Conservatives, but it is also legislation that was improved dramatically by New Democrats, and there's absolutely nothing wrong with that. It was also a significant rebuff of the prime minister's petulance after New Democrats said his choice of Gwyn Morgan to head up the appointments commission was unacceptable. The prime minister stomped around in a huff saying he wouldn't appoint Mr. Morgan to the post and wouldn't even bother with an appointments commission. But NDP amendments established the appointments commission. Despite the prime minister's temper tantrum, the amendments require him to consult with the Opposition party leaders regarding appointments. I have no doubt this will be a major improvement over the old system of doing business with the government, which was described derisively as, "Who do you know in the PMO?"

As the House rose for the summer, I had a certain sense of foreboding at what lay ahead. No House of Commons to hold the government in check at all, within a few weeks, the hijacking of Canada's values by the Conservatives had accelerated. On Canada Day weekend, the government announced and settlement of a major trade dispute with the Americans. I called it "the softwood lumber sellout." It was an agreement about Canada's precious natural resources that hurt the softwood industry, its workers and the communities on which it depends. Harper had traded away, apparently for nothing at all except the nickname "Steve" administered by the President of the United States, Canada's right to establish its own policies regarding our public forests. George W. Bush commented after meeting Stephen Harper that he liked the Canadian prime minister's negotiating style. No wonder! George W. Bush and his administration had won, hands down: a seven-year agreement had been pared to effectively three years—not long enough for investors to rebuild the Canadian industry, a certainty had been established that more and more raw Canadian logs would rumble down the highways to huge American mills, and one billion $1 of Canadian funds needed by our communities to adjust were left on the southern side of the border to be used by Republicans seeking re-election as a slush fund for their communities and for their re-election. However, Mr. Harper did not have the mandate to tell Mr. Bush that there was a softwood deal. That is because this is a minority government and the softwood deal requires a taxation bill to pass the House of Commons to place a levy on exports of Canadian softwood products. The fact that Mr. Harper is ready, at time of writing, to put this matter to a confidence vote rather than work towards a solution with other parties in the House is another example of his government-by-ultimatum approach to politics. Canada would be better served by a prime minister who worked with opposition parties to find common ground, as he said he would on election night, rather than play politics with the schoolyard standoff. Apparently selling out Canadian sovereignty is a price that the Harper Conservatives are happy to pay. Only time will tell if the Canadian people, and their elected parliament will agree. New Democrats will not.

Softwood was not the only item on the agenda of the meeting of Harper and Bush in early July 2006. Harper also opened the door to reconsideration of Canadian participation in the Bush programme to weaponize space through National Missile Defence, the same programme that the NDP and widespread opposition across Canada had forced the Paul Martin Liberals to reject only months before in the previous minority parliament.

Evidence mounts that the Harper Conservatives are taking Canada down a new road. Not one that a majority of Canadians have chosen, mind you. No. This is a road that runs contrary to Canadian values and antithetical to Canadians' best ideas. Examples abound: cancelling the practice of lowering the Canadian flag on government buildings when our soldiers are killed in battle and, despite military opinion and popular opinion to the contrary, refusing to permit Canadians to share in the expression of respect when bodies of the fallen are repatriated, playing the race card in dealing with traditional fishing rights, steering Canada away from its traditional and vital role in the Middle East where balance and mediation were the value that Canada could add to efforts to achieve peace, pushing Canada as an "energy superpower," supplying endless barrels of fuel to gluttonous economies rather than leading the way in environmental stewardship, and much more.

Now is the time for Canadians to reclaim our "shared destiny," as former NDP Saskatchewan Premier Roy Romanow so

eloquently put it in a widely discussed *Walrus* magazine feature article in the spring of 2006. We have a shared mission
to undertake: to achieve our destiny and unique place in the
world—building a society that values leadership concerning
fundamental sustainability of life on the planet, that values
caring for each other and educating one another irrespective
of our personal means or backgrounds, that believes in prosperity with justice, and that is an effective clarion call for
peace, equality, human rights and democracy in the world.

Canadians have the ideas that work to put these values
into action. It is time to abandon the temporary detour that
recent political events have created, and get Canada back on
track.

Index